The Four Supreme Court Land-Use Decisions of 2005:

Separating Fact from Fiction

TABLE OF CONTENTS

Foreword
By Lora Lucero, AICP iii

Chapter 1. Kelo v. City of New London [125 S. Ct. 2655 (June 23, 2005)] 1
Overview 1
The Facts 2
As Argued by APA 2
Oral Argument
*[Excerpted from the transcript of oral arguments before the U.S. Supreme Court,
February 22, 2005, which appeared in the April 2005 issue of* Planning *and
Environmental Law]* 3
The Court's Decision 18
The Case Syllabus 19
Opinion of the Supreme Court 20
The Text of Justice Kennedy's Concurring Opinion 30
The Text of Justice O'Connor's Dissenting Opinion 31
The Text of Justice Thomas's Dissenting Opinion 37
Amicus Curiae Brief
By John D. Echeverria and Thomas W. Merrill 46
Commentary and Reaction 62
Supreme Court Decision Emphasizes the Importance of Planning
By Paul Farmer, AICP 62
Transcript of Television Debate Between Paul Farmer, APA Executive Director, and
Scott Bullock, Senior Attorney, Institute For Justice 62
Commentary: *Kelo v. City of New London*
By Lora A. Lucero, AICP
[Reprinted from the July 2005 issue of Planning and Environmental Law] 68
Confirming a Century of Case Law
By John R. Nolon and Jessica A. Bacher 71
How to Reform Eminent Domain
By Thomas W. Merrill 76
Connecticut Planners Weigh In: Eminent Domain Is Important Tool
By Mark Pellegrini and Donald Poland 78
Public Use Clause Is Virtually Eliminated in Federal Court
By David L. Callies 79
Debunking the Urban (Planning) Legends About *Kelo*
By John M. Baker 80
"Public Use" Goes Valley Girl; Now Means "Public Whatever"
By Michael M. Berger 81
Does *Kelo* Trample on Fundamental Property Rights?
By Lani Williams 82
Alternatives To Eminent Domain
By Frank Schnidman 84
Rumored Death Of Property Rights Is Greatly Exaggerated
By David Parkhurst 85
Domestic Policy Watch: Redevelopment Done Right
By Paul Farmer, AICP 87
Domestic Policy Watch: A Member's Guide to APA's Policy and Advocacy Programs
By Paul Farmer, AICP 90

Chapter 2. *Lingle v. Chevron* [125 S. Ct. 2074 (May 23, 2005)] **95**

Overview **95**
    The Facts 96
    As Argued by APA 96
    The Court's Decision 96

The Case Syllabus **97**

Opinion of the Supreme Court **98**
    The Text of Justice Kennedy's Concurring Opinion 107

Amicus Curiae Brief
    By Edward J. Sullivan and Carrie A. Richter 108

Commentary and Reaction **118**
    Ding Dong, the Witch Is Dead: O'Connor Drops a House on the *Agins* Takings Test
    By Simon Lazar and Dwight H. Merriam, FAICP
    [Reprinted from Planning and Environmental Law, *July 2005]* 118

Chapter 3. *City of Rancho Palos Verdes v. Abrams* [125 S.Ct. 1453 (March 22, 2005)] **131**

Overview **131**
    The Facts 132
    As Argued by APA 132
    The Court's Decision 133

Case Syllabus **133**

Opinion of the Supreme Court **134**
    The Text of Justice Breyer's Concurrence 141
    The Text of Justice Stevens's Concurrence 142

APA Amicus Curiae Brief
    By Richard Ruda and James I. Crowley 144

Chapter 4. *San Remo Hotel, L.P. v. City and County of San Francisco*
[125 S. Ct. 2491 (June 20, 2005)] **159**

Overview **160**
    The Facts 160
    As Argued by APA 160
    The Court's Decision 160

Case Syllabus **161**

Opinion of the Supreme Court **163**
    The Text of Chief Justice Rehnquist's Concurrence 174

Amicus Curiae Brief
    By Timothy J. Dowling and Douglas T. Kendall 176

Afterword
    By Paul Farmer, AICP 189

Foreword

Unless your summer travel plans included extraterrestrial destinations, you've most likely heard of the U.S. Supreme Court's decision in *Kelo v. City of New London*, the hot-button eminent domain case in the 2004 term. Since Justice Steven's opinion for the majority (5-4) merely confirmed a well-established legal doctrine, the media's hyperventilation and the political uproar in many state legislatures has been perplexing and unfortunate. With less fanfare, but certainly of no less importance, the High Court handed down decisions in three other cases of interest to planners this year—*Lingle v. Chevron USA, San Remo Hotel, L.P. v. City and County of San Francisco*, and *City of Rancho Palos Verdes v. Abrams*—but none garnered the public's attention and consternation as much as the *Kelo* opinion.

Taking Justice William J. Brennan's admonition in 1981 to heart—"If a policeman must know the Constitution, then why not a planner?"—this Planning Advisory Service Report provides an overview of these four cases, the text of the Supreme Court opinion (including dissenting and concurring opinions) in each case, the text of the amicus brief that APA filed in each case, and commentary and reaction to each case. The articles in the commentary and reaction section, as well as this Foreword and the Afterword to this report, describe how each of these decisions will affect planners in their daily work.

THE BIGGER PICTURE

Cases that end up in the U.S. Supreme Court are seldom only about the parties involved in the litigation. These cases take on a life of their own with the special interest advocates jockeying for the Court's attention. Agendas are being advanced, and positions are being staked out...in the courts, in Congress, in the state legislatures, at the ballot box through the initiative process, and in the court of public opinion. All of this is clearly observable by those who are looking at the bigger picture.

The agenda of the private property rights movement is to restrict government interference with the use and ownership of private property; to encourage the courts and the judicial branch of government to override or substitute their decisions for the those of local elected officials and the legislative branch of government; and to pit individual property owners against the community.

APA has been criticized for being the "governments' apologist" (the term used by Michael M. Berger, *Planning and Environmental Law*, September 2005, reprinted in this report in Chapter 1's Commentary and Reaction section) in these cases, always siding with the government. Certainly, APA is an advocate with a special interest and a special message for the Court, just as are all of the organizations that file "friend-of-the-court" (*amicus curiae*) briefs, but APA does ***not*** advocate for the government. APA advocates for good planning, for the tools necessary to carry out and implement good planning, for the processes that support good planning, and for the beneficiaries of good planning—the community and its citizens. No other professional organization represents the interests of planners and the planning profession in the courts.

While the Institute for Justice, the Cato Institute, and other private property rights groups advocate for property owners and private property rights, APA advocates for the rights of the community and the public-at-large. The property rights groups prefer to cast the debate as being government versus property owner, but as planners we know the debate must focus on the bigger picture—the community.

What is a community, if not the citizens, the families, and, yes, the property owners who live there, as well as the future residents who may one day call the community home? This is the bigger picture, and we expect our city councilors, county commissioners, and appointed officials to make decisions in the community's best interest. A strong public planning process is how we learn what is in the best interest of the community. So it should come as no surprise that when APA advocates for the community and good planning, we are often supporting the local governments charged with planning for their community's future.

THE PLANNING ISSUES IN EACH OF THESE CASES

Suzette Kelo asked the Court to save her home in New London, Connecticut. Mark Abrams requested that the Court authorize attorneys fees and damages against Rancho Palos Verdes after he had prevailed in his Tele-

*APA does **not** advocate for the government. APA advocates for good planning, for the tools necessary to carry out and implement good planning, for the processes that support good planning, and for the beneficiaries of good planning—the community and its citizens.*

communications Act lawsuit. The owner of the San Remo Hotel in San Francisco wanted the Court to give him a second chance to prove his regulatory takings challenge in federal court. While Chevron USA hoped the Court might second-guess the Hawaii Legislature's decision to enact a rent control statute. What did any of these disputes have to do with good planning and the future of our communities?

The *Kelo* case was about an important planning tool—eminent domain—that, APA argued, needs to be "used only in conjunction with a process of land use planning that includes broad public participation and a careful consideration of alternatives to eminent domain." In his decision for the majority, declining to ban the use of eminent domain for local economic development projects, Justice Stevens mentioned "planning," "plans," and "planner" more than 30 times.

> Given the comprehensive character of the plan, the thorough deliberation that preceded its adoption, and the limited scope of our review," he concluded, "it is appropriate for us, as it was in *Berman*, to resolve the challenges of the individual owners, not on a piecemeal basis, but rather in light of the entire plan. Because that plan unquestionably serves a public purpose, the takings challenged here, satisfy the public use requirement of the Fifth Amendment. (*Kelo v. City of New London*, 125 S. Ct. 2655, 2665 (2005))

Without a doubt, Justice Stevens and the majority understood the importance of planning for community revitalization. One can almost see Justice Stevens tipping his hat to the planners in New London, Connecticut.

The planning issue at stake in the *City of Rancho Palos Verdes* was whether Congress ever intended to put communities on the hook for potentially devastating financial awards to property owners who are successful in challenging state and local zoning and land use requirements under the Telecommunications Act (47 U.S.C. Section 332(c)(7)(B)). APA argued on behalf of the beneficiaries of good planning that the Telecommunications Act already provides a very effective remedy—declaratory and injunctive relief—and Congress never intended to add money damages and attorneys fees as a remedy. In fact, Mark Abrams received his remedy, the conditional use permit to build the antenna tower in his yard. APA explained to the Court:

> Faced with the threat of large claims for attorney's fees and damages by well-financed corporations represented by high-priced counsel, local governments may be deterred from vigorously protecting visual, aesthetic, and safety concerns. Such a result would defeat Congress' intention to allow local governments to retain "the flexibility to treat facilities that create different visual, aesthetic, or safety concerns differently to the extent permitted under generally applicable zoning requirements." (H.R. Conf. Rep. No. 458, 104th Cong., 2d Sess. 208 (1996))

Imagine the chilling effect it would have on communities wishing to adopt reasonable and thoughtful land-use regulations? Justice Scalia, writing for a unanimous Court, agreed that money damages and attorneys fees are not remedies allowed under the Telecommunications Act.

The *San Remo Hotel* case presented an issue of fairness, pure and simple. Should communities be forced to defend against takings claims in state court and, having won, be required to defend themselves again in federal court? APA argued that the property owner was not entitled to two bites at the litigation apple!

> Landowners deserve a fair forum and a full hearing for their constitutional claims, . . . San Remo received its fair hearing already. To grant San Remo's request in this case would unfairly put two hammers to the heads of local officials.

Without a doubt, Justice Stevens and the majority understood the importance of planning for community revitalization. One can almost see Justice Stevens tipping his hat to the planners in New London, Connecticut.

Justice Stevens agreed, and writing for a unanimous Court, decided that one bite at the apple is sufficient. He concluded that:

> State courts are fully competent to adjudicate constitutional challenges to local land-use decisions. Indeed, state courts undoubtedly have more experience than federal courts do in resolving the complex factual, technical, and legal questions related to zoning and land-use regulations.

Perhaps the decision in the 2004 term that will have the greatest impact on planners and the planning profession is *Lingle v. Chevron*. The Court has finally untangled some of the knots in the Fifth Amendment, jettisoning the "substantially advances" test from the Takings Clause. In a breath of fresh air, Justice O'Connor wrote perhaps the clearest, most understandable opinion ever concerning the Court's Takings jurisprudence. Every planner should read it, and it is in this PAS Report.

In a breath of fresh air, Justice O'Connor wrote perhaps the clearest, most understandable opinion ever concerning the Court's Takings jurisprudence. Every planner should read it, and it is in this PAS Report.

The important planning issue at stake in *Lingle* involved "process": Which branch of government (the legislature or the judiciary?) has the responsibility for passing laws and regulations to protect the public welfare and the community's interest? Chevron USA and its allies argued that the rent control statute enacted by the Hawaii Legislature did not "substantially advance a legitimate government purpose" and constituted a regulatory taking. They wanted the Court to second guess the state's determination that the rent control statute substantially advanced the state's concern about high retail gasoline prices and its highly concentrated markets for oil. They also wanted compensation, not merely overturning the statute, if they prevailed.

The State of Hawaii countered that the "substantially advances test," which first appeared in the 1980 *Agins* takings test, was really not a takings test at all, but a due process test. APA supported the arguments made by the state and added:

> The planning and legislative processes that local governments use to consider, formulate, and adopt regulations are by their very nature participatory. Property owners, special interest groups, and members of the general public have ample opportunity to make their views known before elected officials adopt policies that will govern community affairs. If members of the public disagree with decisions made they have an opportunity to seek relief through the legislative or administrative appeals processes. . . . The appropriate way to promote the public's involvement in the development of state and local laws and regulations is through a democratic process that allows for public debate and deliberation based on studies designed to evaluate alternative approaches to achieving community objectives. The process may be time-consuming, but democracy often is.

Justice O'Connor, writing for a unanimous Court, announced that, "Today we correct course. . . . We conclude that this formula prescribes an inquiry in the nature of a due process, not a takings, test, and that it has no proper place in our takings jurisprudence." She went on to explain:

> The "substantially advances" formula suggests a means-ends test: It asks, in essence, whether a regulation of private property is effective in achieving some legitimate public purpose. An inquiry of this nature has some logic in the context of a due process challenge, for a regulation that fails to serve any legitimate governmental objective may be so arbitrary or irrational that it runs afoul of the Due Process Clause. . . . But such a test is not a valid method of discerning whether private property has been "taken" for purposes of the Fifth Amendment.

The *Lingle* decision should bring clarity to takings jurisprudence and reduce the number of takings challenges that hit communities each year.

CONCLUSION

So when you read the materials that follow in this PAS Report, think about the big picture, about the agendas (sometimes hidden, many times not), and how planners and the planning profession can protect and enhance our communities for everyone through good planning practices. The Court's decisions in *Kelo, Rancho Palos Verdes, San Remo,* and *Lingle* support planners and the communities we work in.

Lora Anne Lucero, AICP
Editor, Planning and Environmental Law
Staff Liaison, American Planning Association
Amicus Curiae Committee

CHAPTER 1

Kelo v. City of New London

[125 S. Ct. 2655 (June 23, 2005)]

[*This overview is taken, in large part, from the August 2005 issue of* Zoning Practice, *which was written by Lora Lucero, editor of* Planning and Environmental Law.]

The Fifth Amendment of the U.S. Constitution provides: "[N]or shall private property be taken for public use, without just compensation." This year, the Supreme Court was asked to consider whether economic development is a "public use" for which the power of eminent domain may be exercised. None of the land-use/planning cases on the Supreme Court's docket this term have captured as much media attention as *Kelo v. City of New London* [125 S. Ct. 2655 (June 23, 2005)]. Perhaps Justice O'Connor's scathing dissent has received more air time and ink than the majority's opinion written by Justice John Paul Stevens.

The facts in this case were misplaced in much of the news coverage since the *Kelo* opinion was announced June 23, but they were an important reason why the Supreme Court decided not to expand or restrict the power of eminent domain.

THE FACTS

Since the closure of the Naval Undersea Warfare Center in 1996, New London, Connecticut, has lost more than 1,500 jobs. By 1998, the city's unemployment rate was nearly double that of the state, which designated New London a "distressed municipality."

A private, nonprofit development agency was enlisted to assist the city in planning for the revitalization of the Fort Trumbull area in New London. In February 1998, a pharmaceutical company announced it would build a $300 million research facility adjacent to Fort Trumbull. Hoping the facility would be a catalyst for further revitalization, the city held neighborhood meetings and prepared an economic development plan. The state committed more than $15 million to the effort.

The state reviewed and approved the economic development plan, which called for a waterfront conference hotel, restaurants and shopping, and marinas with a pedestrian riverwalk. On one parcel, 90,000 square feet of research and development office space was planned to complement the pharmaceutical research facility. negotiations with the majority of property owners were successful, but nine owners refused to sell and condemnation proceedings were initiated.

The property owners argued their properties were not blighted and said the taking violated the "public use" requirement of the Fifth Amendment. The city argued that its plan for economic development of the Fort Trumbull area was a proper public use. The Connecticut Supreme Court ruled that all of the proposed takings were valid and that economic development qualified as a valid public use.

AS ARGUED BY APA

Suzette Kelo and the organizations that supported her position asked the Supreme Court to either declare that economic development is never, under any circumstance, a "public use" for the purposes of condemnation or, alternatively, to create a higher standard of judicial review for these types of questions so that courts would look with greater scrutiny at economic development projects.

APA, its Connecticut chapter, and the National Congress for Community Economic Development joined together to urge the Supreme Court to retain its long history of jurisprudence applying a deferential standard of review to public use determinations. The APA amicus brief was written by Professor Thomas W. Merrill of Columbia University and John D. Echeverria of the Georgetown Environmental Law & Policy Institute. (See the full brief below.)

APA wrote:

> Eminent domain is concededly an unsettling power, and is subject to misuse or overuse if not properly constrained. But eminent domain is disruptive for all who experience it, not just those who might be able to persuade a reviewing court that a particular condemnation is not "public" enough. The dangers of eminent domain should be addressed by assuring that it remains a second-best alternative to market exchange as a means of acquiring resources, by encouraging careful planning and public participation in decisions to invoke eminent domain, and by building on current legislative requirements that mandate additional compensation beyond the constitutional minimum for persons who experience uncompensated subjective losses and consequential damages. . . .

The facts in this case were misplaced in much of the news coverage since the Kelo opinion was announced June 23, but they were an important reason why the Supreme Court decided not to expand or restrict the power of eminent domain.

Another source of protection for all property owners is to assure, to the extent possible, that eminent domain is exercised only in conjunction with a process of land-use planning that includes broad public participation and a careful consideration of alternatives to eminent domain.

Integrating the decision to use eminent domain into a sound planning process has a number of desirable consequences. Such a process can help minimize the use of eminent domain, by identifying alternatives to proposed development projects, such as relocating or re-sizing projects, or perhaps forgoing them altogether. It can also reduce public concerns about the use of eminent domain by providing a forum in which the reasons for opposition can be considered, offering explanations for the proposed course of action and possible alternatives, and perhaps instilling a greater degree of understanding on the part of both the proponents and opponents of the proposed project. . . .

ORAL ARGUMENT

[This is an excerpt from the transcript of oral arguments before the U.S. Supreme Court, February 22, 2005, which appeared in the April 2005 issue of Planning and Environmental Law.*]*

Scott G. Bullock, from the Institute for Justice in Washington, D.C., argued on behalf of the property owners. Wesley W. Horton, from the Hartford law firm of Horton, Shields & Knox, argued on behalf of the city and redevelopment agency. In the absence of Chief Justice William H. Rehnquist and Justice John Paul Stevens, Justice Sandra Day O'Connor presided over the oral argument (the first woman to ever do so!). Also attending were Justices Stephen G. Breyer, Ruth Bader Ginsburg, Anthony M. Kennedy, Antonin Scalia, David Hackett Souter, and Clarence Thomas. Case cites are provided in the text.

MR. BULLOCK: Justice O'Connor, and may it please the Court: This case is about whether there are any limits on government's eminent domain power under the public use requirement of the Fifth Amendment. Every home, church, or corner store would produce more tax revenue and jobs if it were a Costco, a shopping mall, or a private office building. But if that's the justification for the use of eminent domain, then any city can take property anywhere within its borders for any private use that might make more money than what is there now.

JUSTICE GINSBURG: Mr. Bullock, you are leaving out that New London was in a depressed economic condition, so this is distinguished from the case where the state has no particular reason for wanting this, but the critical fact on the city side, at least, is that this was a depressed community and they wanted to build it up, get more jobs.

MR. BULLOCK: . . . Every city has problems. Every city would like to have more tax revenue, but that cannot be a justification for taking the property—

JUSTICE GINSBURG: But you concede that on the facts, more than tax revenue was at stake. The community had gone down and down, and the town wanted to build it up.

MR. BULLOCK: It is a desire to try to improve the economy through tax revenue and jobs. That is certainly the case. But that cannot be a justification for the use of eminent domain because if the trickle-down effects of economic development are a justification, then there really is no limit on the—

JUSTICE SCALIA: You don't concede, or do you, that elevating the city from depressed to prosperous is a better justification than elevating a city from prosperous to more prosperous?

MR. BULLOCK: . . . We do not. . . .

JUSTICE GINSBURG: The line you draw is between blight, which *Berman* says was in the public use, blighted conditions okay, but depressed conditions, not the best in line with the—

JUSTICE GINSBURG: Mr. Bullock, you are leaving out that New London was in a depressed economic condition, so this is distinguished from the case where the state has no particular reason for wanting this . . .

JUSTICE BREYER: The question is, if you agree with the empirical statement that there almost always is some public benefit attached, then my question is, why must there be a limit within that broad framework?

MR. BULLOCK: Yes, Your Honor. We think that that is a line that this Court has drawn that is area specific that focuses on the conditions in a particular area. And the condemnations in *Berman* (*Berman v. Parker*, 348 U.S. 26 (1954)) removed the problematic areas. It removed the blight.

JUSTICE O'CONNOR: Oh, but *Berman* spoke, in the opinion, said that the determination of the legislature about these things is virtually conclusive, that there is only the narrowest, narrowest role for the judiciary. What kind of standard are you proposing we should get into here to second-guess the public use aspect?

MR. BULLOCK: Your Honor, it is clear that eminent domain power is broad, but there has to be limits, and that's what we are really talking about here.

JUSTICE O'CONNOR: Well, have we ever in any case from this Court said that the limit has been exceeded?

MR. BULLOCK: In a few cases from earlier in this century, Your Honor, the *Missouri Pacific* case (*Missouri Pacific Railroad v. Nebraska*, 164 U.S. 403 (1896)), the *Thompson v. Consolidated Gas* case (*Thompson v. Consol. Gas Utils. Corp*, 300 U.S. 55 (1937)), but this Court has recognized for over 200 years that there are limits on eminent domain power, that they cannot be used for private cases. And that has been a consistent strain throughout this Court's—

JUSTICE BREYER: Justice Douglas says there that as long as it's an objective within Congress and legislature's legitimate grant of power, they can do it, I mean, as long as there's a—so why does there have to be a limit within that broad limit?

MR. BULLOCK: Well, Your Honor, the limit is that there cannot be takings for private use.

JUSTICE BREYER: Of course, there can't, purely. But there is no taking for private use that you could imagine in reality that wouldn't also have a public benefit of some kind, whether it's increasing jobs or increasing taxes, et cetera. That's a fact of the world. And so given that fact of the world, that is law, why shouldn't the law say, okay, virtually every taking is all right, as long as there is some public benefit which there always is and it's up to the legislature.

MR. BULLOCK: Your Honor, we think that that cuts way too broadly.

JUSTICE BREYER: Because?

MR. BULLOCK: Because then every property, every home, every business can then be taken for any private use.

JUSTICE BREYER: No. It could only be taken if there is a public use and there almost always is. Now, do you agree with that, or do you not agree with my last empirical statement?

MR. BULLOCK: Well, again, the eminent domain power is broad, but there has to be limits.

JUSTICE BREYER: Now, that's, of course, my question. The question is, if you agree with the empirical statement that there almost always is some public benefit attached, then my question is, why must there be a limit within that broad framework?

MR. BULLOCK: Well, . . . with just having a simple public benefit, then there really is no distinction between public and private uses. And that is what we call upon this Court to state, for instance, in the *Berman* case and in the *Midkiff* case (*Hawaii Hous. Auth. v. Midkiff*, 467 U.S. 229 (1984)), which we think are really the outer limits of government's eminent domain—

JUSTICE O'CONNOR: But do you think those were correctly decided or do you take issue with the decision in those two cases?

MR. BULLOCK: We think that those decisions can be consistent with ruling in favor of Petitioners in this particular case, Your Honor, because—

JUSTICE O'CONNOR: But you take the position that a city that is suffering from enormous lack of jobs and depression, economic depression, that there is no public use purpose for taking land to enable the creation of jobs?

MR. BULLOCK: That is correct, Your Honor. We do not—

JUSTICE SOUTER: Well, let's assume that the city instead of taking the property by eminent domain simply used its, its own—some of its own regular tax income to buy up the property, and assembled parcels of land with the purpose of selling them to an industrial developer to raise the tax base and hence ultimately to raise taxes. Would you say just within the meaning of general understanding of proper governmental purposes that the city was acting in a way that had no legitimate public purpose?

MR. BULLOCK: Well, Your Honor, I think the question goes to whether or not the government could use its police power to acquire property and then sell it to a private developer.

JUSTICE SOUTER: Well, I'm not interested in the label. I'm just saying if the government says we need to increase the tax base because we have a depressed city, so we are going to take some of our tax money now, and we are just going to buy up property that people are willing to sell to us, and we are going to assemble parcels. And when we get a big enough one, we are going to sell them to a developer for industrial purposes. And that will raise the tax base. Is there anything illegitimate as a purpose for governmental spending in doing that?

MR. BULLOCK: No, Your Honor. We do not believe that that would be—it's not a public use.

JUSTICE SOUTER: Why isn't there a public purpose here?

MR. BULLOCK: Well, Your Honor, because this case affects the eminent domain power, which is regulated by the Fifth Amendment—

JUSTICE SOUTER: . . . I thought your point was that it was use of eminent domain power for an improper purpose. And you characterize that purpose as conveying property to private owners. Well, in my example, the same thing is going on except that it's not using the eminent domain power. If the purpose in my example is a proper public purpose, why isn't it a proper public purpose when the government does it by eminent domain? What changes about the purpose?

MR. BULLOCK: Your Honor, because of the public use restriction of the Amendment. That's what we really—

JUSTICE SCALIA: Mr. Bullock, do you equate purpose with use? Are the two terms the same? Does the public use requirement mean nothing more than that it have a public purpose?

MR. BULLOCK: No, Your Honor.

JUSTICE SCALIA: That's your answer to Justice Souter.

• • •

JUSTICE SOUTER: If that is your answer, then I suppose the slum clearance cases were wrongly decided.

MR. BULLOCK: Well, your Honor, this Court did hold in *Berman* and *Midkiff* that the police power and eminent domain power are coterminous. That was a holding especially of this Court's opinion in *Midkiff*. And there are certain amici that have been filed in this case . . . that have called upon this Court to re-examine that. And of course, this Court is free to do that.

JUSTICE SOUTER: But you are saying we don't have to re-examine it, but I think your adoption of Justice Scalia's approach puts you in a difficult—I think you're moving in the direction of saying we really have got to overrule the prior cases.

MR. BULLOCK: Your Honor, I think under a—perhaps an original understanding of the takings clause, there was a difference between public

JUSTICE SOUTER: I think you're moving in the direction of saying we really have got to overrule the prior cases.

use and public domain.

JUSTICE SOUTER: Just for the moment, what about my question? And you can get into history, if you want to, and I tend to be interested in that, but my immediate concern is, if you give the answer that you have just given, doesn't it jeopardize the precedent of the slum clearance cases?

MR. BULLOCK: Your Honor, I don't think so, because of the caveat in *Berman* and *Midkiff* that eminent domain cannot be used for private uses. And that is what is really at issue here. What I think is appropriate, though—

JUSTICE KENNEDY: But that's what they were being used for in *Berman* and—everybody knows that private developers were the beneficiaries in *Berman*.

MR. BULLOCK: Your Honor, I believe the justifications focused upon the removal of the offensive conditions in *Berman*, that the public purpose, if you want to call it that, was served once the blight was removed, the public purpose was served once the oligopoly was broken up.

JUSTICE KENNEDY: As I understand, you're testing—you want me to make a distinction between blight, which is a permissible governmental use, governmental objective, and economic revival, which isn't?

JUSTICE KENNEDY: As I understand, you're testing— you want me to make a distinction between blight, which is a permissible governmental use, governmental objective, and economic revival, which isn't?

• • •

MR. BULLOCK: Yes. And we think that that is a line—

JUSTICE KENNEDY: Well, suppose an economist or even the judge might say, well, it's very clear that if this economic depression continues for another five years, we are going to have blight. Blight is in the eye of the beholder, I know that.

MR. BULLOCK: Exactly. And I think that that is really one of the dangers of the majority opinion here is that it puts any property up for grabs. Under the blight statutes, they actually have to—governments have to meet a certain objective criteria to satisfy that this is actually a blighted area.

JUSTICE KENNEDY: Why isn't it an objective criteria to say that we are going to have economic revival, avoid economic downturns?

MR. BULLOCK: Well, Your Honor, because, I think—to get back to the decisions in *Berman* and *Midkiff*, what this Court I think focused on there is that the public use or the public purpose was direct and immediate. It was served directly by the condemnations, and it was immediately served by the removal of the blight and the breaking up of the oligopoly. In economic development condemnations, the only public benefits that come about, if they come about at all, are completely dependent upon private parties actually making a profit. And that those profits then somehow—

• • •

JUSTICE KENNEDY: Precisely the description you gave applied to the railroads in the west.

MR. BULLOCK: Well, Your Honor, those were justified under I think the line of cases that held that those were really essential for land assembly for instrumentalities of commerce. They were—

JUSTICE KENNEDY: And this seems to be really essential for the purpose of developing industrial property to increase the tax base. The argument is, and I don't know of any reason to doubt it, that doing it seriatim by voluntary acquisition and sale doesn't work. So the rationale for this is essentially the rationale for the railroads, for the public utility line condemnations, and so on. There isn't another practical way to do it. And there is a public benefit at the end, and that ought to qualify it as a public use.

MR. BULLOCK: Your Honor, there are many ways to do economic development without condemnation. It happens every single day in this country. And in the states that prohibit the use of eminent domain simply for private business development, those states do make the distinction between blighted areas and simply their communities wanting to take advantage of more tax revenue.

JUSTICE GINSBURG: Even though in *Berman*, there was a department store that was not blighted, and it was permissible because the whole area was to be improved to raze that department store, even though it wasn't contributing in any way to blight.

MR. BULLOCK: Yes, Your Honor. But the Court in *Berman* held that there were certain properties that even though they might have been nonblighted, it was essential to have those properties in order to remove the blight from the area that was at issue. So there was the ability of government to get certain properties even though they might have been nonblighted. Here—

JUSTICE O'CONNOR: Mr. Bullock, would you articulate the test that you would propose the Court adopt. Some amici and others have argued that we should use the substantially advances test, so-called test from regulatory takings. What tests do you articulate?

• • •

MR. BULLOCK: The test should be that the government cannot take property simply so that the new owners can put it to ordinary private uses of land. That's really the test. And the—

JUSTICE O'CONNOR: Well, that's not what's asserted here, of course. Here the city says we are doing this for purposes of enhancing economic development of a very poor city.

MR. BULLOCK: True, Your Honor, but—

JUSTICE O'CONNOR: So what do we do with that alleged purpose? What is your test?

MR. BULLOCK: Well, the test, Your Honor, for—

JUSTICE O'CONNOR: Is it no economic development purpose?

MR. BULLOCK: Yes. Yes. When it's only justified in order to gain the secondary benefits from ordinary private uses of land, and the way that businesses always make use of their land to try to make money or to try to make a profit. That's our bright line rule. But for our second test, if this Court accepts that economic development can be a public use, then we advocate a test of reasonably foreseeable uses and minimum standards in order to counter the dangers posed by such private involvement in the use of eminent domain power.

JUSTICE BREYER: . . . I understand the former. That's a big retreat, and it comes to me now you're getting to what I think is a possible realm of reason here. But the second part now you said "and minimum standards." What minimum standards?

MR. BULLOCK: Well, the dissent in the Connecticut Supreme Court talked a lot about minimum standards that should be in place in order to ensure that public benefits actually come about. Those could be such things as a commencement date for the project, a construction schedule, financial eligibility for the developers, there's a number of different things.

JUSTICE BREYER: No, I mean, are you advocating particular ones?

MR. BULLOCK: Not particular ones, just the standard actually be in place, and we think that the dissent provides some good guide rules for establishing—

JUSTICE SCALIA: Isn't that in effect changing the test from public use to efficient public use? I mean, what's—you know, if I condemn land for a public utility and the public utility turns out to be very inefficient, has the condemnation been invalid?

MR. BULLOCK: No. Your Honor.

JUSTICE SCALIA: Isn't that in effect changing the test from public use to efficient public use? I mean, what's—you know, if I condemn land for a public utility and the public utility turns out to be very inefficient, has the condemnation been invalid?

JUSTICE SCALIA: Do you want us to sit here and evaluate the prospects of each condemnation one by one?

MR. BULLOCK: No, Your Honor, what we are advocating for, and utilities of course are justified, have long been justified under a separate line of cases, common carrier regulations. But what we are talking about are certain minimum standards in place at the time of condemnation to try to have some type of reasonable certainty that the public benefits are to come about so we are not talking about ongoing oversight. We are simply talking about minimum standards at the time of the condemnation.

• • •

JUSTICE SOUTER: . . . [W]hy we would want to draw a distinction between the use of the eminent domain power that takes a parcel of property from private person A and simply then reconveys it to private person B without any particular object in mind except that the city likes B, you know, the mayor is the Democrat and B is the Democrat. That kind of thing. So I can understand the need for some distinction between that case and what we've got here. The question is when you say there have to be minimum standards, I guess, is Do we have a problem historically or in this case about the good faith of the taking so that we need the minimum standards to make sure that we are not getting into the first example?

MR. BULLOCK: Yes, Your Honor. And there is a number of reasons why there has to be reasonably foreseeable uses—

JUSTICE SOUTER: Is there a reason in this case? Is there some doubt here?

MR. BULLOCK: Well, it goes to the doubt about whether or not the public benefits will actually come about in this case. The takings here are really for speculative purposes, pure speculative purposes. And that's where the minimum standards come into play to ensure—

JUSTICE O'CONNOR: But do you really want courts to be in the business of trying to weigh the evidence to see if the utility will be successful or the hospital will be successful or the road will be well constructed? I mean, what kind of a test are you proposing?

MR. BULLOCK: Your Honor, our test is limited really to the condemnations that are completely dependent upon the private businesses actually being successful, and that those benefits coming about so it would not affect utilities or anything like that. But at a minimum, this Court should require that the government actually name a use.

JUSTICE O'CONNOR: Does the record tell us anything about how often takings by eminent domain for economic development occur in this country? Is it frequent? What are we dealing with?

MR. BULLOCK: It is, it is frequent, Your Honor. There's no—we do not know of any study that looks specifically at condemnations for economic development, but after the Michigan court's decision in *Poletown* (*Poletown Neighborhood Council v. City of Detroit*, 304 N.W.2d 455 (Mich. 1981)), they became commonplace. And you had properties— business[es] that were being condemned for casinos, other homes that were taken for automobile manufacturers. And the Michigan Supreme Court saw that as a disaster. And overturned that (in *County of Wayne v. Hathcock*, 684 N.W.2d 765 (Mich. 2004)).

JUSTICE KENNEDY: In all of those cases, I think the economic feasibility or economic success test would have been easily met. I mean, what you're doing is trying to protect some economic value. But I think it's pretty clear that most economists would say this development wouldn't happen unless there is a foreseeable chance of success. Let me ask you this, and it's a little opposite of the particular question presented: Are there any writings or

JUSTICE O'CONNOR: But do you really want courts to be in the business of trying to weigh the evidence to see if the utility will be successful or the hospital will be successful or the road will be well constructed? I mean, what kind of a test are you proposing?

scholarship that indicates that when you have property being taken from one private person ultimately to go to another private person, that what we ought to do is to adjust the measure of compensation, so that the owner—the condemnee—can receive some sort of a premium for the development?

MR. BULLOCK: There may be some scholarship about that. This Court has consistently held that the property owner is simply entitled to just compensation of the appraised value of the property. . . .

• • •

MR. BULLOCK: I believe there has been some scholarship about it, but we think it's vital that there be a public use requirement.

JUSTICE BREYER: Can I ask you about the standard? Go back for a second.

MR. BULLOCK: Yes.

JUSTICE BREYER: I gather that the Iowa courts have a standard that includes whether there is a reasonable likelihood that the intended public use will take place. Now, is that the standard you're advocating?

MR. BULLOCK: It's similar to our reasonable foreseeability test that we set forth in our brief that this Court actually talked about in the *Vester* case (*Cincinnati v. Vester*, 281 U.S. 439 (1930)) as well, and a number of the other state cases that are cited in our brief that establish that there has to be a use for the property and that that use has to be reasonably perceived.

• • •

JUSTICE BREYER: I mean, it seems to me you might—whether there is a reasonable assurance that there will in fact be the public use which the state uses as the justification for taking the property. Is that going to help you that much?

MR. BULLOCK: I think it will provide important minimal standards of protection for—

JUSTICE BREYER: Well, I mean, I don't see how this Court could get into the business of saying you have to have this by a particular day or you have to have witnesses. I mean, we couldn't impose that sort of thing, could we?

MR. BULLOCK: Your Honor, I think just the standard needs to be in place.

JUSTICE BREYER: There needs to be a reasonable assurance.

MR. BULLOCK: Exactly. Or at the very least, a reasonable foreseeability as well, which is at a minimum that is not even in place in this particular case. And the majority of state courts that have looked at this, that is a—

• • •

JUSTICE GINSBURG: But do you do that area by area? I mean, one of the points you made, this is divided into what, seven areas?

MR. BULLOCK: Right.

JUSTICE O'CONNOR: And there's some—to be developed first, you say that your clients lived in parcels that are not likely to be developed soon, if at all. So when making this determination, is development reasonably likely, do you have to do it parcel by parcel or can it be with the whole—

MR. BULLOCK: No, Your Honor. We believe it should be done where the property is actually being conveyed. . . .

JUSTICE GINSBURG: So it's not the area development but this house, will there be—is it reasonably likely that there will be development in that particular plot?

MR. BULLOCK: In this particular parcel, that is correct, Your Honor, and that has been supported by ruling in just about every condemnation—

JUSTICE SOUTER: . . . [G]iven your position, why do you think it's necessary to adopt the test you've just articulated as distinct simply from a good faith requirement. So that if somebody objected and offered to prove bad faith, that would be in effect a defense for the taking?

MR. BULLOCK: Your Honor, because that does not really provide any protection to property owners. The intent to benefit a private party, and the intent to benefit the public are really one and the same in these types of condemnations. And we believe it is imperative at a minimum because the condemnations are dependent upon private parties even being successful that there has to be reasonable foreseeable uses. And also, if this Court so chooses, minimum standards in place to ensure that those benefits actually go to the public. . . .

• • •

MR. HORTON: Justice O'Connor, and may it please the Court: The principal purpose of the takings clause is to provide for just compensation. Now, I want to very briefly state two reasons why you do not want to make a—

JUSTICE O'CONNOR: Well, but it has to be for a valid public use.

• • •

MR. HORTON: I completely agree with that, but if the primary purpose of the takings clause is not to regulate legislative determinations of that, but it seems to me that what the opposition is asking for is two tests. One for *Berman* and *Midkiff* and *National Railroad (Nat'l R.R. Passenger Corp. v. Boston & Maine Corp.*, 503 U.S. 407 (1992)), and another test for *Kelo*. There is no principle basis for a court to make what is really a value judgment about whether a long-term plan to revive an economically depressed city is a public use of a higher or lower rank constitutionally—

JUSTICE BREYER: But he doesn't—he doesn't, his second test does not adopt that. The second test which he was arguing at the end is just that there has to be a reasonable assurance that the public use, and it could include all those things, will in fact take place.

MR. HORTON: Yes, Justice Breyer. And I noted his remark because that's actually in concession because that's the test the Connecticut Supreme Court imposed. And they have—

JUSTICE BREYER: That may be, but what do you think of that test?

MR. HORTON: I don't, I don't agree. I don't think it's necessary to do that, because if you have that test, you have to say, well, what do I do about, about other areas than this. *Berman* is an excellent example of that, because as Justice Ginsburg said, Mr. Berman's property was not blighted. You needed to take Mr. Berman's property in order for the economic development that was going to occur later on. And the question is, Was it reasonably assured that the economic development—in fact, some of the other side's amicus briefs say that that worked out terribly down there, and all it was was discriminating against the poor and, and poverty stricken people and it didn't accomplish any goal—

JUSTICE SCALIA: Mr. Horton, what, what difference does it make that, that New London was in an economic depression? Would it not be fully as much, under your theory of a public use, for a city to say, yes, we are not doing badly, but we could do better. Let's attract some high-tech industry here. You can't possibly draw a line between depressed cities and undepressed cities, can you?

MR. HORTON: I would not draw a line.

JUSTICE SCALIA: You wouldn't. And you wouldn't ask us to do it either.

MR. BULLOCK: The intent to benefit a private party, and the intent to benefit the public are really one and the same in these types of condemnations. And we believe it is imperative at a minimum because the condemnations are dependent upon private parties even being successful that there has to be reasonable foreseeable uses.

MR. HORTON: I would not ask—I have a back-up argument that you do not need to reach that issue here in light of the facts of this case. But I—to be candid with you, my view is that the test you have is—there is no principle—

JUSTICE SCALIA: Any city can do it. And in the hypothetical that Justice Souter gave earlier where, you know, you couldn't take it from A and give it to B, because B is a good Democrat, you could take it from A and give it to B if B is richer, and would pay higher municipal taxes, couldn't you?

MR. HORTON: Yes, Your Honor. But I have a caveat on that. If you're talking about one property, you're very likely to have a *Willowbrook v. Oleck* (528 US 562 (2000)) problem about discrimination, you know, intentional discrimination against somebody else's property.

JUSTICE SCALIA: No. I just want to take property from people who are paying less taxes and give it to people who are paying more taxes. That would be a public use, wouldn't it?

JUSTICE O'CONNOR: For example, Motel 6 and the city thinks, well, if we had a Ritz-Carlton, we would have higher taxes. Now, is that okay?

MR. HORTON: Yes, Your Honor. That would be okay. I—because otherwise you're in the position of drawing the line. I mean, there is, there is a limit. I mean—

JUSTICE KENNEDY: Well, if that, if that's so then the occasional statements that we see in the writing that you can't take from A to give to B is just wrong?

MR. HORTON: No. I don't agree with that. A good example is—well, there is *Missouri Pacific*.

JUSTICE KENNEDY: You think you can't take from A to give to B, that there is some substance and force to that proposition?

MR. HORTON: There is some force to it. I certainly wouldn't—

JUSTICE SCALIA: Let me qualify it. You can take from A to give to B if B pays more taxes?

MR. HORTON: If it's a significant amount. Obviously, there is a cost—

JUSTICE SCALIA: I'll accept that. You can take from A and give to B if B pays significantly more taxes.

MR. HORTON: With that—

JUSTICE SCALIA: You accept that as a proposition?

MR. HORTON: I do, Your Honor.

• • •

JUSTICE KENNEDY: Do you agree that there is substance to that proposition and that that proposition is correct?

MR. HORTON: Yes, Your Honor. I do. And to—

JUSTICE KENNEDY: But isn't that exactly what happened in *Berman*?

MR. HORTON: Your Honor, in *Berman*, the—what has—

JUSTICE KENNEDY: Isn't that exactly what always happens unless it's for a firehouse or a school?

MR. HORTON: Your Honor, my position is that purely taking from one person to give to another that shows no public benefit other than just giving from—taking from one person to another would not be a public use. A good example is the *Missouri Pacific* case. The one case in 200 years of this Court's jurisprudence where you have, in fact, struck such a taking that was not a regulatory taking. I would also point out that there are a few cases around the country where it does not include Justice Scalia's hypothetical about additional taxes. An excellent example of that is the case the other side has cited from New Jersey, *Casino Properties v. Bannon* (727 A.2d 102 (N.J. Super. Ct. 1998)), where the Trump Association just wanted a park-

> *MR. HORTON: Your Honor, my position is that purely taking from one person to give to another that shows no public benefit other than just giving from—taking from one person to another would not be a public use.*

ing lot that was next door. There was no assembly problem. No problem putting small parcels together. There was no talk in the case about taxes or more taxes or more jobs or anything. . . . [T]he trial judge there didn't say it was just for . . . a private purpose, but he said it was overwhelmingly just for the Trump organization's—so, I mean, if you include Justice Scalia's hypothetical about more taxes, then I say that's sufficient, as long as you get over—

JUSTICE GINSBURG: Is that what the Connecticut Supreme Court that we are reviewing said, you—you are arguing, it seems to me, for something that goes beyond what was adjudicated in this case. I mean—

MR. HORTON: Yes.

JUSTICE GINSBURG: It was a finding, a finding before to be a fact in the trial court that this development was going to be primarily for the benefit of the citizens of New London, and not for the benefit of Pfizer or the private developer.

MR. HORTON: Yes, Your Honor. I agree with that and that is why I say my back-up position is you don't need to determine whether you go beyond economic depression of a city in this particular case.

. . .

JUSTICE O'CONNOR: When, when there is no condemnation to acquire property for the direct use of the public, as for a public right-of-way, or a utility path or something, where it's purely economic development, is there any reason why we shouldn't draw a clear line and say that isn't a public purpose. Let them go out and deal with—buy it on the market, on the open market. What's the matter with that?

MR. HORTON: Well, for one thing we have in this case, and this comes back to the point about this particular case, is a severe assembly problem.

• • •

JUSTICE O'CONNOR: So what are these parcels of the people now before us going to be used for?

MR. HORTON: Yes, Your Honor. First of all, it's a long-range plan. If I could have, if I could have the chart, please, if I may show you Your Honor. The—we are out on a peninsula here, and here is Pfizer down here, which at the time of the taking was almost completed. They moved in a month afterwards. Up here is an old state—old fort from the nineteenth century that the state agreed to turn into a state park as part of an overall plan. The overall plan is this whole thing. Now, parcel one is going to be a hotel, is planned for a hotel. Parcel two was planned—

JUSTICE O'CONNOR: Let's talk about the litigants.

• • •

MR. HORTON: . . . They are in parcel 3, and they are in parcel 4-A. Now, the—it's to be developed in phases. The first phase is one and two. The next phase is then three and four, A, and there is also a marina—

JUSTICE O'CONNOR: What's planned for 3 and 4-A?

MR. HORTON: What's planned for 3 is it's going to be office space. And the expectation is there is going to be a demand for class A office space, which is the best-quality office space in this area by 2010. And the expectation is that it will attract the sorts of offices that will feed on Pfizer. They spent $300 million on a site here. In addition, I may point out, this is the Amtrak line going along here. The only way you can get to parcels 1 and is to go right by parcel 3 or go right by parcel 4-A. This is a wastewater treatment facility. Parcel 4-A is for park support or marina support. Now, it isn't more definitive, but obviously, one possible use is for parking here because you've got a wastewater treatment facility here. You've got the

JUSTICE GINSBURG: It was a finding, a finding before to be a fact in the trial court that this development was going to be primarily for the benefit of the citizens of New London, and not for the benefit of Pfizer or the private developer.

park here. You've got the marina here and you've got the other parcels here. It's not like we are talking, as in *Berman*, you're talking about something that's in the parcel. And in *Berman*, they said it's not for the court to decide where the boundary lines ought to be. . . .

• • •

JUSTICE BREYER: Could the courts, under this clause, at least review what you've just said for reasonableness? I mean, look at the reasonableness of a claim that this is for—basically for a public use. Look at the reasonableness of the claim that we should do it this way, rather than excusing the people who don't want to sell their houses no matter what and doing it a little bit differently. Reasonableness is a concept that's already in the Constitution in terms of what the legislature can do, but I'm thinking of the stronger kind of reasonableness review that you might have in an administrative action. Now, is, *Overton Park (Citizens to Preserve Overton Park v. Volpe*, 401 US 402, 419 (1971)), if you want a case. Is that a possible kind of review that you might find appropriate here?

MR. HORTON: No, Your Honor, if what you're defining as reasonableness is being higher than rational basis. Because in that situation, you're applying a higher standard for a taking where we are paying for it than you would be for—

JUSTICE BREYER: Well, the reason that you would apply a somewhat higher standard is because the rational basis, with tremendous deference, applies to the power of Congress to act in an economic area in the absence of a particular constitutional provision designed to protect a minority from the actions of the majority. And if you read that public purpose doctrine, a section here as having that in mind, you might want a somewhat higher level of review. Now, that's the whole thing spelled out. I'm not advocating it. But I am putting it forward to get—to get your reaction.

MR. HORTON: Your Honor, that same type of remark could be made about rational basis equal protection review.

JUSTICE BREYER: Oh, and indeed with equal protection, we very often do have a somewhat higher standard of review.

MR. HORTON: Ah, yes, Your Honor, but the point here is that you should not have a higher standard of review because we are paying for it. It would be ironic to have a higher test than for example in a regulatory taking or even the same test. You have a test in *Nollan (Nollan v. Cal. Coastal Comm'n*, 483 U.S. 825 (1987)) and *Dolan (Dolan v. City of Tigard*, 512 U.S. 374 (1994)), for example, which is an exactions case. So that's to say—

JUSTICE SCALIA: Mr. Horton, you're paying for it, but you're also taking property from somebody who doesn't want to sell it. Does that count for nothing? Yes, you're paying for it, but you're giving the money to somebody who doesn't want the money, who wants to live in the house that she's lived in her whole life. That counts for nothing?

MR. HORTON: No, of course not, Your Honor.

JUSTICE SCALIA: Well, then, let me ask—would, would the reasonableness standard, if the project is indeed reasonable, and there is genuine prospect that all of these good things that you're talking about will happen, why wouldn't private money come in to further the project? Why is it necessary to condemn it if it's so reasonable. Why couldn't you, you—now, you say there is a holdout for one part, parcel. Couldn't the city fund a private purchase of that parcel? Say, you know, we'll make funds available out of our general tax revenue to somebody who wants to come in and put together this system? Of course, that person has to buy out property owners, but we'll, we'll give you money to buy them out at high prices.

JUSTICE SCALIA: Well, then, let me ask—would, would the reasonableness standard, if the project is indeed reasonable, and there is genuine prospect that all of these good things that you're talking about will happen, why wouldn't private money come in to further the project? Why is it necessary to condemn it if it's so reasonable.

MR. HORTON: Your Honor, there are some plaintiffs who are not going to sell at any price. They want to stay there. You've got a severe assembly problem in this case and it's not as though you can say, well, go somewhere else. You have a situation where you've got the Pfizer plant that is being built there. You've got the state park that's there. You've got this Naval underseas facility that just came on the market. That's the only place anything is going to work and it's—and it's five to six square miles of town. I mean, there is no other place to go.

JUSTICE GINSBURG: How much, how much of this was voluntarily sold, is that correct?

MR. HORTON: The large share of it was, but of course, that's because there is always in the background the possibility of being able to condemn it. I mean, that obviously facilitates a lot of voluntary sales. . . . I mean, there is going to be a more severe holdout problem.

JUSTICE BREYER: That may be. Now, that's why I'm back to reasonableness. You see, we are told in the briefs that the people who often might hold out, might be doing so to get more money, but it might also be because they are poor, they are well connected politically, and their only hope is to go to a court and stop this thing. So you'd give them two weapons. Weapon one is you have to pay them. That's correct. Compensation. And weapon two is they can put you to a test of being reasonable. That might be quite a deferential test, so you might have every leg up. But they at least could catch the instances where this is really not reasonable to do to them what you're doing to them that they don't want.

MR. HORTON: . . . First of all, that applies to all sorts of takings. If I'm building a road, let me give you an example of the *Rindge* case (*Rindge Co. v. Los Angeles*, 262 U.S. 700 (1923)) that Your Honors decided in the 1920s. That was the road to nowhere. It was a road that went through a farm to the county line. And the other county had no intention at that point of building a road, but Your Honors said, well, they might get around to it at sometime so it's a good idea to build it now. We had a similar situation in Hartford. There is supposed to be a ring road around Hartford, and the state condemned all this land for a ring road around Hartford. Well, one little bit of it was done and then just this, this year, in very low print in the last page of the newspaper, we see about the state getting around to selling the land because they didn't, they didn't do it. I mean, this can happen in the railroad case (*Nat'l R.R. Passenger Corp. v. Boston & Maine Corp.*, 503 U.S. 407 (1992)) is a good example. . . . If it's—being a common carrier makes all the difference, then how come the ICC just didn't order the Boston & Maine to fix the railroad? . . .

JUSTICE SCALIA: Common carriers are subject to state regulation to a degree that private companies are not. They must, they must treat all comers alike. I mean, I don't think the public utility cases are at all comparable to condemning land in order to get a new company to move in and pay more taxes. I just don't think it's similar.

MR. HORTON: Well, I would like to point out that the—there is a difference, the whole point is about having a test about reasonable assurances, about whether something is going to happen and that's where the railroad case makes a difference.

JUSTICE [?]: I agree with you on that.

MR. HORTON: . . . But coming back to Justice Breyer's point, you made a point about poor people. And I'd like to point out, unless you're going to overrule *Berman*, you know, poor people and minorities are more likely to be vulnerable in the blight cases than in this case. I mean, this is a good example. Economic development can take place anywhere in town. Blight happens in one area of town where the poor and the minorities are likely

MR. HORTON: Your Honor, there are some plaintiffs who are not going to sell at any price. They want to stay there. You've got a severe assembly problem in this case and it's not as though you can say, well, go somewhere else.

to live, and in fact, this very case, we have got middle class people. There is no blight that's been alleged in the condemnation papers. The other thing is if you stick to blight, this is the problem you're going to have. You're going to end up making a blight jurisprudence because—because what's going to happen is the cities are going to say, we can only do this by blight, so they are going to have marginal definitions of blight. Florida, for example, says property is blighted if it's vacant. Is that blight? I mean, you're going to have a big headache in that—

JUSTICE BREYER: No, I'm accepting that you can't make that kind of a distinction. That's where I'm focusing on a test that would possibly apply only where you transfer property from one private person to another, but still wouldn't make those distinctions of blight or not blight.

MR. HORTON: . . . [W]ould the Court make a distinction between a case where the city is doing the developing itself, and another case where the city gives it to a private person[?] I'd like to point out, my client is going to keep the property. It's—it's going to be leased to a developer. It's not going to be sold to the developer. So I mean, if this developer builds a building on this property, and then doesn't comply, they are in big trouble.

MR. HORTON: . . . [W]ould the Court make a distinction between a case where the city is doing the developing itself, and another case where the city gives it to a private person[?]

JUSTICE KENNEDY: It does seem ironic that 100 percent of the premium for the new development goes to the, goes to the developer and to the taxpayers and not to the property owner.

MR. HORTON: Well, that's an interesting point. A question was raised earlier about the other side about whether there should be—

JUSTICE KENNEDY: The compensation measures.

MR. HORTON: The compensation measures. Exactly. . . . But I would point out that's something, you know, in terms of social costs and things like that, that is something that this Court might or might not wish to consider in a just compensation case, but I don't think it should affect whether you take the property or not. It seems to me that . . . you have to assume in this case that there is going to be just compensation.

• • •

JUSTICE SOUTER: Mr. Horton, what do you think is the reason that there are not a lot of examples of the sort that I think one of Justice O'Connor's hypotheticals raised, in which the, I don't know, the Econoline Motel gets condemned so that the Ritz can be built, thereby increasing tax revenue and so on, kind of parcel by parcel augmentations to the tax base and so on. Why aren't there a lot of examples like that?

MR. HORTON: I think there is two good reasons for it, and that it's a theoretical more than a practical problem. First of all, you've got all sorts of transaction costs when you, when you go through eminent domain, as opposed to doing things voluntarily. So you are not going to do things . . . for one piece of property because of the transaction costs involved. I mean, you're never going to make up—unless it's to, you know, to favor the governor's friend or something like that, as you say.

JUSTICE SOUTER: In which case we have a different—

MR. HORTON: In which case you have a different problem. The *Willowbrook v] Oleck* test.

JUSTICE [?]: Okay. So we have transaction costs.

MR. HORTON: Transaction costs, but that is a serious problem. And the other thing, there is the democratic process, Your Honor. I mean, especially if the taxpayers are paying for something and you know, they are getting a bad reason or run around about the reason, you know, that's subject to review. It seems to me democracy can make good decisions and—or bad decisions under the Constitution, but the important thing is that when it's paid for, it's not like regulatory takings which are, you know, the taxpayers don't see that until it's too late. You know, in this type of taking, the tax-payers are seeing up front what's going on.

JUSTICE BREYER: That's true. But now, put yourself in the position of the homeowner. I take it, if it's a forced sale, it's at the market value, the individual, let's say it's someone who has lived in his house his whole life. He bought the house for $50,000. It's worth half a million. He has [$]450,000 profit. He pays 30 percent to the government and the state in taxes, and then he has to live somewhere. Well, I mean, what's he supposed to do? He now has probably [$]350,000 to pay for a house. He gets half a house because that's all he is going to do, all he is going to get for that money after he paid the taxes, or whatever. And I mean, there are a lot of—and he has to move and so forth. So going back to Justice Kennedy's point, is there some way of assuring that the just compensation actually puts the person in the position he would be in if he didn't have to sell his house? Or is he inevitably worse off?

MR. HORTON: Well, I mean, first of all, the—in Connecticut, fortunately, we have relocation loans which are involved here. And they are available in this case. . . . [T]here is $10 million involved in relocation funds.

• • •

JUSTICE SOUTER: I mean, what bothered Justice Breyer I guess bothers a lot of us. And that is, is there a problem of making the homeowner or the property owner whole? But I suppose the answer to that is that goes to the measure of compensation which is not the issue here.

MR. HORTON: Yes. And that's, and I had said that earlier. But another point when I was talking about roads is that applies to—that could apply to any type of case. It doesn't just apply to a case like this.

JUSTICE SCALIA: And that would really overrule a bunch of prior cases and really throw condemnation law into chaos.

• • •

JUSTICE BREYER: What is the remedy? Let's repose the problem to which I want to remedy then. And maybe this isn't the right remedy. But the remedy that they are saying, and I'm really repeating it, is an individual has a house and they want to be really not made a lot worse off, at least not made a lot worse off just so some other people can get a lot more money. Now what, what is the right—is there no constitutional protection? If this isn't the right case, what is?

MR. HORTON: Well, the right case is in the just compensation concept, but going to your, your point, if this were here as just compensation, I would say in terms of just compensation, in deciding what the fair market value is today, you can certainly take into account the economic plan that's going into effect. You know—

JUSTICE KENNEDY: Really? I thought that that was a fundamental of condemnation law that you can not value the property being taken based on what it's going to be worth after the project. That's just—

• • •

MR. HORTON: I may have misspoken on that subject, Your Honor.

• • •

JUSTICE SCALIA: What this lady wants is not more money. No amount of money is going to satisfy her. She is living in this house, you know, her whole life and she does not want to move. She said I'll move if it's being taken for a public use, but by God, you're just giving it to some other private individual because that individual is going to pay more taxes. I—it

JUSTICE BREYER: But now, put yourself in the position of the homeowner. Well, I mean, what's he supposed to do? He gets half a house because that's all he is going to do, all he is going to get for that money after he paid the taxes, or whatever.

seems to me that's, that's an objection in principle, and an objection in principle that the public use requirement of the Constitution seems to be addressed to.

MR. HORTON: But as I say, Your Honor, if public use and public purpose are the same thing, which they are unless you're going to overrule Holmes' decisions from 1905 and 1906.

JUSTICE SCALIA: It wouldn't the first of Holmes' decisions to be overruled.

JUSTICE GINSBURG: Well, I think you'd have to take some substantial chunks of language out of *Berman* as well, because Justice Douglas spoke very expansively in that case.

MR. HORTON: Plus I think Holmes was right when he said that to say that the public actually has to use the property is not an appropriate meaning of the phrase, so I would not think you'd want to revisit that case, even if you want to revisit some other of Holmes' decisions. But the—I guess the best answer I have, Justice Breyer, to your question . . . is simply to go back to the point that the time at which you consider what just compensation is, is in the just compensation proceedings. . . . [C]ertainly this Court can consider if social costs should be taken into account at that time. I'm not saying they should. I haven't thought that through . . . , but it seems to me because my primary answer is that you don't look at that now.

JUSTICE KENNEDY: Well, of course, the tax code does have special provisions for involuntary sales and reinvestments.

MR. HORTON: Yes, it does.

JUSTICE KENNEDY: The tax hypothetical is not accurate.

MR. HORTON: Yes.

JUSTICE SCALIA: Mr. Horton, I'm not proposing that the state has to use the property itself. I'm simply proposing that its use not be a private use which has incidental benefits to the state. That is not enough to justify use of the condemnation power.

MR. HORTON: Well, I don't think—

JUSTICE SCALIA: You can give it to a private entity, you can give it to a railroad, to some public utility. But the use that it's put to by that railroad and public utility is a public use. That's why it's a public utility. It's quite different to say you can give it to a private individual simply because that private individual is going to hire more people and pay more taxes. That, it seems to me, just washes out entirely the distinction between private use and public use.

MR. HORTON: Well, I don't agree, Your Honor, because I think, you know, I think if a person is without a job and if a person is not able to get basic services that they need from the town because the town can't afford it, that's just as important as a trains running on time or eliminating blight. And Justice Breyer, I thought of another answer to your question that has to do with this case. And that is even on a higher test, we win because the Connecticut Supreme Court applied a higher test in this case. And just—I would say that in this case, the essence of federalism is to let various courts make various decisions about what they consider an important public purpose. It may be different in Utah from the way it is in Connecticut, and it's different in Florida, and I don't think this Court should be having a new jurisprudence for this area and having two separate tests, and maybe having a test that even approaches the *Nollan Dolan* test where you certainly want to discourage people from taking these actions. . . .

· · ·

MR. BULLOCK (in rebuttal): . . . Your Honors, first of all, just a couple of matters regarding the Connecticut Supreme Court's decision. The Connecti-

MR. HORTON: I would say that in this case, the essence of federalism is to let various courts make various decisions about what they consider an important public purpose. It may be different in Utah from the way it is in Connecticut, and it's different in Florida, and I don't think this Court should be having a new jurisprudence for this area . . .

cut Supreme Court did not apply the test that we suggest in our case, they explicitly, the majority explicitly declined to apply heightened scrutiny in this, in this instance.

I think the key to understanding their argument is the answer to the question Can you take a Motel 6 and give it to a fancier hotel? Their answer is yes. And that's what's really at stake here. These condemnations are taking place throughout the country. A city in California condemns the 99 cents store in order to give it to Costco. Now, were they giving enormous benefits to Costco? Of course they were. But they did so because they wanted to get the tax revenue, and that's the problem with these types of condemnations, the desire to help a private party and the desire to help the public are really one and the same. The public only benefits if the private party is successful.

All right, the NLDC is a private body. It has a private board of directors, and it is leasing land to a private developer for 99 years at $1 a year. That is private ownership of land. Also, Your Honors, there is no severe assembly problem in this particular case, and in many other development situations. The NLDC and the city have 3 acres that was given to them by the federal government for them to do as they wish. And our homeowners who have lived there a long time and wish to hold on to their properties do not object to that development going on. It is within the rights of the city and the NLDC to do so.

Also, Your Honor, the Rindge case that was cited by the Respondents, they actually knew what was going to go on in that, in that case. They knew what the use was going to be.

And finally, Your Honors, the Respondents talk about the effect that this may have upon poor people. Not all neighborhoods, not all poor neighborhoods are blighted. But the one thing that all poor neighborhoods share in common is that they don't produce much in the way of tax revenue, so you're going to put poor neighborhoods and working class neighborhoods like the ones that exist in Fort Trumbull in jeopardy if the Court affirms the decision below. And that's why so many organizations that are concerned about the rights of senior citizens and the rights of minorities and poor folks like legal services corporations have joined in our side to support the property owners in this case. . . .

THE COURT'S DECISION

The Court's majority opinion mentioned "planning", "plan," and "planner" 39 times. Justice Stevens, along with Justices Stephen G. Breyer, David H. Souter, Ruth Bader Ginsburg, and Anthony M. Kennedy, concluded that "The city has carefully formulated an economic development plan that it believes will provide appreciable benefits to the community. . . .Given the comprehensive character of the plan, and the thorough deliberation that preceded its adoption. . .[the] plan unquestionably serves a public purpose." For more than a century, the Court has "wisely eschewed rigid formulas and intrusive scrutiny in favor of affording legislatures broad latitude in determining what public needs justify the use of the takings power." The Court was unwilling to "second-guess the city's considered judgments about the efficacy of its development plan" or to "second-guess the city's determinations as to what lands it needs to acquire in order to effectuate the project."

The court's ruling, Justice Kennedy said in his concurring opinion, does not "alter the fact that transfers intended to confer benefits on particular, favored private entities, and with only incidental or pretextual public benefits, are forbidden by the Public Use Clause." Those types of condemnations have always been unconstitutional, and they remain unconstitutional.

"The city has carefully formulated an economic development plan that it believes will provide appreciable benefits to the community. . . .Given the comprehensive character of the plan, and the thorough deliberation that preceded its adoption. . .[the] plan unquestionably serves a public purpose."

The *Kelo v. City of New London* decision might be the Supreme Court's strongest validation of the important role of planning since *Euclid* [*Village of Euclid, Ohio v. Ambler Realty Co.*, 272 U.S. 365 (1926)] nearly 80 years ago. What should planners take away from this opinion? First, plans are important because if they are comprehensive and preceded by thorough deliberation–including public participation and public input–then they serve a public purpose and the public interest. The Supreme Court is telling lower courts that they should look to the community's plan to discern what is in the public interest. Second, the courts will refrain from second-guessing the decision of the local and state elected officials about such matters. But the Supreme Court also cautions us that if a condemnation occurs that transfers property from one private owner to another private owner "outside the confines of an integrated development plan," it would certainly raise a suspicion that the condemnation was for a private purpose and not for a public use. *Kelo* is a good decision for planners and the communities they serve.

THE CASE SYLLABUS

After approving an integrated development plan designed to revitalize its ailing economy, respondent city, through its development agent, purchased most of the property earmarked for the project from willing sellers, but initiated condemnation proceedings when petitioners, the owners of the rest of the property, refused to sell. Petitioners brought this state-court action claiming, *inter alia*, that the taking of their properties would violate the "public use" restriction in the Fifth Amendment's Takings Clause. The trial court granted a permanent restraining order prohibiting the taking of the some of the properties, but denying relief as to others. Relying on cases such as *Hawaii Housing Authority* v. *Midkiff*, 467 U.S. 229, and *Berman v. Parker*, 348 U.S. 26, the Connecticut Supreme Court affirmed in part and reversed in part, upholding all of the proposed takings.

Held: The city's proposed disposition of petitioners' property qualifies as a "public use" within the meaning of the Takings Clause.

(a) Though the city could not take petitioners' land simply to confer a private benefit on a particular private party, see, e.g., *Midkiff*, 467 U.S., at 245, the takings at issue here would be executed pursuant to a carefully considered development plan, which was not adopted "to benefit a particular class of identifiable individuals," *ibid*. Moreover, while the city is not planning to open the condemned land–at least not in its entirety–to use by the general public, this "Court long ago rejected any literal requirement that condemned property be put into use for the … public." *Id.*, at 244. Rather, it has embraced the broader and more natural interpretation of public use as "public purpose." See, e.g., *Fallbrook Irrigation Dist.* v. *Bradley*, 164 U.S. 112, 158–164. Without exception, the Court has defined that concept broadly, reflecting its longstanding policy of deference to legislative judgments as to what public needs justify the use of the takings power. *Berman*, 348 U.S. 26; *Midkiff*, 467 U.S. 229; *Ruckelshaus v. Monsanto Co.*, 467 U.S. 986.

(b) The city's determination that the area at issue was sufficiently distressed to justify a program of economic rejuvenation is entitled to deference. The city has carefully formulated a development plan that it believes will provide appreciable benefits to the community, including, but not limited to, new jobs and increased tax revenue. As with other exercises in urban planning and development, the city is trying to coordinate a variety of commercial, residential, and recreational land uses, with the

But the Supreme Court also cautions us that if a condemnation occurs that transfers property from one private owner to another private owner "outside the confines of an integrated development plan," it would certainly raise a suspicion that the condemnation was for a private purpose and not for a public use. Kelo is a good decision for planners and the communities they serve.

hope that they will form a whole greater than the sum of its parts. To effectuate this plan, the city has invoked a state statute that specifically authorizes the use of eminent domain to promote economic development. Given the plan's comprehensive character, the thorough deliberation that preceded its adoption, and the limited scope of this Court's review in such cases, it is appropriate here, as it was in *Berman*, to resolve the challenges of the individual owners, not on a piecemeal basis, but rather in light of the entire plan. Because that plan unquestionably serves a public purpose, the takings challenged here satisfy the Fifth Amendment.

(c) Petitioners' proposal that the Court adopt a new bright-line rule that economic development does not qualify as a public use is supported by neither precedent nor logic. Promoting economic development is a traditional and long accepted governmental function, and there is no principled way of distinguishing it from the other public purposes the Court has recognized. See, *e.g., Berman,* 348 U.S., at 24. Also rejected is petitioners' argument that for takings of this kind the Court should require a "reasonable certainty" that the expected public benefits will actually accrue. Such a rule would represent an even greater departure from the Court's precedent. *E.g., Midkiff,* 467 U.S., at 242. The disadvantages of a heightened form of review are especially pronounced in this type of case, where orderly implementation of a comprehensive plan requires all interested parties' legal rights to be established before new construction can commence. The Court declines to second-guess the wisdom of the means the city has selected to effectuate its plan. *Berman,* 348 U.S., at 26. Pp. 13–20.
268 Conn. 1, 843 A. 2d 500, affirmed.

Justice Stevens delivered the opinion of the Court, in which Justices Kennedy, Souter, Ginsburg, and Breyer joined. Justice Kennedy filed a concurring opinion. Justice O'Connor, J. filed a dissenting opinion, in which Chief Justice Rehnquist and Justices Scalia and Thomas joined. Justice Thomas filed a dissenting opinion.

> *To effectuate this plan, the city has invoked a state statute that specifically authorizes the use of eminent domain to promote economic development.*

TEXT OF THE OPINION OF THE SUPREME COURT

Justice Stevens delivered the opinion of the Court.

In 2000, the city of New London approved a development plan that, in the words of the Supreme Court of Connecticut, was "projected to create in excess of 1,000 jobs, to increase tax and other revenues, and to revitalize an economically distressed city, including its downtown and waterfront areas." 268 Conn. 1, 5, 843 A. 2d 500, 507 (2004). In assembling the land needed for this project, the city's development agent has purchased property from willing sellers and proposes to use the power of eminent domain to acquire the remainder of the property from unwilling owners in exchange for just compensation. The question presented is whether the city's proposed disposition of this property qualifies as a "public use" within the meaning of the Takings Clause of the Fifth Amendment to the Constitution.[1]

The city of New London (hereinafter City) sits at the junction of the Thames River and the Long Island Sound in southeastern Connecticut. Decades of economic decline led a state agency in 1990 to designate the City a "distressed municipality." In 1996, the Federal Government closed the Naval Undersea Warfare Center, which had been located in the Fort Trumbull area of the City and had employed over 1,500 people. In 1998, the City's unemployment rate was nearly double that of the State, and its population of just under 24,000 residents was at its lowest since 1920.

These conditions prompted state and local officials to target New London, and particularly its Fort Trumbull area, for economic revitalization. To this end, respondent New London Development Corporation (NLDC), a private nonprofit entity established some years earlier to assist the City in planning economic development, was reactivated. In January 1998, the State authorized a $5.35 million bond issue to support the NLDC's planning activities and a $10 million bond issue toward the creation of a Fort Trumbull State Park. In February, the pharmaceutical company Pfizer Inc. announced that it would build a $300 million research facility on a site immediately adjacent to Fort Trumbull; local planners hoped that Pfizer would draw new business to the area, thereby serving as a catalyst to the area's rejuvenation. After receiving initial approval from the city council, the NLDC continued its planning activities and held a series of neighborhood meetings to educate the public about the process. In May, the city council authorized the NLDC to formally submit its plans to the relevant state agencies for review.[2] Upon obtaining state-level approval, the NLDC finalized an integrated development plan focused on 90 acres of the Fort Trumbull area.

The Fort Trumbull area is situated on a peninsula that juts into the Thames River. The area comprises approximately 115 privately owned properties, as well as the 32 acres of land formerly occupied by the naval facility (Trumbull State Park now occupies 18 of those 32 acres). The development plan encompasses seven parcels. Parcel 1 is designated for a waterfront conference hotel at the center of a "small urban village" that will include restaurants and shopping. This parcel will also have marinas for both recreational and commercial uses. A pedestrian "riverwalk" will originate here and continue down the coast, connecting the waterfront areas of the development. Parcel 2 will be the site of approximately 80 new residences organized into an urban neighborhood and linked by public walkway to the remainder of the development, including the state park. This parcel also includes space reserved for a new U.S. Coast Guard Museum. Parcel 3, which is located immediately north of the Pfizer facility, will contain at least 90,000 square feet of research and development office space. Parcel 4A is a 2.4-acre site that will be used either to support the adjacent state park, by providing parking or retail services for visitors, or to support the nearby marina. Parcel 4B will include a renovated marina, as well as the final stretch of the riverwalk. Parcels 5, 6, and 7 will provide land for office and retail space, parking, and water-dependent commercial uses. 1 App. 109–113.

The NLDC intended the development plan to capitalize on the arrival of the Pfizer facility and the new commerce it was expected to attract. In addition to creating jobs, generating tax revenue, and helping to "build momentum for the revitalization of downtown New London," *id.*, at 92, the plan was also designed to make the City more attractive and to create leisure and recreational opportunities on the waterfront and in the park.

The city council approved the plan in January 2000, and designated the NLDC as its development agent in charge of implementation. See Conn. Gen. Stat. Section 8–188 (2005). The city council also authorized the NLDC to purchase property or to acquire property by exercising eminent domain in the City's name. Section 8–193. The NLDC successfully negotiated the purchase of most of the real estate in the 90-acre area, but its negotiations with petitioners failed. As a consequence, in November 2000, the NLDC initiated the condemnation proceedings that gave rise to this case.[3]

Local planners hoped that Pfizer would draw new business to the area, thereby serving as a catalyst to the area's rejuvenation. After receiving initial approval from the city council, the NLDC continued its planning activities and held a series of neighborhood meetings to educate the public about the process.

II

Petitioner Susette Kelo has lived in the Fort Trumbull area since 1997. She has made extensive improvements to her house, which she prizes for its water view. Petitioner Wilhelmina Dery was born in her Fort Trumbull house in 1918 and has lived there her entire life. Her husband Charles (also a petitioner) has lived in the house since they married some 60 years ago. In all, the nine petitioners own 15 properties in Fort Trumbull–4 in parcel 3 of the development plan and 11 in parcel 4A. Ten of the parcels are occupied by the owner or a family member; the other five are held as investment properties. There is no allegation that any of these properties is blighted or otherwise in poor condition; rather, they were condemned only because they happen to be located in the development area.

In December 2000, petitioners brought this action in the New London Superior Court. They claimed, among other things, that the taking of their properties would violate the "public use" restriction in the Fifth Amendment. After a seven-day bench trial, the Superior Court granted a permanent restraining order prohibiting the taking of the properties located in parcel 4A (park or marina support). It, however, denied petitioners relief as to the properties located in parcel 3 (office space). 2 App. to Pet. for Cert. 343–350.[4]

After the Superior Court ruled, both sides took appeals to the Supreme Court of Connecticut. That court held, over a dissent, that all of the City's proposed takings were valid. It began by upholding the lower court's determination that the takings were authorized by chapter 132, the State's municipal development statute. See Conn. Gen. Stat. Sections 8–186 et seq. (2005). That statute expresses a legislative determination that the taking of land, even developed land, as part of an economic development project is a "public use" and in the "public interest." 268 Conn., at 18–28, 843 A. 2d, at 515–521. Next, relying on cases such as *Hawaii Housing Authority* v. *Midkiff*, 467 U.S. 229 (1984), and *Berman* v. *Parker*, 348 U.S. 26 (1954), the court held that such economic development qualified as a valid public use under both the Federal and State Constitutions. 268 Conn., at 40, 843 A. 2d, at 527.

Finally, adhering to its precedents, the court went on to determine, first, whether the takings of the particular properties at issue were "reasonably necessary" to achieving the City's intended public use, *id.*, at 82, 843 A. 2d, at 552–553, and, second, whether the takings were for "reasonably foreseeable needs," *id.*, at 93, 843 A. 2d, at 558–559. The court upheld the trial court's factual findings as to parcel 3, but reversed the trial court as to parcel 4A, agreeing with the City that the intended use of this land was sufficiently definite and had been given "reasonable attention" during the planning process. *Id.*, at 120–121, 843 A. 2d, at 574.

The three dissenting justices would have imposed a "heightened" standard of judicial review for takings justified by economic development. Although they agreed that the plan was intended to serve a valid public use, they would have found all the takings unconstitutional because the City had failed to adduce "clear and convincing evidence" that the economic benefits of the plan would in fact come to pass. *Id.*, at 144, 146, 843 A. 2d, at 587, 588 (Zarella, J., joined by Sullivan, C. J., and Katz, J., concurring in part and dissenting in part).

We granted certiorari to determine whether a city's decision to take property for the purpose of economic development satisfies the "public use" requirement of the Fifth Amendment. 542 U.S. ___ (2004).

That statute expresses a legislative determination that the taking of land, even developed land, as part of an economic development project is a "public use" and in the "public interest."

III

Two polar propositions are perfectly clear. On the one hand, it has long been accepted that the sovereign may not take the property of *A* for the sole purpose of transferring it to another private party *B*, even though *A* is paid just compensation. On the other hand, it is equally clear that a State may transfer property from one private party to another if future "use by the public" is the purpose of the taking; the condemnation of land for a railroad with common-carrier duties is a familiar example. Neither of these propositions, however, determines the disposition of this case.

As for the first proposition, the City would no doubt be forbidden from taking petitioners' land for the purpose of conferring a private benefit on a particular private party. See *Midkiff*, 467 U.S., at 245 ("A purely private taking could not withstand the scrutiny of the public use requirement; it would serve no legitimate purpose of government and would thus be void"); *Missouri Pacific R. Co.* v. *Nebraska*, 164 U.S. 403 (1896).[5] Nor would the City be allowed to take property under the mere pretext of a public purpose, when its actual purpose was to bestow a private benefit. The takings before us, however, would be executed pursuant to a "carefully considered" development plan. 268 Conn., at 54, 843 A. 2d, at 536. The trial judge and all the members of the Supreme Court of Connecticut agreed that there was no evidence of an illegitimate purpose in this case.[6] Therefore, as was true of the statute challenged in *Midkiff*, 467 U.S., at 245, the City's development plan was not adopted "to benefit a particular class of identifiable individuals."

On the other hand, this is not a case in which the City is planning to open the condemned land—at least not in its entirety—to use by the general public. Nor will the private lessees of the land in any sense be required to operate like common carriers, making their services available to all comers. But although such a projected use would be sufficient to satisfy the public use requirement, this "Court long ago rejected any literal requirement that condemned property be put into use for the general public." *Id.*, at 244. Indeed, while many state courts in the mid-nineteenth century endorsed "use by the public" as the proper definition of public use, that narrow view steadily eroded over time. Not only was the "use by the public" test difficult to administer (*e.g.*, what proportion of the public need have access to the property? at what price?),[7] but it proved to be impractical given the diverse and always evolving needs of society.[8] Accordingly, when this Court began applying the Fifth Amendment to the States at the close of the 19th century, it embraced the broader and more natural interpretation of public use as "public purpose." See, *e.g.*, *Fallbrook Irrigation Dist.* v. *Bradley*, 164 U.S. 112, 158–164 (1896). Thus, in a case upholding a mining company's use of an aerial bucket line to transport ore over property it did not own, Justice Holmes' opinion for the Court stressed "the inadequacy of use by the general public as a universal test." *Strickley* v. *Highland Boy Gold Mining Co.*, 200 U.S. 527, 531 (1906).[9] We have repeatedly and consistently rejected that narrow test ever since.[10]

The disposition of this case therefore turns on the question whether the City's development plan serves a "public purpose." Without exception, our cases have defined that concept broadly, reflecting our longstanding policy of deference to legislative judgments in this field.

In *Berman* v. *Parker*, 348 U.S. 26 (1954), this Court upheld a redevelopment plan targeting a blighted area of Washington, D. C., in which most of the housing for the area's 5,000 inhabitants was beyond repair. Under the

The disposition of this case therefore turns on the question whether the City's development plan serves a "public purpose." Without exception, our cases have defined that concept broadly, reflecting our longstanding policy of deference to legislative judgments in this field.

plan, the area would be condemned and part of it utilized for the construction of streets, schools, and other public facilities. The remainder of the land would be leased or sold to private parties for the purpose of redevelopment, including the construction of low-cost housing.

The owner of a department store located in the area challenged the condemnation, pointing out that his store was not itself blighted and arguing that the creation of a "better balanced, more attractive community" was not a valid public use. *Id.*, at 31. Writing for a unanimous Court, Justice Douglas refused to evaluate this claim in isolation, deferring instead to the legislative and agency judgment that the area "must be planned as a whole" for the plan to be successful. *Id.*, at 34. The Court explained that "community redevelopment programs need not, by force of the Constitution, be on a piecemeal basis—lot by lot, building by building." *Id.*, at 35. The public use underlying the taking was unequivocally affirmed:

> We do not sit to determine whether a particular housing project is or is not desirable. The concept of the public welfare is broad and inclusive… . The values it represents are spiritual as well as physical, aesthetic as well as monetary. It is within the power of the legislature to determine that the community should be beautiful as well as healthy, spacious as well as clean, well-balanced as well as carefully patrolled. In the present case, the Congress and its authorized agencies have made determinations that take into account a wide variety of values. It is not for us to reappraise them. If those who govern the District of Columbia decide that the Nation's Capital should be beautiful as well as sanitary, there is nothing in the Fifth Amendment that stands in the way. (at 33)

In *Hawaii Housing Authority* v. *Midkiff*, 467 U.S. 229 (1984), the Court considered a Hawaii statute whereby fee title was taken from lessors and transferred to lessees (for just compensation) in order to reduce the concentration of land ownership. We unanimously upheld the statute and rejected the Ninth Circuit's view that it was "a naked attempt on the part of the state of Hawaii to take the property of A and transfer it to B solely for B's private use and benefit." *Id.*, at 235 (internal quotation marks omitted). Reaffirming *Berman*'s deferential approach to legislative judgments in this field, we concluded that the State's purpose of eliminating the "social and economic evils of a land oligopoly" qualified as a valid public use. 467 U.S., at 241–242. Our opinion also rejected the contention that the mere fact that the State immediately transferred the properties to private individuals upon condemnation somehow diminished the public character of the taking. "[I]t is only the taking's purpose, and not its mechanics," we explained, that matters in determining public use. *Id.*, at 244.

In that same Term we decided another public use case that arose in a purely economic context. In *Ruckelshaus* v. *Monsanto, Co.,* 467 U.S. 986 (1984), the Court dealt with provisions of the Federal Insecticide, Fungicide, and Rodenticide Act under which the Environmental Protection Agency could consider the data (including trade secrets) submitted by a prior pesticide applicant in evaluating a subsequent application, so long as the second applicant paid just compensation for the data. We acknowledged that the "most direct beneficiaries" of these provisions were the subsequent applicants, *id.*, at 1014, but we nevertheless upheld the statute under *Berman* and *Midkiff*. We found sufficient Congress' belief that sparing applicants the cost of time-consuming research eliminated a significant barrier to entry in the pesticide market and thereby enhanced competition. 467 U.S., at 1015.

Viewed as a whole, our jurisprudence has recognized that the needs of society have varied between different parts of the Nation, just as they have evolved over time in response to changed circumstances. Our earliest cases in particular embodied a strong theme of federalism, emphasizing the "great respect" that we owe to state legislatures and state courts in discerning local public needs. See *Hairston* v. *Danville & Western R. Co.*, 208 U.S. 598, 606–607 (1908) (noting that these needs were likely to vary depending on a State's "resources, the capacity of the soil, the relative importance of industries to the general public welfare, and the long-established methods and habits of the people").[11] For more than a century, our public use jurisprudence has wisely eschewed rigid formulas and intrusive scrutiny in favor of affording legislatures broad latitude in determining what public needs justify the use of the takings power.

IV

Those who govern the City were not confronted with the need to remove blight in the Fort Trumbull area, but their determination that the area was sufficiently distressed to justify a program of economic rejuvenation is entitled to our deference. The City has carefully formulated an economic development plan that it believes will provide appreciable benefits to the community, including—but by no means limited to—new jobs and increased tax revenue. As with other exercises in urban planning and development,[12] the City is endeavoring to coordinate a variety of commercial, residential, and recreational uses of land, with the hope that they will form a whole greater than the sum of its parts. To effectuate this plan, the City has invoked a state statute that specifically authorizes the use of eminent domain to promote economic development. Given the comprehensive character of the plan, the thorough deliberation that preceded its adoption, and the limited scope of our review, it is appropriate for us, as it was in *Berman*, to resolve the challenges of the individual owners, not on a piecemeal basis, but rather in light of the entire plan. Because that plan unquestionably serves a public purpose, the takings challenged here satisfy the public use requirement of the Fifth Amendment.

To avoid this result, petitioners urge us to adopt a new bright-line rule that economic development does not qualify as a public use. Putting aside the unpersuasive suggestion that the City's plan will provide only purely economic benefits, neither precedent nor logic supports petitioners' proposal. Promoting economic development is a traditional and long accepted function of government. There is, moreover, no principled way of distinguishing economic development from the other public purposes that we have recognized. In our cases upholding takings that facilitated agriculture and mining, for example, we emphasized the importance of those industries to the welfare of the States in question, see, *e.g.*, *Strickley*, 200 U.S. 527; in *Berman*, we endorsed the purpose of transforming a blighted area into a "well-balanced" community through redevelopment, 348 U.S., at 33;[13] in *Midkiff*, we upheld the interest in breaking up a land oligopoly that "created artificial deterrents to the normal functioning of the State's residential land market," 467 U.S., at 242; and in *Monsanto*, we accepted Congress' purpose of eliminating a "significant barrier to entry in the pesticide market," 467 U.S., at 1014–1015. It would be incongruous to hold that the City's interest in the economic benefits to be derived from the development of the Fort Trumbull area has less of a public character than any of those other interests. Clearly, there is no basis for exempting economic development from our traditionally broad understanding of public purpose.

Petitioners contend that using eminent domain for economic development impermissibly blurs the boundary between public and private takings. Again, our cases foreclose this objection. Quite simply, the government's pursuit of a public purpose will often benefit individual pri-

For more than a century, our public use jurisprudence has wisely eschewed rigid formulas and intrusive scrutiny in favor of affording legislatures broad latitude in determining what public needs justify the use of the takings power.

Petitioners urge us to adopt a new bright-line rule that economic development does not qualify as a public use. Putting aside the unpersuasive suggestion that the City's plan will provide only purely economic benefits, neither precedent nor logic supports petitioners' proposal.

Alternatively, petitioners maintain that for takings of this kind we should require a "reasonable certainty" that the expected public benefits will actually accrue. Such a rule, however, would represent an even greater departure from our precedent.

vate parties. For example, in *Midkiff*, the forced transfer of property conferred a direct and significant benefit on those lessees who were previously unable to purchase their homes. In *Monsanto*, we recognized that the "most direct beneficiaries" of the data-sharing provisions were the subsequent pesticide applicants, but benefiting them in this way was necessary to promoting competition in the pesticide market. 467 U.S., at 1014.[14] The owner of the department store in *Berman* objected to "taking from one businessman for the benefit of another businessman," 348 U.S., at 33, referring to the fact that under the redevelopment plan land would be leased or sold to private developers for redevelopment.[15] Our rejection of that contention has particular relevance to the instant case: "The public end may be as well or better served through an agency of private enterprise than through a department of government—or so the Congress might conclude. We cannot say that public ownership is the sole method of promoting the public purposes of community redevelopment projects." *Id.*, at 34.[16]

It is further argued that without a bright-line rule nothing would stop a city from transferring citizen *A*'s property to citizen *B* for the sole reason that citizen *B* will put the property to a more productive use and thus pay more taxes. Such a one-to-one transfer of property, executed outside the confines of an integrated development plan, is not presented in this case. While such an unusual exercise of government power would certainly raise a suspicion that a private purpose was afoot,[17] the hypothetical cases posited by petitioners can be confronted if and when they arise.[18] They do not warrant the crafting of an artificial restriction on the concept of public use.[19]

Alternatively, petitioners maintain that for takings of this kind we should require a "reasonable certainty" that the expected public benefits will actually accrue. Such a rule, however, would represent an even greater departure from our precedent. "When the legislature's purpose is legitimate and its means are not irrational, our cases make clear that empirical debates over the wisdom of takings–no less than debates over the wisdom of other kinds of socioeconomic legislation–are not to be carried out in the federal courts." *Midkiff*, 467 U.S., at 242.[20] Indeed, earlier this Term we explained why similar practical concerns (among others) undermined the use of the "substantially advances" formula in our regulatory takings doctrine. See *Lingle* v. *Chevron U. S. A. Inc.*, 544 U.S. ___, ___ (2005) (slip op., at 14–15) (noting that this formula "would empower–and might often require–courts to substitute their predictive judgments for those of elected legislatures and expert agencies"). The disadvantages of a heightened form of review are especially pronounced in this type of case. Orderly implementation of a comprehensive redevelopment plan obviously requires that the legal rights of all interested parties be established before new construction can be commenced. A constitutional rule that required postponement of the judicial approval of every condemnation until the likelihood of success of the plan had been assured would unquestionably impose a significant impediment to the successful consummation of many such plans.

Just as we decline to second-guess the City's considered judgments about the efficacy of its development plan, we also decline to second-guess the City's determinations as to what lands it needs to acquire in order to effectuate the project. "It is not for the courts to oversee the choice of the boundary line nor to sit in review on the size of a particular project area. Once the question of the public purpose has been decided, the amount and character of land to be taken for the project and the need for a particular tract to complete the integrated plan rests in the discretion of the legislative branch." *Berman*, 348 U.S., at 35–36.

In affirming the City's authority to take petitioners' properties, we do not minimize the hardship that condemnations may entail, notwithstanding the payment of just compensation.[21] We emphasize that nothing in our opinion precludes any State from placing further restrictions on its exercise of the takings power. Indeed, many States already impose "public use" requirements that are stricter than the federal baseline. Some of these requirements have been established as a matter of state constitutional law,[22] while others are expressed in state eminent domain statutes that carefully limit the grounds upon which takings may be exercised.[23] As the submissions of the parties and their *amici* make clear, the necessity and wisdom of using eminent domain to promote economic development are certainly matters of legitimate public debate.[24] This Court's authority, however, extends only to determining whether the City's proposed condemnations are for a "public use" within the meaning of the Fifth Amendment to the Federal Constitution. Because over a century of our case law interpreting that provision dictates an affirmative answer to that question, we may not grant petitioners the relief that they seek.

The judgment of the Supreme Court of Connecticut is affirmed. It is so ordered.

NOTES TO THE SUPREME COURT'S OPINION

1. "[N]or shall private property be taken for public use, without just compensation." U.S. Const., Amdt. 5. That Clause is made applicable to the states by the Fourteenth Amendment. See *Chicago, B. & Q. R. Co. v. Chicago,* 166 U.S. 226 (1897).

2. Various state agencies studied the project's economic, environmental, and social ramifications. As part of this process, a team of consultants evaluated six alternative development proposals for the area, which varied in extensiveness and emphasis. The Office of Planning and Management, one of the primary state agencies undertaking the review, made findings that the project was consistent with relevant state and municipal development policies. See 1 App. 89–95.

3. In the remainder of the opinion we will differentiate between the City and the NLDC only where necessary.

4. While this litigation was pending before the Superior Court, the NLDC announced that it would lease some of the parcels to private developers in exchange for their agreement to develop the land according to the terms of the development plan. Specifically, the NLDC was negotiating a 99-year ground lease with Corcoran Jennison, a developer selected from a group of applicants. The negotiations contemplated a nominal rent of $1 per year, but no agreement had yet been signed. See 268 Conn. 1, 9, 61, 843 A. 2d 500, 509–510, 540 (2004).

5. See also *Calder v. Bull,* 3 Dall. 386, 388 (1798) ("An act of the Legislature (for I cannot call it a law) contrary to the great first principles of the social compact, cannot be considered a rightful exercise of legislative authority... . A few instances will suffice to explain what I mean... [A] law that takes property from A. and gives it to B: It is against all reason and justice, for a people to entrust a Legislature with such powers; and, therefore, it cannot be presumed that they have done it. The genius, the nature, and the spirit, of our State Governments, amount to a prohibition of such acts of legislation; and the general principles of law and reason forbid them" (emphasis deleted)).

6. See 268 Conn., at 159, 843 A. 2d, at 595 (Zarella, J., concurring in part and dissenting in part) ("The record clearly demonstrates that the development plan was not intended to serve the interests of Pfizer, Inc., or any other private entity, but rather, to revitalize the local economy by creating temporary and permanent jobs, generating a significant increase in tax revenue, encouraging spin-off economic activities and maximizing public access to the waterfront"). And while the City intends to transfer certain of the parcels to a private developer in a long-term lease–which developer, in turn, is expected to lease the office space and so forth to other private tenants–the identities of those private parties were not known when the plan was adopted. It is, of course, difficult to accuse the government of having taken *A*'s property to benefit the private interests of *B* when the identity of *B* was unknown.

7. See, e.g., *Dayton Gold & Silver Mining Co. v. Seawell,* 11 Nev. 394, 410, 1876 WL 4573, *11 (1876) ("If public occupation and enjoyment of the object for which land is to be condemned furnishes the only and true test for the right of eminent domain, then the legislature would certainly have the constitutional authority to condemn the lands of any private citizen for the purpose of building hotels and theaters. Why not? A hotel is used

This Court's authority, however, extends only to determining whether the City's proposed condemnations are for a "public use" within the meaning of the Fifth Amendment to the Federal Constitution. Because over a century of our case law interpreting that provision dictates an affirmative answer to that question, we may not grant petitioners the relief that they seek.

by the public as much as a railroad. The public have the same right, upon payment of a fixed compensation, to seek rest and refreshment at a public inn as they have to travel upon a railroad").

8. From upholding the Mill Acts (which authorized manufacturers dependent on power-producing dams to flood upstream lands in exchange for just compensation), to approving takings necessary for the economic development of the West through mining and irrigation, many state courts either circumvented the "use by the public" test when necessary or abandoned it completely. See Nichols, The Meaning of Public Use in the Law of Eminent Domain, 20 B. U. L. Rev. 615, 619–624 (1940) (tracing this development and collecting cases). For example, in rejecting the "use by the public" test as overly restrictive, the Nevada Supreme Court stressed that "[m]ining is the greatest of the industrial pursuits in this state. All other interests are subservient to it. Our mountains are almost barren of timber, and our valleys could never be made profitable for agricultural purposes except for the fact of a home market having been created by the mining developments in different sections of the state. The mining and milling interests give employment to many men, and the benefits derived from this business are distributed as much, and sometimes more, among the laboring classes than with the owners of the mines and mills. ... The present prosperity of the state is entirely due to the mining developments already made, and the entire people of the state are directly interested in having the future developments unobstructed by the obstinate action of any individual or individuals." *Dayton Gold & Silver Mining Co.,* 11 Nev., at 409–410, 1876 WL, at *11.

9. See also *Clark* v. *Nash,* 198 U.S. 361 (1905) (upholding a statute that authorized the owner of arid land to widen a ditch on his neighbor's property so as to permit a nearby stream to irrigate his land).

10. See, e.g., *Mt. Vernon-Woodberry Cotton Duck Co.* v. *Alabama Interstate Power Co.,* 240 U.S. 30, 32 (1916) ("The inadequacy of use by the general public as a universal test is established"); *Ruckelshaus* v. *Monsanto Co.,* 467 U.S. 986, 1014–1015 (1984) ("This Court, however, has rejected the notion that a use is a public use only if the property taken is put to use for the general public").

11. See also *Clark,* 198 U.S., at 367–368; *Strickley* v. *Highland Boy Gold Mining Co.,* 200 U.S. 527, 531 (1906) ("In the opinion of the legislature and the Supreme Court of Utah the public welfare of that State demands that aerial lines between the mines upon its mountain sides and railways in the valleys below should not be made impossible by the refusal of a private owner to sell the right to cross his land. The Constitution of the United States does not require us to say that they are wrong"); *O'Neill* v. *Leamer,* 239 U.S. 244, 253 (1915) ("States may take account of their special exigencies, and when the extent of their arid or wet lands is such that a plan for irrigation or reclamation according to districts may fairly be regarded as one which promotes the public interest, there is nothing in the Federal Constitution which denies to them the right to formulate this policy or to exercise the power of eminent domain in carrying it into effect. With the local situation the state court is peculiarly familiar and its judgment is entitled to the highest respect").

11. Cf. *Village of Euclid* v. *Ambler Realty Co.,* 272 U.S. 365 (1926).

12. It is a misreading of *Berman* to suggest that the only public use upheld in that case was the initial removal of blight. See Reply Brief for Petitioners 8. The public use described in *Berman* extended beyond that to encompass the purpose of *developing* that area to create conditions that would prevent a reversion to blight in the future. See 348 U.S., at 34–35 ("It was not enough, [the experts] believed, to remove existing buildings that were insanitary or unsightly. It was important to redesign the whole area so as to eliminate the conditions that cause slums. . . . The entire area needed redesigning so that a balanced, integrated plan could be developed for the region, including not only new homes, but also schools, churches, parks, streets, and shopping centers. In this way it was hoped that the cycle of decay of the area could be controlled and the birth of future slums prevented"). Had the public use in *Berman* been defined more narrowly, it would have been difficult to justify the taking of the plaintiff's nonblighted department store.

14. Any number of cases illustrate that the achievement of a public good often coincides with the immediate benefiting of private parties. See, *e.g., National Railroad Passenger Corporation* v. *Boston & Maine Corp.,* 503 U.S. 407, 422 (1992) (public purpose of "facilitating Amtrak's rail service" served by taking rail track from one private company and transferring it to another private company); *Brown* v. *Legal Foundation of Wash.,* 538 U.S. 216 (2003) (provision of legal services to the poor is a valid public purpose). It is worth noting that in *Hawaii Housing Authority* v. *Midkiff,* 467 U.S. 229 (1984), *Monsanto,* and *Boston & Maine Corp.,* the property in question retained the same use even after the change of ownership.

15. Notably, as in the instant case, the private developers in *Berman* were required by contract to use the property to carry out the redevelopment plan. See 348 U.S., at 30.

16. Nor do our cases support Justice O'Connor's novel theory that the government may only take property and transfer it to private parties when the initial taking eliminates some "harmful property use." *Post*, at 8 (dissenting opinion). There was nothing "harmful" about the nonblighted department store at issue in *Berman*, 348 U.S. 26; see also n. 13, *supra*; nothing "harmful" about the lands at issue in the mining and agriculture cases, see, *e.g.*, *Strickley*, 200 U.S. 527; see also nn. 9, 11, *supra*; and certainly nothing "harmful" about the trade secrets owned by the pesticide manufacturers in *Monsanto*, 467 U.S. 986. In each case, the public purpose we upheld depended on a private party's *future* use of the concededly nonharmful property that was taken. By focusing on a property's future use, as opposed to its past use, our cases are faithful to the text of the Takings Clause. See U.S. Const., Amdt. 5. ("[N]or shall private property be taken for public use, without just compensation"). Justice O'Connor's intimation that a "public purpose" may not be achieved by the action of private parties, see *post*, at 8, confuses the *purpose* of a taking with its *mechanics*, a mistake we warned of in *Midkiff*, 467 U.S., at 244. See also *Berman*, 348 U.S., at 33–34 ("The public end may be as well or better served through an agency of private enterprise than through a department of government").

17. Courts have viewed such aberrations with a skeptical eye. See, *e.g.*, *99 Cents Only Stores* v. *Lancaster Redevelopment Agency*, 237 F. Supp. 2d 1123 (CD Cal. 2001); cf. *Cincinnati* v. *Vester*, 281 U.S. 439, 448 (1930) (taking invalid under state eminent domain statute for lack of a reasoned explanation). These types of takings may also implicate other constitutional guarantees. See *Village of Willowbrook* v. *Olech*, 528 U.S. 562 (2000) (per curiam).

18. Cf. *Panhandle Oil Co.* v. *Mississippi ex rel. Knox*, 277 U.S. 218, 223 (1928) (Holmes, J., dissenting) ("The power to tax is not the power to destroy while this Court sits").

19. A parade of horribles is especially unpersuasive in this context, since the Takings Clause largely "operates as a conditional limitation, permitting the government to do what it wants so long as it pays the charge." *Eastern Enterprises* v. *Apfel*, 524 U.S. 498, 545 (1998) (Kennedy, J., concurring in judgment and dissenting in part). Speaking of the takings power, Justice Iredell observed that "[i]t is not sufficient to urge, that the power may be abused, for, such is the nature of all power–such is the tendency of every human institution: and, it might as fairly be said, that the power of taxation, which is only circumscribed by the discretion of the Body, in which it is vested, ought not to be granted, because the Legislature, disregarding its true objects, might, for visionary and useless projects, impose a tax to the amount of nineteen shillings in the pound. We must be content to limit power where we can, and where we cannot, consistently with its use, we must be content to repose a salutary confidence." *Calder*, 3 Dall., at 400 (opinion concurring in result).

20. See also *Boston & Maine Corp.*, 503 U.S., at 422–423 ("[W]e need not make a specific factual determination whether the condemnation will accomplish its objectives"); *Monsanto*, 467 U.S., at 1015, n. 18 ("Monsanto argues that EPA and, by implication, Congress, misapprehended the true 'barriers to entry' in the pesticide industry and that the challenged provisions of the law create, rather than reduce, barriers to entry... . Such economic arguments are better directed to Congress. The proper inquiry before this Court is not whether the provisions in fact will accomplish their stated objectives. Our review is limited to determining that the purpose is legitimate and that Congress rationally could have believed that the provisions would promote that objective").

21. The *amici* raise questions about the fairness of the measure of just compensation. See, *e.g.*, Brief for American Planning Association et al. as *Amici Curiae* 26–30. While important, these questions are not before us in this litigation.

22. See, *e.g.*, *County of Wayne* v. *Hathcock*, 471 Mich. 445, 684 N. W. 2d 765 (2004).

23. Under California law, for instance, a city may only take land for economic development purposes in blighted areas. Cal. Health & Safety Code Ann. Sections 33030–33037 (West 1997). See, *e.g.*, *Redevelopment Agency of Chula Vista* v. *Rados Bros.*, 95 Cal. App. 4th 309 (2002).

24. For example, some argue that the need for eminent domain has been greatly exaggerated because private developers can use numerous techniques, including secret negotiations or precommitment strategies, to overcome holdout problems and assemble lands for genuinely profitable projects. See Brief for Jane Jacobs as *Amicus Curiae* 13–15; see also Brief for John Norquist as *Amicus Curiae*. Others argue to the contrary, urging that the need for eminent domain is especially great with regard to older, small cities like New London, where centuries of development have created an extreme overdivision of land and thus a real market impediment to land assembly. See Brief for Connecticut Conference for Municipalities et al. as *Amici Curiae* 13, 21; see also Brief for National League of Cities et al. as *Amici Curiae*.

TEXT OF JUSTICE KENNEDY'S CONCURRING OPINION

I join the opinion for the Court and add these further observations.

This Court has declared that a taking should be upheld as consistent with the Public Use Clause, U.S. Const., Amdt. 5., as long as it is "rationally related to a conceivable public purpose." *Hawaii Housing Authority v. Midkiff*, 467 U.S. 229, 241 (1984); see also *Berman v. Parker*, 348 U.S. 26 (1954). This deferential standard of review echoes the rational-basis test used to review economic regulation under the Due Process and Equal Protection Clauses, see, e.g., *FCC v. Beach Communications, Inc.*, 508 U.S. 307, 313–314 (1993); *Williamson v. Lee Optical of Okla., Inc.*, 348 U.S. 483 (1955). The determination that a rational-basis standard of review is appropriate does not, however, alter the fact that transfers intended to confer benefits on particular, favored private entities, and with only incidental or pretextual public benefits, are forbidden by the Public Use Clause.

A court applying rational-basis review under the Public Use Clause should strike down a taking that, by a clear showing, is intended to favor a particular private party, with only incidental or pretextual public benefits, just as a court applying rational-basis review under the Equal Protection Clause must strike down a government classification that is clearly intended to injure a particular class of private parties, with only incidental or pretextual public justifications. See *Cleburne v. Cleburne Living Center, Inc.*, 473 U.S. 432, 446–447, 450 (1985); *Department of Agriculture v. Moreno*, 413 U.S. 528, 533–536 (1973). As the trial court in this case was correct to observe, "Where the purpose [of a taking] is economic development and that development is to be carried out by private parties or private parties will be benefited, the court must decide if the stated public purpose–economic advantage to a city sorely in need of it–is only incidental to the benefits that will be confined on private parties of a development plan." 2 App. to Pet. for Cert. 263. See also ante, at 7.

A court confronted with a plausible accusation of impermissible favoritism to private parties should treat the objection as a serious one and review the record to see if it has merit, though with the presumption that the government's actions were reasonable and intended to serve a public purpose. Here, the trial court conducted a careful and extensive inquiry into "whether, in fact, the development plan is of primary benefit to ... the developer [i.e., Corcoran Jennison], and private businesses which may eventually locate in the plan area [e.g., Pfizer], and in that regard, only of incidental benefit to the city." 2 App. to Pet. for Cert. 261. The trial court considered testimony from government officials and corporate officers; id., at 266–271; documentary evidence of communications between these parties, ibid.; respondents' awareness of New London's depressed economic condition and evidence corroborating the validity of this concern, id., at 272–273, 278–279; the substantial commitment of public funds by the State to the development project before most of the private beneficiaries were known, id., at 276; evidence that respondents reviewed a variety of development plans and chose a private developer from a group of applicants rather than picking out a particular transferee beforehand, id., at 273, 278; and the fact that the other private beneficiaries of the project are still unknown because the office space proposed to be built has not yet been rented, id., at 278.

The trial court concluded, based on these findings, that benefiting Pfizer was not "the primary motivation or effect of this development plan"; instead, "the primary motivation for [respondents] was to take advantage of Pfizer's presence." Id., at 276. Likewise, the trial court concluded that "[t]here is nothing in the record to indicate that ... [respondents] were motivated by a desire to aid [other] particular private entities." Id., at 278. See also ante, at 7–8. Even the dissenting justices on the Connecticut Su-

The trial court concluded, based on these findings, that benefiting Pfizer was not "the primary motivation or effect of this development plan"; instead, "the primary motivation for [respondents] was to take advantage of Pfizer's presence."

preme Court agreed that respondents' development plan was intended to revitalize the local economy, not to serve the interests of Pfizer, Corcoran Jennison, or any other private party. 268 Conn. 1, 159, 843 A. 2d 500, 595 (2004) (Zarella, J., concurring in part and dissenting in part). This case, then, survives the meaningful rational basis review that in my view is required under the Public Use Clause.

Petitioners and their amici argue that any taking justified by the promotion of economic development must be treated by the courts as per se invalid, or at least presumptively invalid. Petitioners overstate the need for such a rule, however, by making the incorrect assumption that review under *Berman and Midkiff* imposes no meaningful judicial limits on the government's power to condemn any property it likes. A broad per se rule or a strong presumption of invalidity, furthermore, would prohibit a large number of government takings that have the purpose and expected effect of conferring substantial benefits on the public at large and so do not offend the Public Use Clause.

My agreement with the Court that a presumption of invalidity is not warranted for economic development takings in general, or for the particular takings at issue in this case, does not foreclose the possibility that a more stringent standard of review than that announced in *Berman and Midkiff* might be appropriate for a more narrowly drawn category of takings. There may be private transfers in which the risk of undetected impermissible favoritism of private parties is so acute that a presumption (rebuttable or otherwise) of invalidity is warranted under the Public Use Clause. Cf. *Eastern Enterprises v. Apfel*, 524 U.S. 498, 549–550 (1998) (Kennedy, J., concurring in judgment and dissenting in part) (heightened scrutiny for retroactive legislation under the Due Process Clause). This demanding level of scrutiny, however, is not required simply because the purpose of the taking is economic development.

This is not the occasion for conjecture as to what sort of cases might justify a more demanding standard, but it is appropriate to underscore aspects of the instant case that convince me no departure from *Berman and Midkiff* is appropriate here. This taking occurred in the context of a comprehensive development plan meant to address a serious citywide depression, and the projected economic benefits of the project cannot be characterized as de minimus. The identity of most of the private beneficiaries were unknown at the time the city formulated its plans. The city complied with elaborate procedural requirements that facilitate review of the record and inquiry into the city's purposes. In sum, while there may be categories of cases in which the transfers are so suspicious, or the procedures employed so prone to abuse, or the purported benefits are so trivial or implausible, that courts should presume an impermissible private purpose, no such circumstances are present in this case.

For the foregoing reasons, I join in the Court's opinion.

> *This taking occurred in the context of a comprehensive development plan meant to address a serious citywide depression, and the projected economic benefits of the project cannot be characterized as de minimus. . . . The city complied with elaborate procedural requirements that facilitate review of the record and inquiry into the city's purposes.*

THE TEXT OF JUSTICE O'CONNOR'S DISSENTING OPINION

Justice O'Connor, with whom The Chief Justice, Justice Scalia, and Justice Thomas join, dissented.

Over two centuries ago, just after the Bill of Rights was ratified, Justice Chase wrote:

> An act of the Legislature (for I cannot call it a law) contrary to the great first principles of the social compact, cannot be considered a rightful exercise of legislative authority. . . . A few instances will suffice to explain what I mean. . . . [A] law that takes property from A. and gives it to B: It is against all reason and justice, for a people to entrust a Legislature with such powers; and, therefore, it cannot be presumed that they have done it. *Calder v. Bull*, 3 Dall. 386, 388 (1798) (emphasis deleted).

Today the Court abandons this long-held, basic limitation on government power. Under the banner of economic development, all private property is now vulnerable to being taken and transferred to another private owner, so long as it might be upgraded—*i.e.*, given to an owner who will use it in a way that the legislature deems more beneficial to the public—in the process. To reason, as the Court does, that the incidental public benefits resulting from the subsequent ordinary use of private property render economic development takings "for public use" is to wash out any distinction between private and public use of property–and thereby effectively to delete the words "for public use" from the Takings Clause of the Fifth Amendment. Accordingly I respectfully dissent.

I

Petitioners are nine resident or investment owners of 15 homes in the Fort Trumbull neighborhood of New London, Connecticut. Petitioner Wilhelmina Dery, for example, lives in a house on Walbach Street that has been in her family for over 100 years. She was born in the house in 1918; her husband, petitioner Charles Dery, moved into the house when they married in 1946. Their son lives next door with his family in the house he received as a wedding gift, and joins his parents in this suit. Two petitioners keep rental properties in the neighborhood.

In February 1998, Pfizer Inc., the pharmaceuticals manufacturer, announced that it would build a global research facility near the Fort Trumbull neighborhood. Two months later, New London's city council gave initial approval for the New London Development Corporation (NLDC) to prepare the development plan at issue here. The NLDC is a private, nonprofit corporation whose mission is to assist the city council in economic development planning. It is not elected by popular vote, and its directors and employees are privately appointed. Consistent with its mandate, the NLDC generated an ambitious plan for redeveloping 90 acres of Fort Trumbull in order to "complement the facility that Pfizer was planning to build, create jobs, increase tax and other revenues, encourage public access to and use of the city's waterfront, and eventually 'build momentum' for the revitalization of the rest of the city." App. to Pet. for Cert. 5.

Petitioners own properties in two of the plan's seven parcels–Parcel 3 and Parcel 4A. Under the plan, Parcel 3 is slated for the construction of research and office space as a market develops for such space. It will also retain the existing Italian Dramatic Club (a private cultural organization) though the homes of three plaintiffs in that parcel are to be demolished. Parcel 4A is slated, mysteriously, for " 'park support.' " *Id.*, at 345–346. At oral argument, counsel for respondents conceded the vagueness of this proposed use, and offered that the parcel might eventually be used for parking. Tr. of Oral Arg. 36.

To save their homes, petitioners sued New London and the NLDC, to whom New London has delegated eminent domain power. Petitioners maintain that the Fifth Amendment prohibits the NLDC from condemning their properties for the sake of an economic development plan. Petitioners are not hold-outs; they do not seek increased compensation, and none is opposed to new development in the area. Theirs is an objection in principle: They claim that the NLDC's proposed use for their confiscated property is not a "public" one for purposes of the Fifth Amendment. While the government may take their homes to build a road or a railroad or to eliminate a property use that harms the public, say petitioners, it cannot take their property for the private use of other owners simply because the new owners may make more productive use of the property.

Petitioners are not hold-outs; they do not seek increased compensation, and none is opposed to new development in the area. Theirs is an objection in principle: They claim that the NLDC's proposed use for their confiscated property is not a "public" one for purposes of the Fifth Amendment.

II

The Fifth Amendment to the Constitution, made applicable to the States by the Fourteenth Amendment, provides that "private property [shall not] be taken for public use, without just compensation." When interpreting the Constitution, we begin with the unremarkable presumption that every word in the document has independent meaning, "that no word was unnecessarily used, or needlessly added." *Wright* v. *United States*, 302 U.S. 583, 588 (1938). In keeping with that presumption, we have read the Fifth Amendment's language to impose two distinct conditions on the exercise of eminent domain: "the taking must be for a 'public use' and 'just compensation' must be paid to the owner." *Brown* v. *Legal Foundation of Wash.*, 538 U.S. 216, 231–232 (2003).

These two limitations serve to protect "the security of Property," which Alexander Hamilton described to the Philadelphia Convention as one of the "great obj[ects] of Gov[ernment]." 1 Records of the Federal Convention of 1787, p. 302 (M. Farrand ed. 1934). Together they ensure stable property ownership by providing safeguards against excessive, unpredictable, or unfair use of the government's eminent domain power–particularly against those owners who, for whatever reasons, may be unable to protect themselves in the political process against the majority's will.

While the Takings Clause presupposes that government can take private property without the owner's consent, the just compensation requirement spreads the cost of condemnations and thus "prevents the public from loading upon one individual more than his just share of the burdens of government." *Monongahela Nav. Co.* v. *United States*, 148 U.S. 312, 325 (1893); see also *Armstrong* v. *United States*, 364 U.S. 40, 49 (1960). The public use requirement, in turn, imposes a more basic limitation, circumscribing the very scope of the eminent domain power: Government may compel an individual to forfeit her property for the *public's* use, but not for the benefit of another private person. This requirement promotes fairness as well as security. Cf. *Tahoe-Sierra Preservation Council, Inc.* v. *Tahoe Regional Planning Agency*, 535 U.S. 302, 336 (2002) ("The concepts of 'fairness and justice' . . . underlie the Takings Clause").

Where is the line between "public" and "private" property use? We give considerable deference to legislatures' determinations about what governmental activities will advantage the public. But were the political branches the sole arbiters of the public-private distinction, the Public Use Clause would amount to little more than hortatory fluff. An external, judicial check on how the public use requirement is interpreted, however limited, is necessary if this constraint on government power is to retain any meaning. See *Cincinnati* v. *Vester*, 281 U.S. 439, 446 (1930) ("It is well established that . . . the question [of] what is a public use is a judicial one").

Our cases have generally identified three categories of takings that comply with the public use requirement, though it is in the nature of things that the boundaries between these categories are not always firm. Two are relatively straightforward and uncontroversial. First, the sovereign may transfer private property to public ownership—such as for a road, a hospital, or a military base. See, *e.g., Old Dominion Land Co.* v. *United States*, 269 U.S. 55 (1925); *Rindge Co.* v. *County of Los Angeles*, 262 U.S. 700 (1923). Second, the sovereign may transfer private property to private parties, often common carriers, who make the property available for the public's use–such as with a railroad, a public utility, or a stadium. See, *e.g., National Railroad Passenger Corporation* v. *Boston & Maine Corp.*, 503 U.S. 407 (1992); *Mt. Vernon-Woodberry Cotton Duck Co.* v. *Alabama Interstate Power Co.*, 240 U.S. 30 (1916). But "public ownership" and "use-by-the-public" are some-

Where is the line between "public" and "private" property use? We give considerable deference to legislatures' determinations about what governmental activities will advantage the public. But were the political branches the sole arbiters of the public-private distinction, the Public Use Clause would amount to little more than hortatory fluff.

times too constricting and impractical ways to define the scope of the Public Use Clause. Thus we have allowed that, in certain circumstances and to meet certain exigencies, takings that serve a public purpose also satisfy the Constitution even if the property is destined for subsequent private use. See, *e.g., Berman* v. *Parker*, 348 U.S. 26 (1954); *Hawaii Housing Authority* v. *Midkiff*, 467 U.S. 229 (1984).

This case returns us for the first time in over 20 years to the hard question of when a purportedly "public purpose" taking meets the public use requirement. It presents an issue of first impression: Are economic development takings constitutional? I would hold that they are not. We are guided by two precedents about the taking of real property by eminent domain. In *Berman*, we upheld takings within a blighted neighborhood of Washington, D. C. The neighborhood had so deteriorated that, for example, 64.3 percent of its dwellings were beyond repair. 348 U.S., at 30. It had become burdened with "overcrowding of dwellings," "lack of adequate streets and alleys," and "lack of light and air." *Id.,* at 34. Congress had determined that the neighborhood had become "injurious to the public health, safety, morals, and welfare" and that it was necessary to "eliminat[e] all such injurious conditions by employing all means necessary and appropriate for the purpose," including eminent domain. *Id.,* at 28. Mr. Berman's department store was not itself blighted. Having approved of Congress' decision to eliminate the harm to the public emanating from the blighted neighborhood, however, we did not second-guess its decision to treat the neighborhood as a whole rather than lot-by-lot. *Id.,* at 34–35; see also *Midkiff,* 467 U.S., at 244 ("it is only the taking's purpose, and not its mechanics, that must pass scrutiny").

In *Midkiff,* we upheld a land condemnation scheme in Hawaii whereby title in real property was taken from lessors and transferred to lessees. At that time, the State and Federal Governments owned nearly 49 percent of the State's land, and another 47 percent was in the hands of only 72 private landowners. Concentration of land ownership was so dramatic that on the State's most urbanized island, Oahu, 22 landowners owned 72.5 percent of the fee simple titles. *Id.,* at 232. The Hawaii Legislature had concluded that the oligopoly in land ownership was "skewing the State's residential fee simple market, inflating land prices, and injuring the public tranquility and welfare," and therefore enacted a condemnation scheme for redistributing title. *Ibid.*

In those decisions, we emphasized the importance of deferring to legislative judgments about public purpose. Because courts are ill-equipped to evaluate the efficacy of proposed legislative initiatives, we rejected as unworkable the idea of courts' " 'deciding on what is and is not a governmental function and . . . invalidating legislation on the basis of their view on that question at the moment of decision, a practice which has proved impracticable in other fields.' " *Id.,* at 240–241 (quoting *United States ex rel. TVA* v. *Welch,* 327 U.S. 546, 552 (1946)); see *Berman, supra,* at 32 ("[T]he legislature, not the judiciary, is the main guardian of the public needs to be served by social legislation"); see also *Lingle* v. *Chevron U.S.A., Inc.,* 544 U.S. __ (2005). Likewise, we recognized our inability to evaluate whether, in a given case, eminent domain is a necessary means by which to pursue the legislature's ends. *Midkiff, supra,* at 242; *Berman, supra,* at 103.

Yet for all the emphasis on deference, *Berman* and *Midkiff* hewed to a bedrock principle without which our public use jurisprudence would collapse: "A purely private taking could not withstand the scrutiny of the public use requirement; it would serve no legitimate purpose of government and would thus be void." *Midkiff,* 467 U.S., at 245; *id.,* at 241 ("[T]he Court's cases have repeatedly stated that 'one person's property may not be taken for the benefit of another private person without a justifying public purpose, even though compensation be paid' " (quoting *Thompson* v. *Consolidated Gas Util. Corp.*, 300 U.S. 55, 80 (1937))); see also *Missouri Pacific R. Co.* v. *Nebraska*, 164 U.S. 403, 417 (1896). To protect that principle, those decisions reserved "a role for courts to play in reviewing a legislature's judgment of what constitutes a public use ... [though] the Court in *Berman* made clear that it is 'an extremely narrow' one." *Midkiff, supra*, at 240 (quoting *Berman, supra*, at 32).

The Court's holdings in *Berman* and *Midkiff* were true to the principle underlying the Public Use Clause. In both those cases, the extraordinary, precondemnation use of the targeted property inflicted affirmative harm on society—in *Berman* through blight resulting from extreme poverty and in *Midkiff* through oligopoly resulting from extreme wealth. And in both cases, the relevant legislative body had found that eliminating the existing property use was necessary to remedy the harm. *Berman, supra*, at 28–29; *Midkiff, supra*, at 232. Thus a public purpose was realized when the harmful use was eliminated. Because each taking *directly* achieved a public benefit, it did not matter that the property was turned over to private use. Here, in contrast, New London does not claim that Susette Kelo's and Wilhelmina Dery's well-maintained homes are the source of any social harm. Indeed, it could not so claim without adopting the absurd argument that any single-family home that might be razed to make way for an apartment building, or any church that might be replaced with a retail store, or any small business that might be more lucrative if it were instead part of a national franchise, is inherently harmful to society and thus within the government's power to condemn.

> *The Court today significantly expands the meaning of public use. It holds that the sovereign may take private property currently put to ordinary private use, and give it over for new, ordinary private use, so long as the new use is predicted to generate some secondary benefit for the public.*

In moving away from our decisions sanctioning the condemnation of harmful property use, the Court today significantly expands the meaning of public use. It holds that the sovereign may take private property currently put to ordinary private use, and give it over for new, ordinary private use, so long as the new use is predicted to generate some secondary benefit for the public—such as increased tax revenue, more jobs, maybe even aesthetic pleasure. But nearly any lawful use of real private property can be said to generate some incidental benefit to the public. Thus, if predicted (or even guaranteed) positive side-effects are enough to render transfer from one private party to another constitutional, then the words "for public use" do not realistically exclude *any* takings, and thus do not exert any constraint on the eminent domain power.

There is a sense in which this troubling result follows from errant language in *Berman* and *Midkiff*. In discussing whether takings within a blighted neighborhood were for a public use, *Berman* began by observing: "We deal, in other words, with what traditionally has been known as the police power." 348 U.S., at 32. From there it declared that "[o]nce the object is within the authority of Congress, the right to realize it through the exercise of eminent domain is clear." *Id.*, at 33. Following up, we said in *Midkiff* that "[t]he 'public use' requirement is coterminous with the scope of a sovereign's police powers." 467 U.S., at 240. This language was unnecessary to the specific holdings of those decisions. *Berman* and *Midkiff* simply did not put such language to the constitutional test, because the takings in those cases were within the police power but also for "public use" for the reasons I have described. The case before us now demonstrates why, when deciding if a taking's purpose is constitutional, the police power and "public use" cannot always be equated. The Court protests that it does not sanction the bare transfer from A to B for B's benefit. It suggests two limitations on what can be taken after today's decision. First, it maintains a role for courts in ferreting out takings whose sole purpose is to bestow a benefit on

For who among us can say she already makes the most productive or attractive possible use of her property? The specter of condemnation hangs over all property. Nothing is to prevent the State from replacing any Motel 6 with a Ritz-Carlton, any home with a shopping mall, or any farm with a factory.

the private transferee—without detailing how courts are to conduct that complicated inquiry. *Ante*, at 7. For his part, Justice Kennedy suggests that courts may divine illicit purpose by a careful review of the record and the process by which a legislature arrived at the decision to take–without specifying what courts should look for in a case with different facts, how they will know if they have found it, and what to do if they do not. *Ante*, at 2–3 (concurring opinion). Whatever the details of Justice Kennedy's as-yet-undisclosed test, it is difficult to envision anyone but the "stupid staff[er]" failing it. See *Lucas v. South Carolina Coastal Council*, 505 U.S. 1003, 1025–1026, n. 12 (1992). The trouble with economic development takings is that private benefit and incidental public benefit are, by definition, merged and mutually reinforcing. In this case, for example, any boon for Pfizer or the plan's developer is difficult to disaggregate from the promised public gains in taxes and jobs. See App. to Pet. for Cert. 275–277.

Even if there were a practical way to isolate the motives behind a given taking, the gesture toward a purpose test is theoretically flawed. If it is true that incidental public benefits from new private use are enough to ensure the "public purpose" in a taking, why should it matter, as far as the Fifth Amendment is concerned, what inspired the taking in the first place? How much the government does or does not desire to benefit a favored private party has no bearing on whether an economic development taking will or will not generate secondary benefit for the public. And whatever the reason for a given condemnation, the effect is the same from the constitutional perspective—private property is forcibly relinquished to new private ownership.

A second proposed limitation is implicit in the Court's opinion. The logic of today's decision is that eminent domain may only be used to upgrade—not downgrade—property. At best this makes the Public Use Clause redundant with the Due Process Clause, which already prohibits irrational government action. See *Lingle*, 544 U.S. __. The Court rightfully admits, however, that the judiciary cannot get bogged down in predictive judgments about whether the public will actually be better off after a property transfer. In any event, this constraint has no realistic import. For who among us can say she already makes the most productive or attractive possible use of her property? The specter of condemnation hangs over all property. Nothing is to prevent the State from replacing any Motel 6 with a Ritz-Carlton, any home with a shopping mall, or any farm with a factory. Cf. *Bugryn v. Bristol*, 63 Conn. App. 98, 774 A. 2d 1042 (2001) (taking the homes and farm of four owners in their 70's and 80's and giving it to an "industrial park"); *99 Cents Only Stores v. Lancaster Redevelopment Authority*, 237 F. Supp. 2d 1123 (CD Cal. 2001) (attempted taking of 99 Cents store to replace with a Costco); *Poletown Neighborhood Council v. Detroit*, 410 Mich. 616, 304 N. W. 2d 455 (1981) (taking a working-class, immigrant community in Detroit and giving it to a General Motors assembly plant), overruled by *County of Wayne v. Hathcock*, 471 Mich. 415, 684 N. W. 2d 765 (2004); Brief for the Becket Fund for Religious Liberty as *Amicus Curiae* 4–11 (describing takings of religious institutions' properties); Institute for Justice, D. Berliner, Public Power, Private Gain: A Five-Year, State-by-State Report Examining the Abuse of Eminent Domain (2003) (collecting accounts of economic development takings).

The Court also puts special emphasis on facts peculiar to this case: The NLDC's plan is the product of a relatively careful deliberative process; it proposes to use eminent domain for a multipart, integrated plan rather than for isolated property transfer; it promises an array of incidental benefits (even aesthetic ones), not just increased tax revenue; it comes on the heels of a legislative determination that New London is a depressed municipality. See, *e.g., ante*, at 16 ("[A] one-to-one transfer of property, executed outside the confines of an integrated development plan, is not presented in this case"). Justice Kennedy, too, takes great comfort in these facts. *Ante*, at 4 (concurring opinion). But none has legal significance to blunt the force of today's holding. If legislative prognostications about the secondary public benefits of a new use can legitimate a taking, there is nothing in the Court's rule or in Justice Kennedy's gloss on that rule to prohibit property transfers generated with less care, that are less comprehensive, that happen to result from less elaborate process, whose only projected advantage is the incidence of higher taxes, or that hope to transform an already prosperous city into an even more prosperous one.

Finally, in a coda, the Court suggests that property owners should turn to the States, who may or may not choose to impose appropriate limits on economic development takings. *Ante*, at 19. This is an abdication of our responsibility. States play many important functions in our system of dual sovereignty, but compensating for our refusal to enforce properly the Federal Constitution (and a provision meant to curtail state action, no less) is not among them.

The Court suggests that property owners should turn to the States, who may or may not choose to impose appropriate limits on economic development takings. . . . This is an abdication of our responsibility.

• • •

It was possible after *Berman* and *Midkiff* to imagine unconstitutional transfers from A to B. Those decisions endorsed government intervention when private property use had veered to such an extreme that the public was suffering as a consequence. Today nearly all real property is susceptible to condemnation on the Court's theory. In the prescient words of a dissenter from the infamous decision in *Poletown*, "[n]ow that we have authorized local legislative bodies to decide that a different commercial or industrial use of property will produce greater public benefits than its present use, no homeowner's, merchant's or manufacturer's property, however productive or valuable to its owner, is immune from condemnation for the benefit of other private interests that will put it to a 'higher' use." 410 Mich., at 644–645, 304 N. W. 2d, at 464 (opinion of Fitzgerald, J.). This is why economic development takings "seriously jeopardiz[e] the security of all private property ownership." *Id.*, at 645, 304 N. W. 2d, at 465 (Ryan, J., dissenting).

Any property may now be taken for the benefit of another private party, but the fallout from this decision will not be random. The beneficiaries are likely to be those citizens with disproportionate influence and power in the political process, including large corporations and development firms. As for the victims, the government now has license to transfer property from those with fewer resources to those with more. The Founders cannot have intended this perverse result. "[T]hat alone is a *just* government," wrote James Madison, "which *impartially* secures to every man, whatever is his *own*." For the National Gazette, Property, (Mar. 29, 1792), reprinted in 14 Papers of James Madison 266 (R. Rutland et al. eds. 1983).

I would hold that the takings in both Parcel 3 and Parcel 4A are unconstitutional, reverse the judgment of the Supreme Court of Connecticut, and remand for further proceedings.

THE TEXT OF JUSTICE THOMAS'S DISSENTING OPINION
Long ago, William Blackstone wrote that "the law of the land . . . postpone[s] even public necessity to the sacred and inviolable rights of private property." 1 Commentaries on the Laws of England 134–135 (1765) (hereinafter Blackstone). The Framers embodied that principle in the Constitution, allowing the government to take property not for "public necessity," but instead for "public use." Amdt. 5. Defying this understanding, the Court

replaces the Public Use Clause with a "'[P]ublic [P]urpose'" Clause, *ante*, at 9–10 (or perhaps the "Diverse and Always Evolving Needs of Society" Clause, *ante*, at 8 (capitalization added)), a restriction that is satisfied, the Court instructs, so long as the purpose is "legitimate" and the means "not irrational," *ante*, at 17 (internal quotation marks omitted). This deferential shift in phraseology enables the Court to hold, against all common sense, that a costly urban-renewal project whose stated purpose is a vague promise of new jobs and increased tax revenue, but which is also suspiciously agreeable to the Pfizer Corporation, is for a "public use."

I cannot agree. If such "economic development" takings are for a "public use," any taking is, and the Court has erased the Public Use Clause from our Constitution, as Justice O'Connor powerfully argues in dissent. *Ante*, at 1–2, 8–13. I do not believe that this Court can eliminate liberties expressly enumerated in the Constitution and therefore join her dissenting opinion. Regrettably, however, the Court's error runs deeper than this. Today's decision is simply the latest in a string of our cases construing the Public Use Clause to be a virtual nullity, without the slightest nod to its original meaning. In my view, the Public Use Clause, originally understood, is a meaningful limit on the government's eminent domain power. Our cases have strayed from the Clause's original meaning, and I would reconsider them.

The Fifth Amendment provides:

> No person shall be held to answer for a capital, or otherwise infamous crime, unless on a presentment or indictment of a Grand Jury, except in cases arising in the land or naval forces, or in the Militia, when in actual service in time of War or public danger; nor shall any person be subject for the same offence to be twice put in jeopardy of life or limb, nor shall be compelled in any criminal case to be a witness against himself, nor be deprived of life, liberty, or property, without due process, of law; *nor shall private property be taken for public use, without just compensation.*" (Emphasis added.)

It is the last of these liberties, the Takings Clause, that is at issue in this case. In my view, it is "imperative that the Court maintain absolute fidelity to" the Clause's express limit on the power of the government over the individual, no less than with every other liberty expressly enumerated in the Fifth Amendment or the Bill of Rights more generally. *Shepard* v. *United States*, 544 U. S. ___, ___ (2005) (slip op., at 2) (Thomas, J., concurring in part and concurring in judgment) (internal quotation marks omitted).

Though one component of the protection provided by the Takings Clause is that the government can take private property only if it provides "just compensation" for the taking, the Takings Clause also prohibits the government from taking property except "for public use." Were it otherwise, the Takings Clause would either be meaningless or empty. If the Public Use Clause served no function other than to state that the government may take property through its eminent domain power–for public or private uses–then it would be surplusage. See *ante*, at 3–4 (O'Connor, J., dissenting) ; see also *Marbury* v. *Madison*, 1 Cranch 137, 174 (1803) ("It cannot be presumed that any clause in the constitution is intended to be without effect"); *Myers* v. *United States*, 272 U. S. 52, 151 (1926). Alternatively, the Clause could distinguish those takings that require compensation from those that do not. That interpretation, however, "would permit private property to be taken or appropriated for private use without any compensation whatever." *Cole* v. *La Grange*, 113 U. S. 1, 8 (1885) (interpreting same language in the Missouri Public Use Clause). In other words, the Clause would require the government to compensate for takings done "for public use," leaving it free to take property for purely private uses without the payment of compensation. This would contradict a bedrock principle well established by the time of the founding: that all takings required the payment of compensation. 1 Blackstone 135; 2 J. Kent, Commentaries on American Law 275 (1827) (hereinafter Kent); J. Madison, for the National Property Gazette, (Mar. 27, 1792), in 14 Papers of James Madison 266, 267 (R. Rutland et al. eds. 1983) (arguing that no property shall be taken *directly* even for public use without indemnification to the owner").[1] The Public Use Clause, like the Just Compensation Clause, is therefore an express limit on the government's power of eminent domain.

The most natural reading of the Clause is that it allows the government to take property only if the government owns, or the public has a legal right to use, the property, as opposed to taking it for any public purpose or necessity whatsoever. At the time of the founding, dictionaries primarily defined the noun "use" as "[t]he act of employing any thing to any purpose." 2 S. Johnson, A Dictionary of the English Language 2194 (4th ed. 1773) (hereinafter Johnson). The term "use," moreover, "is from the Latin *utor*, which means 'to use, make use of, avail one's self of, employ, apply, enjoy, etc." J. Lewis, Law of Eminent Domain Section 165, p. 224, n. 4 (1888) (hereinafter Lewis). When the government takes property and gives it to a private individual, and the public has no right to use the property, it strains language to say that the public is "employing" the property, regardless of the incidental benefits that might accrue to the public from the private use. The term "public use," then, means that either the government or its citizens as a whole must actually "employ" the taken property. See *id.*, at 223 (reviewing founding-era dictionaries).

Granted, another sense of the word "use" was broader in meaning, extending to "[c]onvenience" or "help," or"[q]ualities that make a thing proper for any purpose." 2 Johnson 2194. Nevertheless, read in context, the term "public use" possesses the narrower meaning. Elsewhere, the Constitution twice employs the word "use," both times in its narrower sense. Claeys, Public-Use Limitations and Natural Property Rights, 2004 Mich. St. L. Rev. 877, 897 (hereinafter Public Use Limitations). Article 1, Section10 provides that "the net Produce of all Duties and Imposts, laid by any State on Imports or Exports, shall be for the Use of the Treasury of the United States," meaning the Treasury itself will control the taxes, not use it to any beneficial end. And Article I, Section 8 grants Congress power "[t]o raise and support Armies, but no Appropriation of Money to that Use shall be for a longer Term than two Years." Here again, "use" means "employed to raise and support Armies," not anything directed to achieving any military end. The same word in the Public Use Clause should be interpreted to have the same meaning.

Tellingly, the phrase "public use" contrasts with the very different phrase "general Welfare" used elsewhere in the Constitution. See *ibid.* ("Congress shall have Power To . . . provide for the common Defence and general Welfare of the United States"); preamble (Constitution established "to promote the general Welfare"). The Framers would have used some such broader term if they had meant the Public Use Clause to have a similarly sweeping scope. Other founding-era documents made the contrast between these two usages still more explicit. See Sales, Classical Republicanism and the Fifth Amendment's "Public Use" Requirement, 49 Duke L. J. 339, 368 (2000) (hereinafter Sales) (noting contrast between, on the one hand, the term "public use" used by 6 of the first 13 States and, on the other, the terms "public exigencies" employed in the Massachusetts Bill of Rights and the Northwest Ordinance, and the term "public necessity" used in the Vermont Constitution of 1786). The Constitution's text, in short, suggests that the Takings Clause authorizes the taking of property only if the public has a right to employ it, not if the public realizes any conceivable benefit from the taking.

When the government takes property and gives it to a private individual, and the public has no right to use the property, it strains language to say that the public is "employing" the property, regardless of the incidental benefits that might accrue to the public from the private use.

The Takings Clause is a prohibition, not a grant of power: The Constitution does not expressly grant the Federal Government the power to take property for any public purpose whatsoever. Instead, the Government may take property only when necessary and proper to the exercise of an expressly enumerated power.

The Constitution's common-law background reinforces this understanding. The common law provided an express method of eliminating uses of land that adversely impacted the public welfare: nuisance law. Blackstone and Kent, for instance, both carefully distinguished the law of nuisance from the power of eminent domain. Compare 1 Blackstone 135 (noting government's power to take private property with compensation), with 3 *id.*, at 216 (noting action to remedy "*public* . . .nuisances, which affect the public and are an annoyance to *all* the king's subjects"); see also 2 Kent 274–276 (distinguishing the two). Blackstone rejected the idea that private property could be taken solely for purposes of any public benefit. "So great . . . is the regard of the law for private property," he explained, "that it will not authorize the least violation of it; no, not even for the general good of the whole community." 1 Blackstone 135. He continued: "If a new road . . . were to be made through the grounds of a private person, it might perhaps be extensively beneficial to the public; but the law permits no man, or set of men, to do this without the consent of the owner of the land." *Ibid.* Only "by giving [the landowner] full indemnification" could the government take property, and even then "[t]he public [was] now considered as an individual, treating with an individual for an exchange." *Ibid.* When the public took property, in other words, it took it as an individual buying property from another typically would: for one's own use. The Public Use Clause, in short, embodied the Framers' understanding that property is a natural, fundamental right, prohibiting the government from "tak[ing] *property* from A. and giv[ing] it to B." *Calder* v. *Bull,* 3 Dall. 386, 388 (1798); see also *Wilkinson* v. *Leland,* 2 Pet. 627, 658 (1829); *Vanhorne's Lessee* v. *Dorrance,* 2 Dall. 304, 311 (CC Pa. 1795).

The public purpose interpretation of the Public Use Clause also unnecessarily duplicates a similar inquiry required by the Necessary and Proper Clause. The Takings Clause is a prohibition, not a grant of power: The Constitution does not expressly grant the Federal Government the power to take property for any public purpose whatsoever. Instead, the Government may take property only when necessary and proper to the exercise of an expressly enumerated power. See *Kohl* v. *United States,* 91 U. S. 367, 371–372 (1876) (noting Federal Government's power under the Necessary and Proper Clause to take property "needed for forts, armories, and arsenals, for navy-yards and light-houses, for custom-houses, post offices, and court-houses, and for other public uses"). For a law to be within the Necessary and Proper Clause, as I have elsewhere explained, it must bear an "obvious, simple, and direct relation" to an exercise of Congress' enumerated powers, *Sabri* v. *United States,* 541 U. S. 600, 613 (2004) (Thomas, J., concurring in judgment), and it must not "subvert basic principles of" constitutional design, *Gonzales* v. *Raich, ante,* at __ (Thomas, J., dissenting). In other words, a taking is permissible under the Necessary and Proper Clause only if it serves a valid public purpose. Interpreting the Public Use Clause likewise to limit the government to take property only for sufficiently public purposes replicates this inquiry. If this is all the Clause means, it is, once again, surplusage. See *supra,* at 3. The Clause is thus most naturally read to concern whether the property is used by the public or the government, not whether the purpose of the taking is legitimately public.

II

Early American eminent domain practice largely bears out this understanding of the Public Use Clause. This practice concerns state limits on eminent domain power, not the Fifth Amendment, since it was not until the late nineteenth century that the Federal Government began to use the power of eminent domain, and since the Takings Clause did not even arguably limit state power until after the passage of the Fourteenth Amendment. See Note, The Public Use Limitation on Eminent Domain: An Advance Requiem, 58 Yale L. J. 599, 599–600, and nn. 3–4 (1949); *Barron ex rel. Tiernan* v. *Mayor of Baltimore*, 7 Pet. 243, 250–251 (1833) (holding the Takings Clause inapplicable to the States of its own force). Nevertheless, several early state constitutions at the time of the founding likewise limited the power of eminent domain to "public uses." See Sales 367–369, and n. 137 (emphasis deleted). Their practices therefore shed light on the original meaning of the same words contained in the Public Use Clause.

States employed the eminent domain power to provide quintessentially public goods, such as public roads, toll roads, ferries, canals, railroads, and public parks. Lewis Sections 166, 168–171, 175, at 227–228, 234–241, 243. Though use of the eminent domain power was sparse at the time of the founding, many States did have so-called Mill Acts, which authorized the owners of grist mills operated by water power to flood upstream lands with the payment of compensation to the upstream landowner. See, *e.g., id.*, Section178, at 245–246; *Head* v. *Amoskeag Mfg. Co.*, 113 U. S. 9, 16–19, and n. (1885). Those early grist mills "were regulated by law and compelled to serve the public for a stipulated toll and in regular order," and therefore were actually used by the public. Lewis Section 178, at 246, and n. 3; see also *Head, supra*, at 18–19. They were common carriers—quasi-public entities. These were "public uses" in the fullest sense of the word, because the public could legally use and benefit from them equally. See Public Use Limitations 903 (common-carrier status traditionally afforded to "private beneficiaries of a state franchise or another form of state monopoly, or to companies that operated in conditions of natural monopoly").

To be sure, some early state legislatures tested the limits of their state-law eminent domain power. Some States enacted statutes allowing the taking of property for the purpose of building private roads. See Lewis Section167, at 230.

These statutes were mixed; some required the private landowner to keep the road open to the public, and others did not. See *id.*, Section167, at 230–234. Later in the 19th century, moreover, the Mill Acts were employed to grant rights to private manufacturing plants, in addition to grist mills that had common-carrier duties. See, *e.g.,* M. Horwitz, The Transformation of American Law 1780–1860, pp. 51–52 (1977).

These early uses of the eminent domain power are often cited as evidence for the broad "public purpose" interpretation of the Public Use Clause, see, *e.g., ante,* at 8, n. 8 (majority opinion); Brief for Respondents 30; Brief for American Planning Assn. et al. as *Amici Curiae* at 6–7, but in fact the constitutionality of these exercises of eminent domain power under state public use restrictions was a hotly contested question in state courts throughout the nineteenth and into the twentieth century. Some courts construed those clauses to authorize takings for public purposes, but others adhered to the natural meaning of "public use."[2] As noted above, the earliest Mill Acts were applied to entities with duties to remain open to the public, and their later extension is not deeply probative of whether that subsequent practice is consistent with the original meaning of the Public Use Clause. See *McIntyre* v. *Ohio Elections Comm'n,* 514 U. S. 334, 370 (1995) (Thomas, J., concurring in judgment). At the time of the founding, "[b]usiness corporations were only beginning to upset the old corporate model, in which the raison d'être of chartered associations was their service to the public," Horwitz, *supra,* at 49–50, so it was natural to those who framed the first Public Use Clauses to think of mills as inherently public entities. The disagreement among state courts, and state legislatures' attempts to circumvent public use limits on their eminent domain power,

These early uses of the eminent domain power are often cited as evidence for the broad "public purpose" interpretation of the Public Use Clause, but in fact the constitutionality of these exercises of eminent domain power under state public use restrictions was a hotly contested question in state courts throughout the nineteenth and into the twentieth century.

cannot obscure that the Public Use Clause is most naturally read to authorize takings for public use only if the government or the public actually uses the taken property.

III

Our current Public Use Clause jurisprudence, as the Court notes, has rejected this natural reading of the Clause. *Ante*, at 8–10. The Court adopted its modern reading blindly, with little discussion of the Clause's history and original meaning, in two distinct lines of cases: first, in cases adopting the "public purpose" interpretation of the Clause, and second, in cases deferring to legislatures' judgments regarding what constitutes a valid public purpose. Those questionable cases converged in the boundlessly broad and deferential conception of "public use" adopted by this Court in *Berman* v. *Parker,* 348 U. S. 26 (1954), and *Hawaii Housing Authority* v. *Midkiff,* 467 U. S. 229 (1984), cases that take center stage in the Court's opinion. See *ante,* 10–12. The weakness of those two lines of cases, and consequently *Berman* and *Midkiff,* fatally undermines the doctrinal foundations of the Court's decision. Today's questionable application of these cases is further proof that the "public purpose" standard is not susceptible of principled application. This Court's reliance by rote on this standard is ill advised and should be reconsidered.

Today's questionable application of these cases is further proof that the "public purpose" standard is not susceptible of principled application. This Court's reliance by rote on this standard is ill advised and should be reconsidered.

A

As the Court notes, the "public purpose" interpretation of the Public Use Clause stems from *Fallbrook IrrigationDist.* v. *Bradley,* 164 U. S. 112, 161–162 (1896). *Ante,* at 11. The issue in *Bradley* was whether a condemnation for purposes of constructing an irrigation ditch was for a public use. 164 U. S., at 161. This was a public use, Justice Peckham declared for the Court, because "[t]o irrigate and thus to bring into possible cultivation these large masses of otherwise worthless lands would seem to be a public purpose and a matter of public interest, not confined to landowners, or even to any one section of the State." *Ibid.* That broad statement was dictum, for the law under review also provided that "[a]ll landowners in the district have the right to a proportionate share of the water." *Id.,* at 162. Thus, the "public" did have the right to use the irrigation ditch because all similarly situated members of the public—those who owned lands irrigated by the ditch—had a right to use it. The Court cited no authority for its dictum, and did not discuss either the Public Use Clause's original meaning or the numerous authorities that had adopted the "actual use" test (though it at least acknowledged the conflict of authority in state courts, see *id.,* at 158; *supra,* at 9, and n. 2). Instead, the Court reasoned that "[t]he use must be regarded as a public use, or else it would seem to follow that no general scheme of irrigation can be formed or carried into effect." *Bradley, supra,* at 160–161. This is no statement of constitutional principle: Whatever the utility of irrigation districts or the merits of the Court's view that another rule would be "impractical given the diverse and always evolving needs of society," *ante,* at 8, the Constitution does not embody those policy preferences any more than it "enact[s] Mr. Herbert Spencer's Social Statics." *Lochner* v. *New York,* 198 U. S. 45, 75 (1905) (Holmes, J., dissenting); but see *id.,* at 58–62 (Peckham, J., for the Court).

This Court's cases followed *Bradley*'s test with little analysis. In *Clark* v. *Nash,* 198 U. S. 361 (1905) (Peckham, J., for the Court), this Court relied on little more than a citation to *Bradley* in upholding another condemnation for the purpose of laying an irrigation ditch. 198 U. S., at 369–370. As in *Bradley,* use of the "public purpose" test was unnecessary to the result the Court reached. The government condemned the irrigation ditch for the purpose of ensuring access to water in which "[o]ther land owners adjoining the defendant in error . . . might share," 198 U. S., at 370, and therefore *Clark* also involved a condemnation for the purpose of ensuring access to a resource to which similarly situated members of the public had a legal right of access. Likewise, in *Strickley* v. *Highland Boy Gold Mining Co.,* 200 U. S. 527 (1906), the Court upheld a condemnation establishing an aerial right-of-way for a bucket line operated by a mining company, relying on little more than *Clark,* see *Strickley, supra,* at 531. This case, too, could have been disposed of on the narrower ground that "the plaintiff [was] a carrier for itself and others," 200 U. S., at 531–532, and therefore that the bucket line was legally open to the public. Instead, the Court unnecessarily rested its decision on the "inadequacy of use by the general public as a universal test." *Id.,* at 531. This Court's cases quickly incorporated the public purpose standard set forth in *Clark* and *Strickley* by barren citation. See, *e.g., Rindge Co.* v. *County of Los Angeles,* 262 U. S. 700, 707 (1923); *Block* v. *Hirsh,* 256 U. S. 135, 155 (1921); *Mt. Vernon-Woodberry Cotton Duck Co.* v. *Alabama Interstate Power Co.,* 240 U. S. 30, 32 (1916); *O'Neill* v. *Leamer,* 239 U. S. 244, 253 (1915).

B

A second line of this Court's cases also deviated from the Public Use Clause's original meaning by allowing legislatures to define the scope of valid "public uses." *United States* v. *Gettysburg Electric R. Co.,* 160 U. S. 668 (1896), involved the question whether Congress' decision to condemn certain private land for the purpose of building battlefield memorials at Gettysburg, Pennsylvania, was for a public use. *Id.,* at 679–680. Since the Federal Government was to use the lands in question, *id.,* at 682, there is no doubt that it was a public use under any reasonable standard. Nonetheless, the Court, speaking through Justice Peckham, declared that "when the legislature has declared the use or purpose to be a public one, its judgment will be respected by the courts, unless the use be palpably without reasonable foundation." *Id.,* at 680. As it had with the "public purpose" dictum in *Bradley, supra,* the Court quickly incorporated this dictum into its Public Use Clause cases with little discussion. See, *e.g., United States ex rel. TVA* v. *Welch,* 327 U. S. 546, 552 (1946); *Old Dominion Land Co.* v. *United States,* 269 U. S. 55, 66 (1925).

There is no justification, however, for affording almost insurmountable deference to legislative conclusions that a use serves a "public use." To begin with, a court owes no deference to a legislature's judgment concerning the quintessentially legal question of whether the government owns, or the public has a legal right to use, the taken property. Even under the "public purpose" interpretation, moreover, it is most implausible that the Framers intended to defer to legislatures as to what satisfies the Public Use Clause, uniquely among all the express provisions of the Bill of Rights. We would not defer to a legislature's determination of the various circumstances that establish, for example, when a search of a home would be reasonable, see, *e.g., Payton* v. *New York,* 445 U. S. 573, 589–590 (1980), or when a convicted double-murderer may be shackled during a sentencing proceeding without on-the-record findings, see *Deck* v. *Missouri,* 544 U. S. ___ (2005), or when state law creates a property interest protected by the Due Process Clause, see, *e.g., Castle Rock* v. *Gonzales, post,* at __; *Board of Regents of State Colleges* v. *Roth,* 408 U. S. 564, 576 (1972); *Goldberg* v. *Kelly,* 397 U. S. 254, 262–263 (1970).

Still worse, it is backwards to adopt a searching standard of constitutional review for nontraditional property interests, such as welfare benefits, see, *e.g., Goldberg, supra,* while deferring to the legislature's determi-

A second line of this Court's cases also deviated from the Public Use Clause's original meaning by allowing legislatures to define the scope of valid "public uses."

nation as to what constitutes a public use when it exercises the power of eminent domain, and thereby invades individuals' traditional rights in real property. The Court has elsewhere recognized "the overriding respect for the sanctity of the home that has been embedded in our traditions since the origins of the Republic," *Payton, supra*, at 601, when the issue is only whether the government may search a home. Yet today the Court tells us that we are not to "second-guess the City's considered judgments," *ante*, at 18, when the issue is, instead, whether the government may take the infinitely more intrusive step of tearing down petitioners' homes. Something has gone seriously awry with this Court's interpretation of the Constitution. Though citizens are safe from the government in their homes, the homes themselves are not. Once one accepts, as the Court at least nominally does, *ante*, at 6, that the Public Use Clause is a limit on the eminent domain power of the Federal Government and the States, there is no justification for the almost complete deference it grants to legislatures as to what satisfies it.

> Once one permits takings for public purposes in addition to public uses, no coherent principle limits what could constitute a valid public use—at least, none beyond Justice O'Connor's (entirely proper) appeal to the text of the Constitution itself.

C

These two misguided lines of precedent converged in *Berman* v. *Parker,* 348 U. S. 26 (1954), and *Hawaii Housing Authority* v. *Midkiff,* 467 U. S. 229 (1984). Relying on those lines of cases, the Court in *Berman* and *Midkiff* upheld condemnations for the purposes of slum clearance and land redistribution, respectively. "Subject to specific constitutional limitations," *Berman* proclaimed, "when the legislature has spoken, the public interest has been declared in terms well-nigh conclusive. In such cases the legislature, not the judiciary, is the main guardian of the public needs to be served by social legislation." 348 U. S., at 32. That reasoning was question begging, since the question to be decided was whether the "specific constitutional limitation" of the Public Use Clause prevented the taking of the appellant's (concededly "nonblighted") department store. *Id.,* at 31, 34. *Berman* also appeared to reason that any exercise by Congress of an enumerated power (in this case, its plenary power over the District of Columbia) was *per se* a "public use" under the Fifth Amendment. *Id.,* at 33. But the very point of the public Use Clause is to limit that power. See *supra,* at 3–4.

More fundamentally, *Berman* and *Midkiff* erred by equating the eminent domain power with the police power of States. See *Midkiff,* 467 U. S., at 240 ("The 'public use' requirement is . . . coterminous with the scope of a sovereign's police powers"); *Berman,* 348 U. S., at 32. Traditional uses of that regulatory power, such as the power to abate a nuisance, required no compensation whatsoever, see *Mugler* v. *Kansas,* 123 U. S. 623, 668–669 (1887), in sharp contrast to the takings power, which has always required compensation, see *supra,* at 3, and n. 1. The question whether the State can take property using the power of eminent domain is therefore distinct from the question whether it can regulate property pursuant to the police power. See, *e.g., Lucas* v. *South Carolina Coastal Council,* 505 U. S. 1003, 1014 (1992); *Mugler, supra,* at 668–669. In *Berman,* for example, if the slums at issue were truly "blighted," then state nuisance law, see, *e.g., supra,* at 5–6; *Lucas, supra,* at 1029, not the power of eminent domain, would provide the appropriate remedy. To construe the Public Use Clause to overlap with the States' police power conflates these two categories.[3]

The "public purpose" test applied by *Berman* and *Midkiff* also cannot be applied in principled manner. "When we depart from the natural import of the term 'public use,' and substitute for the simple idea of a public possession and occupation, that of public utility, public interest, common benefit, general advantage or convenience . . . we are afloat without any certain principle to guide us." *Bloodgood* v. *Mohawk & Hudson R. Co.,* 18 Wend. 9, 60–61 (NY 1837) (opinion of Tracy, Sen.). Once one permits takings for public purposes in addition to public uses, no coherent principle limits what could constitute a valid public use—at least, none beyond Justice O'Connor's (entirely proper) appeal to the text of the Constitution itself. See *ante*, at 1–2, 8–13 (dissenting opinion). I share the Court's skepticism about a public use standard that requires courts to second-guess the policy wisdom of public works projects. *Ante*, at 16–19. The "public purpose" standard this Court has adopted, however, demands the use of such judgment, for the Court concedes that the Public Use Clause would forbid a purely private taking. *Ante*, at 7–8. It is difficult to imagine how a court could find that a taking was purely private except by determining that the taking did not, in fact, rationally advance the public interest. Cf. *ante*, at 9–10 (O'Connor, J., dissenting) (noting the complicated inquiry the Court's test requires). The Court is therefore wrong to criticize the "actual use" test as "difficult to administer." *Ante*, at 8. It is far easier to analyze whether the government owns or the public has a legal right to use the taken property than to ask whether the taking has a "purely private purpose"—unless the Court means to eliminate public use scrutiny of takings entirely. *Ante*, at 7–8, 16–17. Obliterating a provision of the Constitution, of course, guarantees that it will not be misapplied.

For all these reasons, I would revisit our Public Use Clause cases and consider returning to the original meaning of the Public Use Clause: that the government may take property only if it actually uses or gives the public a legal right to use the property.

IV

The consequences of today's decision are not difficult to predict, and promise to be harmful. So-called "urban renewal" programs provide some compensation for the properties they take, but no compensation is possible for the subjective value of these lands to the individuals displaced and the indignity inflicted by uprooting them from their homes. Allowing the government to take property solely for public purposes is bad enough, but extending the concept of public purpose to encompass any economically beneficial goal guarantees that these losses will fall disproportionately on poor communities. Those communities are not only systematically less likely to put their lands to the highest and best social use, but are also the least politically powerful. If ever there were justification for intrusive judicial review of constitutional provisions that protect "discrete and insular minorities," *United States* v. *Carolene Products Co.*, 304 U. S. 144, 152, n. 4 (1938), surely that principle would apply with great force to the powerless groups and individuals the Public Use Clause protects. The deferential standard this Court has adopted for the Public Use Clause is therefore deeply perverse. It encourages "those citizens with disproportionate influence and power in the political process, including large corporations and development firms" to victimize the weak. *Ante*, at 11 (O'Connor, J., dissenting).

Those incentives have made the legacy of this Court's "public purpose" test an unhappy one. In the 1950's, no doubt emboldened in part by the expansive understanding of "public use" this Court adopted in *Berman*, cities "rushed to draw plans" for downtown development. B. Frieden & L. Sagalayn, Downtown, Inc. How America Rebuilds Cities 17 (1989). "Of all the families displaced by urban renewal from 1949 through 1963, 63 percent of those whose race was known were nonwhite, and of these families, 56 percent of nonwhites and 38 percent of whites had incomes low enough to qualify for public housing, which, however, was seldom available to them." *Id.*, at 28. Public works projects in the 1950's and 1960's destroyed predominantly minority communities in St. Paul, Minnesota, and Balti-

Allowing the government to take property solely for public purposes is bad enough, but extending the concept of public purpose to encompass any economically beneficial goal guarantees that these losses will fall disproportionately on poor communities.

The APA is centrally concerned with redirecting growth and development into the nation's central cities, inner suburbs, and other areas already served by infrastructure and supported by urban services. It believes that it is critically important to preserve the ability of local governments to use redevelopment tools and techniques, including eminent domain when appropriate, to achieve well-defined public purposes. The APA also believes that an open and inclusive public participation process should be part of all redevelopment planning.

more, Maryland. *Id.*, at 28–29. In 1981, urban planners in Detroit, Michigan, uprooted the largely "lower-income and elderly" Poletown neighborhood for the benefit of the General Motors Corporation. J. Wylie, Poletown: Community Betrayed 58 (1989). Urban renewal projects have long been associated with the displacement of blacks; "[i]n cities across the country, urban renewal came to be known as 'Negro removal.'" Pritchett, The "Public Menace" of Blight: Urban Renewal and the Private Uses of Eminent Domain, 21 Yale L. & Pol'y Rev. 1, 47 (2003). Over 97 percent of the individuals forcibly removed from their homes by the "slum-clearance" project upheld by this Court in *Berman* were black. 348 U. S., at 30. Regrettably, the predictable consequence of the Court's decision will be to exacerbate these effects.

• • •

The Court relies almost exclusively on this Court's prior cases to derive today's far-reaching, and dangerous, result. See *ante*, at 8–12. But the principles this Court should employ to dispose of this case are found in the Public Use Clause itself, not in Justice Peckham's high opinion of reclamation laws, see *supra*, at 11. When faced with a clash of constitutional principle and a line of unreasoned cases wholly divorced from the text, history, and structure of our founding document, we should not hesitate to resolve the tension in favor of the Constitution's original meaning. For the reasons I have given, and for the reasons given in Justice O'Connor's dissent, the conflict of principle raised by this boundless use of the eminent domain power should be resolved in petitioners' favor. I would reverse the judgment of the Connecticut Supreme Court.

AMICUS CURIAE BRIEF

FILED ON BEHALF OF THE AMERICAN PLANNING ASSOCIATION, THE CONNECTICUT CHAPTER OF APA, AND THE NATIONAL CONGRESS FOR COMMUNITY ECONOMIC DEVELOPMENT IN SUPPORT OF THE CITY OF NEW LONDON, CONNECTICUT

By John D. Echeverria, Georgetown University Environmental Law and Policy Institute, Washington, D.C., and Thomas W. Merrill, Charles Keller Beekman Professor of Law, Columbia University, New York, N.Y.

QUESTION PRESENTED
Whether this Court should change the settled meaning of the "public use" limitation of the Just Compensation Clause by ruling either (i) that property cannot be taken by eminent domain solely for economic development, or (ii) that courts should apply a heightened standard of review in considering legislative determinations of public use.

IDENTITY AND INTEREST OF AMICI CURIAE[1]
The American Planning Association (APA) is a non-profit public interest and research organization founded in 1978 to advance the art and science of planning at the local, regional, state, and national levels. It represents more than 37,000 practicing planners, officials, and citizens involved, on a day-to-day basis, in formulating and implementing planning policies and land-use regulations. The organization has 46 regional chapters, including the Connecticut Chapter with 446 members, which joins in filing this amicus brief, as well as nineteen divisions devoted to specialized planning interests. The APA is centrally concerned with redirecting growth and development into the nation's central cities, inner suburbs, and other areas

already served by infrastructure and supported by urban services. It believes that it is critically important to preserve the ability of local governments to use redevelopment tools and techniques, including eminent domain when appropriate, to achieve well-defined public purposes. The APA also believes that an open and inclusive public participation process should be part of all redevelopment planning. To the extent possible, the APA believes that communities should use incentives—such as increased development densities and favorable zoning policies—as their primary redevelopment tool, and should resort to eminent domain only as a tool of last resort when incentives are insufficient to implement redevelopment plans.

Founded in 1970, the National Congress for Community Economic Development ("NCCED") is the representative and advocate for the community-based development industry. NCCED represents over 3,600 community development corporations ("CDCs") across America; its membership encompasses a broad range of geographic, ethnic, racial, political, social, and economic interests, including neighborhood housing and community action agencies, farmworker organizations, public officials, financial institutions, municipalities, businesses and individuals. Community development corporations produce affordable housing and create jobs through business and commercial development activities, and are a vital force in empowering low-income communities across the nation to achieve economic and social progress.

SUMMARY OF ARGUMENT

Petitioners ask this Court to impose a restrictive gloss on the words "public use" in the Just Compensation Clause, interpreting those words to mean that property cannot be condemned solely for economic development. This is not the first time courts have been asked to police the ends to which the power of eminent domain is devoted. From roughly 1840 through the 1930s, many state courts applying state constitutional law sought to limit eminent domain to projects that were "used by the public," a project that was eventually abandoned as unworkable and unduly restrictive. Significantly, however, during that same period this Court never endorsed a restrictive reading of public use as a matter of federal constitutional law. To the contrary, it specifically approved condemnations designed to promote economic development, and consistently applied a highly deferential standard of review to public use determinations. This history is instructive in considering petitioners' proposals that this Court restrict the use of eminent domain for economic development, or adopt a more intrusive standard of review. It reveals that these proposals are not only unwise, but would require a radical departure from a jurisprudence that has been long settled.

Petitioners and their amici advance only two specific legal arguments in support of their proposals. Petitioners request that the Court emulate the reasoning of *County of Wayne v. Hathcock*, 471 Mich. 445, 684 N.W.2d 765 (2004).

But *Hathcock* rests on an idiosyncratic state constitutional methodology; would invite manipulation; and could lead to a variety of undesirable consequences in different areas of the law. Petitioners' amici suggest that *Nollan v. California Coastal Commission*, 483 U.S. 825 (1987), and *Dolan v. City of Tigard*, 512 U.S. 374 (1994), require a higher standard of review of public use determinations. However, there is no justification for transposing a standard of review designed to identify uncompensated expropriations to the wholly different context in which government agencies agree to pay just compensation for the property interests they acquire.

Eminent domain is concededly an unsettling power, and is subject to misuse or overuse if not properly constrained. But eminent domain is disruptive for all who experience it, not just those who might be able to persuade a reviewing court that a particular condemnation is not "public" enough. The dangers of eminent domain should be addressed by assuring that it remains a second-best alternative to market exchange as a means of acquiring resources, by encouraging careful planning and public participation in decisions to invoke eminent domain, and by building on current legislative requirements that mandate additional compensation beyond the constitutional minimum for persons who experience uncompensated subjective losses and consequential damages.

ARGUMENT

I. History Teaches That "Public Use" Should be Given a Broad Interpretation That Includes Economic Development

The briefs filed in this case by petitioners and their amici can be read to imply that this Court in *Berman v. Parker*, 348 U.S. 26 (1954), and *Hawaii Hous. Auth. v. Midkiff*, 467 U.S. 229 (1984), abdicated a constitutional role it had previously performed in protecting property owners from overly zealous exercises of the power of eminent domain, and that the law should now be restored to its former glory. Nothing could be further from the truth. Petitioners are the ones who seek a sharp break with settled constitutional understandings. They are urging the adoption of novel constitutional limitations on the exercise of eminent domain that have never had, and never should have, any basis in federal constitutional law.

A. The rise and fall of "use by the public." There is little affirmative evidence that the Framers understood the words "for public use" in the Just Compensation Clause to incorporate any kind of substantive limitation on the ends to which the power of eminent domain may be devoted. These words may have been intended merely to describe the type of taking for which just compensation must be given—a taking of specific private property by public authority as opposed to some other type of taking, such as a taking by tort or taxation.[2] Nevertheless, "for public use" has been read throughout our history as imposing an implied limitation on the exercise of eminent domain—that it can be used only for public and not private uses—and this Court has accepted this interpretation. *Brown v. Legal Found. of Washington*, 538 U.S. 216, 231-32 (2003); *Thompson v. Consol. Gas Utils. Corp.*, 300 U.S. 55, 80 (1937).

As an implied limitation on the power of eminent domain, the core case of a forbidden private use has always been clear: when the government takes A's property and gives it to B, with no public justification other than the legislature's preference for B over A. *See Mo. Pac. Ry. v. Nebraska*, 164 U.S. 403, 417 (1896). What has been less clear is just what sort of justification is necessary to elevate a taking from the A to B category and transform it into a public use.

Historically speaking, three different interpretations of "public use" can be discerned.[3] The most restrictive interpretation requires that the government actually hold title to the property after the condemnation. The next-most-restrictive definition is that public use means "use by the public." Under this definition, public title to the property is irrelevant; what is decisive is whether the property is accessible as a matter of right to the public. The third and broadest definition is that public use means public benefit or advantage. Under this conception, neither title to the property after condemnation, nor access to the property by the general public, is necessary. Instead, property can be taken for any objective that the legislature rationally determines to be a sufficient public justification.

The dangers of eminent domain should be addressed by assuring that it remains a second-best alternative to market exchange as a means of acquiring resources . . .

As an implied limitation on the power of eminent domain, the core case of a forbidden private use has always been clear: when the government takes A's property and gives it to B, with no public justification other than the legislature's preference for B over A.

The narrowest possible definition—that public use means public ownership—has always been regarded as a fairly uncontroversial type of taking. Many routine examples of eminent domain—such as the acquisition of land for a highway—fit this definition. But public ownership has almost universally been regarded as too narrow to serve as a comprehensive definition of public use. Starting in the early years of the nineteenth century, States frequently delegated the power of eminent domain to privately owned turnpike, canal and railroad corporations. Later, such delegations were extended to privately owned gas, electric, and telephone utilities. The widespread practice of delegating the power of eminent domain to these sorts of privately owned common carriers and public utilities meant that courts almost never regarded public title to condemned property as a complete definition of public use.[4]

During the colonial and early national periods, the understanding about the permissible scope of eminent domain appears to have been, at least implicitly, the broad view–that the power could be used for any purpose consistent with public benefit or advantage.[5] The issue received little attention by courts, presumably because land was plentiful and eminent domain was little used. Around 1840, however, a judicial reaction began to set in. Many state courts began to endorse the more restrictive "use by the public" test.[6] This permitted eminent domain to be delegated to railroads, turnpike companies, and the like, because these were common carriers subject to duties to serve the public on a nondiscriminatory basis. But, by definition, it would not permit eminent domain to be used by other types of enterprises, such as manufacturing plants or mining operations.

Almost immediately, those state courts that had endorsed the "use by the public" reading began to encounter cases in which the test appeared to be unduly restrictive. Mill Acts, which permitted riparian owners to build dams flooding the property of upstream owners, were a primary focus of controversy. With respect to gristmills that ground grain for area farmers, one could characterize the enterprise as being subject to common carrier-type duties, and hence as satisfying the "use by the public" criterion.[7] But as the nineteenth century unfolded, Mill Acts increasingly came to include other types of mill dams, such as those powering textile plants and other types of manufacturing operations. Courts that had embraced the "use by the public" test struggled with these applications.[8] Similar problems were encountered when public utility companies began to acquire easements for electric and telephone distribution lines across private property, and many States, especially in the West, adopted statutes broadly permitting eminent domain to be used to facilitate the construction of mining operations, irrigation projects, and drainage districts. State courts that had adopted the "use by the public" test engaged in a variety of contortions in an effort generally to sustain these exercises of eminent domain.[9] By the beginning of the twentieth century, as one commentator observed, "there had developed a massive body of case law, irreconcilable in its inconsistency, confusing in its detail and defiant of all attempts at classification."[10]

The *coup de grace* to the "use by the public" test was delivered in the 1930s. Beginning with the National Industrial Recovery Act, followed by the Housing Acts of 1937 and 1949, Congress began appropriating significant federal funds to state and local government authorities to assist in the process of slum removal and construction of public housing.[11] Many of these projects entailed the use of eminent domain either to clear deteriorated properties and/or to acquire sites for public housing. Following the lead of the New York Court of Appeals,[12] state courts uniformly rejected claims that these condemnations violated the public use limitation. From this point on, the "use by the public" test faded into obscurity. It is today the law in at most only a few States.[13]

B. This court has consistently embraced the broad view of public use. Throughout the roughly 100 years that witnessed the rise and fall of the "use by the public" standard in the state courts, this Court never once sought to impose such a restriction on eminent domain as a matter of federal constitutional law. Four cases decided by this Court around the turn of the twentieth century involving the development of natural resources are particularly instructive. These cases involved challenges to the use of eminent domain to construct a ditch to remove water from a drainage district, *O'Neill v. Leamer*, 239 U.S. 244 (1915); to construct ditches to bring water to irrigation districts, *Clark v. Nash*, 198 U.S. 361 (1905); *Fallbrook Irrigation Dist. v. Bradley*, 164 U.S. 112 (1896); and to build an aerial bucket line to transport minerals taken from a mine, *Strickley v. Highland Boy Gold Mining Co.*, 200 U.S. 527, 531 (1906). They establish three propositions of importance to the present controversy.

First, in none of the four cases did the general public have any right of access to the property condemned. The Court specifically rejected the contention that a lack of public access made the exercise of the power of eminent domain constitutionally problematic. Speaking for the Court in *Strickley*, Justice Holmes noted "the inadequacy of use by the public as a universal test." 200 U.S. at 531. The Court soon reaffirmed this conclusion in a variety of contexts not involving the development of natural resources.[14] Given that the two contending approaches to interpretation of public use at the time were the "use by the public" test and the public benefit or advantage test, the Court's explicit rejection of the narrow test represented a firm embrace of the broad public benefit or advantage interpretation.

The Court stressed that the conditions that might justify the exercise of eminent domain vary greatly from one section of the country to another, making it inappropriate to lay down a single federal rule binding on all States.

Second, the Court stressed that the conditions that might justify the exercise of eminent domain vary greatly from one section of the country to another, making it inappropriate to lay down a single federal rule binding on all States. In *Clark*, the Court upheld a Utah statute that had been applied to permit the condemnation of a ditch to convey water for irrigation to a single farm. Justice Peckham (who in other contexts was quite skeptical of state intervention in economic affairs, *see Lochner v. New York*, 198 U.S. 45 (1905)) wrote that whether such a purpose is a valid public use will "depend upon many different facts":

> Those facts must be general, notorious, and acknowledged in the State, and the state courts may be assumed to be exceptionally familiar with them. They are not the subjects of judicial investigation as to their existence, but the local courts know and appreciate them. They understand the situation that led to the demand for the enactment of the statute, and they also appreciate the results upon the growth and prosperity of the State, which in all probability would flow from the denial of its validity. 198 U.S. at 368.

Given the variability of conditions from one State to another, Justice Peckham concluded: "[W]here the right of condemnation is asserted under a state statute, we are always, where it can fairly be done, strongly inclined to hold with the state courts, when they uphold a state statute providing for such condemnation." *Id.*

Third, the public rationale for the takings in each of these cases was the State's determination that the property was needed in order to enhance the productivity of particular resources. The Court recognized that the takings in these cases could not be justified on public health and safety grounds, *see Fallbrook Irrigation Dist.*, 164 U.S. at 163, or on the ground that large numbers of persons directly benefited from the takings, *see Clark, supra; Stickley, supra.* Instead, in each case the condemnation was justified because of its impact on "the growth and prosperity of the state," *Clark, supra*, 198 U.S. at 368, or "the prosperity of the community," *Fallbrook Irrigation Dist.*, 164 U.S. at 163—in other words, *because it was needed to promote economic development*. Each of these decisions therefore stands for the proposition that condemnation for the sole purpose of economic development *is* a legitimate public use, provided a State so determines and this judgment is a rational one in light of the circumstances of the property and the needs of the public. Petitioners cite some of these decisions in footnotes (*see* Pet. Br. at 22 n.18, 33 n.31). But they have not explained why they should now be overruled based on a novel theory that the power of eminent domain cannot be used to promote economic development.[15]

Throughout the period when many state courts followed the "use by the public" standard, this Court invalidated only one state action as an impermissible private use. This was an order of the Nebraska Board of Transportation directing a railroad to allow a group of farmers to construct an elevator on railroad property on terms and conditions similar to those previously extended to two other firms. *Mo. Pac. Ry. v. Nebraska*, 164 U.S. 403 (1896). The Court observed that the challenged order was not framed or defended as an exercise of the power of eminent domain for public use, that the beneficiaries were private individuals associated for their own benefit, that they had not been incorporated for any public purpose, and that they did not represent that the new elevator would be open to use by the public. *Id.* at 416. On these assumptions, the Court held that "[t]he taking by a State of the private property of one person or corporation, for the private use of another, is not due process of law . . . ." *Id.* at 417. *Missouri Pacific* stands for the proposition that when government takes property from A and gives it to B, and fails altogether to advance a rational public purpose justification for the taking, this violates the public use limitation. There is no reason to believe that this does not remain good law.

As the federal government grew in the scope of its activities, this Court also began to encounter public use challenges to the exercise of eminent domain by federal authorities. The Court in these cases adhered to the broad conception of public use, permitting eminent domain to be used for a variety of ends, including acquiring land for a park, *Shoemaker v. United States*, 147 U.S. 282 (1893); acquiring the site of the Battle of Gettysburg for a national memorial, *United States v. Gettysburg Elec. Ry.*, 160 U.S. 668 (1896); acquiring land to retransfer to persons whose property had been flooded by a federal reservoir, *Brown v. United States*, 263 U.S. 78 (1923); and acquiring homes that had been cut off from access to the outside world by a federal reservoir. *United States ex rel. TVA v. Welch*, 327 U.S. 546 (1946). From its earliest encounters with the public use issue, the Court's understanding of the applicable standard of review remained essentially unchanged. In *Gettysburg Electric*, the Court said: "[W]hen the legislature has declared the use or purpose to be a public one, its judgment will be respected by the courts, unless the use be palpably without reasonable foundation." 160 U.S. at 680. In *Old Dominion Land Co. v. United States*, 269 U.S. 55, 66 (1925), the Court said: "Congress has declared the purpose to be a public use, by implication if not by express words. . . . Its decision is entitled to deference until it is shown to involve an impossibility." In *Welch*, after quoting the foregoing standard, the Court said: "Any departure from this judicial restraint would result in courts deciding on what is and is not a governmental function and in their invalidating legislation on the basis of their view on that question at the moment of decision, a practice which has proved impracticable in other fields." 327 U.S. at 551-52.

Against this background, it is clear that *Berman v. Parker*, 348 U.S. 26 (1954), and *Hawaii Hous. Auth. v. Midkiff*, 467 U.S. 229 (1984), represented no break with the past. Those decisions simply restated the settled jurisprudence established by this Court more than fifty years before *Berman* was decided. Under that jurisprudence, the determination of what ends constitute a public use is for the legislature to make, without any artificial restrictions on legislative choice such as the "use by the public" test. Legislative determinations of public use are subject to judicial review, but only under the highly deferential rationality standard that applies to constitutional challenges to social and economic legislation more generally.

In the years since *Berman* and *Midkiff,* litigation over the public use issue has settled into a stable pattern.[16] Federal courts, following the teachings of *Berman* and *Midkiff,* have played a minor role in the process, and have been highly deferential to legislative determinations of public use. There are 31 published federal appellate decisions resolving public use controversies since *Berman.* Only one of these decisions holds that a condemnation is not for a public use, and that decision turns largely on the conclusion that the taking was not an authorized public use under Indiana state law.[17] The outcome in state courts, not surprisingly in a federal system, is somewhat more variable. There have been 513 state appellate decisions resolving public use controversies since *Berman,* the vast majority of which interpret "public use" language in state constitutions rather than the parallel language found in the federal Constitution. These decisions are also deferential to legislative determinations of public use, but less so than federal appellate decisions. Altogether, about one in six of these decisions (17 percent) holds that a challenged taking is not for a proper public use, mostly under state constitutional law.

In short, the law of public use has been and largely remains state constitutional law, reflecting the vagaries and traditions of each individual state. State courts have not failed to scrutinize the use of eminent domain to assure that States do not take property from A and give it to B without an adequate public justification. They have in fact invalidated a sizeable number of takings as lacking a sufficient public use. The Connecticut Supreme Court's decision in this case, decided by a four-to-three margin, reflects the kind of careful consideration that state appellate courts continue to give to these issues. Federal courts, however, have stood to one side, and have allowed the state courts to police this issue. Petitioners and their amici have offered no compelling argument as to why this settled division of constitutional authority, reflecting over a century of unbroken federal constitutional precedent established by this Court, should now be upended.

II. Petitioners And Their Amici Have Advanced No Principled Legal Basis For Adopting A Novel And Restrictive Approach To Public Use

Given the longstanding and settled meaning of "public use," petitioners and their amici offer surprisingly little by way of legal argument that would justify adopting a novel and restrictive approach to the public use limitation.

Petitioners' primary argument is to urge the Court to emulate the reasoning of a recent Michigan Supreme Court decision construing the Michigan Constitution (Pet. Br. 18-27). Their secondary argument is that the Court should adopt a more searching standard of review of public use determinations than the one reflected in its past decisions (Pet. Br. 30-40). Although petitioners offer no specific legal argument in support of this secondary argument, some of petitioners' amici contend that the Court's decisions involving exactions require adopting an intermediate standard of review for public use cases. None of these claims has merit.

A. The public use standard recently adopted as a matter of Michigan constitutional law in Hathcock is unworthy of emulation. Petitioners invite the Court to adopt as a matter of federal constitutional law the restrictive definition of public use recently adopted as a matter of Michigan con-

Under that jurisprudence, the determination of what ends constitute a public use is for the legislature to make, without any artificial restrictions on legislative choice such as the "use by the public" test.

In short, the law of public use has been and largely remains state constitutional law, reflecting the vagaries and traditions of each individual state.

stitutional law in *County of Wayne v. Hathcock*, 471 Mich. 445, 684 N.W.2d 765 (2004). *Hathcock* involved a challenge to the use of eminent domain to acquire a number of parcels of land in Wayne County adjacent to the Detroit Airport. The project started when the airport was expanded, exacerbating noise pollution of nearby properties. With the aid of a grant from the Federal Aviation Administration, the County began to purchase nearby property affected by noise. The County eventually determined to acquire 1,300 acres in all, and to use the property to develop a business and technology park that would promote economic development in the County. Scattered within this tract were 19 individual parcels whose owners declined to sell, which the County sought to acquire by eminent domain.

As explained in Part I, courts historically have assumed that "public use" should be defined in terms of a single variable: public ownership, use by the public, or public benefit or advantage. *Hathcock* breaks new ground by combining these definitions into a more complex, multi-part definition of what is *not* a public use. Specifically, the decision holds that property is not dedicated to public use when it is taken for the use of a private for-profit enterprise, unless one of three circumstances applies: (1) the condemnation is for a highway, railroad, canal, pipeline or similar "instrumentality of commerce" that requires the assembly of many contiguous parcels of land and hence presents the potential for an extreme holdout problem; (2) the private transferee will remain accountable to the public for its use of the property because it will be subject to continuing regulatory oversight; or (3) property has been selected for condemnation based on some attribute or condition of the condemned property of "independent public significance" such as being blighted. 471 Mich. at 472-76, 684 N.W.2d at 781-83. The Michigan Supreme Court, finding that the County did not propose to retain title to the land in the technology park, and that the project did not otherwise fit any of the categories where eminent domain was permitted, held the taking was not for a valid public use. 471 Mich. at 476-78, 684 N.W.2d at 781-83.

There are a number of reasons not to emulate the *Hathcock* decision. First, *Hathcock* rests on an interpretative method unique to Michigan constitutional law, which deviates sharply from federal constitutional law. *Hathcock* sought to fix the meaning of broad constitutional language by incorporating the particular applications of that language that a "legally sophisticated" reader would recognize to exist at the time of ratification. *See* 471 Mich. at 468-71, 684 N.W.2d at 779-80 (purporting to derive this methodology from the writings of the nineteenth-century Michigan jurist Thomas Cooley). The current version of the Michigan Constitution was ratified in 1963. The court asked: What would a legally sophisticated reader of the constitutional text in 1963 understand by the term "public use"? The answer: Such a reader would have examined Michigan decisional law on the subject, and would have understood that law to comprise only those uses that had been previously recognized by the Michigan judiciary prior to 1963, namely, public ownership, condemnations for common carriers facing extreme holdout problems, condemnations for other private entities subject to close regulatory supervision, and elimination of blighted property. Use of eminent domain for any other purpose would have been understood to be impermissible.

Whatever merits it may have as a matter of Michigan constitutional law, *Hathcock*'s methodology is inconsistent with the way this Court generally interprets the Federal Constitution. Although the Court is guided by its under-standing of the general concepts the Framers understood they were constitutionalizing, it does not treat the "broad and majestic" Clauses of that document[18] as incorporating a specific list of permitted applications

The court asked: What would a legally sophisticated reader of the constitutional text in 1963 understand by the term "public use"? The answer: Such a reader would have examined Michigan decisional law on the subject, and would have understood that law to comprise only those uses that had been previously recognized by the Michigan judiciary prior to 1963, . . .

Proper economic development planning looks to a wide range of factors, including not just the condition of existing properties, but also the potential for future economic activity in the area, population densities, proximity to transportation facilities, the presence or absence of public amenities, and other variables.

that a "legally sophisticated" reader would recognize at the time of ratification.[19] To some degree the Seventh Amendment's right to jury trial in suits at common law has been interpreted this way.[20] But there is a textual basis for this: the Seventh Amendment directs that the right to trial by jury in suits at common law "shall be preserved." Ordinarily, however, constitutional provisions are not construed as incorporating contemporaneous applications frozen in time. For example, the Commerce Clause, the First Amendment, the Fourth Amendment and the Equal Protection Clause have not been construed this way. Indeed, the other elements of the Takings Clause—most prominently, the word "taken"—have not been construed as having a fixed historical meaning.[21] It would be very odd, to say the least, to interpret one word of the Takings Clause ("taken") as a general concept whose application is to be determined over time, and three other words ("for public use") in an historically frozen fashion.

Interpreting the "public use" language in the Federal Constitution in a historically frozen manner would obviously have deeply unsettling consequences. The Fifth Amendment has not been amended since it was adopted in 1791. If only those projects recognized as proper objects of eminent domain in 1791 were deemed permissible, huge swathes of settled eminent domain law would now have to be repudiated as unconstitutional. If we decide that 1868, when the Fourteenth Amendment was adopted, is the appropriate reference point, then the effect would be only slightly less invasive. Takings for public utility lines, pipelines, water reclamation projects, and urban renewal were all unrecognized as of 1868.

Second, *Hathcock*'s attempt to limit the use of eminent domain for economic development to cases where property is "blighted" would generate undesirable consequences. Such a limitation could work to the disadvantage of poor and minority communities, which could be more readily subject to condemnation based on a finding of blight than middle-class communities.[22] More broadly, it would seriously distort the process of development planning, by skewing economic development projects toward locations most plausibly characterized as blighted. Proper economic development planning looks to a wide range of factors, including not just the condition of existing properties, but also the potential for future economic activity in the area, population densities, proximity to transportation facilities, the presence or absence of public amenities, and other variables.[23] The straightjacket *Hathcock* seeks to impose on eminent domain could under-mine the quality of planning for economic development, to the detriment of all the community.

Any constitutionally mandated finding of "blight" would also be subject to manipulation. This Court observed in *Lucas* that "the distinction between 'harm-preventing' and 'benefit-conferring' regulation is often in the eyes of the beholder" and cautioned against using this distinction as a basis for interpretation of the Just Compensation Clause.[24] Restricting the use of eminent domain to blighted areas would confront similar imponderables, as municipalities and property owners would contest whether particular takings are blight prevention programs ("harm-preventing") or "mere" economic development programs ("benefit-conferring"). Federal courts could arbitrate these disputes only by developing a jurisprudence of "blight," and closely reviewing the factual records in state eminent domain proceedings to make sure that the States are conforming to the federalized standard.

Third, *Hathcock*'s restrictive definition of public use could limit the options of government in solving important social problems in a variety of areas. Of particular relevance to the issues in this case, *Hathcock*'s limitations could severely restrict government efforts to combat urban sprawl.

Developers of new shopping centers, townhouse complexes, and business centers need large tracts of land to configure their projects in ways that will attract customers. The easiest way to acquire large tracts of land is to buy up greenfields at the outer fringes of urban areas. Large sites in existing urban centers are hard to come by because of the high transaction costs of land assembly. One way to reduce the advantage developers currently see in greenfield development is to use eminent domain to assemble tracts of land in high-density urban areas. But *Hathock* seems to say that, outside the context of property found to be blighted, this will be possible only if the government retains title to the property. *Hathcock* observes dismissively that "the landscape of our country is flecked with shopping centers, office parks, clusters of hotels, and centers of entertainment and commerce." 471 Mich. at 477, 684 N.W.2d at 783. What it fails to observe is that these are mostly located along arterial highways at the perimeter of urban areas. The only meaningful land assembly option *Hathcock* leaves for fighting sprawl is state ownership of shopping centers, townhouse complexes or business centers—not a very appealing idea.

Hathcock could have other unhappy consequences as well, many undoubtedly unforeseeable. For example, *Hathcock* might call into question federal legislation providing for compulsory licensing of intellectual property rights.[25] The statutes that incorporate these provisions represent an exercise of the power of eminent domain in the sense that the government authorizes one party (the licensee) to "take" the rights of another person (the intellectual property owner) without permission, in return for the payment of just compensation. Yet these devices also do not appear to fit into any of *Hathcock*'s permitted "exceptions."[26] Similarly, *Hathcock* could call into question statutes that exist in about half the States authorizing private landowners to condemn rights of way to landlocked property. Michigan has specifically disapproved such takings,[27] but other States permit them, and *Hathcock*'s test for public use would arguably wipe out any room for state variation in terms of these longstanding practices.[28]

These and other uncertainties suggest that the primary effect of *Hathcock*'s complex and poorly defined test would simply be to transfer discretion over approval of projects that involve the use of eminent domain from politically accountable bodies to courts. The decision would almost surely impose a new source of litigation costs, as lawyers for property owners and public authorities debated different aspects of the multi-part rule. This Court should decline petitioners' invitation to subject state and local authorities throughout the Nation to this unjustifiable headache.

B. There is no basis for transplanting the heightened standard of review applicable to development exactions to public use cases. Petitioners argue in the alternative that this Court should jettison its longstanding commitment to deferential review of legislative determinations of public use. Although petitioners offer no specific legal argument that would justify this step, several of petitioners' amici contend that the Court's decisions in *Nollan v. California Coastal Comm'n*, 483 U.S. 825 (1987), and *Dolan v. City of Tigard*, 512 U.S. 374 (1994), should be read effectively to overrule the Court's public use precedents and compel use of a heightened standard of review in eminent domain cases. *See, e.g.*, Brief of Cascade Policy Institute *et al.*; Brief Amicus Curiae of Professors David L. Callies *et al.* In fact, those decisions do not in any way alter or undermine the Court's settled standard of review for public use determinations.

Nollan and *Dolan* establish a special legal standard to deal with the situation where government officials, in the course of making individual land-use permitting decisions, seek to attach conditions requiring owners to grant the public permanent physical access to their property. Under *Loretto*

One way to reduce the advantage developers currently see in greenfield development is to use eminent domain to assemble tracts of land in high-density urban areas.

v. Teleprompter Manhattan CATV Corp., 458 U.S. 419, 426 (1982), these types of requirements, if imposed directly, would constitute per se takings. The question the Court faced in *Nollan* and *Dolan* is whether it makes a difference if such requirements are imposed, not directly, but as conditions of regulatory permits the government might simply deny altogether without incurring takings liability. The Court resolved the question by ruling that such "exactions" do not effect a taking so long as (1) there is an essential "nexus" between the exaction and the government's regulatory purposes in establishing the permitting scheme, *Nollan, supra*, 483 U.S. at 837, and (2) there is a "rough proportionality" between the impact of the proposed development and the property right exacted, *Dolan, supra*, 512 U.S. at 319. The Court acknowledged that application of these tests entails a more heightened standard of review than the traditionally deferential, rational-basis standard. *See Dolan, supra*, 512 U.S. at 391.

The heightened standard established in Nollan *and* Dolan *for exactions does not extend to the quite different context of public use determinations for the exercise of eminent domain. A critical difference is that government affirmatively offers to pay just compensation in an eminent domain case, whereas the very question at issue in an exactions case is whether the government has affected an appropriation for which it must pay compensation.*

The heightened standard established in *Nollan* and *Dolan* for exactions does not extend to the quite different context of public use determinations for the exercise of eminent domain. A critical difference is that government affirmatively offers to pay just compensation in an eminent domain case, whereas the very question at issue in an exactions case is whether the government has affected an appropriation for which it must pay compensation. *Nollan* and *Dolan* themselves make this distinction clear by indicating that the government in each case could have acquired the property rights in question in those cases, regardless of whether the nexus and proportionality tests were met, so long as it was willing to pay compensation. *See Nollan, supra*, 483 U.S. at 842 ("if [California] wants an easement across the Nollan's property, it must pay for it"); *Dolan*, 512 U.S. at 396. The standard for deciding whether government can evade paying for an appropriation should not govern the very different question of whether government can take property upon payment of just compensation.

Furthermore, *Nollan* and *Dolan* represent an application of the doctrine of unconstitutional conditions, which has no bearing on eminent domain cases. While reaffirming the government's broad authority to regulate land uses, *Nollan* and *Dolan* focus on the danger that government could use its ad hoc regulatory authority as leverage to extract interests in property that are unrelated to government's regulatory objectives. As the Court stated in *Nollan*, where there is no "essential nexus" between an exaction and government's regulatory objectives, there is a risk that a permitting decision can be converted into "an out-and-out plan of extortion." *Nollan*, 483 U.S. at 837. The same risk of potential misuse of government authority does not exist where government mandates a straightforward exchange of property for compensation equal to the fair market value of the property taken.

Consistent with the specific nature of the problem these cases address, the Court has made clear that *Nollan* and *Dolan* have only a narrow scope. Petitioners' suggestion that *Nollan* mandates a complete rethinking of the pubic use standard was implicitly rejected by the Court's decision in *National R.R. Passenger Corp. v. Boston & Maine Corp.*, 503 U.S. 407 (1992), issued five years after *Nollan* was decided, in which the Court applied, without any dissent, the deferential rational basis test in a public use case involving property retransfer to a private party. Subsequently, in *City of Monterey v. Del Monte Dunes at Monterey, Ltd.*, 526 U.S. 687, 702 (1999), the Court ruled that the rough proportionality test of *Dolan* (and, by clear implication, the companion *Nollan* essential nexus test) does not extend "beyond the special context of exactions—land use decisions conditioning approval of development on the dedication of property to public use." In any event, in *Dolan* the Court said that the heightened standard of review for exactions does not apply to "legislative determinations" that do not present the same risk of improper leveraging as ad hoc permitting decisions. 512 U.S. at 385. Thus, the heightened standard established by *Nollan* and *Dolan* does not apply to New London's legislative determination, made in conjunction with a comprehensive planning process involving full public participation, to use the eminent domain power to affect a compensated taking.

III. Heightened Public Use Review Is Not The Answer To Misuse Or Overuse Of Eminent Domain

Eminent domain is admittedly an unsettling power. To be wrenched from one's home or business by order of the government is a deeply disruptive experience—with or without the payment of compensation. Such coercive power should be used sparingly. Heightened judicial review under the public use requirement, however, would provide a poor mechanism for protecting property owners against the misuse or overuse of eminent domain. Such review would aid only the lucky few who could persuade a panel of judges that the purpose of a particular exercise of eminent domain is not sufficiently "public." To be displaced by eminent domain is a potentially disorienting event for any property owner who experiences it, whatever the justification for the condemnation. What is needed are more general mechanisms that will assure that eminent domain is used as a last resort, not a first resort, and that mitigate the harshness of eminent domain for all who experience it.

Fortunately, there is reason to believe that those mechanisms are already in place. They do not work perfectly, and there is unquestionably room for refinements that would provide additional protections for property owners. But constructive solutions to eminent domain abuse or overuse lie in directions other than developing novel substantive limitations on the ends to which eminent domain can be used, or injecting federal courts into local land use planning processes through a heightened standard of review.

A. Keeping eminent domain a second-best option. As a general rule, it is cheaper to acquire resources through voluntary exchange in the market than it is to obtain them through eminent domain. Market exchange is of course not without cost. But the costs of eminent domain are generally greater. This is confirmed by the fact that when government units want to acquire property for which there is a thick market— such as personal property—they invariably make open market purchases or use competitive bidding, rather than having to resort to eminent domain.[29]

Eminent domain is generally more expensive because the power is cabined by a variety of procedural requirements that entail significant cost and delay for agencies seeking to acquire resources. The power of eminent domain must be properly delegated by the legislature to the body that is conducting the condemnation; the condemning authority typically must formally determine under applicable law that the exercise of eminent domain is "necessary" in order to achieve the stated public purpose; many States require that the property be properly appraised by the condemning authority before proceeding to negotiate over its acquisition; many States require that the authority make a good faith effort to acquire the property through voluntary negotiation before proceeding to condemnation; many States allow condemnees to demand trial by jury on the question of just compensation; in all States, the Due Process Clause requires that the condemnee be given a full and fair opportunity for a hearing to determine whether all legal requirements for eminent domain have been satisfied, and to contest in court the amount of compensation she will receive.[30]

Eminent domain is admittedly an unsettling power. To be wrenched from one's home or business by order of the government is a deeply disruptive experience—with or without the payment of compensation. Such coercive power should be used sparingly.

One other procedural requirement, of course, is important. The legislature or its delegate must make an actual determination that condemnation is for a public use before exercising the power of eminent domain. We do not believe that a restrictive judicial gloss should be imposed on the meaning of public use, or that courts should apply a heightened standard of review to public use determinations. But we *do* believe it is important that some politically accountable body determine that the exercise of eminent domain is for a public use, and that judicial review of such determinations remain available, even if under a deferential standard. The prospect of judicial review and potential invalidation of public use determinations, especially in state courts where review has been more intrusive than in federal courts, adds another important increment to the expected costs of acquiring resources through eminent domain.

Perhaps the most constructive contribution courts can make in protecting against misuse or overuse of eminent domain is to insist that the procedural requirements associated with the exercise of eminent domain be faith-fully followed in every case. These requirements not only provide valuable protections *ex post* for individual property owners when they have been singled out for condemnation. Perhaps more importantly, by increasing the costs and the delay associated with acquiring resources by eminent domain, they provide important protection *ex ante* to all property owners, by creating a powerful incentive for authorities with condemnation authority to use market transactions wherever possible. Strict enforcement of procedural requirements, in other words, makes eminent domain largely self-regulating, in the sense that it will only be used in situations where the costs of negotiated exchange are prohibitive.

B. Integrating eminent domain into land-use planning. Another source of protection for all property owners is to assure, to the extent possible, that eminent domain is exercised only in conjunction with a process of land use planning that includes broad public participation and a careful consideration of alternatives to eminent domain.

Integrating the decision to use eminent domain into a sound planning process has a number of desirable consequences. Such a process can help minimize the use of eminent domain, by identifying alternatives to proposed development projects, such as relocating or resizing projects, or perhaps forgoing them altogether. It can also reduce public concerns about the use of eminent domain, by providing a forum in which the reasons for opposition can be considered, offering explanations for the proposed course of action and possible alternatives, and perhaps instilling a greater degree of understanding on the part of both the proponents and opponents of the proposed project. To the extent the need to undertake a planning process including public participation magnifies the cost differential between eminent domain and market transactions, these processes also provide a further disincentive to use eminent domain.

We do not suggest that a mandate to engage in a sound planning process can be extracted from the "public use" requirement of the Fifth Amendment. Planning processes, including public participation and a requirement of considering alternatives, have other roots, most prominently the administrative law traditions surrounding the local land-use planning. We do think, however, that the presence of these features is relevant to this Court's consideration of whether the public use determination of New London and the New London Development Corporation was a rational one. New London and its Development Corporation engaged in an extensive planning process before determining that it was necessary to exercise the power of eminent domain; they provided multiple opportunities for public participation in the planning process; and they gave extensive con-

We do not believe that a restrictive judicial gloss should be imposed on the meaning of public use, or that courts should apply a heightened standard of review to public use determinations. But we do believe it is important that some politically accountable body determine that the exercise of eminent domain is for a public use, and that judicial review of such determinations remain available, even if under a deferential standard.

New London and its Development Corporation engaged in an extensive planning process before determining that it was necessary to exercise the power of eminent domain; they provided multiple opportunities for public participation in the planning process; and they gave extensive consideration to alternative plans before settling on the final plan.

sideration to alternative plans before settling on the final plan. *See* Resp. Br. at 4-9. We would urge the Court to note these features of the instant case as relevant factors confirming that the public use determination was rational—without of course necessarily suggesting that they are constitutionally required. We would also suggest that the Court note other recent decisions in the lower courts, such as *S.W. Ill. Dev. Auth. v. Nat'l City Envt'l, L.L.C.*, 199 Ill.2d 225, 768 N.E.2d 1 (2002), where eminent domain decisions were *not* accompanied by any significant degree of planning or public participation, and where the state courts held that the taking was not for a public use—without of course necessarily suggesting that the same result would be required by the Federal Constitution. The Court can instruct by example as well as by mandate.

C. Providing additional compensation for takings of occupied structures. The default standard for determining just compensation is fair market value—what a willing buyer would pay a willing seller of the property, taking into account all possible uses to which the property might be put other than the use contemplated by the taker.[31] This standard, however, sometimes fails to provide full indemnification to all property owners whose property is taken by eminent domain. The most obvious shortfall is the subjective value that individual owners attach to their properties. Subjective value has many sources. Owners may have made modifications to the property to suit their individual needs and preferences; they may treasure friendships they have formed in the neighborhood; they may simply enjoy the security that comes from being in familiar surroundings. These values are ignored under the fair market value test.[32] Another important shortfall involves consequential damages caused by a taking of property, including moving expenses, attorneys fees, loss or damage to tangible personal property, and loss of business good will. The constitutional formula does not provide any compensation for any of these values either.[33] These systematic shortfalls in compensation help account for the intensity of opposition many homeowners express even to compensated takings.

Adjusting compensation awards to provide more complete indemnification would be a far more effective reform of the existing system of eminent domain than increasing federal judicial review of public use determinations. Additional compensation would reduce the burden imposed on particular individuals by the imposition of uncompensated residual losses. It would provide a further incentive for public authorities to forego eminent domain, if at all possible, in favor of market exchange. And it would provide a targeted and calibrated remedy for the concerns about uncompensated losses suffered by certain property owners, homeowners in particular,[34] without erecting an unnecessary general barrier to the use of the eminent domain power as a tool for economic development.

The Constitution requires "just compensation," not fair market value, and it is possible that constitutional compensation standards could be modified in ways that would provide more complete compensation for persons who experience uncompensated subjective losses and consequential damages. The Court has been reluctant to endorse deviations from the market value standard, however, because differentiating between claimants who experience such losses and those who do not would create administrative problems for courts.[35] Legislatures are in a much better position to identify categories of claimants who deserve additional compensation, and to develop administrable mechanisms for providing such compensation. Congress has shown the way, through the landmark Uniform Relocation Assistance Act of 1970, 42 U.S.C. Section 4601 et seq. The Relocation Act requires that all real property condemnations undertaken by the federal government provide, in addition to compensation for

Adjusting compensation awards to provide more complete indemnification would be a far more effective reform of the existing system of eminent domain than increasing federal judicial review of public use determinations.

the fair market value of the property taken, additional compensation for moving expenses, direct losses of tangible personal property, reasonable expenses of searching for a substitute business or farm, and certain other incidental expenses. *Id.* Sections 4622(a), 4653. Federal agencies may not make financial grants to state agencies that will result in takings of real property without first receiving adequate assurances that the state agency will follow similar policies. *Id.* Section 4630. Pursuant to these requirements, Relocation Act awards will be provided to the petitioners in this case. *See* Resp. Br. at 8.

The additional compensation mandated by the Relocation Act, which has not been significantly amended since it was adopted, obviously goes only part way toward solving the problem of uncompensated subjective losses and consequential damages. But the Act targets the properties of greatest concern: occupied residential structures and operating businesses and farms. A logical further step for reform would be to amend the Act to provide a further increment in compensation for classes of property at risk for significant uncompensated losses, perhaps by providing a percentage bonus above fair market value.[36] Petitioners and their supporters would be well advised to channel their energies toward pursuing this kind of reform of eminent domain – and in directing their proposals to the appropriate legislative bodies – rather than asking this Court to adopt unprecedented restrictions on the purposes to which the eminent domain power can be devoted.

For the foregoing reasons, the judgment of the Supreme Court of Connecticut should be affirmed.

NOTES FOR THE AMICUS CURIAE BRIEF

1. Counsels for the parties have consented to the filing of this brief. No counsel for a party in this case authored this brief in whole or in part, and no person or entity, other than amici or their counsel, made a monetary contribution to the brief 's preparation or submission.

2. *See* David A. Dana & Thomas W. Merrill, *Property: Takings* 8-25 (2002); Matthew P. Harrington, *"Public Use" and the Original Understanding of the So-Called "Takings" Clause*, 53 Hastings L.J. 1245 (2002).

3. For useful surveys of the history of interpretation of the public use limitation, *see* Errol E. Meidinger, *The "Public Uses" of Eminent Domain: History and Policy*, 11 Envtl. L. 1, 4-41 (1980); Lawrence Berger, *The Public Use Requirement in Eminent Domain*, 57 Or. L. Rev. 203, 204-25 (1978); Philip Nichols, Jr., *The Meaning of Public Use in the Law of Eminent Domain*, 20 B.U.L. Rev. 615 (1940).

4. For a rare judicial expression of the public title view, *see Bloodgood v. Mohawk & Hudson R.R.*, 18 Wend. 9, 60-61 (N.Y. 1837) (concurring opinion of Senator Tracey).

5. *See* Meidinger, *supra* note 3, at 25; Berger, *supra* note 3, at 207.

6. *See* Nichols, *supra* note 3, at 617-18; Comment, *The Public Use Limitation on Eminent Domain: An Advance Requiem*, 58 Yale L.J. 599, 603-04 (1949).

7. *See Head v. Amoskeag Mfg. Co.*, 113 U.S. 9, 18-19 (1885). 8

8. *See* Nichols, *supra* note 3, at 620-21.

9. *See* Dayton G. & S. Mining Co. v. Seawell, 11 Nev. 394, 400-01 (1876).

10. Comment, *supra* note 6, at 605-06.

11. *See* Berger, *supra* note 3, at 214-17; Nichols, *supra* note 3, at 629-33.

12. New York City Hous. Auth. v. Muller, 270 N.Y. 333, 1 N.E.2d 153 (1936).

13. See, e.g., Karesh v. City Council, 271 S.C. 339, 247 S.E.2d 342 (S.C. 1978).

14. *See Mt. Vernon-Woodberry Cotton Duck Co. v. Ala. Interstate Power Co.*, 240 U.S. 30, 32 (1916); *Block v. Hirsh*, 256 U.S. 135, 155 (1921); *Rindge Co. v. Los Angeles County*, 262 U.S. 700, 707 (1923).

15. Petitioners suggest that these cases involved "instrumentalities of commerce" (Pet. Br. at 21). But if the private ditches and aerial bucket line were "instrumentalities of

commerce," then so is every private driveway in the country. The stated justification for the taking in each case was that it would enhance the productivity of resources, and the Court upheld each of the takings on the assumption that this was the "public use."

16. The data in this paragraph are drawn from Corey J. Wilk, *The Struggle Over the Public Use Clause: Survey of Holdings and Trends, 1986-2003*, 39 Real. Prop. Prob. & Tr. J. 251 (2004); Thomas W. Merrill, *The Economics of Public Use*, 72 Cornell L. Rev. 61 (1986).

17. *Daniels v. Area Plan Comm'n. of Allen County*, 306 F.3d 445 (7th Cir. 2002).

18. *Board of Regents v. Roth*, 408 U.S. 564, 571 (1972).

19. *See* Antonin Scalia, *A Matter of Interpretation* 140-41 (Amy Gutmann ed., 1997).

20. *See*, e.g., *Atlas Roofing Co. v. Occupational Safety & Health Review Comm'n*, 430 U.S. 442 (1977).

21. *See Lucas v. S.C. Coastal Council*, 505 U.S. 1003, 1014 (1992) (observing that Takings Clause was originally understood to reach only direct appropriations of property or practical ousters from possession).

22. Scholars have concluded that traditional urban renewal as practiced from the 1940s through the 1960s tended to have a disproportionate impact on minority communities. *See* Wendell E. Pritchett, *The "Public Menace" of Blight: Urban Renewal and the Private Uses of Eminent Domain*, 21 Yale L. & Pol'y Rev. 1 (2003).

23. The American Planning Association policy guide on redevelopment, ratified in April 2004, provides a summary of the principles that planning professionals follow in designing urban redevelopment projects. See http://www.planning.org/policyguides/redevelopment.htm.

24. 505 U.S. at 1024.

25. *See*, e.g., 17 U.S.C., Section 115 (compulsory license for making and distributing phono records).

26. This Court has held this type of statutory scheme satisfies the public use requirement, at least in the context of licensing the use of trade secret information for federal regulatory purposes. *Ruckelshaus v. Monsanto Co.*, 467 U.S. 986, 1014-16 (1984).

27. *See Tolksdorf v. Griffith*, 464 Mich. 1, 626 N.W.2d 163 (2001).

28. *See* Kristin Kanski, Case Note, 30 Wm. Mitchell L. Rev. 725, 729-30 & n.34 (2003) (collecting state statutes).

29. *See* Merrill, *supra* note 16, at 80.

30. For an overview of eminent domain procedures, *see* 7 *Nichols on Eminent Domain* (Patrick J. Rohan & Melvin A. Reskins, eds., 3d ed. 2004).

31. *See*, e.g., *United States v. 564.54 Acres*, 441 U.S. 506, 511-12 (1979); *United States v. Miller*, 317 U.S. 369, 374 (1943).

32. See, e.g., *United States v. 50 Acres of Land*, 469 U.S. 24, 35-36 (1984).

33. *Miller, supra,* 317 U.S. at 376.

34. As recognized in one amicus brief in support of petitioners, "A fair market price is not everyone's price. Some may come out ahead, in the sense that they would have been willing to sell for less. Some will find the price is fair. But others will be paid less than they were willing to sell for." Brief of Cascade Policy Institute, at 7-8. *See also* Serge F. Kovaleski and Debbi Wilgoren, *Landowners Feel Stadium Squeeze; Twenty Acres Earmarked for Baseball Isn't the District's – Yet*, Wash. Post, September 26, 2004 at C1 (describing the different reaction of different property owners to the prospect of eminent domain being used to acquire land for a new baseball stadium for the District of Columbia).

35. *See*, e.g., *564.54 Acres of Land*, 441 U.S. at 511-13; 516-17.

36. Some of the Mill Acts provided for awards equal to 150% of the damages found to have been sustained, *see Head v. Amoskeag Mfg. Co.*, 113 U.S. 9, 10 n.1 (1885); and the English practice at one time was to provide compensation equal to 110 percent of market value. *See* Merrill, *supra* note 16, at 92 n.97.

COMMENTARY AND REACTION

5.1. SUPREME COURT DECISION EMPHASIZES THE IMPORTANCE OF PLANNING

By Paul Farmer, AICP, Executive Director and CEO, APA

The Supreme Court faced a difficult decision in the *Kelo v. City of New London* case. In the 5-4 opinion issued today, the Court emphasized the importance of linking eminent domain to a community's comprehensive plan. This decision validates the essential role of planning in ensuring fairness in the eminent domain process.

> *The Court's decision need not strike fear into every property owner's mind; it will not open the floodgates for eminent domain use. The Court specifically mentions that a determining factor in their decision was the city's "comprehensive character of the plan" and the "thorough deliberation that preceded [the plan's] adoption."*

The Court's decision need not strike fear into every property owner's mind; it will not open the floodgates for eminent domain use. The Court specifically mentions that a determining factor in their decision was the city's "comprehensive character of the plan" and the "thorough deliberation that preceded [the plan's] adoption." The Justices determined that the plan and the thorough planning process ensured that the project truly met the Constitution's "public use" standard.

Using eminent domain for the benefit of the community as a whole is never easy. It is one of many valuable tools planners and elected officials use to create communities that enrich people's lives. Without eminent domain, adapting to the challenges presented by growth and change would be even more difficult, if not impossible.

Eminent domain is a tool that should be used with caution, and only as a last resort. The Court stressed that cities and planners have the power to exercise eminent domain if it is done thoughtfully and is consistent with the implementation of a community's comprehensive development plan.

The American Planning Association (APA) strongly believes that citizens should be justly compensated with fair market value when eminent domain is used. Furthermore, APA holds that it is important to preserve the ability of local governments to use redevelopment tools and techniques, including eminent domain when appropriate, to achieve well-defined public purposes to create communities of lasting value.

This decision, coupled with the 9-0 decisions handed down in the Lingle and San Remo cases issued earlier this term, shows that the Supreme Court is "staying the course" with long-standing principles of U.S. land-use law. The court has refused to introduce radical and potentially troubling new concepts into a system that fairly balances rights and responsibilities.

The opinion, albeit difficult, underscores the importance of the planning process. The planning process involves everyone: residents, businesses, civic leaders, elected officials and planners alike. It's not easy, but a democratic planning process with meaningful public participation is the appropriate way to proceed. This community engagement is necessary to keep our cities growing and prosperous.

5.2. TRANSCRIPT OF DEBATE ON E&E TV BETWEEN PAUL FARMER, APA EXECUTIVE DIRECTOR, AND SCOTT BULLOCK, SENIOR ATTORNEY, INSTITUTE FOR JUSTICE

[Reprinted from E&ETV with permission from Environment & Energy Publishing, LLC. http://www.eenews.net. 202-628-6500. Copyright 2005. All rights reserved.]

The Supreme Court's decision has been hotly debated since it was released in June. Media have raised the questions: Is the ruling an expansion of the government's eminent domain powers? Will the decision lead to more takings in other cities, or are property rights advocates overstating the potential fallout? How are state and federal lawmakers reacting to the decision?

APA Executive Director Paul Farmer and Scott Bullock, a senior attorney with the Institute for Justice who argued the case before the high court, went head to head over Kelo for the web-based discussion program, On Point, which airs daily on E&ETV.

BRIAN STEMPECK: We're here to talk about a major Supreme Court decision we saw last month. It was a 5 to 4 decision that basically upheld the actions of the city of New London, Conn., in taking some property for economic development. Scott, I wanted to ask you, I know you were unhappy with the decision. You are one of the attorneys at the Institute for Justice who argued the case and this is a quote I saw from you in the newspaper, it said, quote, "Every home or church could be replaced by a Costco, a shopping mall or private building that would produce more tax dollars." Is that really true? What's your feelings on how the Court ruled?

SCOTT BULLOCK: It is true, and Justice O'Connor made the same point in her dissent. She said under the Court's ruling a Motel 6 can be taken for a Ritz-Carlton, a home can be taken for a shopping mall, any farm can be taken for a factory. Those aren't hypotheticals, those unfortunately are actually happening. Just two weeks ago the village of Sunset Hills, Mo., approved the taking of 85 homes and small businesses to build a shopping mall. Lower-tax-producing businesses are taken for higher-tax-producing businesses. This is happening in America. The Supreme Court gave its stamp of approval to it. I think it was a terrible decision, but the good news is that this has really awakened people to what is happening with eminent domain abuse and you're seeing a number of efforts by state legislators and citizens fighting back against this decision.

BRIAN STEMPECK: But haven't we been seeing this for quite some time? I mean typically when you talk about eminent domain it's a city or a state taking property for a railroad, for a utility, for things like that, for power lines. In this case, it's for private development, but this has been going on for some years. Whenever they build a baseball stadium it seems like something like this happens. What's new about this case that stands out from what's been happening for the past 20 or 30 years?

SCOTT BULLOCK: Well, what is new about this is that the Supreme Court for the first time said that the government can take land and use eminent domain purely for private economic development. Its decisions before said that they could take land in so-called blighted neighborhoods, but here there was no finding of blight. There was no allegation this neighborhood was blighted. It just happened to be desired by the city and private developers. So for the Supreme Court to say that it doesn't matter the condition of your property, it doesn't matter where it is, for the government be able to use eminent domain to take it and give to other private parties is an expansion of eminent domain authority and it's something that has rightly alarmed home and small business owners throughout the country.

BRIAN STEMPECK: Paul, what's your reaction to the case? The American Planning Association was one of the groups that sided with the city of New London. Is what Scott's saying true? Could a shopping mall developer, can they now come in and take over a church?

PAUL FARMER: I don't think what he's saying is true at all. I think that it's a vast overstatement of what the Supreme Court said. I think you need to read the majority decision. We don't believe it changed anything. People's property was no more at risk the day after the decision than the day before the decision. This is something that's gone back 200 years in practice. It's gone back in legal precedent for over a hundred years. The Court had been ruling that property could be taken for economic development purposes

I think that it's a vast overstatement of what the Supreme Court said. I think you need to read the majority decision. We don't believe it changed anything. People's property was no more at risk the day after the decision than the day before the decision. This is something that's gone back 200 years in practice.

We believe that a very robust citizen participation process is the best safeguard to see that any governmental authority is used correctly and we believe that's the case with eminent domain.

long before they ruled that it could be taken in conditions of blight, which was 1954 in *Berman v. Parker*. The economic development cases go back way before that. We believe, and we said this in our friend of the court brief that this really is an issue that ought to be decided at the state level and the local level and we see that activity going on now. The Supreme Court simply said they weren't going to intervene so that federal courts became the places where these decisions were made. These decisions ought to be left close to home, close to the voters. We believe that a very robust citizen participation process is the best safeguard to see that any governmental authority is used correctly and we believe that's the case with eminent domain. We don't think that we need sweeping new laws. We didn't need a sweeping new law from the Supreme Court. We didn't get it. We do believe that many state laws can be improved. We did a lot of work for seven years looking at state enabling laws in a whole variety of ways and that information is free and available on the Web. We think there are some states that have very good state enabling laws regarding the use of eminent domain and that power. We think there are many that could be improved. So we stand ready to assist in a reasoned discussion of how to improve those.

BRIAN STEMPECK: Scott, the city's basic argument in this case was that this is an area that's pretty underprivileged economically. The unemployment in the area was twice the average of the rest of the city. Why shouldn't city planners have the right to go in there and say we have a new development that's going to add a thousand new jobs? What's wrong with that argument?

SCOTT BULLOCK: Well it's fundamentally un-American for the government to take property from one private owner and hand it over to another private owner just because the government happens to prefer that new owner and thinks that new owner would make more productive use of the land than the current owners would. There's nothing wrong with governments using whatever incentives they wish to encourage economic development and that's a policy choice that cities can make and choose to make. But when eminent domain is involved there are specific limitations upon that in the Constitution. The Constitution says very clearly private property shall not be taken for public use without just compensation. So there's a constitutional limit. Unfortunately, the Supreme Court did not apply at that constitutional limit. That's why it's now up to state courts, why it's up to state legislators to do this. You know the ironic thing about the situation in new London, and it's true in many of these projects, New London has ample land available in the Fort Trumbull area to do development projects. They have twice the land area available now to do development projects than New York has to rebuild the World Trade Center. The people who live there have about an acre and a half total of land. They can do development, but they can still respect the rights of these people and that's true in just about every situation I've seen.

BRIAN STEMPECK: Paul, what's your reaction to what Scott is saying? I know that the majority of the decision, what they're saying is basically we think that economic redevelopment is in fact public use.

PAUL FARMER: Right.

BRIAN STEMPECK: Explain what the Court meant by that.

PAUL FARMER: Well the Court has made very clear that they were relying on a hundred years of precedent, where that was the way that the clause of the Constitution had been interpreted. The majority decision made it very clear they were not interpreting the Constitution any differently than it had been for a hundred years. This was essentially a state's rights case that said we're not going to change. We're going to stay with the precedent we relied on and this is a matter that ought to be left to local government and a local government under their laws. We think that eminent domain should be used very, very sparingly. We are not in favor of any kind of widespread use. We think it should be monitored very carefully. We think that it should be used only in very, very open processes. California has a very good way of doing it, where they require development plans to be approved in very open processes before authorization would occur. We think that's a good way to do it. We think that there ought to be just compensation that goes beyond market value, because we think that you do need to compensate people for the years that they have held land, held property and invested in it and our brief said that. We think that there ought to be that type of additional compensation.

BRIAN STEMPECK: Yeah, well—

PAUL FARMER: But I'm sure there are lots of areas we probably would find that we agree on this.

BRIAN STEMPECK: Now while Scott is saying this is basically an expansion of eminent domain, some people looking at this case have said, well maybe, hold on a second, the Supreme Court basically said—New London city planners had a lot of documents they used to back up their decision to take this land.

PAUL FARMER: Right.

BRIAN STEMPECK: A lot of economic studies saying we need this for this type of development. Does this actually raise the bar for eminent domain, saying that if you're going to do this you need to justify it with these types of studies?

PAUL FARMER: Oh I think you can read this as raising the bar. I think one commentator called this a yellow blinking light. I think it says that you need to be very careful and that you need to show that you have the proper studies. You have had the public processes that have allowed imports of all parties into this. These are very critical decisions and these are very critical decisions whether it's being done for economic development or a highway for example. And many, many more homes have been taken for highways as an example, than for economic development of this type we're talking about.

BRIAN STEMPECK: Scott, what's your reaction? I mean do you agree with that? That this could actually limit the use of eminent domain in some places?

SCOTT BULLOCK: Well I think there are very few limits that have been imposed by the Supreme Court upon this. I think the emphasis in the majority opinion on there being a plan in New London was really disconnected from reality. Virtually every situation of eminent domain for private development is done according to a plan. The government puts together a plan. The developer puts together a plan. That's really no check on the fundamental question of whether you're going to use eminent domain for private economic development. That should not be a hard question. An overwhelming majority of people in this country are opposed to this, as just about any poll that has come out in the wake of this decision demonstrates. People are opposed to this. This is an issue that cuts across party lines, cuts across ideological lines. People just simply think it's wrong to take somebody's home and give it to Costco or take a smaller business and give it to a larger business. And I think you're finally now going to see some real momentum in state legislatures to change the law in the legal institution.

BRIAN STEMPECK: Wait a second. I want to follow up on this. Let's use an example that's close to home here. In Washington we're going to be building a new baseball stadium —

We think that eminent domain should be used very, very sparingly. We are not in favor of any kind of widespread use. We think it should be monitored very carefully. We think that it should be used only in very, very open processes. California has a very good way of doing it, . . .

SCOTT BULLOCK: Yup.

BRIAN STEMPECK: — in the southeast part of the city and probably going to see a scenario similar to this, where the city basically has to get some land from some homeowners who don't want to leave or some property owners who don't want to leave that area in order to build the stadium. How do you get that job done? How do you build that stadium without invoking eminent domain?

SCOTT BULLOCK: Well stadiums are kind of a separate category. Stadiums are typically public bodies. They're public entities, or at least they're largely controlled by public bodies, at least many stadiums are, probably most of them are. So if it's publicly owned or the public has equal right of access to it, that's a public use. There are certain situations—a stadium up in Massachusetts, the courts struck down because it was essentially done for one private party and the private party had total say over how the stadium was going to be used. So that's a separate category. I'll tell you another instance of eminent domain abuse that's happening in our nation's capital is the city of Washington wants to take a shopping mall in southeast Washington that's fully leased, servicing its customers, because they want more high-end retail in that section of the city. So that's a classic example of taking from one private owner and handing it over to another private owner and that's what's been opened up in the wake of the Court's decision.

PAUL FARMER: Let's follow the distinction that Scott's trying to make. As I understand it, you wouldn't be able to take property to provide, let's say, grocery shopping for poor people in inner city neighborhoods, but it's OK to take property so you can build a baseball stadium so people can sit in skyboxes. And as I understand it, the Texas Rangers had eminent domain used on their behalf when they built their ballpark and I think we know who was a managing partner of the team at the time. And the Texas bill that has gone through the Legislature, that it's not yet approved because the two houses couldn't reach agreement, exempted sports arenas from the prohibition against the use for economic development. I think that one of the things that shows is the very difficult distinctions that have to be made and those distinctions have to be made, that's what legislatures have to do. They're very difficult to do. Again, our approach is let's have a very reasoned thoughtful way of looking at that through the state legislatures. There's some very good existing models out there to look at. Don't rush just to sort of make political points so that you can either get a bill passed or are even if you don't, be able to use that in your campaign for reelection the next time you're running.

BRIAN STEMPECK: You're of course talking about some of the state legislatures, but we are seeing a big reaction right now on the federal level. A lot of members of Congress have come out saying they don't like this bill. There's been a half a dozen bills introduced to deal with the decision in different ways. Scott, if you could talk a little bit about some of the legislation that's out there and what it would do. How can a U.S. member of Congress tried reverse this decision?

SCOTT BULLOCK: Well, Congress can't reverse the decision.

BRIAN STEMPECK: Right.

SCOTT BULLOCK: It's an interpretation by the Supreme Court of the U.S. Constitution and the Supreme Court has final say on that, but Congress can do something that can be very effective and that is to limit or eliminate federal spending for projects that use eminent domain for private development purposes. There's a number of pieces of legislation that's pending. They've got something that will demonstrate that Congress is against the use of eminent domain for private development and I think you're going to

I think that one of the things that shows is the very difficult distinctions that have to be made and those distinctions have to be made, that's what legislatures have to do. They're very difficult to do. Again, our approach is let's have a very reasoned thoughtful way of looking at that through the state legislatures.

see some real momentum, hopefully when Congress reconvenes, to get some of this legislation passed. We know of at least 26 states that are looking at this and in a vast majority of these cases this is an easy call. You know, a roadway, a public facility, a courthouse, that's a public use. Costco is not a public use, Novis Development Corporation's $165 million shopping mall in Sunset Hills isn't a public use. These are very easy calls in a vast majority of cases to make and the lines can be fairly easily drawn.

BRIAN STEMPECK: Paul, what's your reaction to that?

PAUL FARMER: The Supreme Court has spent 200 years trying to make these distinctions and I think it's interesting that for Scott it's an easy distinction to make, because the Supreme Court has not been able to find so easily that they can make that distinction. And even this case, when you look at the various opinions, the concurring and dissenting opinions, you see this back and forth as they try to craft what the distinction should be. We go back to the fact, again, that you need to work very carefully as you look at these laws. This is not something to rush in on with a lot of sentiment and the like. These are decisions that will change 200 years of practice. These are decisions that could change a hundred years of the legal precedents. It just needs to be done very, very carefully and I would like to say that something the Supreme Court made very clear is that it is absolutely the law the land that if Costco spotted a piece of land and said I want that piece of land. Now would you use eminent domain to take those houses for me? This Supreme Court decision says absolutely not. That can't be done. That it's only after you go through a public process and determine what your needs are that you then can assemble the land.

SCOTT BULLOCK: I don't think that's what the Supreme Court says in this case. I don't think there's any limit on that whatsoever. Costco, and we've seen this time and time again, developers can come up with ideas, citizens can petition governments for what they want to do and if the government goes through a process and they say this is what we want done — New London's a perfect example of that. Pfizer Corporation went to New London and said we'd like to have these things in the redevelopment area. We'd just like to have them. This is what we would like. The city said all right, we'll go through the process. They added everything that Pfizer wanted, they had the public hearings, they went through with the process and at the end of the day everything that Pfizer wanted in this neighborhood was made a part of the plan. So I think that the Court puts no limits on that whatsoever and that's why it is so vital for legislatures to step in and say that eminent domain simply should not be used for private development purposes.

BRIAN STEMPECK: Paul, your response?

PAUL FARMER: Well, you're re-arguing the point you lost on before the Supreme Court. You made those same arguments. The Supreme Court rejected that —

SCOTT BULLOCK: And the Court got it wrong.

PAUL FARMER: — argument and so I think that —

SCOTT BULLOCK: The Court got it wrong.

PAUL FARMER: Well I think the Court got it right after 200 years of getting it right and I think that you're trying to go and take the law to a place it has not been in 200 years. It's a radical change in the law you're seeking and we believe that the property system in this country works very well. It's worked very well for many, many people over many years and you shouldn't make radical changes in the property system of this country without sufficient thought.

BRIAN STEMPECK: We're running out of time, so I'm going to have to stop you guys there. I've got one last question for you both, maybe we can

We go back to the fact, again, that you need to work very carefully as you look at these laws. This is not something to rush in on with a lot of sentiment and the like. These are decisions that will change 200 years of practice.

It's a radical change in the law you're seeking and we believe that the property system in this country works very well. It's worked very well for many, many people over many years and you shouldn't make radical changes in the property system of this country without sufficient thought.

agree on this one. They're talking about taking Judge Souter's house in New Hampshire and turning it into a hotel, perhaps calling it the Lost Liberty Hotel with a restaurant called the Just Desserts Cafe. Some pretty bad puns there. What's going to happen to Judge Souter's place, take it or leave it? Paul?

PAUL FARMER: I don't think that it's anything more than political grandstanding and it's freedom of speech and it's nice theater.

BRIAN STEMPECK: Scott, are you going to be staying at this hotel?

SCOTT BULLOCK: We do want to focus on trying to save people's homes and small businesses, that's a distraction. We want to focus on the legislation. There's nothing radical about the Fifth Amendment to the U.S. Constitution.

BRIAN STEMPECK: All right, well it sounds like I think Judge Souter might need a good lawyer. I'd like to thank you both for being here. I'm Brian Stempeck. This is On Point. Thanks for watching.

COMMENTARY: *KELO V. CITY OF NEW LONDON*

By Lora A. Lucero, AICP
[Reprinted from the July 2005 issue of Planning and Environmental Law.*]*

The 2004-2005 term added some excitement to the lives of land use attorneys and planners. In addition to jettisoning the "substantially advances" test from takings jurisprudence (see Dwight Merriam's July 2005 Commentary below discussing *Lingle v. Chevron* No. 04-163), the Justices clarified that a property owner doesn't get two bites of the apple, in both state and federal courts, when bringing his takings claim (*San Remo Hotel v. City of San Francisco* No. 04-340); and Section 1983 damages and attorneys fees are not available to someone challenging a zoning decision pursuant to the Telecommunications Act (*City of Rancho Palos Verdes* No. 03-1601). Each were 9-0 decisions.

The unanimity was gone on June 23, 2005, when the Court announced the *Kelo* decision. In a 5-4 opinion, Justice Stevens declared that economic development is a valid public use for the purpose of condemnation. (*Kelo v. City of New London* No. 04-108) The fallout in the days and weeks that followed was astonishing, particularly given the fact that the decision was not a radical departure from more than 50 years of precedent.

Justice O'Connor's dissent has received more air time and ink than Justice Stevens's opinion for the majority. The headlines have included "Justices Affirm Property Seizures,"[1] "Supreme Court Rules Cities May Seize Homes,"[2] "High court Oks personal property seizures,"[3] "Seizing land for private use OK'd; Court backs city vs. homeowners,"[4] and "High Court Backs Seizure of Land for Development."[5]

Did the Supreme Court emasculate the Fifth Amendment? Based on much of the coverage in the popular media, one might get that impression, and citizens are wondering if any protections for private property remain. Apparently, even Justice Souter's New Hampshire farmhouse may be targeted for condemnation if the letter sent by a California resident to the town officials in Weare, New Hampshire, is something more than just a publicity stunt. Dubbing the project the "Lost Liberty Hotel," the letter was posted on conservative radio show host Rush Limbaugh's website.[6]

U.S. Senator John Cornyn (R-Tex.) introduced legislation four days after the *Kelo* decision was announced, entitled The Protection of Homes, Small Businesses, and Private Property Act of 2005. The act would not allow eminent domain to be used to solely further private economic development. It would apply to all exercises of eminent domain power by the federal government, and all exercises of eminent domain power by state and local government through the use of federal funds.

To balance the rhetoric, some facts are in order.[7] Connecticut law authorizes condemnation for economic development purposes. Since the closure of the Naval Undersea Warfare Center in 1996, the city of New London has lost more than 1,500 jobs. By 1998, the city's unemployment rate was nearly double that of the state. The state designated the community a "distressed municipality" and committed more than $15 million to reversing the loss.

A private nonprofit development agency was enlisted to assist the city in planning for the revitalization of the Fort Trumbull area. In February 1998, a pharmaceutical company announced it would build a $300 million research facility adjacent to Fort Trumbull. Hoping the facility would be a catalyst for further revitalization, neighborhood meetings were held and economic development plans were prepared. The state reviewed and approved the plans which called for a waterfront conference hotel, restaurants and shopping, and marinas with a pedestrian riverwalk. On one parcel, 90,000 square feet of research and development office space was planned to complement the pharmaceutical research facility. Negotiations with the majority of property owners were successful, but nine owners refused to sell and condemnation proceedings were initiated.

John Baker, an attorney with the firm of Greene Espel PLLP in Minneapolis, provided a more dispassionate response to *Kelo* critics on an ABA land use listserv following the decision. Baker writes:

Kelo presented a collision between conservative jurisprudence and conservative political outcomes. If conservative jurisprudence is to be intellectually honest, it must prevail in a collision of that kind. On this issue, the pillars of conservative jurisprudence—textualism, originalism, and federalism—all failed to support the property owners' position.

Textualism failed because the reference to "public use" in the Fifth Amendment is not phrased as a requirement.

Originalism failed because there is no meaningful historical evidence that the framers intended the takings clause to restrict when government may pay just compensation to acquire property by eminent domain. As *National Review* contributing editor Jonathon Adler wrote, "While the Fifth Amendment clearly requires compensation for takings of any sort, there is little evidence the Founders sought to limit the purposes for which eminent domain could be used." The treatment of the "public use" phrase in the Fifth Amendment as a separate requirement really began in earnest with New York's highest court in 1837. In the era of Lochner, the notion flourished, and appropriately faded in the mid-20th Century, along with the other relics of economic judicial activism. And contrary to the rhetoric of those seeking to incite backlash, *Kelo* did nothing to expand the powers of government; it simply confirmed the continued vitality of rules that have been firmly in place for more than 50 years.

Finally, federalism failed to support the property owners' position, because federal judges are in no better position than elected officials to decide whether a particular purpose is sufficiently beneficial to the public to be considered a "public" use.

The *Kelo* cert petition was an effort to accomplish revolutionary legal change, and it darned near succeeded. I think the activists with Institute for Justice knew exactly what they were doing when they took a case involving sound planning all the way to the Supreme Court. Had the Supreme Court found "public use" lacking in that situation, cities could not have easily distinguished the decision as one involving "an extreme set of facts not present here.[8]

The American Planning Association filed an amicus curiae brief supporting the City of New London, authored by Tom Merrill at Columbia University and John Echeverria at Georgetown Environmental Law & Policy

To balance the rhetoric, some facts are in order. Connecticut law authorizes condemnation for economic development purposes. Since the closure of the Naval Undersea Warfare Center in 1996, the city of New London has lost more than 1,500 jobs. By 1998, the city's unemployment rate was nearly double that of the state.

Institute. The National Congress for Community Economic Development[9] joined us. We urged the Court to stay the course, retain the broad interpretation of "public use" that includes economic development and the Court's deferential standard of review in such cases. APA also echoed what many amici[10] pointed out to the Court—that condemnation abuses occur and perhaps the measure of just compensation needs to be reconsidered.

Eminent domain is concededly an unsettling power, and is subject to misuse or overuse if not properly constrained. But eminent domain is disruptive for all who experience it, not just those who might be able to persuade a reviewing court that a particular condemnation is not "public" enough. The dangers of eminent domain should be addressed by assuring that it remains a second-best alternative to market exchange as a means of acquiring resources, by encouraging careful planning and public participation in decisions to invoke eminent domain, and by building on current legislative requirements that mandate additional compensation beyond the constitutional minimum for persons who experience uncompensated subjective losses and consequential damages.[11]

The dangers of eminent domain should be addressed by assuring that it remains a second-best alternative to market exchange as a means of acquiring resources, by encouraging careful planning and public participation in decisions to invoke eminent domain, and by building on current legislative requirements that mandate additional compensation beyond the constitutional minimum for persons who experience uncompensated subjective losses and consequential damages.

APA's amicus brief stood apart from the others in advocating the importance of integrating eminent domain into land use planning.

Another source of protection for all property owners is to assure, to the extent possible, that eminent domain is exercised only in conjunction with a process of land use planning that includes broad public participation and a careful consideration of alternatives to eminent domain. Integrating the decision to use eminent domain into a sound planning process has a number of desirable consequences. Such a process can help minimize the use of eminent domain, by identifying alternatives to proposed development projects, such as relocating or re-sizing projects, or perhaps forgoing them altogether. It can also reduce public concerns about the use of eminent domain, by providing a forum in which the reasons for opposition can be considered, offering explanations for the proposed course of action and possible alternatives, and perhaps instilling a greater degree of understanding on the part of both the proponents and opponents of the proposed project.[12]

Justice Stevens and the majority focused on the important role of planning in the redevelopment process. The City of New London's program of economic rejuvenation was entitled to the Court's deference, Justice Stevens wrote, because the "City has carefully formulated an economic development plan that it believes will provide appreciable benefits to the community, including . . . new jobs and increased tax revenue. . . . Given the comprehensive character of the plan, the thorough deliberation that preceded its adoption, and the limited scope of our review, it is appropriate for us, as it was in *Berman*, to resolve the challenges of the individual owners, not on a piecemeal basis, but rather in light of the entire plan."[13] Someone counted more than 30 references to "plan," "planning," and "planner" in the majority's opinion.

Justice Kennedy provided the critical fifth vote. He wrote in concurrence:

> The determination that a rational-basis standard of review is appropriate does not, however, alter the fact that transfers intended to confer benefits on particular, favored private entities, and with only incidental or pretextual public benefits, are forbidden by the Public Use Clause." Further in his opinion, he continued "This taking occurred in the context of a comprehensive development plan meant to address a serious city-wide depression, and the projected economic benefits of the project cannot be characterized as *de minimus*. The identity of most of the private beneficiaries were unknown at the time the city formulated its plans. The city complied with elaborate procedural requirements that facilitate review of the record and inquiry into the city's purposes. In sum, while there may be categories of

cases in which the transfers are so suspicious, or the procedures employed so prone to abuse, or the purported benefits are so trivial or implausible, that courts should presume an impermissible private purpose, no such circumstances are present in this case.[14]

Contrary to the opinion of many of Kelo's supporters, the decision might be viewed as a "win" for all sides because the debate is not over. It now moves into the halls of Congress and the state legislatures. Our democratically elected officials will have a voice in shaping the next generation of eminent domain codes.

Contrary to the opinion of many of Kelo's supporters, the decision might be viewed as a "win" for all sides because the debate is not over. It now moves into the halls of Congress and the state legislatures. Our democratically elected officials will have a voice in shaping the next generation of eminent domain codes.

NOTES FOR COMMENTARY

1. *Washington Post*, June 24, 2005.

2. *Chicago Tribune*, June 24, 2005.

3. CNN.com, June 23, 2005.

4. *USA Today*, June 24, 2005.

5. *The Boston Globe*, June 24, 2005.

6. www.rushlimbaugh.com/home/today.guest.html

7. The facts are taken from Justice Stevens's majority opinion.

8. Landuse@mail.abanet.org

9. www.ncced.org. Founded in 1970, The National Congress for Community Economic Development is the trade association for community development corporations (CDCs) and the community economic development (CED) industry.

10. There were 25 amicus curiae briefs filed in support of Petitioner Kelo and 12 amicus curiae briefs filed in support of Respondent City of New London.

11. Amicus Curiae Brief of the American Planning Association, *Kelo v. City of New London*, p. 3

12. *Id.* at pp. 25-26

13. Opinion of Justice Stevens for the majority. *Kelo v. City of New London*, June 23, 2005, 545 U.S. __ (2005).

14. Concurring opinion of Justice Kennedy. *Kelo v. City of New London*, June 23, 2005, 545 U.S. __ (2005).

CONFIRMING A CENTURY OF CASE LAW

By John R. Nolon and Jessica A. Bacher

[Reprinted with permission from the June 29, 2005, edition of the New York Law Journal *© 2005 ALM Properties, Inc. All rights reserved. Further duplication without permission is prohibited.]*

John Nolon is a Professor at Pace University School of Law, Counsel to its Land Use Law Center, and Visiting Professor at Yale's School of Forestry and Environmental Studies. Jessica Bacher is an Adjunct Professor at Pace University School of Law and a Staff Attorney for the Land Use Law Center.

In *Kelo v. City of New London*, the U.S. Supreme Court affirmed the long-standing principle that governments can condemn private land in order to carry out area-wide redevelopment projects. No. 04-108, 2005 U.S. LEXIS 5011 (June 23, 2005). The decision, which affirms the legal status quo, has been spun as a grievous invasion of property rights that now threatens every American home. *Kelo* would warrant the public attention it is getting if it had gone the other way, if one more justice had sided with the dissent. The *Kelo* facts involve the taking of private land in a designated redevelopment area in a state designated distressed city. It is the prior law and the Court's holding in this limited context that is the subject of this column.

In most states, including New York, had the Court gone the other way, the decision would have muddied clear and long-settled state court precedents; used federal courts to dictate state-defined property rights and public interests; cast a shadow over a procedure that has led to the revival of distressed downtowns, urban neighborhoods, and waterfronts throughout the country; limited one of the few fiscal remedies available to economically distressed cities; and strapped their ability to redevelop dangerous brownfields located in poor neighborhoods—a matter of environmental justice.

The Legal Question

In *Kelo,* the question was whether the taking by condemnation of title to unblighted single-family homes for the purpose of transferring ownership to a private developer to accomplish a large-scale waterfront redevelopment project constituted a public use under the Fifth Amendment. The terms of the Amendment allow such takings, but only if they accomplish a public use and require the payment of just compensation to the condemnees. At issue is the critical matter of whether distressed cities, like New London, when specifically authorized by state legislation, can carry out programs to increase jobs, strengthen their tax bases, revitalize neighborhoods, and stabilize property values by condemning the land of private property owners who are not willing to sell to the government at a negotiated price.

Public sympathies for Ms. Kelo and her fellow petitioners run high. Their homes are not blighted, two or three of them have lived in the neighborhood for decades, and their futures are clouded by having to use the compensation they will receive to relocate and build new lives among new neighbors. On the other side is the stark reality of life in New London and other cities throughout the country that are struggling to revitalize themselves so that they can provide public services and a decent quality of life for the disproportionately high percentage of homeless, jobless, and income-strapped citizens they shelter.

New York Law

In an amici curiae brief filed in *Kelo,* the Empire State Development Corporation noted its success in transforming neighborhoods surrounding the New York Stock Exchange, Seven World Trade Center, and in the 42nd Street Redevelopment Area, using authority to condemn private properties and convey them to private development companies under the strict procedures established in statutes adopted by the New York State legislature. Its brief notes that "despite private benefits, the predominant economic and social benefits have accrued to the public."

In *Rosenthal & Rosenthal Inc. v. The New York State Urban Development Corporation,* 771 F.2d 44 (2d Cir. 1985), the Second Circuit affirmed a District Court decision upholding the taking of the petitioners' unblighted buildings which were needed for the 42nd Street Redevelopment Project. The District Court found that the proposed taking was rationally related to a conceivable public purpose. The Second Circuit noted that "the power of eminent domain is a fundamental and necessary attribute of sovereignty, superior to all private property rights." It rested its decision on the U.S. Supreme Court's decision the previous year in *Hawaii Housing Authority v. Midkiff,* 467 U.S. 229 (1984), concluding that "courts long have recognized that the compensated taking of private property for urban renewal or community redevelopment is not proscribed by the Constitution." The Supreme Court denied certiorari in *Rosenthal* in 1986. 475 U.S. 1018 (1986).

We heard from the Court of Appeals on the subject in 1986 in a unanimous opinion written by Judge Kaye in a case that also challenged the Urban Development Corporation's (UDC) condemnations in the 42nd Street Redevelopment Project area. *Jackson v. New York State Urban Development Corporation,* 494 N.E.2d 429 (N.Y. 1986). The court noted that, as required by the state Eminent Domain Procedure Law (EDPL), the UDC had made a reasoned determination that the condemnation would serve a valid public purpose and that the scope of the court's review under the statute is narrow. The EDPL is representative of statutes in a number of states that guide and limit the power of government to exercise the power of eminent domain. Under this statute the condemning authority must provide public notice, hold a public hearing, specify the public use, benefit, and purpose of the project. The court cited the U.S. Supreme Court's opinion in *Hawaii Housing Authority* for the proposition that the due process requirements of the Constitution are satisfied where there is a rational relationship to a conceivable public purpose.

Various industrial companies, including several oil refineries, challenged the City of Syracuse Industrial Development Agency for condemning their properties to further a waterfront redevelopment master plan for an 800 acre area on the south shore of Onondaga Lake known as "oil city." *Sun Company, Inc. v. City of Syracuse IDA*, 625 N.Y.S.2d 371 (N.Y. App. Div. 1995). The area was located next to several low-income neighborhoods in Syracuse where a disproportionately large percentage of welfare recipients, jobless, and poverty level households resided. This is a classic environmental justice context. The court followed the tests outlined in *Jackson* and found that the purpose of the taking was to accomplish a proper use and that this determination was not without a proper foundation. The petitioners' motion for leave to appeal was denied by the Court of Appeals in 1997. 679 N.E.2d 643 (N.Y. 1997).

The *Kelo* Decision

The majority in the *Kelo* case, a 5-4 decision written by Justice Stevens, held that the purpose for the taking was a legitimate public use, clearing the way for the New London Development Corporation to condemn title from nine individual owners who held onto 15 parcels of the 115 private lots in the redevelopment area. Justice Stevens noted: " For more than a century, our public use jurisprudence has wisely eschewed rigid formulas and intrusive scrutiny in favor of affording legislatures broad latitude in determining what public needs justify the use of the takings power."

The dissenting opinion, drafted by Justice O'Connor, agreed with the petitioners who argued that the Court should establish a new "heightened scrutiny" test for takings designed to accomplish economic development purposes. Such takings could be classified as invalid per se, presumptively invalid, or invalid if the condemning authority could not prove with reasonable certainty that significant public benefits will be accomplished. Interestingly, O'Connor's impassioned dissent argues against the approach she adopted a few weeks earlier in the landmark decision *Lingle v. Chevron U.S.A. Inc.*, No. 04-163, 2005 U.S. LEXIS 4342 (May 23, 2005). That decision, which she authored, changed the rules for determining whether governmental regulations constitute a taking of property without compensation under the Fifth Amendment. *Lingle* repealed a 25 year-old standard that invalidated a government regulation as a taking if it fails to substantially advance a legitimate public purpose. In *Lingle*, Justice O'Connor eliminated the test because it requires "courts to scrutinize the efficacy of a vast array of state and federal regulations–a task for which courts are not well suited. Moreover, it would empower–and often require–the courts to substitute their predictive judgments for those of elected legislatures and expert agencies." This aligns squarely with the rationale of *Midkiff* in which the Court noted that "empirical debates over the wisdom of takings–no less than debates over the wisdom of other kinds of socioeconomic legislation– are not to be carried out in the federal courts."

Under existing case law, the Court defers to public use determinations of condemning authorities, regardless of the context. If New London had decided that Ms. Kelo's parcel were needed for a public road or to be conveyed to a utility company for telephone, transportation, or gas line conveyance, both the majority and dissenting justices would defer to the determination that the purpose for which the land was taken was a public one, within the meaning of the Fifth Amendment. The dissenters, however, believe that when the purpose is to further the economic objectives of the community, a stricter test should be used.

The cases cited by the majority involved the validation of takings of private property in order to advance economic development, such as accomplishing the revival of a blighted urban neighborhood in *Berman v. Parker*, 348 U.S. 26 (1954), and eliminating the social and economic evils of a land oligopoly by requiring land transfers from lessors to lessees in *Hawaii Housing Authority*.

In these cases, compensation was paid and the court deferred to the government's public use determination. The majority noted that in *Berman*, taking a nonblighted department store to effect area wide redevelopment of a blighted area was within the scope of the police power. The *Berman* Court noted that "the concept of the public welfare is broad and inclusive. . . . The values it represents are spiritual as well as physical, aesthetic as well as monetary. It is within the power of the legislature to determine that the community should be beautiful as well as healthy, spacious as well as clean, well-balanced as well as carefully patrolled."

The minority, apparently content with deference in these prior economic development cases, distinguished them from *Kelo* in that the condemned property in *Berman* and *Midkiff* "inflicted affirmative harm on society" and the taking, therefore, was necessary to "eliminate the existing property use to remedy the harm." Dismissing the broad description of the police power in *Berman* as "errant language," the dissent approached *Kelo* as if it were a case of first impression. It would limit deference to cases where the condemned property had "veered to such an extreme that the public was suffering as a consequence," thinking, apparently, that the unblighted parcels of Kelo and her fellow petitioners were not harmful to the area redevelopment plan in the same way that the petitioner's unblighted department store in the District of Columbia was harmful to the area redevelopment plan in *Berman*. In both cases, however, the acquisition of all parcels in the redevelopment area was essential to the projects' success.

The city council in New London, a legislative body, determined—in effect—that the petitioners' properties, in fact, were "harmful" to the interest of its citizens. Recall that it was operating under authority of a state statute aimed at promoting economic redevelopment in distressed cities and that New London was designated a distressed city by the state. The city council and the state legislature understood the context of the system of public finance where the real property tax is the balancing factor in the creation of the municipal budget. The median household income of New London's residents is 40 percent less than the state median; its poverty rate is twice that of the state's; and its unemployment rate 30 percent higher than the rest of the state.

When the city's redevelopment plan for its waterfront was initiated—with its promise of hundreds of new jobs and greatly enhanced property taxes—the city's population had been shrinking and it had just lost a major employer. Under our system of government, its options were limited; the constraints on its ability to increase municipal revenue seriously affected its ability, like that of most distressed cities, to meet the pressing needs of its poor and moderate income neighborhoods and households. The City needed

The dissenters, however, believe that when the purpose is to further the economic objectives of the community, a stricter test should be used.

all the parcels in the area to carry out an areawide plan. Not securing them, therefore, would be harmful to the city and its residents.

The Parade of Horribles

The petitioners were represented by an advocacy litigation group that raised public awareness of the fact that some public takings are abusive. The specter of corrupt, or misguided, local officials condemning title to property of private property owners primarily to benefit private developers was on the mind of the minority. In response, the majority made it clear that "[s]uch a one-to-one transfer of property, executed outside the confines of an integrated development plan, is not presented in this case." Kennedy, in a concurring opinion, reminded the minority that under the rational basis test, giving due deference to the public use determination, the Court can invalidate a condemnation by finding, in a particular case, that the public benefits achieved by such a suspicious transfer are only incidental to the benefits that will be conferred on the private parties.

The dissent disparages Kennedy's confidence in the rational-basis test as sufficient to ferret out privately motivated takings, by applying the "stupid staffer" test: suggesting that only the most inept administrations could fail to paper over a private deal and make it appear public in nature. The dissent is apparently unaware of numerous cases called to the Court's attention in *amici* briefs submitted in *Kelo*. In *99 Cents Only Store v. Lancaster Redevelopment Agency*, for example, a federal district court in California invalidated the condemnation of a store to accommodate the interest of an adjacent Costco's expansion plans; it found that the redevelopment agency's only purpose "was to satisfy the private expansion demands of Costco." 237 F. Supp. 2d 1123 (C.D. Cal 2001). In *Bailey v. Meyers*, 76 P.3d 898 (Ariz. 2003), the state court held that the taking of a brake shop for a hardware store to advance economic development lacked the requisite public purpose. Donald Trump's attempt to get the Casino Reinvestment Development Authority in New Jersey to condemn the parcels of a few landowners who had refused to sell to expand his hotel and casino was thwarted by the state court; it found that the Authority had given Trump a blank check regarding future development on the site. *Casino Reinvestment Development Authority v. Banin*, 727 A.2d 102 (N.J. Sup. Ct.1998).

Under state law, in fact, courts have invalidated condemnations in Arizona, California, Georgia, Illinois, Indiana, Michigan, Missouri, New Jersey, and Virginia. In all these cases, there was no sustaining public presence of the type involved in all redevelopment projects. In cases involving no more than a one-to-one transfer of title between businesses, as a *de facto* matter, the court's suspicion is aroused and, under the rational-basis test, it senses a lack of public involvement and purpose. This enables state courts to invalidate such condemnations, saving the homes of average Americans and the businesses of moms and pops, dulling the edge of the hard-cutting rhetoric of those alarmed by the majority's decision in *Kelo*.

Kennedy's caveat regarding how the rational basis test can be used to invalidate one-to-one transfers is a strong cautionary message to condemning authorities. Reading the 5-4 decision as a reminder to act reasonably, legislatures should, as most do, justify the use of condemnation as a necessary means of achieving clearly stated public goals in redevelopment projects. Where there is little public presence in the development and imprecise means of securing the intended public benefits, there is less evident rationality and more vulnerability to invalidation.

There is a further response to the alarmists. Redevelopment projects don't gestate in back rooms with greedy politicians waiting as midwives to the birth of private wealth. They are subject to onerous, transparent, and lengthy

The specter of corrupt, or misguided, local officials condemning title to property of private property owners primarily to benefit private developers was on the mind of the minority.

There is a further response to the alarmists. Redevelopment projects don't gestate in back rooms with greedy politicians waiting as midwives to the birth of private wealth. They are subject to onerous, transparent, and lengthy processes that provide all the details of the project and invite public participation and extensive debate.

processes that provide all the details of the project and invite public participation and extensive debate. In New London, the public was asked what it thought about the redevelopment project as the project was debated, shaped, and decided over 20 months—nearly two years. In New York, under the State Environmental Quality Review Act, redevelopment projects generate foot-high environmental impact statements that include a hard look at their impact on community character and neighborhood change and contain lengthy chapters on all the economic and environmental consequences of the project.

Public hearings, ULURP proceedings in New York City, reviews of impact statements, open meeting laws, conflict of interest rules, and a host of other legal protections ensure that the public knows who is involved, how they were chosen, what the proposed benefits are, and who will suffer. When such projects are approved, this public process has mediated the claims of those affected such as Ms. Kelo and her neighbors and the evidence that the greater public will be benefited by jobs, public revenues, and property improvement. ■

HOW TO REFORM EMINENT DOMAIN

By Thomas W. Merrill

Thomas Merrill is Charles Keller Beekman Professor at Columbia Law School. He filed a brief amicus curiae on behalf of the American Planning Association in *Kelo v. City of New London.*

The Supreme Court's ruling in *Kelo v. New London*, declining to ban the use of eminent domain for local economic development projects, has triggered a firestorm of criticism. The cause has now been taken up in Congress, where the House has passed a resolution condemning the decision, and legislation has been introduced to overturn it. Much of the criticism of the decision is poorly informed about the history and practice of eminent domain. But the spotlight on the power to take property, and the push to do something to reassure property owners that this power will be held in check, are welcome developments.

The question Congress and other legislative bodies must now consider is what form the legislative response should take. The initial impulse, reflected in the proposed legislation, is to ban the use of eminent domain for projects the sponsors think are unworthy. But the history of controversy over when the " public use" requirement has been satisfied suggests that coming up a workable definition of what is permitted and what is forbidden to local governments is no easy task. If thousands of federal and state judges, struggling with this question for nearly 200 years, have been unable to come up with a satisfactory formula, it is unlikely that modern legislators will succeed in their rush to enact a response to *Kelo.*

For example, the statutes proposed by House Judiciary Chair James Sensenbrenner (R-Wis.) and Senator John Cornyn (R-Tex.) would prohibit any state or local government receiving federal funds from using eminent domain for " economic development purposes." But what exactly does that mean? Virtually all exercises of eminent domain—whether for highways, utility lines, or industrial parks —are designed to promote economic development. The language of these bills could raise legal doubts about even the most conventional exercise of eminent domain.

The project that has raised such ire in New London, Connecticut, is not designed solely for economic development purposes. It will also provide a marina, a public walkway along the Thames River, a site for Coast Guard museum, and public parking facilities for the museum and a nearby state park.

Do the sponsors mean to prohibit eminent domain when it is used *solely* for economic development? Well, the project that has raised such ire in New London, Connecticut, is not designed solely for economic development purposes. It will also provide a marina, a public walkway along the Thames River, a site for Coast Guard museum, and public parking facilities for the museum and a nearby state park. So if we ban eminent domain for projects designed solely for economic development, this would quite likely not cover the New London Redevelopment project and any number of similar projects.

The prohibitory approach, even if we could solve the definitional dilemmas, also requires that there be someone to enforce the ban. Do the sponsors intend to create a new federal cause of action permitting eminent domain opponents to take local officials to federal court for a ruling on whether their projects are permissible? Do we really want federal judges deciding whether local development projects should be allowed to go forward or not?

And where are the lawyers going to come from to represent the landowners who object to their property being taken for economic development? Property owners currently rely on lawyers who work for a percentage of any additional compensation they obtain for the owners. These lawyers have a strong incentive to argue that their clients are entitled to more money, since that will automatically increase their fees. But their incentives to argue that the taking is prohibited are obviously more problematic; if they push too hard and the argument actually prevails, there may be no money to pay their fees.

A better reform idea would be to require more complete compensation for persons whose property is taken by eminent domain. The constitutional standard requires fair market value, no more and no less. Congress modified this when it passed the Uniform Relocation Act in 1970, which requires some additional compensation for moving expenses and loss of personal property. Congress could modify the Relocation Act again, in order to nudge the compensation formula further in the direction of providing truly "just" compensation.

For example, Congress could require that when occupied homes, businesses or farms are taken, the owner is entitled to a percentage bonus above fair market value, equal to one percentage point for each year the owner has continuously occupied the property. This would provide significant additional compensation for the Susette Kelos and Wilhelmina Derys who are removed from homes they have lived in for much of their lives.

Alternatively, Congress could require that when a condemnation produces a gain in the underlying land values due to the assembly of multiple parcels, some part of this assembly gain has to be shared with the people whose property is taken. Under current law, all of the assembly gain goes to the condemning authority, or the entity to which the property is transferred after the condemnation.

Either one of these adjustments in the measure of just compensation – or others that might be advanced if Congress held serious hearings on the matter – would do more to protect homeowners against eminent domain than declaring a federal prohibition on takings for economic development. Adjustments in compensation would protect all property owners – those whose property is taken for highways and public housing projects, as well as those whose property is taken for economic development projects. Such a requirement would be vigorously enforced by the attorneys who represent property owners in condemnation proceedings. Providing additional compensation in cases of greatest concern would discourage local governments from using eminent domain in these cases, without prohibiting its use altogether. Perhaps most importantly, assuring a more "just" measure of compensation would leave the ultimate decision about when to exercise this power in the hands of local elected officials, where it has long been lodged, and where it belongs. ■

A better reform idea would be to require more complete compensation for persons whose property is taken by eminent domain. The constitutional standard requires fair market value, no more and no less.

CONNECTICUT PLANNERS WEIGH IN: EMINENT DOMAIN IS IMPORTANT TOOL

By Mark Pellegrini and Donald Poland

Mark Pellegrini is president of the Connecticut Chapter of APA and Donald Poland is vice president of the Connecticut Chapter of APA. The Chapter joined national APA in filing an amicus curiae brief in support of the City of New London.

The day after the *Kelo* decision, *The Hartford Courant*, Connecticut's only state-wide newspaper, ran a two-thirds page photo of a saddened Suzette Kelo on her front porch with the headline "5-4 for the Taking" on its front page. The imagery and the lead paragraphs describing the Supreme Court's decision contributed greatly to the emotional response by many people in Connecticut and around the country. Dozens of opinion letters and commentary by local residents, politicians, land-use lawyers, and planners argued both sides of the case. The editorial commentary continues to this day.

Governor Rell, after the decision, expressed her hope that the few remaining homes in the project area could be incorporated into the development plan. Others called for a greater degree of compensation. The minority leader of the state legislature called for a special session to take action to rein in what was being described as rampant abuse of the eminent domain power and a failure to protect ordinary citizens.

The majority leaders of the Connecticut House and Senate sent a letter to all Connecticut municipalities urging them to honor a voluntary moratorium on the use of eminent domain until the state legislature could study this issue further and decide what refinement or adjustments, if any, might be warranted.

There can be little doubt that in the current climate Connecticut municipalities will be even more reluctant to use eminent domain until the state legislature takes action, which it appears determined to take in the 2006 session. The State's Office of Legislative Research has begun drafting reports on the implications of the *Kelo* decision and the use of eminent domain in Connecticut. It is cataloging all sections of the state statutes that provide authority for the use of eminent domain, for what purpose, and by what governmental or quasi-governmental body.

Practically and politically, the use of eminent domain is always a last resort. Not only is it controversial, it is often very costly and time consuming. Nevertheless, there are circumstances where the use of such power is essential.

The legislature's Planning and Development and Judiciary committees held a joint public hearing on July 28, 2005 and invited representatives for Kelo, the New London Development Corporation, the City of New London and others to testify. A second hearing is scheduled August 25, 2005, when testimony will be heard from the general public.

The Connecticut Chapter of the APA (CCAPA) has been following this case very closely for several years, and joined APA's amicus brief to argue for the importance of eminent domain. Under certain circumstances, in certain types of municipalities, it is important to have this power available to reposition communities or parts of communities when the private market has failed to revitalize such areas. Any use of eminent domain for a public purpose, but not solely for private gain, should only occur after there is a rigorous, open, and fair public planning process. The process should articulate the goals for development and the purposes to be served, and consider alternatives both for the development itself and the mechanisms by which to accomplish it.

Practically and politically, the use of eminent domain is always a last resort. Not only is it controversial, it is often very costly and time consuming. Nevertheless, there are circumstances where the use of such power is essential. In particular, the use of eminent domain can benefit communities and residents when aging city centers, first-tier suburbs, or vacant, abandoned, or deteriorated areas are redeveloped.

The CCAPA will continue to monitor and provide testimony to the various legislative committees as proposed legislation moves through the 2006 session. We believe there is room to further clarify and improve the eminent domain statutes. Amendments are worth exploring that will strengthen the planning and public participation processes; place individual development plans into a broader context of the development plan for the entire community; articulate the public purposes for which this power can be used and how those public purposes will be measured; and adjust the method for calculating just compensation. ■

PUBLIC USE CLAUSE IS VIRTUALLY ELIMINATED IN FEDERAL COURT

By David L. Callies

A bare majority of the *Kelo* Court upheld the exercise of eminent domain for the purpose of economic revitalization. Heavily relying on its previous decisions in *Berman v. Parker* [348 U.S. 26 (1954)] and *HHA v. Midkiff* [467 U.S. 229 (1984)], the Court stated it was too late in the game to revisit its present expansive view of public use. There is no difference in modern eminent domain practice between public use and public purpose, at least in federal court. Indeed, the Court, by a narrow 5/4 vote, specifically equated public use and public purpose before holding that condemning land for economic revitalization was simply another small step along the continuum of permitting public benefits to be sufficient indicia of meeting public use/public purpose requirements. As the Court also noted, it is now up to the states to decide whether or not to increase the burden on the government's exercise of compulsory purchase powers. The federal bar is presently set so low as to be little more than a speed bump.

The Court bluntly rejected any suggestion that it formulate a more rigorous test. To require government to show that public benefits would actually accrue with reasonable certainty or that the implementation of a development plan would actually occur would take the Court into factual inquiries already rejected earlier in the term when the Court rejected the "substantially advances a legitimate state interest" test for regulatory takings in *Lingle v. Chevron U.S.A. Inc.* [125 S. Ct. 2074 (2005)]. In a nod to federalism and states rights, the Court closed by leaving to the states any remedy for such hardships posed by the condemnations in New London.

Only Justice Kennedy's concurrence suggests some small role remains for federal courts in determining that a particular exercise of eminent domain might fall short of the required public use requirement: "There may be private transfers in which the risk of undetected impermissible favoritism of private parties is so acute that a presumption (rebuttable or otherwise) of invalidity is warranted under the Public Use Clause." [2005 U.S. LEXIS 5011, *43 (Kennedy, J., concurring)]

The argument for a judicial hands-off is not so strong as the Court's majority suggests however. Justice O'Connor, who wrote the broadly-worded *Midkiff* opinion for a unanimous Court in 1984, observed that the question of what is a public use is a judicial, not a legislative one. If economic development takings meet the public use requirement, there is no longer any distinction between private and public use of property, the effect of which is "to delete the words 'for public use' from the Takings Clause of the Fifth Amendment." [2005 U.S. LEXIS 5011, *46 (O'Connor, J., dissenting)]

There was very little left of the public use clause – at least in federal court – even before the *Kelo* decision. While a growing handful of state decisions (and federal decisions applying state law on property) found economic revitalization public purposes invalid on constitutional grounds, [*See, e.g.*, the decisions in *Hathcock*, 2005 U.S. LEXIS 5011, *26-28] an equal number of decisions agreed with the Connecticut Supreme Court that this was a valid public use. Clearly, this is also the view of hundreds of state and local revitalization and redevelopment agencies.

David L. Callies is the Benjamin A. Kudo Professor of Law at the University of Hawaii's William S. Richardson School of Law. He filed a brief amicus curiae on behalf of 13 law professors in support of the property owners.

Whether one reads the Court's previous jurisprudence on public use broadly, as Justice Stevens does for the Court's majority, or more narrowly, as does the dissent, it is difficult to argue with the conclusions reached separately by Justice O'Connor: the public use clause is virtually eliminated in federal court. What yellow light of caution the handful of recent cases signaled has now turned back to green, and the government may once more acquire private property by eminent domain on the slightest of public purpose pretexts unless such a use is inconceivable or involves an impossibility, the tests following *Midkiff* in 1984. In other words, it's now all about process, and process only.

There is no doubt that state and local governments will do much good in terms of public welfare and public benefits flowing from economic revitalization under such a relaxed standard, as they have often done in the past. And yet, the public use clause is more than simple policy; it is a bedrock principle contained in the Bill of Rights amendments to our Federal Constitution, designed not to further the goals and desires of the majority, but as a shield against majoritarian excesses at the expense of an otherwise defenseless minority—like the Kelos. Surely we could have found grounds to preserve that shield in federal court.■

DEBUNKING THE URBAN (PLANNING) LEGENDS ABOUT *KELO*

By John M. Baker

John M. Baker is a founding partner of Greene Espel P.L.L.P., a Minneapolis-based firm with a longstanding commitment to representation of public bodies and officials. He holds a degree in political science from the University of Iowa and a law degree from the University of Michigan.

If you rely upon headlines, AM radio, and op-ed pieces for your news about our highest court, you should be stunned to learn the following. More than 50 years ago in Berman v. Parker, the U.S. Supreme Court unanimously recognized that judges are particularly unsuited to tell public officials what is and is not a public purpose, and what use of eminent domain does or does not further such a purpose.

In *Kelo*, the petitioners asked the Supreme Court to do something it had never done before—strike "economic development" and "tax base enhancement" from the set of "conceivable public purposes." The property owners didn't seriously dispute that those were valid governmental objectives, or that condemning property can rationally further those goals. They wanted those objectives stricken from the list of "public purposes" so that property owners would win more often. It was an effort at revolutionary change that nearly succeeded.

If you rely upon headlines, AM radio, and op-ed pieces for your news about our highest court, you should be stunned to learn the following. More than 50 years ago in *Berman v. Parker*, the U.S. Supreme Court unanimously recognized that judges are particularly unsuited to tell public officials what is and is not a public purpose, and what use of eminent domain does or does not further such a purpose. In *Berman*, as in *Kelo*, the government took property that belonged to one private party, condemned it, and sold it to another private party. As in *Kelo*, the plaintiff's property in *Berman* was not blighted, but the surrounding area was. Yet the U.S. Constitution did not prohibit the government from deciding to purchase the property through eminent domain, so long as it paid its owner just compensation and provided the owner with due process.

Thirty years later, in another unanimous ruling in *Hawaii Housing Authority v. Midkiff*, the U.S. Supreme Court again held that the "public use" requirement does not prevent governments from condemning the property of one person, paying him or her just compensation, and selling it to another, so long as there was a "conceivable public purpose" behind the action, and the acquisition was rationally related to that purpose.

In *Kelo*, the law *did* become more favorable to property owners, but in an incremental (rather than revolutionary) way. The 5-4 majority created one new way for property owners to win—by demonstrating that the government's justifications are simply pretexts for a real intention to benefit a single private party. Justice Kennedy, a critical fifth vote, included "further observations" in a concurring opinion. Those "observations" hint that he might switch sides in "cases in which the transfers are so suspicious, or the procedures employed are so prone to abuse, or the purported benefits are so trivial or implausible, that courts should assume an impermissible private purpose." However, because Justice Kennedy also joined the opinion of the court (and not just its judgment), and no other justice joined his opinion, his "observations" are, for the time being, simply that.

Yet the actual words of the Supreme Court majority now seem unimportant. Six days after the decision was released, a remarkable coalition of House members– Jim Sensenbrenner *and* John Conyers, Tom DeLay *and* Barney Frank – took to the floor to express "the grave disapproval of the House" regarding the majority opinion. Some legislative gestures, including the "grave disapproval" resolution and another passed the same day to bar federal funds from "enforcing the judgment" in Kelo, have no real effect. Others—such as the Sensenbrenner bill in the House and the Cornyn bill in the Senate—would coerce local governments into paying inflated prices to holdouts when eminent domain is needed for economic development.

How can so great a backlash follow a decision that, in reality, changes so little? When there is an underdog as sympathetic as Suzette Kelo. When the most respected Supreme Court Justice paints a vivid (but inaccurate) picture of what her colleagues have actually done, and the headline writers and congressional staffers latch onto it. When candidates who have won elections by scaring citizens about the dangers of social security reform, terrorism, or gay marriage see the political value of now scaring citizens into believing that they will lose their homes to a Wal-Mart if you vote against them.

In the current climate of misunderstanding about eminent domain, it may be difficult for many legislators to vote against all eminent domain "reform" efforts. The greatest risk is that the ideologues of the property rights movement use this momentum and fear as an opportunity to enact into legislation the rest of their agenda that failed in the courts. ■

In the current climate of misunderstanding about eminent domain, it may be difficult for many legislators to vote against all eminent domain "reform" efforts. The greatest risk is that the ideologues of the property rights movement use this momentum and fear as an opportunity to enact into legislation the rest of their agenda that failed in the courts.

"PUBLIC USE" GOES VALLEY GIRL; NOW MEANS "PUBLIC WHATEVER"

By Michael M. Berger

Anyone who has dealt with people in their teens lately (at least since the movie "Clueless" put Valley Girl phraseology into the national consciousness) is familiar with the typical response to any sort of adult directive: "What . . . ever!" Who would have thought that the U.S. Supreme Court would decide that is now the answer to the constitutional question—"What is a public use?"

Critical reaction around the country to the *Kelo* decision has been jaw-dropping. Even former President Clinton criticized the ruling, noting "I never thought it would happen"—although his two appointees to the Court provided decisive votes for the 5-4 majority. [Josh Gerstein, "Clinton: Court Was 'Wrong' on Eminent Domain," The New York Sun, July 14, 2005]

Legislators around the country have been listening to the groundswell of public disbelief. They began immediately introducing curative legislation—either at the state level, to prevent state and local government from acting in the newly approved manner, or at the federal level, by exercising Congress' power over the purse to preclude the use of federal funds for similar takings.

What happened? How did the so-called "progressive" group of Supreme Court Justices manage to come up with what one editorial called "not only one of the most unpopular court decisions in memory but one of the worst, as well"? [Editorial, "The Court Errs Badly," *The Huntsville (Alabama) Times*, June 25, 2005]

Michael M. Berger is a Partner and Co-Chair of the Appellate Practice Group in the Los Angeles office of Manatt, Phelps & Phillips. Mr. Berger filed an amicus curiae brief in support of the property owners in *Kelo* on behalf of the American Farm Bureau Federation.

Simply put, the Court's majority (led by Justice Stevens) yielded to the siren song of the governments' apologists (including, as usual, the American Planning Association, which routinely supports the government position in the Supreme Court, no matter the issue) and opted for extreme deference to local government decision making. The Court refused to "second guess" the city's determination that the way out of its general economic decline was to convert these middle-class homes (whose only offense was that they produced little in the way of taxes) into a "planned" commercial/office development that would hopefully yield "more," and to compel the owners to sell if they would not do so voluntarily. (The fact that the city really had no concrete plan for these particular properties at this time seemed of no moment to the Court.)

Curiously, having established a rule that legislative decisions about land use warrant deference, the opinion cautioned that condemnations that are obviously intended simply to provide benefit to some favored private party, so that the public benefit is incidental, should be subjected to scrutiny. Justice Kennedy's separate concurring opinion amplified on this same theme. The problem, as pointed out in the dissents written by Justices O'Connor and Thomas, is that the majority opinion is clueless as to how such scrutiny would take place and how that sort of approved "second guessing" could be constitutionally differentiated from the prohibited "second guessing" outlawed here. (Or, indeed, how the disapproved "second guessing" differs from ordinary judicial review of constitutionality.)

The problem, of course, is that the Constitution should give no one a free pass. Separation of powers is a fine concept, and there is room for some amount of deference but, by the time of *Marbury v. Madison* [5 U.S. 137 (1803)], the idea that legislative determinations were beyond the review of the judiciary was passé.

After *Kelo*, review is uncertain. The majority opinion appears to accept a form of abject judicial deference, so long as the government mouths the right words in its resolution. Whether there is actually any room to raise the kind of questions noted in Justice Kennedy's concurrence remains—at this writing—an open question at best. Justice Kennedy seemed to be operating on the theory that due process review could provide a meaningful brake on unconstitutional action. That will happen only if the Court allows more intrusiveness than it does into a "public use" determination. Time will tell.

Nearly a decade ago, a commentary in *Time* magazine sarcastically concluded that "eminent domain" is "a legal term meaning 'we can do anything we want.'" [Steve Lopez, "In the Name of Her Father," *Time*, July 14, 1996, p.4] The U.S. Supreme Court recently wrote that comment into American constitutional law. ■

DOES *KELO* TRAMPLE ON FUNDAMENTAL PROPERTY RIGHTS?

By Lani Williams

I strongly feel the *Kelo* decision came out as it should have. However, many people around the country feel that a fundamental right has been trampled upon. Brilliant minds can debate the pros and cons of the decision and its affect on land-use law. I have nothing to add to the intricacies of land-use law that has not already been the subject of dueling editorials. However, two things come to mind about the opinion, held by many citizens, that the *Kelo* decision attacks fundamental property rights.

The first is the nature of fundamental rights in the United States. We speak of certain rights as "fundamental" under the Constitution. Often

Lani Williams is the Associate Counsel for the International Municipal Lawyers Association. IMLA joined the National League of Cities, National Conference of State Legislatures, U.S. Conference of Mayors, Council of State Governments, National Association of Counties, and the International City/County Management Association in filing this is interpreted to mean that these rights are "absolute," which they are not. For instance, while we all have a "fundamental" right to engage in free speech under the First Amendment, none of us have a right to shout "Fire!" in a crowded theatre. [Schenck v. United States, 249 U.S. 47, 52 (1919)]. Similarly, while the Fourth Amendment guarantees the "fundamental" right to be free from searches absent a warrant, our society has recognized the necessity to qualify that right in certain circumstances. [Michigan v. Tyler, 436 U.S. 499, 509 (1978) (exigent circumstances); Carroll v. United States, 267 U.S. 132 (1925) (automobile exception); Chimel v. California, 395 U.S. 752, 763 (1969) (search incident to arrest)]. And, as the Supreme Court has recognized, the right to own property is qualified by the government's ability to zone its use, and even to take that property for a public use, in exchange for just compensation. The *Kelo* decision did not change this right, though perhaps it broadened our understanding of the right. Yet many in the general public feel that the right to own property should be absolutely protected from any government "interference."

The second striking aspect of *Kelo* is that citizens are so disturbed by the ruling that they largely have turned, not to their local officials for recourse and solutions, but to Congress, a legislative body much further removed from the day to day concerns than the local mayor and council. What qualifies as a "public use" at the local level should not be decided by the federal government, even when federal dollars are at stake. I doubt whether a federal definition of public use can adequately take into account the differing needs of communities in today's global economy. A community's direction should be decided by local citizens through their local elected officials, not by federal mandates.

The quest for a national solution is particularly interesting because the vast majority of citizens have never been, and will never be, affected by an eminent domain action. Local governments are reticent to use this power (and have been so historically) because of the turmoil it creates in the community. Yet, in spite of the fact that eminent domain is rarely used, citizens do not trust their local governments to treat them equitably should their property be deemed necessary for a public purpose. I would have hoped that in dealing with crises on the local front, citizens would feel more secure in turning to their local elected officials for assistance, as well as to voice their opposition to planned projects. Apparently, they do not. The most disturbing result from the *Kelo* decision is that local government seems no longer to be connected with its constituency, seems to have lost the public's trust, and seems to have lost the public's confidence in being able to govern justly.

Local government employees and advocates must learn to engage our constituencies so they do not feel disenfranchised. Only then can decisions, like the one in *Kelo,* be supported by the public. Certainly, there will still be people whose homes will be taken and who will feel bitter about their losses. But hopefully with greater trust and confidence, there will be fewer people who feel they are powerless to influence the direction of local government. Only in this way can local governments win the war for continued self-sufficiency and self-direction, which affects not only the limited *Kelo* case, or even merely the use of eminent domain, but everything local government does. ■

an amicus curiae brief in support of the City of New London. The brief was authored by Timothy J. Dowling and Jennifer Bradley of the Community Rights Counsel in Washington, D.C., and Richard Ruda, Chief Counsel of the State and Local Legal Center.

What qualifies as a "public use" at the local level should not be decided by the federal government, even when federal dollars are at stake. I doubt whether a federal definition of public use can adequately take into account the differing needs of communities in today's global economy.

Frank Schnidman is a Senior
Fellow at the Center for Urban
and Environmental Solutions
(CUES) at Florida Atlantic
University and the Executive
Director of the Community
Redevelopment Agency of North
Miami, Florida. Mr. Schnidman
filed an amicus curiae brief in
support of Kelo and the property
owners on behalf of John
Norquist, President of the
Congress for New Urbanism.

*Kelo is likely to become the
most important property rights
case ever decided, not because
of its holding, but because of
the backlash.*

ALTERNATIVES TO EMINENT DOMAIN

By Frank Schnidman

Local government should not use the power of eminent domain in purely economic development projects to transfer property from one private property owner to another when the "public use" is simply increasing the tax base and hopefully creating additional jobs.

During my professional career, beginning with the "Great Society" of President Lyndon Johnson and his federal "Model Cities" program, I have witnessed a variety of federal, state, and local government efforts to address both community redevelopment and economic development needs. Politicians always wanted to have a ribbon-cutting ceremony before the next re-election campaign, so time was of the essence in getting projects planned and built. Nothing much has changed with the politicians. But the development industry, in my opinion, has changed considerably in the last 50 years, as well as the way we finance new development and redevelopment.

When the WWII veterans returned home and spurred the great demand for new housing, the Housing Act of 1949 was passed, and commercial and retail developers were seeking suburban locations for new shopping and business centers, the development industry was led by a group of entrepreneurial organizations which were privately owned, local or regional in focus, and planning and building a small number of projects each year. In the twenty-first century, the development industry is now led by large corporations with access to Wall Street for funding, with a need to issue quarterly progress reports to their shareholders.

Fifty years ago the large developers were working on a few projects while quietly assembling land for the ones soon to be announced. Today it is not uncommon for a large developer to have numerous projects in many areas of a state or even nationwide, and always looking for more projects because of the variety of sources for equity and non-equity finance to support the size of their organizations. Key players in the development industry now have the same mentality as the politician looking for the ribbon cutting before the next re-election campaign. This has resulted in an effort to move the process along more rapidly.

Politicians want immediate results and developers want local government "incentives" to "fast-track" the projects, not only from the regulatory perspective, but also for land assembly. Because of the increased use of Tax Increment Financing (TIF) and even developer-financed eminent domain actions, the funds are available at the local level to allow local government to fast-track redevelopment and economic development projects through eminent-domain-led land assembly.

I have witnessed both appropriate and inappropriate uses of the power of eminent domain with this convergence of municipal revitalization plans and the private sector's need for building sites. I have grown more concerned as I've seen projects move forward that target private property for for-profit ventures when the economic benefits have not been rigorously examined, the impacts on the community have not been thoroughly investigated, and the property to be taken is neither slum nor blighted.

When the *Kelo* appeal was accepted by the Supreme Court, I drafted an *amicus brief* for John Norquist, President of the Congress for New Urbanism. John is the former Mayor of Milwaukee and author of *The Wealth of Cities.* Combining his experience with the slum and blight of Milwaukee with my experience in land assembly, we prepared a resource for the Supreme Court to show the Justices that the sky would not fall on the government's efforts to revitalize cities if they chose to rule in favor of Suzette Kelo and the other property owners. (Read the Norquist brief amicus curiae at www.cuesfau.org/cra)

There are an array of tools and techniques commonly used for land assembly by the public and private sectors that do not require eminent domain. Incentives for landowner-organized assembly is a tool with great potential;, the primary incentive being greater sales price. (*See*, M. Crouch, "A Neighborhood in North Carolina is Put Up for Sale," *New York Times*, August 14, 2005, Real Estate, p. 16, col.1) There are also numerous third-party, private sector assemblage opportunities, through either a broker, speculator or even a developer herself. In the brief, we carefully explained the ways that the public and private sectors have been using land assembly historically and currently, in the U.S. and overseas, to assemble land without forcing owners from their property.

We were disappointed by the breath of the deference to local government decision making found in the Court's opinion. Justice Stevens cited our brief in support of the proposition that "the necessity and wisdom of using eminent domain to promote economic development are certainly matters of legitimate public debate," but then simply stated that the case was about the definition of "public use," and "[b]ecause of over a century of our case law interpreting that provision," the Court found in favor of the city.

Kelo is likely to become the most important property rights case ever decided, not because of its holding, but because of the backlash. To John Norquist and myself, the heightened concern over the use of eminent domain is important because it will force policy makers, as well as the development industry, to explore options and alternatives. We hope that our brief will serve as a guidebook for the public and private sectors as they begin their exploration. ■

RUMORED DEATH OF PROPERTY RIGHTS IS GREATLY EXAGGERATED

By David Parkhurst

The Supreme Court's *Kelo* decision blew open, rather than closed, the debate on the use of eminent domain for economic development purposes. It touched a raw nerve for most people about the boundaries between property rights of individuals and the authority of government. Despite the fury that erupted following the decision, the Court's opinion preserves the opportunity for municipalities to contribute to the national discussion about the legal, policy, and personal aspects of eminent domain.

From a legal perspective, the rumored death of property rights is greatly exaggerated. The *Kelo* decision did not expand the use or powers of eminent domain. Nor did the decision overturn existing restrictions imposed at the state or local levels. In fact, some legal scholars argue that the *Kelo* decision places new limits on state and local authority. A public process involving comprehensive planning, identifiable public benefits, reasonable promise of results, and an evident public need are four elements outlined in the *Kelo* decision that courts should now consider when evaluating the use of eminent domain for economic development purposes. The decision simply reaffirmed years of precedent that economic development is a "public use" under the Takings Clause.

The Takings Clause, moreover, retains its constitutional requirement that property owners receive just compensation for their property acquired by eminent domain.

Cities are now under an even brighter spotlight when it comes to the use of eminent domain. There will be more pressure to demonstrate that the

David Parkhurst is the Principal Legislative Counsel for Policy and Federal Relations of the National League of Cities. The NLC joined the International Municipal Lawyers Association, National Conference of State Legislatures, U.S. Conference of Mayors, Council of State Governments, National Association of Counties, and the International City/County Management Association in filing an amicus curiae brief in support of the City of New London. The brief was authored by Timothy J. Dowling and Jennifer Bradley of the Community Rights Counsel in Washington, D.C., and Richard Ruda, Chief Counsel of the State and Local Legal Center.

Sadly, but not surprisingly, the outcry created by the Kelo decision sounded loudest from the halls of Congress. . . . This congressional approach risks creating unintended consequences for federal housing, community development, and historic preservation programs in its march to restrict the use of eminent domain.

The press has incorrectly reported that the Kelo *decision greatly expands local government authority giving city leaders permission to take grandma's house without warning and without adequate compensation. This feeds the public's fears that bulldozers, which allegedly stand at grandma's gate, engines roaring, are heading next for their homes.*

use of eminent domain will occur sparingly and only after exhausting all other options. The *Kelo* decision, moreover, did not condone eminent domain abuse. "There may be private transfers in which the risk of undetected impermissible favoritism of private parties is so acute that a presumption of invalidity is warranted under the Public Use Clause," wrote Justice Kennedy in his concurrence.

From a public policy perspective, the *Kelo* decision affirmed that eminent domain, a power derived from state law, is one best left to the states and their political subdivisions. Sadly, but not surprisingly, the outcry created by the *Kelo* decision sounded loudest from the halls of Congress. Members of Congress have introduced bills that would prevent states and cities from using federal funds to exercise eminent domain for economic development. In most cases, sponsors of these bills have left "economic development" undefined, or attempted to define it only by carving out what is not meant by it. This congressional approach risks creating unintended consequences for federal housing, community development, and historic preservation programs in its march to restrict the use of eminent domain.

Congress has also attempted to limit future use of eminent domain through the appropriations process. On June 30, 2005, without one public hearing and no record of verified abuses, the House of Representatives adopted an amendment onto its housing appropriations bill (H.R. 3058) that would prohibit the use of federal funds to "enforce the judgment" in the *Kelo* case. The Senate Appropriations Committee averted an anti-*Kelo* amendment to its housing appropriations bill, which awaits action by the full Senate this fall, to allow for consideration that is more deliberate.

The political rhetoric of members of Congress who disagree with the *Kelo* decision, which includes both liberal Democrats and conservative Republicans, miscasts the decision as granting constitutional carte blanche for cities to take away private property, most likely owned by vulnerable populations, and give it to private developers for private gain, in the name of economic development.

From a personal perspective, the anxiety people feel about eminent domain is real. Examples of governmental abuse of eminent domain to construct the interstate highway system and for urban renewal make people suspicious about how governments intend to use eminent domain following the *Kelo* decision. This history imposes a duty on local officials to explain governmental use of eminent domain with greater sensitivity to its personal impact on individuals. Ironically, national opinion polls show Americans prefer and have more trust in their local governments than in state or national government. The press has incorrectly reported that the *Kelo* decision greatly expands local government authority giving city leaders permission to take grandma's house without warning and without adequate compensation. This feeds the public's fears that bulldozers, which allegedly stand at grandma's gate, engines roaring, are heading next for their homes.

Municipal leaders have a responsibility to engage in public conversation about eminent domain that can help dispel inaccuracies and stereotypes. Property rights activists, on the other hand, need to understand there is a delicate balance between minimizing the burdens on individuals and maximizing benefits to the community. The art of compromise is essential going forward. ▪

DOMESTIC POLICY WATCH: REDEVELOPMENT DONE RIGHT

By W. Paul Farmer, AICP
APA Executive Director

[This article is the July 2005 posting in a series that examines the federal domestic agenda. As planners, we have views about issues of public policy. APA's adopted policies may be found at www.planning.org/policyguides. The purpose of this series is to add to the discourse about issues of great importance. These are not partisan issues. Rather, they are fundamental issues that will influence our communities for decades.

In addition, From Washington, *APA's twice-monthly electronic update on federal initiatives, is free to APA members. To read past issues of* From Washington, *or to subscribe, visit the APA website at http://www.planning.org/fromwashington/index.htm. To read other issues of* Domestic Policy Watch, *please go to www.planning.org/domesticagenda/index.htm.*

Member responses to this article and others in the Domestic Policy Watch *series are encouraged and will be posted on the APA website. Visit www.planning.org/legislation/member/feedback.htm to respond.]*

The U.S. Supreme Court term that concluded last month was extremely successful for planning. APA filed amicus briefs in four important cases. The Court properly clarified longstanding disputes in regulatory takings by jettisoning the "substantially advances" test (*Lingle*), held that takings claims cannot be retried in federal court after a state court ruling (*San Remo*), protected communities from excessive damages and litigation when facing telecommunications zoning challenges (*Rancho Palos Verdes*), and, in the most publicized case, preserved economic development as a legitimate public use for the use of eminent domain (*Kelo*).

Our briefs, published in this PAS Report and available at www.planning.org/amicusbriefs/, proved persuasive in upholding the importance of good planning. APA was on the winning side in all four decisions. Three of the four decisions were unanimous, showing that good planning is nonpartisan. With the exception of the *Kelo* case, these decisions, although important, caused barely a ripple in the public mind. *Kelo*, of course, triggered a tidal wave of media coverage. Most of all of the coverage was misleading at best and downright wrong at worst.

With conservative think tanks and so-called property rights organizations fanning the flames, many commentators and lawmakers have rushed in to condemn the decision and call for legislative remedies. Within days of the ruling, multiple bills had been introduced in Congress, each with an eye toward undoing the handiwork of the majority on the High Court.

The House of Representatives showed its disdain for the Constitution's separation of powers by overwhelmingly approving a nonbinding resolution opposing the decision and more narrowly adopting an amendment to prevent funds from being used to enforce the decision. The House Majority Leader and several key committee chairmen, after testing the wind of political sentiment, called a special news conference to promise swift corrective action. Special interests dedicated to undermining local governments marshaled $3 million in just 24 hours following the decision. Talk radio simmered with images of bureaucrats preparing to seize homes in the name of corporate profit.

APA was on the winning side in all four decisions. Three of the four decisions were unanimous, showing that good planning is nonpartisan. . . . Kelo, of course, triggered a tidal wave of media coverage. Most of all of the coverage was misleading at best and downright wrong at worst.

In 2004, the APA Board of Directors adopted a Policy Guide on Public Redevelopment (www.planning.org/ policyguides/ redevelopment.htm). This guide outlines key principles and recommends specific legislation to craft redevelopment policies. The policy guide makes clear our commitment to planning that is democratic, inclusive, accountable, comprehensive, and empowering.

APA has written much on the *Kelo* case and decision. This PAS Report brings together many of those resources. I want to take this opportunity to set the record straight on some vital facts:

No new powers were created as a result of the decision. The decision simply upheld existing legal precedent dating back 100 years and reaffirmed many times in the last 50 years. The justices reaffirmed that economic development qualifies as a "public use" under the Fifth Amendment. No city in America can do anything after *Kelo* that they couldn't do before the ruling. The petitioners were the ones asking for new powers, namely the ability to have local eminent domain decisions subject to review by federal judges.

Citizens are not more vulnerable to the use of eminent domain in light of the Kelo decision. Just the opposite is true. Cities will be under more scrutiny than ever. Officials should welcome this spotlight and continue to pursue eminent domain in only the rarest circumstances.

State laws and constitutions governing eminent domain were not overturned. In my home state of Illinois, state law would have prevented the situation in *Kelo* from ever arising. Many states have eminent domain standards stricter than those under review in *Kelo*. The decision did nothing to change, amend, or undermine these laws. We are certainly going to see similar restrictions introduced in other states.

The Court affirmed that a thorough and engaged planning process protects the values of citizens and their community. The most important aspect of the decision in *Kelo* is the fact that the Court specifically noted that communities are granted deference in the determination of public use based primarily on the fact that an open, participatory, and comprehensive planning process was involved. Planning is the appropriate forum for public debate and decision making. Good plans outline the collective vision of a community. The Court explicitly challenged backroom deals and made it very clear that the ruling would have been different had the private entity initiated the project requiring exercise of eminent domain.

While the *Kelo* decision did not make dramatic changes in longstanding eminent domain jurisprudence, it has presented planners and APA with an important challenge —helping communities do redevelopment the right way. Justice Stevens noted in his opinion that "nothing in the opinion precludes any state from placing further restrictions" on the exercise of eminent domain. He called the "necessity and wisdom of using eminent domain to promote economic development" a "legitimate public debate."

This debate will now unfold in state legislatures across the nation. It is a debate we should welcome and one we must inform and influence with principles of good planning. We should promote legislation that embraces a comprehensive approach to redevelopment. Redevelopment policy is an essential component of efforts to redirect growth into the nation's cities, inner suburbs, and other areas already served by infrastructure and supported by urban services. We should ensure planning that is transparent and inclusive.

APA recently testified before the House of Representatives Saving America's Cities Working Group on the needs of urban communities. APA was among many national organizations calling for better efforts to address redevelopment and revitalization. Debate at the state level over eminent domain provides an opportunity to improve the redevelopment process in a way that bolsters the future of our communities while allaying the fears of property owners.

As in so many areas of state law related to planning, redevelopment statutes in many states are outdated, ill conceived, or nonexistent. In 2004, the

APA Board of Directors adopted a Policy Guide on Public Redevelopment (www.planning.org/policyguides/redevelopment.htm). This guide outlines key principles and recommends specific legislation to craft redevelopment policies. The policy guide makes clear our commitment to planning that is democratic, inclusive, accountable, comprehensive, and empowering. Our vision of redevelopment creates communities of lasting value. Creation of such communities is the best guarantor of everyone's property rights.

What does "redevelopment done right" look like? Redevelopment, including any use of eminent domain, should be directly linked to a plan. Redevelopment plans should be consistent with adopted comprehensive plans. Both plans should be subject to rigorous public involvement. Legislation governing redevelopment authorities should include a clearly defined process for designating redevelopment areas. Whenever possible, a designated and well-defined redevelopment authority should be a prerequisite to eminent domain use. Public-private partnerships for redevelopment should be constructed to ensure they are fair, open, equitable, transparent, and accountable for acting in the public interest. Public notice and participation processes should be required and outreach should include citizens, property owners, businesses, and civic institutions. Lastly, as we argued in our brief to the Supreme Court, eminent domain compensation should in certain circumstances exceed the fair market value standard.

One of the important principles at stake in *Kelo* that has been mostly lost in the ensuing media frenzy is the notion that local officials are the most directly accountable to local citizens. APA has argued that eminent domain is justly a last resort tool because of its enormous impacts on the lives of individual citizens. Given the stakes involved in redevelopment decisions and eminent domain decisions, the best means of ensuring fairness is to lodge ultimate responsibility with locally elected officials. Ironically, many opponents of the *Kelo* decision believe the very federal judges they frequently decry as "activist" and "disconnected" would be more appropriate arbiters of local fairness than those directly accountable at the ballot box. That is a proposition APA rejects.

Other ironies abound. Just weeks after criticizing the *Kelo* decision that found economic development to be an appropriate use of eminent domain, a governor announced that a long-stalled highway would be built, requiring the "seizure" of 58 houses. And the governor's justification for the road and the use of eminent domain? You guessed it. Economic development.

As state legislators debate the best approach for their state, it is important to keep in mind that redevelopment, including eminent domain, is critical for job creation, economic revitalization, and improved quality of life. Eminent domain is a powerful tool—its prudent use, when exercised in the sunshine of public scrutiny, can help achieve a greater public good that benefits the entire community.

The use of eminent domain should not be categorically rejected based on misunderstanding of the court's verdict in *Kelo*. Simply eliminating use of eminent domain in all but the most direct of public uses may well impose serious financial burdens on citizens. In Minnesota, a fiscal impact study mandated by legislation eliminating eminent domain power for economic development uncovered a dramatic new tax burden. In urban and inner-ring suburban areas, development often involves complex land assembly where eminent domain can be a vital tool.

Congress is preparing to consider various proposals to limit eminent domain for "economic development." But what exactly does that mean?

> *The use of eminent domain should not be categorically rejected based on misunderstanding of the court's verdict in Kelo. Simply eliminating use of eminent domain in all but the most direct of public uses may well impose serious financial burdens on citizens.*

That prohibition could go well beyond the category of projects that are the intended target. The issues of definition and, eventually, of enforcement raise as many problems as they purport to solve.

Many more homeowners have lost their homes and the principal value of their homes through changing economic circumstances, neglect, and disinvestment than through the use of eminent domain for economic development. Are our currently outraged and activist legislators willing to address these problems or just grandstand on a suddenly popular crusade?

Congress should move cautiously to avoid untended consequences to a variety of federal programs and the health of communities. Congressional action could, unlike the *Kelo* decision, undermine current state law. Congress might be better equipped to deal with the compensation issue by addressing the Uniform Relocation Act. Adjusting the compensation rules may prove a more effective incentive for preventing eminent domain abuse. However, the most appropriate forum for reform of the redevelopment process is the states.

On *Kelo*, the Supreme Court got it right. However, our work is only beginning. Planners and APA must be leaders in the reform of redevelopment practices nationwide. Let us move forward united in the commitment to revitalize our communities in a way that builds value and serves citizens. Let us resolve to get redevelopment done, and done right. ■

DOMESTIC POLICY WATCH: A MEMBER'S GUIDE TO APA'S POLICY AND ADVOCACY PROGRAMS

By W. Paul Farmer, AICP
APA Executive Director

[This article is the August 2005 posting in a series that examines the federal domestic agenda. As planners, we have views about issues of public policy. APA's adopted policies may be found at www.planning.org/policyguides. The purpose of this series is to add to the discourse about issues of great importance. These are not partisan issues. Rather, they are fundamental issues that will influence our communities for decades.

In addition, From Washington, *APA's twice-monthly electronic update on federal initiatives, is free to APA members. To read past issues of* From Washington, *or to subscribe, visit the APA website at http://www.planning.org/ fromwashington/index.htm. To read other issues of* Domestic Policy Watch, *please go to www.planning.org/domesticagenda/index.htm.*

Member responses to this article and others in the Domestic Policy Watch *series are encouraged and will be posted on the APA website. Visit www.planning.org/ legislation/member/feedback.htm to respond.]*

This year, APA has been extremely active with member delegate assemblies, on Capitol Hill, and in the courts on behalf of good planning. One highlight was the Legislative & Policy Conference held this spring and jointly sponsored by ASLA. With threats to the Community Development Block Grant program, final negotiations over the long-stalled transportation reauthorization, and recent action on eminent domain and takings, the first half of 2005 has been filled with policy debates critical to the planning process.

In the wake of our advocacy on these important issues and with Congress now off on the month-long August recess, I thought it was a good time to give APA members an overview of how APA makes decisions on public policy issues. Advocacy is an essential part of APA's mission, so it is important that members understand and actively participate in our ongoing policy process.

APA's policy and advocacy programs, like good planning, are grounded in an open, democratic, participatory process and driven by solid data and information. Because issues arise in different contexts—legislative, executive, judicial—and at different levels of government—federal, state, local—APA has adopted a multifaceted approach to adopting and advocating positions.

There are three main vehicles that guide APA's legislative and advocacy programs: policy guides, legislative priorities, and amicus activities. While each component builds on work and action from the other two, all three mechanisms are instrumental in their own right.

Policy guides lay the foundation for our advocacy efforts with broad principles and recommendations for action. Each year, these guides are used to develop legislative priorities and an agenda that provide greater detail on specific issues and bills under active consideration. This process involves taking the board-approved list of priorities and recasting them into a legislative agenda that targets specific pieces of proposed legislation or regulatory actions. In addition to focusing our efforts, the format allows APA to put forward a proactive agenda for positive change.

Complementing these legislative efforts is our amicus, or friend of the court, activity designed to promote important legal principles that are critical to planning. Like our legislative priorities, APA's amicus work is grounded in our policy guides. All of these efforts are guided by APA's Board of Directors and appointed committees. Primary, ongoing volunteer work occurs through the Legislative and Policy Committee and the Amicus Committee. Broader participation occurs annually through development of policy guides.

Policy Guides

Policy guides spell out APA's position on topics of vital importance to the practice of planning. These guides lay out what we stand for and detail the action needed at all levels of government to ensure good planning that leads to communities of lasting value. These guides are official statements of APA and the planning profession on public policy issues. While APA represents a diverse membership, it comes together around certain fundamental principles and policies that are necessary to promote and further the success of our communities.

APA policies are developed with thorough member involvement and participation. Any APA member may suggest a topic for a policy guide to the Legislative and Policy Committee. The committee is appointed by the APA President and currently is chaired by Steve Preston, FAICP. The committee carefully evaluates the policy environment for planning and identifies issue areas for new guides.

Once topics are selected, a task force is formed. Any APA member can serve on a task force and the committee works to ensure that task forces represent APA's diversity in order to account for geographic distribution as well as areas of expertise. The task force carefully reviews the issue at hand and prepares a formal draft guide. The draft is then circulated to APA chapters and divisions for formal comment. Additionally, draft guides are posted online so that all APA members can offer input.

Following consideration of all comments and subsequent editing, the Legislative and Policy Committee votes on the final draft of the new guide. Once the committee approves the guide, it is forwarded to the National Delegate Assembly for approval. The Delegate Assembly comprises pro-

APA's policy and advocacy programs, like good planning, are grounded in an open, democratic, participatory process and driven by solid data and information.

portional representation from every APA chapter, based on the size of chapter membership. These assemblies are typically conducted during the APA annual conference where delegates extensively debate and revise the proposed guide. A guide receiving majority support from a Delegate Assembly is then sent to the APA Board of Directors for ratification. The board considers the guide and is the sole body empowered to give final approval for adoption.

All subsequent APA policy and advocacy actions spring from the statements of position and principle articulated in approved policy guides. Adopted guides broadly discuss the issue, outline pertinent facts and findings, and identify specific policies and general recommendations for an improved social and political environment for planning to play its most effective role. Guides are intentionally written for an audience of policymakers, elected officials, and community leaders.

There are 22 current guides. The most recently adopted guide deals with planning for community safety and security. A new guide on air quality is under development, as is an update of our guide on housing.

Legislative Priorities

APA's policy advocacy efforts set the course for positive change in America's communities by giving direction to the actions of lawmakers, public officials, professional planners, and engaged citizens. APA advocates policies at the federal and state level to improve planning in the nation's communities. Each year the Legislative and Policy Committee proposes, and the board adopts, a set of legislative priorities. These legislative priorities reflect the major areas of emphasis for APA's policy advocacy efforts. The list also helps define APA in the eyes of our members, friends, foes, and policy makers.

Adopted priorities are intended to serve as a basic guide—a blueprint—for our legislative and policy action. To implement these legislative priorities, APA drafts an annual Federal Policy Agenda for Congress. The current agenda for the 109th Congress can be found at www.planning.org/priorities/fedpolicy109.htm.

Legislative priorities identify the most pressing and important policy issues for a given year. Policy guides cover a wide range of issues, so legislative priorities are adopted to guide the efforts of the Legislative and Policy Committee and APA staff. Priorities are adopted to maintain a focus on the most important and timely issues related to the objectives contained in our policy guides. The priorities bridge the broad principles in policy guides and the more focused, bill-specific legislative agenda. All three tools—policy guides, legislative agenda, and legislative priorities—guide APA's decisions on specific legislative positions and advocacy.

Legislative priorities are drafted annually and listed in three general categories: National Primary, National Secondary, and State. The two national categories distinguish between those priorities that will require APA to take a leading position and those that require APA to be a partner. The categories also guide our organization's allocation of resources and energy. Determinations are based on the status of legislation affecting the issue, current events and context, existing APA policy statements on the issue, and the degree of our involvement with other organizations and interest groups. Priorities are reflected in the program, agenda, and messages for the annual Legislative & Policy Conference and Planner's Day on Capitol Hill. The State category reinforces our intent to support and enhance chapter legislative programs by assisting their efforts with respect to critical policy issues identified by the Committee, staff, and Chapter Presidents Council.

All subsequent APA policy and advocacy actions spring from the statements of position and principle articulated in approved policy guides.

To implement these legislative priorities, APA drafts an annual Federal Policy Agenda for Congress. The current agenda for the 109th Congress can be found at www.planning.org/priorities/fedpolicy109.htm.

APA's Legislative and Policy Committee works year-round to guide our progress and define our positions as the legislative process moves forward. We actively promote our priorities throughout the year through testimony, briefings, formal letters and comments, legislative coalitions, and grassroots advocacy.

APA's current priorities (www.planning.org/priorities/) call for the following three national primary priorities:

- Opposing efforts to expand "takings" doctrines and federal attempts to preempt local planning authority

- Supporting reauthorization of the nation's transportation laws based on principles of increased choice, access, equity, flexibility, public engagement, and livability through planning

- Addressing the nation's growing housing crisis by increasing choice, expanding affordability, and maintaining resources for vital federal community development programs, including a distinct Community Development Block Grant program.

Additional priorities include a focus on coastal issues, hazard mitigation planning, energy, land conservation, and redevelopment.

Amicus Activities

In the mid-1980s, APA recognized the need to be an advocate for planning not only in the legislature but also in the courts. APA established an Amicus Curiae Committee to identify important cases where "friend of the court" briefs could be written to support vital legal precedent and principles related to planning. APA's amicus actions are an extension of our advocacy on behalf of principles rooted in policy guides. The committee continues today in this tradition and, in fact, is more active than ever.

APA has filed amicus briefs in a wide array of cases. They have proven influential, with numerous citations in judicial opinions, including several direct references in U.S. Supreme Court decisions. The committee, which is appointed by the APA president, reviews cases under consideration in state and federal appellate courts. Most often, APA briefs focus on issues of local planning authority and regulatory takings. In recent years, APA has filed briefs in a number of cases dealing with religious land use, billboard controls, and regulation of adult businesses. This year was particularly active with APA filing a record five amicus briefs before the U.S. Supreme Court. Because the amicus effort is centered on legal principles, not simply the facts of an individual case, the committee by tradition has not participated in cases at the trial court level.

Often APA members or chapters bring cases to the attention of this Committee. The Amicus Committee works closely with the Legislative and Policy Committee and the Planning and Law Division. As a matter of process, the committee carefully reviews each potential case. Once a decision is made to participate, the committee identifies an attorney willing to draft an amicus brief. The nation's leading legal experts on planning and land-use law write APA's briefs pro bono. Often, APA amicus briefs are joined by other state and national organizations that share our values and opinions on a given case. The Amicus Committee and staff carefully vet draft briefs before filing and review relevant policy guides to assure consistency. State court briefs also are provided to chapters for review and comment.

The current chair of APA's Amicus Committee is Patricia E. Salkin, Associate Dean and Director of the Government Law Center at Albany Law School. Copies of briefs, case overviews, and court decisions in selected cases are available online.

Often, APA amicus briefs are joined by other state and national organizations that share our values and opinions on a given case. The Amicus Committee and staff carefully vet draft briefs before filing and review relevant policy guides to assure consistency.

Your membership in APA gives you access to the tools and services of our policy program. You have the opportunity to be involved in shaping APA policy. Your voice, vision, and values are at the core of our policy positions and legislative process.

Get Involved

Member involvement strengthens APA's policy advocacy. Members are encouraged to participate in developing policy guides, drafting legislative priorities, and advocating for good planning. There are a variety of ways to increase your participation in our policy process. Every chapter has a legislative liaison that guides state level advocacy and coordinates with APA national on federal issues. Contact your chapter's liaison (see www.planning.org/advocacy/network.htm for a list)to learn more about state issues and how you can be part of your chapter's review of policy guides and priorities. Subscribe to the free e-newsletter, *From Washington, available at* www.planning.org/fromwashington/index.htm. Join APA's grassroots network, the Planners Legislative Action Network at www.planning.org/legislation/plan.htm and get all the latest alerts, updates, and analysis on policy issues. PLAN is free to members and a great way to make your voice heard with the people you elect to represent your interests on Capitol Hill and at the statehouse.

Of course, the most basic guidance for our association is found in our Articles of Incorporation, which begin:

> The association is organized exclusively for charitable, educational, literary and scientific research purposes to advance the art and science of planning and the activity of planning — physical, economic and social — at the local, regional, state and national levels; the objective of the Association is to encourage planning that will contribute to public well-being by developing communities and environments that meet more effectively the needs of people and of society.

I encourage you to consider our articles, policy guides, priorities, and amicus briefs. They all are available online. These, admittedly, provide a rather comprehensive view. If you have questions about APA policy or want to get involved by serving on a committee, working on a policy guide, or commenting on policy material, contact us at govtaffairs@planning.org.

Advocacy of the policies and programs essential to good planning is a major part of APA's mission. Your membership in APA gives you access to the tools and services of our policy program. You have the opportunity to be involved in shaping APA policy. Your voice, vision, and values are at the core of our policy positions and legislative process. Together we can make a difference for our nation's communities.█

CHAPTER 2

Lingle v. Chevron

[125 S. Ct. 2074 (May 23, 2005)]

[*This overview is reprinted from the August 2005 issue of* Zoning Practice, *which was written by Lora Lucero, editor of* Planning and Environmental Law.]

On May 23, the U.S. Supreme Court said, "Today we correct course." In the *Lingle* decision, written by Justice Sandra Day O'Connor and joined by all the other Justices, the Supreme Court jettisoned the "substantially advances" test that made its way into regulatory takings law a quarter century ago in *Agins v. City of Tiburon*, 447 U.S. 255 (1980). In the process, they provided much-needed clarity in takings jurisprudence.

THE FACTS

The controversy arose in Hawaii when that state's legislature passed Act 257 in June 1997. Among other things, the statute limits the amount of rent an oil company may charge a lessee-dealer to 15 percent of the dealer's gross profits from gasoline sales. Chevron U.S.A. Inc. was the largest refiner and marketer of gasoline in Hawaii at the time, controlling 60 percent of the market for gasoline produced or refined in state and 30 percent of the wholesale market on the island of Oahu. The legislature was concerned about the effects of this market concentration on retail gasoline prices and thought the rent cap would help.

Chevron U.S.A. Inc. sued the state, claiming that Act 257 effected an unconstitutional regulatory taking because it did not substantially advance a legitimate governmental purpose. Hawaii responded that Chevron was using the wrong test. The "substantially advances" test is a due process test, the state argued, not a takings test. The substantially advances test requires the court to take a closer look at the legislation passed by local and state governments—a higher level of scrutiny than the more deferential rational basis test the courts use when they review regulatory takings claims.

After a trial with a battle of economists (one for the state and one for Chevron), the trial court and the Ninth Circuit Court of Appeals concluded that Chevron was right. Act 257 did not substantially advance any legitimate state interest. Hawaii asked the U.S. Supreme Court to review the decision.

AS ARGUED BY APA

Although it was not a typical land-use case, APA filed an amicus brief, drafted by Professor Tom Roberts of Wake Forest Law School and Ed Sullivan of Garvey Schubert Barer in Portland, Oregon, because of the importance of the outcome on future regulatory takings cases. APA urged the Court to jettison the "substantially advances" test in regulatory takings cases:

> The adoption of legislation, particularly at the local government level, aided by the planning process, involves the participation of all segments of the community working to define the public interest. Allowing judges to second-guess legislation will undermine the public's role in the democratic process. Intermediate judicial scrutiny is neither needed nor justified to protect those who are well represented in legislative halls.

THE COURT'S DECISION

Justice O'Connor acknowledged that "the language the Court selected [in the *Agins* opinion] was regrettably imprecise." The "substantially advances" test, she said, asks whether a regulation of private property is effective in achieving some legitimate public purpose:

> An inquiry of this nature has some logic in the context of a due process challenge, for a regulation that fails to serve any legitimate governmental objective may be so arbitrary or irrational that it runs afoul of the Due Process Clause. . . . But such a test is not a valid method of discerning whether private property has been "taken" for purposes of the Fifth Amendment. . . . Instead of addressing a challenged regulation's effect on private property, the "substantially advances" inquiry probes the regulation's underlying validity.

By removing the "substantially advances" test as a valid method of identifying regulatory takings, courts will not be second-guessing the wisdom of the legislation enacted by state legislatures and city councils. One wonders if we will see more due process challenges now, with the elimination of the "substantially advances" test in takings cases.

By removing the "substantially advances" test as a valid method of identifying regulatory takings, courts will not be second-guessing the wisdom of the legislation enacted by state legislatures and city councils.

Justice O'Connor's *Lingle* opinion is a must-read for planners and follows. Although the decision will likely have a greater impact on the work of land-use attorneys, planners will find that the decision changes the dynamics between applicants and zoning boards, perhaps taking some of the steam out of frivolous threats to file a regulatory takings claim against the city.

THE CASE SYLLABUS

Concerned about the effects of market concentration on retail gasoline prices, the Hawaii Legislature passed Act 257, which limits the rent oil companies may charge dealers leasing company-owned service stations. Respondent Chevron U. S. A. Inc., then one of the largest oil companies in Hawaii, brought this suit seeking a declaration that the rent cap effected an unconstitutional taking of its property and an injunction against application of the cap to its stations. Applying *Agins* v. *City of Tiburon*, 447 U.S. 255, 260—where this Court declared that government regulation of private property "effects a taking if [it] does not substantially advance legitimate state interests"—the District Court held that the rent cap effects an uncompensated taking in violation of the Fifth and Fourteenth Amendments because it does not substantially advance Hawaii's asserted interest in controlling retail gas prices. The Ninth Circuit affirmed.

The "substantially advances" formula is not a valid method of identifying compensable regulatory takings. It prescribes an inquiry in the nature of a due process test, which has no proper place in the Court's takings jurisprudence.

Held: Agins' **"substantially advance[s]" formula is not an appropriate test for determining whether a regulation effects a Fifth Amendment taking. Pp. 6–19.**

(a) The paradigmatic taking requiring just compensation is a direct government appropriation or physical invasion of private property. See, *e.g.*, *United States* v. *Pewee Coal Co.*, 341 U.S. 114. Beginning with *Pennsylvania Coal Co.* v. *Mahon*, 260 U.S. 393, however, the Court recognized that government regulation of private property may be so onerous that its effect is tantamount to a direct appropriation or ouster. Regulatory actions generally will be deemed *per se* takings for Fifth Amendment purposes (1) where government requires an owner to suffer a permanent physical invasion of her property, see *Loretto* v. *Teleprompter Manhattan CATV Corp.*, 458 U.S. 419, or (2) where regulations completely deprive an owner of *"all* economically beneficial us[e]" of her property, *Lucas* v. *South Carolina Coastal Council*, 505 U.S. 1003, 1019. Outside these two categories (and the special context of land-use exactions discussed below), regulatory takings challenges are governed by *Penn Central Transportation Co.* v. *New York City*, 438 U.S. 104, 124. *Penn Central* identified several factors—including the regulation's economic impact on the claimant, the extent to which it interferes with distinct investment-backed expectations, and the character of the government action—that are particularly significant in determining whether a regulation effects a taking. Because the three inquiries reflected in *Loretto*, *Lucas*, and *Penn Central* all aim to identify regulatory actions that are functionally equivalent to a direct appropriation of or ouster from private property, each of them focuses upon the severity of the burden that government imposes upon property rights. Pp. 6–10.

(b) The "substantially advances" formula is not a valid method of identifying compensable regulatory takings. It prescribes an inquiry in the nature of a due process test, which has no proper place in the Court's takings jurisprudence. The formula unquestionably was derived from due process precedents, since *Agins* supported it with citations to *Nectow* v. *Cambridge*, 277 U.S. 183, 185, and *Village of Euclid* v. *Ambler Realty Co.*, 272 U.S. 365, 395. Although *Agins'* reliance on those precedents is understandable when

The "substantially advances" inquiry reveals nothing about the magnitude or character of the burden a particular regulation imposes upon private property rights or how any regulatory burden is distributed among property owners.

viewed in historical context, the language the Court selected was imprecise. It suggests a means-ends test, asking, in essence, whether a regulation of private property is *effective* in achieving some legitimate public purpose. Such an inquiry is not a valid method of discerning whether private property has been "taken" for Fifth Amendment purposes. In stark contrast to the three regulatory takings tests discussed above, the "substantially advances" inquiry reveals nothing about the *magnitude or character of the burden* a particular regulation imposes upon private property rights or how any regulatory burden is *distributed* among property owners. Thus, this test does not help to identify those regulations whose effects are functionally comparable to government appropriation or invasion of private property; it is tethered neither to the text of the Takings Clause nor to the basic justification for allowing regulatory actions to be challenged under the Clause. Moreover, the *Agins* formula's application as a takings test would present serious practical difficulties. Reading it to demand heightened means-ends review of virtually all regulation of private property would require courts to scrutinize the efficacy of a vast array of state and federal regulations—a task for which they are not well suited. It would also empower—and might often require—courts to substitute their predictive judgments for those of elected legislatures and expert agencies. Pp. 10–15.

(c) The Court's holding here does not require it to disturb any of its prior holdings. Although it applied a "substantially advances" inquiry in *Agins* itself, see 447 U.S., at 261–262, and arguably in *Keystone Bituminous Coal Assn.* v. *DeBenedictis*, 480 U.S. 470, 485–492, it has never found a compensable taking based on such an inquiry. Moreover, in most of the cases reciting the *Agins* formula, the Court has merely assumed its validity when referring to it in dicta. See, *e.g., Tahoe-Sierra Preservation Council, Inc.* v. *Tahoe Regional Planning Agency*, 535 U.S. 302, 334. Although *Nollan* v. *California Coastal Commission*, 483 U.S. 825, 834, and *Dolan* v. *City of Tigard*, 512 U.S. 374, 385, drew upon *Agins'* language, the rule those cases established is entirely distinct from the "substantially advances" test: They involved a special application of the "doctrine of unconstitutional conditions," which provides that the government may not require a person to give up the constitutional right to receive just compensation when property is taken for a public use in exchange for a discretionary benefit that has little or no relationship to the property. *Ibid.* Pp. 16–18.

(d) A plaintiff seeking to challenge a government regulation as an uncompensated taking of private property may proceed by alleging a "physical" taking, a *Lucas*-type total regulatory taking, a *Penn Central* taking, or a land-use exaction violating the *Nollan* and *Dolan* standards. Because Chevron argued only a "substantially advances" theory, it was not entitled to summary judgment on its takings claim. Pp. 18–19.
363 F.3d 846, reversed and remanded.

O'Connor, J., delivered the opinion for a unanimous Court. Kennedy, J., filed a concurring opinion.

OPINION OF THE SUPREME COURT

Justice O'Connor delivered the opinion of the Court.

On occasion, a would-be doctrinal rule or test finds its way into our case law through simple repetition of a phrase—however fortuitously coined. A quarter century ago, in *Agins* v. *City of Tiburon*, 447 U.S. 255 (1980), the Court declared that government regulation of private property "effects a taking if [such regulation] does not substantially advance legitimate state interests ... ." *Id.*, at 260. Through reiteration in a half dozen or so decisions since *Agins*, this language has been ensconced in our Fifth Amendment takings jurisprudence. See *Monterey* v. *Del Monte Dunes at Monterey, Ltd.*, 526 U.S. 687, 704 (1999) (citing cases).

In the case before us, the lower courts applied *Agins*' "substantially advances" formula to strike down a Hawaii statute that limits the rent that oil companies may charge to dealers who lease service stations owned by the companies. The lower courts held that the rent cap effects an uncompensated taking of private property in violation of the Fifth and Fourteenth Amendments because it does not substantially advance Hawaii's asserted interest in controlling retail gasoline prices. This case requires us to decide whether the "substantially advances" formula announced in *Agins* is an appropriate test for determining whether a regulation effects a Fifth Amendment taking. We conclude that it is not.

This case requires us to decide whether the "substantially advances" formula announced in Agins is an appropriate test for determining whether a regulation effects a Fifth Amendment taking. We conclude that it is not.

I

The State of Hawaii, whose territory comprises an archipelago of 132 islands clustered in the midst of the Pacific Ocean, is located over 1,600 miles from the U.S. mainland and ranks among the least populous of the 50 States. Because of Hawaii's small size and geographic isolation, its wholesale market for oil products is highly concentrated. When this lawsuit began in 1997, only two refineries and six gasoline wholesalers were doing business in the State. As of that time, respondent Chevron U. S. A. Inc. was the largest refiner and marketer of gasoline in Hawaii: It controlled 60 percent of the market for gasoline produced or refined in-state and 30 percent of the wholesale market on the State's most populous island, Oahu.

Gasoline is sold at retail in Hawaii from about 300 different service stations. About half of these stations are leased from oil companies by independent lessee-dealers, another 75 or so are owned and operated by "open" dealers, and the remainder are owned and operated by the oil companies. Chevron sells most of its product through 64 independent lessee-dealer stations. In a typical lessee-dealer arrangement, Chevron buys or leases land from a third party, builds a service station, and then leases the station to a dealer on a turnkey basis. Chevron charges the lessee-dealer a monthly rent, defined as a percentage of the dealer's margin on retail sales of gasoline and other goods. In addition, Chevron requires the lessee-dealer to enter into a supply contract, under which the dealer agrees to purchase from Chevron whatever is necessary to satisfy demand at the station for Chevron's product. Chevron unilaterally sets the wholesale price of its product.

The Hawaii Legislature enacted Act 257 in June 1997, apparently in response to concerns about the effects of market concentration on retail gasoline prices. See 1997 Haw. Sess. Laws no. 257, Section 1. The statute seeks to protect independent dealers by imposing certain restrictions on the ownership and leasing of service stations by oil companies. It prohibits oil companies from converting existing lessee-dealer stations to company-operated stations and from locating new company-operated stations in close proximity to existing dealer-operated stations. Haw. Rev. Stat. Sections 486H–10.4(a), (b) (1998 Cum. Supp.). More importantly for present purposes, Act 257 limits the amount of rent that an oil company may charge a lessee-dealer to 15 percent of the dealer's gross profits from gasoline sales plus 15 percent of gross sales of products other than gasoline. Section 486H–10.4(c).

Thirty days after Act 257's enactment, Chevron sued the Governor and Attorney General of Hawaii in their official capacities (collectively Hawaii) in the United States District Court for the District of Hawaii, raising several federal constitutional challenges to the statute. As pertinent here, Chevron claimed that the statute's rent cap provision, on its face, effected a taking of Chevron's property in violation of the Fifth and Fourteenth Amendments. Chevron sought a declaration to this effect as well as an injunction against the application of the rent cap to its stations. Chevron swiftly moved for summary judgment on its takings claim, arguing that the rent cap does not substantially advance any legitimate government interest. Hawaii filed a cross-motion for summary judgment on all of Chevron's claims.

To facilitate resolution of the summary judgment motions, the parties jointly stipulated to certain relevant facts. They agreed that Act 257 reduces by about $207,000 per year the aggregate rent that Chevron would otherwise charge on 11 of its 64 lessee-dealer stations. On the other hand, the statute allows Chevron to collect more rent than it would otherwise charge at its remaining 53 lessee-dealer stations, such that Chevron could increase its overall rental income from all 64 stations by nearly $1.1 million per year. The parties further stipulated that, over the past 20 years, Chevron has not fully recovered the costs of maintaining lessee-dealer stations in any State through rent alone. Rather, the company recoups its expenses through a combination of rent and product sales. Finally, the joint stipulation states that Chevron has earned in the past, and anticipates that it will continue to earn under Act 257, a return on its investment in lessee-dealer stations in Hawaii that satisfies any constitutional standard.

The District Court granted summary judgment to Chevron, holding that "Act 257 fails to substantially advance a legitimate state interest, and as such, effects an unconstitutional taking in violation of the Fifth and Fourteenth Amendments." *Chevron U.S. A. Inc.* v. *Cayetano*, 57 F. Supp. 2d 1003, 1014 (1998). The District Court accepted Hawaii's argument that the rent cap was intended to prevent concentration of the retail gasoline market—and, more importantly, resultant high prices for consumers—by maintaining the viability of independent lessee-dealers. *Id.*, at 1009–1010. The court concluded that the statute would not substantially advance this interest, however, because it would not actually reduce lessee-dealers' costs or retail prices. It found that the rent cap would allow incumbent lessee-dealers, upon transferring occupancy rights to a new lessee, to charge the incoming lessee a premium reflecting the value of the rent reduction. Accordingly, the District Court reasoned, the incoming lessee's overall expenses would be the same as in the absence of the rent cap, so there would be no savings to pass along to consumers. *Id.*, at 1010–1012. Nor would incumbent lessees benefit from the rent cap, the court found, because the oil company lessors would unilaterally raise wholesale fuel prices in order to offset the reduction in their rental income. *Id.*, at 1012–1014.

On appeal, a divided panel of the Court of Appeals for the Ninth Circuit held that the District Court had applied the correct legal standard to Chevron's takings claim. *Chevron U.S. A. Inc.* v. *Cayetano*, 224 F.3d 1030, 1033–1037 (2000). The Court of Appeals vacated the grant of summary judgment, however, on the ground that a genuine issue of material fact remained as to whether the Act would benefit consumers. *Id.*, at 1037–1042. Judge William Fletcher concurred in the judgment, maintaining that the "reasonableness" standard applicable to "ordinary rent and price control laws" should instead govern Chevron's claim. *Id.*, at 1048.

On remand, the District Court entered judgment for Chevron after a one-day bench trial in which Chevron and Hawaii called competing expert witnesses (both economists) to testify. 198 F. Supp. 2d 1182 (2002). Finding Chevron's expert witness to be "more persuasive" than the State's expert, the District Court once again concluded that oil companies would raise wholesale gasoline prices to offset any rent reduction required by Act 257, and that the result would be an increase in retail gasoline prices. *Id.*, at 1187–1189. Even if the rent cap did reduce lessee-dealers' costs, the court found, they would not pass on any savings to consumers. *Id.*, at 1189. The court went on to reiterate its determination that Act 257 would enable incumbent lessee-dealers to sell their leaseholds at a premium, such that incoming lessees would not obtain any of the benefits of the rent cap. *Id.*, at 1189–1190. And while it acknowledged that the rent cap could preclude oil companies from constructively evicting dealers through excessive rents, the court found no evidence that Chevron or any other oil company would attempt to charge such rents in the absence of the cap. *Id.*, at 1191. Finally, the court concluded that Act 257 would in fact decrease the number of lessee-dealer stations because the rent cap would discourage oil companies from building such stations. *Id.*, at 1191–1192. Based on these findings, the District Court held that "Act 257 effect[ed] an unconstitutional regulatory taking given its failure to substantially advance any legitimate state interest." *Id.*, at 1193.

The Ninth Circuit affirmed, holding that its decision in the prior appeal barred Hawaii from challenging the application of the "substantially advances" test to Chevron's takings claim or from arguing for a more deferential standard of review. 363 F.3d 846, 849–855 (2004). The panel majority went on to reject Hawaii's challenge to the application of the standard to the facts of the case. *Id.*, at 855–858. Judge Fletcher dissented, renewing his contention that Act 257 should not be reviewed under the "substantially advances" standard. *Id.*, at 859–861. We granted certiorari, 543 U.S. ___ (2004), and now reverse.

II

A

The Takings Clause of the Fifth Amendment, made applicable to the States through the Fourteenth, see *Chicago, B. & Q. R. Co.* v. *Chicago*, 166 U.S. 226 (1897), provides that private property shall not "be taken for public use, without just compensation." As its text makes plain, the Takings Clause "does not prohibit the taking of private property, but instead places a condition on the exercise of that power." *First English Evangelical Lutheran Church of Glendale* v. *County of Los Angeles*, 482 U.S. 304, 314 (1987). In other words, it "is designed not to limit the governmental interference with property rights *per se*, but rather to secure *compensation* in the event of otherwise proper interference amounting to a taking." *Id.*, at 315 (emphasis in original). While scholars have offered various justifications for this regime, we have emphasized its role in "bar[ring] Government from forcing some people alone to bear public burdens which, in all fairness and justice, should be borne by the public as a whole." *Armstrong* v. *United States*, 364 U.S. 40, 49 (1960); see also *Monongahela Nav. Co.* v. *United States*, 148 U.S. 312, 325 (1893).

The paradigmatic taking requiring just compensation is a direct government appropriation or physical invasion of private property. See, *e.g.*, *United States* v. *Pewee Coal Co.*, 341 U.S. 114 (1951) (Government's seizure and operation of a coal mine to prevent a national strike of coal miners effected a taking); *United States* v. *General Motors Corp.*, 323 U.S. 373 (1945) (Government's occupation of private warehouse effected a taking). Indeed, until the Court's watershed decision in *Pennsylvania Coal Co.* v. *Mahon*, 260 U.S. 393 (1922), "it was generally thought that the Takings Clause reached *only* a 'direct appropriation' of property, or the functional equivalent of a 'practical ouster of [the owner's] possession.' " *Lucas* v. *South Carolina Coastal Council*, 505 U.S. 1003,

The rub, of course, has been—and remains—how to discern how far is "too far." In answering that question, we must remain cognizant that "government regulation—by definition—involves the adjustment of rights for the public good."

1014 (1992) (citations omitted and emphasis added; brackets in original); see also *id.*, at 1028, n. 15 ("[E]arly constitutional theorists did not believe the Takings Clause embraced regulations of property at all").

Beginning with *Mahon*, however, the Court recognized that government regulation of private property may, in some instances, be so onerous that its effect is tantamount to a direct appropriation or ouster—and that such "regulatory takings" may be compensable under the Fifth Amendment. In Justice Holmes' storied but cryptic formulation, "while property may be regulated to a certain extent, if regulation goes too far it will be recognized as a taking." 260 U.S., at 415. The rub, of course, has been—and remains—how to discern how far is "too far." In answering that question, we must remain cognizant that "government regulation—by definition—involves the adjustment of rights for the public good," *Andrus* v. *Allard*, 444 U.S. 51, 65 (1979), and that "Government hardly could go on if to some extent values incident to property could not be diminished without paying for every such change in the general law," *Mahon, supra*, at 413.

Our precedents stake out two categories of regulatory action that generally will be deemed *per se* takings for Fifth Amendment purposes. First, where government requires an owner to suffer a permanent physical invasion of her property—however minor—it must provide just compensation. See *Loretto* v. *Teleprompter Manhattan CATV Corp.*, 458 U.S. 419 (1982) (state law requiring landlords to permit cable companies to install cable facilities in apartment buildings effected a taking). A second categorical rule applies to regulations that completely deprive an owner of "*all* economically beneficial us[e]" of her property. *Lucas*, 505 U.S., at 1019 (emphasis in original). We held in *Lucas* that the government must pay just compensation for such "total regulatory takings," except to the extent that "background principles of nuisance and property law" independently restrict the owner's intended use of the property. *Id.*, at 1026–1032.

Outside these two relatively narrow categories (and the special context of land-use exactions discussed below, see *infra*, at 16–18), regulatory takings challenges are governed by the standards set forth in *Penn Central Transp. Co.* v. *New York City*, 438 U.S. 104 (1978). The Court in *Penn Central* acknowledged that it had hitherto been "unable to develop any 'set formula' " for evaluating regulatory takings claims, but identified "several factors that have particular significance." *Id.*, at 124. Primary among those factors are "[t]he economic impact of the regulation on the claimant and, particularly, the extent to which the regulation has interfered with distinct investment-backed expectations." *Ibid.* In addition, the "character of the governmental action"—for instance whether it amounts to a physical invasion or instead merely affects property interests through "some public program adjusting the benefits and burdens of economic life to promote the common good"—may be relevant in discerning whether a taking has occurred. *Ibid.* The *Penn Central* factors—though each has given rise to vexing subsidiary questions—have served as the principal guidelines for resolving regulatory takings claims that do not fall within the physical takings or *Lucas* rules. See, *e.g.*, *Palazzolo* v. *Rhode Island*, 533 U.S. 606, 617–618 (2001); *id.*, at 632–634 (O'Connor, J., concurring).

Although our regulatory takings jurisprudence cannot be characterized as unified, these three inquiries (reflected in *Loretto, Lucas,* and *Penn Central*) share a common touchstone. Each aims to identify regulatory actions that are functionally equivalent to the classic taking in which government directly appropriates private property or ousts the owner from his domain. Accordingly, each of these tests focuses directly upon the severity of the burden that government imposes upon private property rights. The Court has held that physical takings require compensation because of the unique burden they impose: A permanent physical invasion, however minimal the economic cost it entails, eviscerates the owner's right to exclude others from entering and using her property—perhaps the most fundamental of all property interests. See *Dolan* v. *City of Tigard*, 512 U.S. 374, 384 (1994); *Nollan* v. *California Coastal Comm'n*, 483 U.S. 825, 831–832 (1987); *Loretto, supra*, at 433; *Kaiser Aetna* v. *United States*, 444 U.S. 164, 176 (1979). In the *Lucas* context, of course, the complete elimination of a property's value is the determinative factor. See *Lucas, supra*, at 1017 (positing that "total deprivation of beneficial use is, from the landowner's point of view, the equivalent of a physical appropriation"). And the *Penn Central* inquiry turns in large part, albeit not exclusively, upon the magnitude of a regulation's economic impact and the degree to which it interferes with legitimate property interests.

B

In *Agins* v. *City of Tiburon*, a case involving a facial takings challenge to certain municipal zoning ordinances, the Court declared that "[t]he application of a general zoning law to particular property effects a taking if the ordinance does not substantially advance legitimate state interests, see *Nectow* v. *Cambridge*, 277 U.S. 183, 188 (1928), or denies an owner economically viable use of his land, see *Penn Central Transp. Co.* v. *New York City*, 438 U.S. 104, 138, n. 36 (1978)." 447 U.S., at 260. Because this statement is phrased in the disjunctive, *Agins'* "substantially advances" language has been read to announce a stand-alone regulatory takings test that is wholly independent of *Penn Central* or any other test. Indeed, the lower courts in this case struck down Hawaii's rent control statute as an "unconstitutional regulatory taking," 198 F. Supp. 2d, at 1193, based solely upon a finding that it does not substantially advance the State's asserted interest in controlling retail gasoline prices. See *supra*, at 6–7. Although a number of our takings precedents have recited the "substantially advances" formula minted in *Agins*, this is our first opportunity to consider its validity as a freestanding takings test. We conclude that this formula prescribes an inquiry in the nature of a due process, not a takings, test, and that it has no proper place in our takings jurisprudence.

There is no question that the "substantially advances" formula was derived from due process, not takings, precedents. In support of this new language, *Agins* cited *Nectow* v. *Cambridge*, 277 U.S. 183, a 1928 case in which the plaintiff claimed that a city zoning ordinance "deprived him of his property without due process of law in contravention of the Fourteenth Amendment," *id.*, at 185. *Agins* then went on to discuss *Village of Euclid* v. *Ambler Realty Co.*, 272 U.S. 365 (1926), a historic decision holding that a municipal zoning ordinance would survive a substantive due process challenge so long as it was not "clearly arbitrary and unreasonable, having no *substantial relation to the public health, safety, morals, or general welfare.*" *Id.*, at 395 (emphasis added); see also *Nectow, supra*, at 188 (quoting the same "substantial relation" language from *Euclid*).

When viewed in historical context, the Court's reliance on *Nectow* and *Euclid* is understandable. *Agins* was the Court's first case involving a challenge to zoning regulations in many decades, so it was natural to turn to these seminal zoning precedents for guidance. See Brief for United States as *Amicus Curiae* in *Agins* v. *City of Tiburon*, O. T. 1979, No. 602, pp. 12–13 (arguing that *Euclid* "set out the principles applicable to a determination of the facial validity of a zoning ordinance attacked as a violation of the Takings Clause of the Fifth Amendment"). Moreover, *Agins'* apparent commingling of due process and takings inquiries had some precedent in the Court's then-recent decision in *Penn Central*. See 438 U.S., at 127 (stating in

Although a number of our takings precedents have recited the "substantially advances" formula minted in Agins, this is our first opportunity to consider its validity as a freestanding takings test.

dicta that "[i]t is ... implicit in *Goldblatt* [v. *Hempstead*, 369 U.S. 590 (1962),] that a use restriction on real property may constitute a 'taking' if not reasonably necessary to the effectuation of a substantial public purpose, see *Nectow* v. *Cambridge, supra*"). But see *Goldblatt, supra*, at 594–595 (quoting " 'reasonably necessary' " language from *Lawton* v. *Steele*, 152 U.S. 133, 137 (1894), a due process case, and applying a deferential " 'reasonableness' " standard to determine whether a challenged regulation was a "valid exercise of the ... police power" under the Due Process Clause). Finally, when *Agins* was decided, there had been some history of referring to deprivations of property without due process of law as "takings," see, *e.g.*, *Rowan* v. *Post Office Dept.*, 397 U.S. 728, 740 (1970), and the Court had yet to clarify whether "regulatory takings" claims were properly cognizable under the Takings Clause or the Due Process Clause, see *Williamson County Regional Planning Comm'n* v. *Hamilton Bank of Jefferson City*, 473 U.S. 172, 197–199 (1985).

Although Agins' reliance on due process precedents is understandable, the language the Court selected was regrettably imprecise.

Although *Agins'* reliance on due process precedents is understandable, the language the Court selected was regrettably imprecise. The "substantially advances" formula suggests a means-ends test: It asks, in essence, whether a regulation of private property is *effective* in achieving some legitimate public purpose. An inquiry of this nature has some logic in the context of a due process challenge, for a regulation that fails to serve any legitimate governmental objective may be so arbitrary or irrational that it runs afoul of the Due Process Clause. See, *e.g.*, *County of Sacramento* v. *Lewis*, 523 U.S. 833, 846 (1998) (stating that the Due Process Clause is intended, in part, to protect the individual against "the exercise of power without any reasonable justification in the service of a legitimate governmental objective"). But such a test is not a valid method of discerning whether private property has been "taken" for purposes of the Fifth Amendment.

In stark contrast to the three regulatory takings tests discussed above, the "substantially advances" inquiry reveals nothing about the *magnitude or character of the burden* a particular regulation imposes upon private property rights. Nor does it provide any information about how any regulatory burden is *distributed* among property owners. In consequence, this test does not help to identify those regulations whose effects are functionally comparable to government appropriation or invasion of private property; it is tethered neither to the text of the Takings Clause nor to the basic justification for allowing regulatory actions to be challenged under the Clause.

Chevron appeals to the general principle that the Takings Clause is meant " 'to bar Government from forcing some people alone to bear public burdens which, in all fairness and justice, should be borne by the public as a whole.' " Brief for Respondent 17–21 (quoting *Armstrong*, 364 U.S., at 49). But that appeal is clearly misplaced, for the reasons just indicated. A test that tells us nothing about the actual burden imposed on property rights, or how that burden is allocated cannot tell us when justice might require that the burden be spread among taxpayers through the payment of compensation. The owner of a property subject to a regulation that *effectively* serves a legitimate state interest may be just as singled out and just as burdened as the owner of a property subject to an *ineffective* regulation. It would make little sense to say that the second owner has suffered a taking while the first has not. Likewise, an ineffective regulation may not significantly burden property rights at all, and it may distribute any burden broadly and evenly among property owners. The notion that such a regulation nevertheless "takes" private property for public use merely by virtue of its ineffectiveness or foolishness is untenable.

Instead of addressing a challenged regulation's effect on private property, the "substantially advances" inquiry probes the regulation's underlying validity. But such an inquiry is logically prior to and distinct from the question whether a regulation effects a taking, for the Takings Clause presupposes that the government has acted in pursuit of a valid public purpose. The Clause expressly requires compensation where government takes private property *"for public use."* It does not bar government from interfering with property rights, but rather requires compensation "in the event of *otherwise proper interference* amounting to a taking." *First English Evangelical Lutheran Church*, 482 U.S., at 315 (emphasis added). Conversely, if a government action is found to be impermissible—for instance because it fails to meet the "public use" requirement or is so arbitrary as to violate due process—that is the end of the inquiry. No amount of compensation can authorize such action.

Chevron's challenge to the Hawaii statute in this case illustrates the flaws in the "substantially advances" theory. To begin with, it is unclear how significantly Hawaii's rent cap actually burdens Chevron's property rights. The parties stipulated below that the cap would reduce Chevron's aggregate rental income on 11 of its 64 lessee-dealer stations by about $207,000 per year, but that Chevron nevertheless expects to receive a return on its investment in these stations that satisfies any constitutional standard. See *supra*, at 4. Moreover, Chevron asserted below, and the District Court found, that Chevron would recoup any reductions in its rental income by raising wholesale gasoline prices. See *supra*, at 5. In short, Chevron has not clearly argued—let alone established—that it has been singled out to bear any particularly severe regulatory burden. Rather, the gravamen of Chevron's claim is simply that Hawaii's rent cap will not actually serve the State's legitimate interest in protecting consumers against high gasoline prices. Whatever the merits of that claim, it does not sound under the Takings Clause. Chevron plainly does not seek compensation for a taking of its property for a legitimate public use, but rather an injunction against the enforcement of a regulation that it alleges to be fundamentally arbitrary and irrational.

Finally, the "substantially advances" formula is not only *doctrinally* untenable as a takings test—its application as such would also present serious practical difficulties. The *Agins* formula can be read to demand heightened means-ends review of virtually any regulation of private property. If so interpreted, it would require courts to scrutinize the efficacy of a vast array of state and federal regulations—a task for which courts are not well suited. Moreover, it would empower—and might often require—courts to substitute their predictive judgments for those of elected legislatures and expert agencies.

Although the instant case is only the tip of the proverbial iceberg, it foreshadows the hazards of placing courts in this role. To resolve Chevron's takings claim, the District Court was required to choose between the views of two opposing economists as to whether Hawaii's rent control statute would help to prevent concentration and supracompetitive prices in the State's retail gasoline market. Finding one expert to be "more persuasive" than the other, the court concluded that the Hawaii Legislature's chosen regulatory strategy would not actually achieve its objectives. See 198 F. Supp. 2d, at 1187–1193. Along the way, the court determined that the State was not entitled to enact a prophylactic rent cap without actual evidence that oil companies had charged, or would charge, excessive rents. See *id.*, at 1191. Based on these findings, the District Court enjoined further enforcement of Act 257's rent cap provision against Chevron. We find the proceedings below remarkable, to say the least, given that we have long eschewed such heightened scrutiny when addressing substantive due process challenges to government regulation. See, *e.g.*, *Exxon Corp.* v. *Governor*

Finally, the "substantially advances" formula is not only doctrinally untenable as a takings test—its application as such would also present serious practical difficulties.

of Maryland, 437 U.S. 117, 124–125 (1978); *Ferguson* v. *Skrupa*, 372 U.S. 726, 730–732 (1963). The reasons for deference to legislative judgments about the need for, and likely effectiveness of, regulatory actions are by now well established, and we think they are no less applicable here.

For the foregoing reasons, we conclude that the "substantially advances" formula announced in *Agins* is not a valid method of identifying regulatory takings for which the Fifth Amendment requires just compensation. Since Chevron argued only a "substantially advances" theory in support of its takings claim, it was not entitled to summary judgment on that claim.

III

We emphasize that our holding today—that the "substantially advances" formula is not a valid takings test—does not require us to disturb any of our prior holdings. To be sure, we applied a "substantially advances" inquiry in *Agins* itself, see 447 U.S., at 261–262 (finding that the challenged zoning ordinances "substantially advance[d] legitimate governmental goals"), and arguably also in *Keystone Bituminous Coal Assn.* v. *DeBenedictis*, 480 U.S. 470, 485–492 (1987) (quoting " 'substantially advance[s]' " language and then finding that the challenged statute was intended to further a substantial public interest). But in no case have we found a compensable taking based on such an inquiry. Indeed, in most of the cases reciting the "substantially advances" formula, the Court has merely assumed its validity when referring to it in dicta. See *Tahoe-Sierra Preservation Council, Inc.* v. *Tahoe Regional Planning Agency*, 535 U.S. 302, 334 (2002); *Del Monte Dunes*, 526 U.S., at 704; *Lucas*, 505 U.S., at 1016; *Yee* v. *Escondido*, 503 U.S. 519, 534 (1992); *United States* v. *Riverside Bayview Homes, Inc.*, 474 U.S. 121, 126 (1985).

It might be argued that this formula played a role in our decisions in *Nollan* v. *California Coastal Comm'n*, 483 U.S. 825 (1987), and *Dolan* v. *City of Tigard*, 512 U.S. 374 (1994). See Brief for Respondent 21–23. But while the Court drew upon the language of *Agins* in these cases, it did not apply the "substantially advances" test that is the subject of today's decision. Both *Nollan* and *Dolan* involved Fifth Amendment takings challenges to adjudicative land-use exactions—specifically, government demands that a landowner dedicate an easement allowing public access to her property as a condition of obtaining a development permit. See *Dolan*, *supra*, at 379–380 (permit to expand a store and parking lot conditioned on the dedication of a portion of the relevant property for a "greenway," including a bike/pedestrian path); *Nollan*, *supra*, at 828 (permit to build a larger residence on beachfront property conditioned on dedication of an easement allowing the public to traverse a strip of the property between the owner's seawall and the mean high-tide line).

In each case, the Court began with the premise that, had the government simply appropriated the easement in question, this would have been a *per se* physical taking. *Dolan*, *supra*, at 384; *Nollan*, *supra*, at 831–832. The question was whether the government could, without paying the compensation that would otherwise be required upon effecting such a taking, demand the easement as a condition for granting a development permit the government was entitled to deny. The Court in *Nolan* answered in the affirmative, provided that the exaction would substantially advance the same government interest that would furnish a valid ground for denial of the permit. 483 U.S., at 834–837. The Court further refined this requirement in *Dolan*, holding that an adjudicative exaction requiring dedication of private property must also be " 'rough[ly] proportiona[l]' . . . both in nature and extent to the impact of the proposed development." 512 U.S., at 391; see also *Del Monte Dunes*, *supra*, at 702 (emphasizing that we have not extended this standard "beyond the special context of [such] exactions").

Although *Nollan* and *Dolan* quoted *Agins'* language, see *Dolan, supra*, at 385; *Nollan, supra*, at 834, the rule those decisions established is entirely distinct from the "substantially advances" test we address today. Whereas the "substantially advances" inquiry before us now is unconcerned with the degree or type of burden a regulation places upon property, *Nollan* and *Dolan* both involved dedications of property so onerous that, outside the exactions context, they would be deemed *per se* physical takings. In neither case did the Court question whether the exaction would substantially advance *some* legitimate state interest. See *Dolan, supra*, at 387–388; *Nollan, supra*, at 841. Rather, the issue was whether the exactions substantially advanced the *same* interests that land-use authorities asserted would allow them to deny the permit altogether. As the Court explained in *Dolan*, these cases involve a special application of the "doctrine of 'unconstitutional conditions,' " which provides that "the government may not require a person to give up a constitutional right—here the right to receive just compensation when property is taken for a public use—in exchange for a discretionary benefit conferred by the government where the benefit has little or no relationship to the property." 512 U.S., at 385. That is worlds apart from a rule that says a regulation affecting property constitutes a taking on its face solely because it does not substantially advance a legitimate government interest. In short, *Nollan* and *Dolan* cannot be characterized as applying the "substantially advances" test we address today, and our decision should not be read to disturb these precedents.

· · ·

 Twenty-five years ago, the Court posited that a regulation of private property "effects a taking if [it] does not substantially advance [a] legitimate state interes[t]." *Agins, supra*, at 260. The lower courts in this case took that statement to its logical conclusion, and in so doing, revealed its imprecision. Today we correct course. We hold that the "substantially advances" formula is not a valid takings test, and indeed conclude that it has no proper place in our takings jurisprudence. In so doing, we reaffirm that a plaintiff seeking to challenge a government regulation as an uncompensated taking of private property may proceed under one of the other theories discussed above—by alleging a "physical" taking, a *Lucas*-type "total regulatory taking," a *Penn Central* taking, or a land-use exaction violating the standards set forth in *Nollan* and *Dolan*. Because Chevron argued only a "substantially advances" theory in support of its takings claim, it was not entitled to summary judgment on that claim. Accordingly, we reverse the judgment of the Ninth Circuit and remand the case for further proceedings consistent with this opinion.

It is so ordered.

TEXT OF JUSTICE KENNEDY'S CONCURRING OPINION

This separate writing is to note that today's decision does not foreclose the possibility that a regulation might be so arbitrary or irrational as to violate due process. *Eastern Enterprises* v. *Apfel*, 524 U.S. 498, 539 (1998) (Kennedy, J., concurring in judgment and dissenting in part). The failure of a regulation to accomplish a stated or obvious objective would be relevant to that inquiry. Chevron voluntarily dismissed its due process claim without prejudice, however, and we have no occasion to consider whether Act 257 of the 1997 Hawaii Session Laws "represents one of the rare instances in which even such a permissive standard has been violated." *Apfel, supra*, at 550. With these observations, I join the opinion of the Court.

Edward J. Sullivan is a principal in the firm of Garvey, Schubert, Barer in Portland, Oregon. He has edited five editions of the Oregon State Bar's Continuing Legal Education Publications on Land Use and has written numerous law review articles on land use and administrative law. Carrie Richter is an attorney with Garvey, Schubert, Barer in Portland, Oregon.

The adoption of legislation, particularly at the local government level, aided by the planning process, involves the participation of all segments of the community working to define the public interest. Allowing judges to second-guess legislation will undermine the public's role in the democratic process.

APA'S AMICUS CURIAE BRIEF

By Edward J. Sullivan and Carrie A. Richter, Garvey Schubert Barer, Portland, Oregon[1]

QUESTIONS PRESENTED

1. Whether the Just Compensation Clause authorizes a court to invalidate state economic legislation on its face and enjoin enforcement of the law on the basis that the legislation does not substantially advance a legitimate state interest, without regard to whether the challenged law diminishes the economic value or usefulness of any property.

2. Whether a court, in determining under the Just Compensation Clause whether state economic legislation substantially advances a legitimate state interest, should apply a deferential standard of review equivalent to that traditionally applied to economic legislation under the Due Process and Equal Protection Clauses, or may instead substitute its judgment for that of the legislature by determining de novo, by a preponderance of the evidence at trial, whether the legislation will be effective in achieving its goals.

SUMMARY OF ARGUMENT

Courts should not substitute their views of the wisdom or efficiency of state economic legislation under the guise of the Takings Clause.

The Takings Clause conveys a straightforward message: when government physically takes property, it must pay. Yet, no property of Respondent was physically taken by the statute.

Regulations that destroy all economic value of property also may fall within the compensation command of the Takings Clause based on the principle that such a denial is the functional equivalent of a confiscation. Yet, the statute did not deprive Respondent's property of economically viable use.

Principle does not support moving the Fourteenth Amendment's substantially advances test into the Takings Clause of the Fifth Amendment. The question of the validity of government action is not a part of the takings inquiry, and it ought not become so based on the historical confusion between due process and takings.

The adoption of legislation, particularly at the local government level, aided by the planning process, involves the participation of all segments of the community working to define the public interest. Allowing judges to second-guess legislation will undermine the public's role in the democratic process. Intermediate judicial scrutiny is neither needed nor justified to protect those who are well represented in legislative halls.

ARGUMENT

I. Whether Legislation Substantially Advances a Legitimate State Interest Is Not a Question Within the Purview of the Takings Clause

A. Neither the language nor the purpose of the Takings Clause supports the use of the substantially advances test. The Ninth Circuit's decision invalidating Hawaii's statute on the grounds that it represents unwise and ineffective legislation is wrongly based on the Takings Clause of the Fifth Amendment. The Takings Clause—"nor shall property be taken for a public use without just compensation"—on its face limits the eminent domain power, not the police power. The Court has subjected the police power to the Takings Clause, but only in cases where regulations have an economic impact that is tantamount to a confiscation of property. Except insofar as the exercise of the power of eminent domain must be for a public use, ill-advised governmental action is not within the purview the Takings Clause. As Chief Justice Rehnquist has said:

> This basic understanding of the [Fifth] Amendment makes clear that it is designed not to limit the governmental interference with property rights per se, but rather to secure compensation in the event of an otherwise proper interference amounting to a taking. First English Evangelical Lutheran Church of Glendale v. County of Los Angeles, 482 U.S. 304, 314-315 (1987).

The substantially advances test, drawn from *Agins v. City of Tiburon*, 447 U.S. 255 (1980), and used by the Ninth Circuit in the case at bar, assesses the validity of government action pursuant to the police power. This question, however, precedes the takings question. If a court finds a regulation does not substantially advance a legitimate state interest, the case is over and the regulation is invalidated. If a court finds the law does substantially advance a legitimate state interest, then the court may move to the question of whether that law has gone too far in the imposition of economic harm on a property owner and thus been converted into a taking. The substantially advances test, already answered, should not be reexamined as part of the takings inquiry.

The Court has subjected the police power to the Takings Clause, but only in cases where regulations have an economic impact that is tantamount to a confiscation of property.

The plain language of the Takings Clause cannot support a requirement that a law substantially advance a legitimate state interest. The mandate is straightforward. If government takes property for a public use, it must pay. While deciding what constitutes a "taking" or a "public use" or qualifies as "property" or suffices as "just compensation" may be difficult, they are questions that must be asked. What is not covered, and no reading, however tortured, can supply it, is whether the government is doing a good job in legislating to promote the general welfare.

While the Court "has . . . not read [the Takings Clause] literally," *Penn Central Transportation Co. v. New York City*, 438 U.S. 104, 142 (1978) (Rehnquist, J., dissenting), it has gone beyond the language of the Amendment to transmute regulations into takings in only the narrow circumstance where a regulation is the functional equivalent of a confiscation. Thus, while the operative language of the clause connotes a physical invasion or seizure, under *Pennsylvania Coal v. Mahon*, 260 U.S. 393 (1922), an otherwise valid regulation can be converted into a taking if it goes "too far." *Id.* at 415. In language perhaps more familiar to the law, such a regulation constitutes a "constructive taking" based on the reasoning that a "total deprivation of beneficial use is, from the landowner's point of view, the equivalent of a physical appropriation." *Lucas v. South Carolina Coastal Council*, 505 U.S. 1003, 1017 (1992).

In contrast to the *Agins* supposed substantially advances takings test, *Pennsylvania Coal's* regulatory takings equation is a principled interpretation of the Takings Clause. Over the years, the Court has steadfastly viewed the purpose of the Fifth Amendment's Takings Clause to prevent government from forcing one property owner "alone [to] bear public burdens which, in all fairness and justice, should be borne by the public as a whole." *Armstrong v. United States*, 364 U.S. 40, 49 (1960). For the greater good, the property owner yields the land but his loss is mitigated by the payment of compensation and the burden of paying is shared by the public by use of public funds. As explained in *Pennsylvania Coal*, the Takings Clause prevents government from "forgetting that a strong public desire to improve the public condition is not enough to warrant achieving the desire by a shorter cut than the constitutional way of paying for the change." 262 U.S. at 416.

A concern for excessive economic impact does not enter into the antecedent question of whether a law substantially advances a legitimate state interest. That question is applicable to all legislation and is grounded on the proposition that there are some things government may not do under any circumstance. The Takings Clause only comes into play where an otherwise valid measure is alleged to have gone too far and extracted too much. It is at this point that the "fairness and justice," which are the guideposts for the Takings Clause, come into play. *Tahoe-Sierra Preservation Council, Inc. v. Tahoe Regional Planning Agency*, 535 U.S. 302, 334 (2003).

B. No explanation has been forthcoming as to how the substantially advances test fits within either the language or purpose of the Takings Clause. The entry of the "substantially advance" language into the takings lexicon was either a mistake or a momentous change in takings jurisprudence that was announced without fanfare or explanation. The former is the more likely explanation. *Agins v. City of Tiburon*, 447 U.S. 255 (1980), drew the substantially advances test from *Nectow v. City of Cambridge*, 277 U.S. 183 (1928), a substantive due process case.[2] The Court in *Agins* said:

> The application of a general zoning law to particular property effects a taking if the ordinance does not substantially advance legitimate state interests, see *Nectow v. Cambridge*, . . . , or denies an owner economically viable use of his land, see *Penn Central*. . . . The determination that governmental action constitutes a taking is, in essence, a determination that the public at large, rather than a single owner, must bear the burden of an exercise of state power in the public interest. 447 U.S. at 260.

Glaringly absent from the above quoted language is an explanation that links the *Nectow* rule in the first clause of the first sentence, that a valid exercise of the police power must substantially advance a legitimate state interest, to the ultimate goal set out in the second sentence of determining whether it is fair to burden a single landowner with the cost of an otherwise valid police power measure.

No principled explanation has been offered as to how a law that does not substantially advance a legitimate state interest can be a taking within the language or purpose of the Takings Clause. On numerous occasions the Court has stated that a regulation that does not substantially advance a legitimate state interest is a taking, but as the Court observed in *City of Monterey v. Del Monte Dunes at Monterey, Ltd.*, 526 U.S. 687 (1999), it has yet to offer "a thorough explanation of the nature or applicability of the requirement that a regulation substantially advance legitimate public interests outside the context of required dedications or exactions." *Id.* at 704.[3] Lower courts have likewise failed to explain how the test fits within the Fifth Amendment. This lack of an explanation is understandable since, outside the context of physical exactions, a regulation that does not substantially advance a legitimate state interest cannot be viewed as the functional equivalent of a physical appropriation, the touchstone of the regulatory takings doctrine.

In most of the instances when the Court has ex-pressed the *Nectow* or *Agins* substantially advances language as a takings test, it has done so in dicta. On the few occasions when the Court has applied the test and said that a particular regulation is not a taking because it passes the substantially advances test, it has not only not paused to discuss why it is relevant to ask that question but in those cases, the landowner's so-called takings claim was in fact an effort to secure an invalidation of the law in question, not to seek compensation. In *Keystone Bituminous Coal Ass'n v. DeBenedictis*, 480 U.S. 470 (1987), the Court declared the Pennsylvania prohibition of mining so as to cause surface subsidence substantially advanced a state interest and then moved on to the question of economic impact. The answer to the former question was virtually a given, and, while four justices dissented, none took issue with this conclusion. The serious question of

On numerous occasions the Court has stated that a regulation that does not substantially advance a legitimate state interest is a taking, but . . . it has yet to offer "a thorough explanation of the nature or applicability of the requirement that a regulation substantially advance legitimate public interests outside the context of required dedications or exactions."

the case for the majority and the dissent was whether the statute went too far in the economic harm it imposed on owners of the mineral estates.

In *Del Monte Dunes*, the Court upheld the trial judge's decision to allow the jury to determine the city's takings' liability, which included ascertaining whether the city's permit denials substantially advanced the stated purposes of its regulations. Since the city itself had proposed the jury instructions that included the *Agins* question, the Court "decline[d] the suggestions of amici" to address the issue. 526 U.S. at 704. These uses of the substantially advances test hardly constitute endorsements of the test since its application was not contested in *Keystone* and was assumed in *Del Monte Dunes*.

It is not a strong endorsement of *Agins* as a takings test to say that the courts have repeated it often. Yet, no other reason is forthcoming. Repeated inconsequential reiterations should not be used to knowingly validate a test that stems from an erroneous reading of authority and cannot be tied to the language or purposes of the Takings Clause. Merely wishing to have intermediate scrutiny applied to regulations of property is also insufficient.

C. The historical confusion between due process and regulatory takings led to the mistaken application of the substantially advances test of the former into the latter. Confusion has been a constant companion of the regulatory takings doctrine. This confusion can be traced to the doctrine's origins, which is usually said to have been the 1922 *Pennsylvania Coal v. Mahon* decision. 260 U.S. 393 (1922). With the advantage of hindsight we can look back and say that the regulatory takings doctrine originated in the 1922 *Pennsylvania Coal* decision, but at the time the decision was handed down it was not clear that anything new had been done. When the Court spoke of regulations as takings in *Pennsylvania Coal*, it was difficult to distinguish that idea from then prevailing views of substantive due process.[4]

In the latter part of the nineteenth century and early twentieth century, the jurisprudence of the Court was that the validity of a police power regulation depended on whether the measure promoted the public interest by a means reasonably necessary to accomplish the purpose and was "not unduly oppressive upon individuals." *Lawton v. Steele*, 152 U.S. 133, 137 (1894). *Pennsylvania Coal*'s holding that otherwise valid regulations that went "too far" were takings in effect restated the *Lawton* due process "unduly onerous" test. The result has been a confusion of tongues and minds, as courts have spoken of "due process takings." *See Williamson County Regional Planning Commission v. Hamilton Bank of Johnson City*, 473 U.S. 172, 199 (1985); *GJR Investments, Inc. v. County of Es-cambia*, 132 F.3d 1359, 1364 (11th Cir. 1998).

Certain features of the *Pennsylvania Coal* opinion caused or aided this confusion. The state by definition must be a party to a takings claim yet the case was between private parties. The Takings Clause has a self-executing compensation remedy, but invalidation, not compensation, was the remedy awarded. In other words what happened in the case duplicates what would have happened had the Court not mentioned the Takings Clause and relied instead on the Fourteenth Amendment's Due Process Clause. So great was the confusion that it was not known for decades whether the remedy from a regulatory taking was a Fourteenth Amendment declaration of invalidity coupled with an injunction or a Fifth Amendment taking requiring the assessment of compensation due. The historically accurate reading is merely an academic point today.[5] But, the fact of the confusion is of great importance because it goes to the heart of the error made by the Ninth Circuit in this case.

The confusion created by *Pennsylvania Coal* between due process and takings concerned the excessive impact of a regulation, not whether the

It is not a strong endorsement of Agins *as a takings test to say that the courts have repeated it often. Yet, no other reason is forthcoming.*

regulation substantially advanced a legitimate state interest. For Justice Holmes the legitimacy of the action was a given:

We assume, of course, that the statute was passed upon the conviction that an exigency existed that would warrant it, and we assume that an exigency exists that would warrant the exercise of eminent domain. But the question at bottom is upon whom the loss of the changes desired should fall. *Pennsylvania Coal*, 260 U.S. at 416.

The confusion, instead, dealt with the third "unduly onerous" prong, which came to be confused with the "too far" test. Consequently, some courts viewed *Pennsylvania Coal* as a due process case, believing that Justice Holmes spoke merely "symbolically" in using takings language or as this Court said in *Williamson County*, he may have spoken "loosely." 472 U.S. at 198.

In *Goldblatt v. Town of Hempstead*, 369 U.S. 590 (1962), the Court distinguished between takings and due process. The Court there held that a ban on excavation as applied to a sand and gravel business was not a taking because there was no showing of a reduction in the value of the property. *Id.* at 594. After reaching this conclusion, the Court looked at the validity of the ban, concluding that it did substantially advance a legitimate state interest. In reaching this conclusion this Court did not mention the Takings Clause but the Court did rely on the leading substantive due process case of *Lawton v. Steele*, 152 U.S. 155 (1894). *Goldblatt*, 369 U.S. at 594. Despite *Goldblatt*, the confusion reemerged in *Agins*.

First English Evangelical Lutheran Church of Glendale v. County of Los Angeles, 482 U.S. 304 (1987), partially resolved the confusion by settling the debate as to whether claims of excessive economic impact were action-able under the Takings Clause. The Court there held that regulations that went "too far," or, put another way, were excessive in their impact upon the affected property owner, were real, as opposed to symbolic, takings. Thus, a judicial finding of a taking by regulation triggered the "self-executing compensation remedy" of the Takings Clause. *First English, Id.* at 315.

A lingering question as to claims of severe economic impact from regulations is whether the Takings Clause is the exclusive home to such claims. The question is answered by the doctrine that where there is an explicit textual source in the constitution it must be used to determine liability rather than generalized notions of substantive due process. *See Graham v. Connor*, 490 U.S. 386 (1989) (claims of excessive force during arrest must be brought under the Fourth Amendment) and *Whitley v. Albers*, 475 U.S. 312 (1986) (injuries suffered in a prison riot must be heard under the Eighth Amendment). Though the Fifth Amendment is not an explicit textual source for compensation from excessive regulations, the reasoning of *Graham* and *Whitely*, as well as *Pennsylvania Coal* and *First English* call for application of the rule.

While this Court has not specifically addressed whether the Fifth Amendment Takings Clause qualifies as sufficiently explicit under the *Graham-Whitley* doctrine, the functional equivalence of regulatory takings to physical appropriations should yield that conclusion. And several circuit courts have so held. *See Banks v. City of Whitehall*, 344 F.3d 550 (6th Cir. 2003); *John v. City of Houston*, 214 F.3d 573, 583-583 (5th Cir. 2000). There is no merit in having two independent yet virtually identical causes of actions. Thus, allegations of excessive economic impact should be exclusively within the province of the Fifth Amendment's Takings Clause. But, that does not mean that allegations of arbitrary legislation likewise should be subsumed by the Takings Clause. *See* Julian C. Juergensmeyer and Thomas E. Roberts, Land Use Planning and Development Regulation Law Section 10.12 C (Thom-son-West 2003).

While the *Graham-Whitely* issue is not directly before the Court in this case, it is important to recognize its relevance to clarifying the distinction between regulatory takings and due process. The thrust of those cases, along with *Penn-*

sylvania Coal and *First English,* is that at the most the Due Process Clause can provide a check on the validity of legislation, while the Takings Clause deals with the question of whether otherwise valid government actions either confiscate or effectively confiscate property so as to become takings.

The strand of confusion that remains is the one in this case and it is of more recent origin, dating back only to the 1980 *Agins* case. The Court can remove that confusion in this case by applying the principled standard of the Takings Clause that has heretofore guided its decisions: The Fifth Amendment regulatory takings claim assumes the legitimacy of the regulation but demands that where the effect of the regulation is so great that it is the functional equivalent of a physical appropriation the landowner must be compensated.[6]

D. Nollan's essential nexus test applies to physical exactions, and is not dependent on the substantially advances test. In *Nollan v. California Coastal Commission*, 483 U.S. 825 (1987), the Court applied the "substantially advances" test in the context of a physical exaction. The Court purportedly used the *Agins* test to find a taking but, though superficially applicable to the facts of the case, the *Agins* formulation was irrelevant to the holding reached in the case. In *Nollan,* when the owners of a beachfront lot sought permission to build a larger house, the state coastal commission conditioned the permit on the granting of an easement to allow the public to walk along the beachfront side of the lot. The Court had no quarrel with the legitimacy of the state-asserted interests (to protect the public's ability to see the beach from the street, to prevent congestion on the beach, and to overcome psychological barriers to the use of the beach resulting from increased shoreline development), but the Court was not convinced that the required lateral access easement along the beach front would promote them.

While this Court in *Nollan* found that the interests asserted by the state would not have been substantially advanced by the easement sought, the Court's concern was the state's justification for singling out the Nollans to contribute land for the public use, which the Court found wanting. The lack of a sufficient nexus between what the Nollans proposed to do and what the state was asking in return led the Court to conclude that the state's problems were not of the Nollans' making. If California wanted an easement, the Court said it would have to pay for it. This was the heart of the opinion. What was important was not whether the law substantially advanced a legitimate state interest but whether the government was attempting to force the property owners "alone bear public burdens which, in all fairness and justice, should be borne by the public as a whole." *Armstrong v. United States,* 364 U.S. 40, 49 (1960).

Although the regulation at issue in *Nollan* did not substantially advance a legitimate state interest, the question did not need to be asked in order to decide whether a taking had occurred. While the means and ends did not link up in *Nollan,* imagine what would have happened had the state "come clean" so to speak, and simply admitted that it wanted the easement to aid public passage on the beach. Obtaining an easement unquestionably would have substantially advanced a legitimate state interest, and thus not run afoul of the *Agins* test. No one, however, would contend that it therefore was not a taking. Yet, that is where *Agins* leads.

Nollan does not deal with issues of regulatory takings but rather establishes the essential nexus test for physical exactions. When the state conditions development permission on a landowner dedicating property to public use it may do so without paying compensation only if the dedicated land is "reasonably necessary," *Nollan,* 483 U.S. at 834, to prevent or counteract anticipated public effects of the landowner's actions. The only difficulty with *Nollan* is that asking the wrong question runs the risk of unfair results in that it does not answer the question of who should bear the burden in question. The corrective step needed is to recognize that the use of the word "substantially" was unnecessary to the essential nexus test. A land exaction may be required because of its use or because of its location. While acquiring the land by either method substantially advances a legitimate interest, compulsory dedication should only be imposed on those whose use is related to the interest the state is promoting. Those who own land the state happens to need but who are not contributors to or involved in the project or program that creates the need should be compensated.

In *Dolan v. City of Tigard*, 512 U.S. 374 (1994), the Court added a rough proportionality requirement to physical exactions. In *Dolan*, the Court remanded a case to the state court requiring the city to show that its demand for land for a greenway and pedestrian pathway was roughly proportional to the new burdens that would be placed on the city by the landowner's increased development.

The *Nollan* and *Dolan* requirements, that government carry the burden of justifying the need for exacting land, are based directly on the language of the Takings Clause. Physical takings of land must be compensated unless the state can show that the exaction is a legitimate condition of development permission. Planners have incorporated these rules into the planning process. A year after the *Dolan* decision, *Amicus* American Planning Association incorporated the principle of fact-based decision making in its 1995 Policy Guide on Takings.[7] The Policy Guide advises planners to establish a sound basis for land use and environmental regulations through comprehensive planning and background studies. The Policy Guide states that "a thoughtful comprehensive plan or program that sets forth overall community goals and objectives and which establishes a rational basis for land use regulations helps lay the foundation for a strong defense against any takings claim." *Id.*

II. The Invalidation Remedy That Necessarily Follows From a Finding That a Law Does Not Substantially Advance a Legitimate State Interest Contradicts the Express, Self-Executing Compensation Remedy of the Takings Clause

The Ninth Circuit's invalidation of Hawaii's law turns a blind eye to the self-executing compensation remedy of the Takings Clause and thereby reveals the *Agins* masquerade. In *First English Evangelical Lutheran Church v. County of Los Angeles*, 482 U.S. 304 (1987), the Court held that the remedy for a regulatory taking, as with a physical taking, is compensation. As discussed above in Part I. C., this decision ended the debate as to whether the *Pennsylvania Coal* decision spoke merely symbolically of excessive regulations as takings by concluding that it did not. A regulatory taking was a true, not a symbolic, taking, insofar as the self-executing compensation remedy is concerned. 482 U.S. at 315. As Justice Kennedy has explained:

> The [Takings] Clause operates as a conditional limitation, permitting the government to do what it wants so long as it pays the charge. The Clause presupposes what the government intends to do is otherwise constitutional. *Eastern Enterprises v. Apfel*, 524 U.S. 498, 545 (1998) (concurring in the judgment and dissenting in part).

An act that does not substantially advance a legitimate state interest as required by the federal constitution is void, *Nectow v. City of Cambridge*, 277 U.S. 183 (1928), and a void act cannot be a taking. Allowing an ordinance found to not substantially advance legitimate state interests to remain in effect by treating it as an exercise of the power of eminent domain is not constitutionally permissible. Yet, the plain meaning of the *Agins* formula coupled with the express mandate of the Fifth Amendment means that an ordinance that does not substantially advance a legitimate state interest can remain in force if compensation is paid.

Numerous courts have made the point that where an ordinance is invalidated as an improper exercise of the police power, any loss sustained for the period the ordinance applied to the property is not a compensable exercise of the power of eminent domain. *Pheasant Bridge Corp. v. Township of Warren*, 169 N.J. 282, 777 A.2d 334, 343 (2001), *cert. denied*, 535 U.S. 1077 (2002), *Sea Cabins on Ocean IV Homeowners Ass'n, Inc. v. City of North Myrtle Beach*, 345 S.C. 418, 548 S.E.2d 595, 604 (2001), *Miller & Son Paving, Inc. v. Plumstead Twp.*, 717 A.2d 483 (Pa.1998), *cert. denied*, 525 U.S. 1121 (1999), *Landgate, Inc. v. California Coastal Commission*, 17 Cal.4th 1006, 953 P.2d 1188, 1195, 73 Cal.Rptr.2d 841, 848, *cert. denied*, 525 U.S. 876 (1998). *See also Board Machine, Inc. v. U.S.*, 49 Fed.Ct. 325, 328 (2001) (unauthorized action of government official not within the pur view of the takings clause). *See generally* John D. Echeverria, Taking and Errors, 51 Ala.L.Rev. 1047 (2000).

Since the exercise of the power of eminent domain requires legitimate government action, a judicial finding of illegal or unauthorized action precludes the constitutional trigger of compensation. Even if the period of time from application to declaration of invalidity were viewed as a taking for a public use, that would not end the inquiry. A second analysis would follow under the *Penn Central* factors to determine whether a taking had occurred.

While retrospective monetary relief could be labeled compensation for a temporary taking, characterizing a monetary award for the past effects of a law found invalid for failing to substantially advance a legitimate state interest as a taking means that the government took property by an illegal act. Since an award of just compensation "presupposes what the government intends to do is otherwise constitutional," *Eastern Enterprises*, 524 U.S. 498, 545 (1998) (Kennedy, J., concurring in the judgment and dissenting in part), awarding compensation for some-thing the government did unconstitutionally is a constitutional impossibility.

Despite the Fifth Amendment's self-executing compensation remedy for a taking, *First English*, 482 U.S. at 315, the Court has recognized that an exception must be made in the unusual situation where monetary relief would be ineffective. For example, in *Eastern Enterprises v. Apfel*, 524 U.S. 498 (1998), coal companies sued to escape having to pay money into a retirement fund for miners. Finding the act to impose retroactive liability and constitute a taking, it made no sense to have the coal company comply with the law by paying money into the fund (and thus complete the taking) only to turn around and order the fund to give the money back to the coal company as compensation. But, as Justice Kennedy pointed out in his concurrence, this feature itself suggested that the takings clause was inapposite. 524 U.S. at 540.

Invalidation is the exception, not the rule. Asking that invalidation be recognized as a commonplace remedy for a taking reveals the flawed basis of the Respondent's argument.

III. Incorporating the Substantially Advances Test Into the Takings Clause In Order To Apply Intermediate Scrutiny To Judge the Wisdom and Efficacy of Government Regulation Undermines the Legislative Process and Compromises Orderly planning

A. The legislative and planning processes followed across the country, particularly at the local level, are the epitome of participatory democracy and deserve to be accorded substantial deference by the Court. The planning and legislative processes that local governments use to consider, formulate, and adopt regulations are by their very nature participatory. Property owners, special interest groups, and members of the general public

The legislative and planning processes followed across the country, particularly at the local level, are the epitome of participatory democracy and deserve to be accorded substantial deference by the Court.

Judicial second-guessing destroys the public effort that the planning process embodies.

have ample opportunity to make their views known before elected officials adopt policies that will govern community affairs. If members of the public disagree with decisions made they have an opportunity to seek relief through the legislative or administrative appeals processes. In many states, they can engage in direct lawmaking by use of the initiative or referendum. And, they have the power at the polls to turn out of office those they believe have not served them well.

The appropriate way to promote the public's involvement in the development of state and local laws and regulations is through a democratic process that allows for public debate and deliberation based on studies designed to evaluate alternative approaches to achieving community objectives. The process may be time-consuming but democracy often is. For example, this Court recognized the importance of the decision making process in *Tahoe-Sierra Preservation Council, Inc. v. Tahoe Regional Planning Agency,* 535 U.S. 302 (2002), observing that the moratorium imposed by the regional agency allowed it "to obtain the benefit of comments and criticisms from interested parties, such as the petitioners, during its deliberations." 535 U.S. at 340. The district court in *Tahoe-Sierra* noted the complexity of the planning task, and found the agency had acted reasonably and in good faith, and did not waste time in enacting a new plan. 34 F. Supp. 2d 1226, 1250 (D. Nev. 1999). Courts should defer to the legislative judgments that flow from this process.

Involving the public in formulating legislation through public review and comments are concepts that are integral to the planning process. The Code of Ethics of the American Institute of Certified Planners,[8] whose membership includes more than 14,000 certified professional planners, places particular emphasis on the planning profession's special responsibility to serve the public interest and to involve the public in the process of balancing among divergent interests. To the planning profession the public interest is not an abstract concept but rather a set of principles that is defined through debate and with the full participation of citizens. To that end, the planner has special obligations that include striving to provide full, clear and accurate information on planning issues to citizens and governmental decision makers. The planner's Code of Ethics requires that every effort be made "to give citizens the opportunity to have a meaningful impact on the development of plans and programs. Participation should be broad enough to include people who lack formal organization or influence."[9] Endorsing the Ninth Circuit's second-guessing of legislation would undermine the public's role in defining the public interest. And, as Judge J. Harvie Wilkinson has observed, in these times we can ill afford to do this:

> The very impersonality of global trends and national bureaucracy will leave state and local governments among the few places where a sense of civic connection with governing institutions can still be felt. J. Harvie Wilkinson, III, Chief Judge, United States Court of Appeals for the Fourth Circuit, "Is There a Distinctive Conservative Jurisprudence?" 73 U.Colo.L.Rev. 1383, 1392-93 (2002).

B. *Judicial second-guessing destroys the public effort that the planning process embodies.* Intermediate judicial scrutiny is neither needed nor justified to protect those who are well represented in legislative halls. Property owners, developers, and financial institutions, along with special interest groups such as homebuilders and realtors associations, as well as environmental organizations, all have an opportunity to speak up on how their communities should develop and grow. The economic and political influence of those wishing to develop land or to prevent land from being developed will wax and wane. One group will be strong in some communities and weak in others. Legislators who disfavor growth will be replaced by those who favor growth or vice-versa. But those who are affected, particularly property owners, have a powerful voice in what happens.

The Court recognized in *Dolan v. City of Tigard* that "cities have long engaged in the commendable task of land use planning, made necessary by increasing urbanization." 512 U.S. 374, 396 (1994). Engagement in this task calls for a process that may be messy at times and may result in laws that are imperfect in design, but those imperfections are the essence of our democratic system. To permit a judge who thinks a law is imperfect or unwise, with the stroke of a pen, to undermine this democratic process violates the fundamental mandate of our constitutional government that separates the legislative, judicial, and executive branches.

CONCLUSION
The decision of the court of appeals should be reversed.

Notes for Amicus Brief in *Chevron v. Lingle*

1. Counsel for the parties did not author this brief in whole or in part. No person or entity other than the *amicus*, its members, and its counsel made a monetary contribution to the preparation or submission of this brief. The parties have consented to the filing of *amicus* briefs.

2. While the declaration in *Agins* is commonly viewed as the source of the supposed incorporation of the Fourteenth Amendment test into the Fifth Amendment, two years earlier, the Court used "substantially advances" language in *Penn Central*.

3. Five members of the Court have expressed serious reservations about the test, see *Eastern Enterprises v. Apfel*, 524 U.S. 498 (1998) (Kennedy, J., concurring in the judgment but dissenting in part, and, Breyer, J., joined by Stevens, J., Ginsburg, J., and Souter, J., dissenting.

4. For a complete historical analysis, see Edward J. Sullivan, Emperors and Clothes: The Genealogy and Operation of the *Agins'* Tests, 33 Urb. Law. 343, 345-348 (2001). *See also* Julian C. Juergensmeyer and Thomas E. Roberts, Land Use Planning and Development Regulation Law ◊ 10.9 (Thomson-West 2003).

5. Professor James Ely notes that the Court had intimated that regulations could become takings before 1922. *See* James W. Ely, Jr., The Fuller Court and Takings Jurisprudence, 1996 J. Sup.Ct. History, voi. II at 120. Then again, Professor Brauneis notes problems with viewing *Pennsylvania Coal* itself as a takings case. *See* Robert Brauneis, The Foundation of Our "Regulatory Takings" Jurisprudence: The Myth and Meaning of Justice Holmes's Opinion in *Pennsylvania Coal v. Mahon*, 106 Yale L.J. 613 (1996).

6. Legitimacy of the exercise of eminent domain must of course be shown to meet the Public Use clause. That issue and such public use cases like *Hawai'i Housing Authority v. Midkiff*, 467 U.S. 229 (1984) and *Kelo v. City of New London*, 268 Conn. 1, 843 A.2d 500 (2004), *cert. granted*, 125 S.Ct. 27, 73 USLW 3178, 73 USLW 3204 (Sep. 28, 2004) (NO. 04-108) are different from regulatory takings actions in that they check unlawful government action rather than compensate for excessive regulation.

7. American Planning Association, Policy Guide on Takings (April 1995). http://www.planning.org/policyguides/takings.html.

8. The American Institute of Certified Planners, known as AICP, is a subsidiary institute of *amicus* American Planning Association. http://www.planning.org/aicp/

9. AICP Code of Ethics and Professional Conduct (Adopted October 1978, amended October 1991).

Simon Lazar is a J.D. candidate at Harvard Law School. Dwight H. Merriam, FAICP, is the founder and senior member of the Land Use Group at Robinson & Cole LLP and former president of the American Institute of Certified Planners.

This Agins *either/or analysis appeared to be at odds with the multifactor test set forth in* Penn Central Transportation Co. v. City of New York *just two years earlier.*

COMMENTARY AND REACTION

Ding Dong the Witch Is Dead:[1] O'Connor Drops a House on the *Agins* Takings Test

By Simon Lazar and Dwight H. Merriam, FAICP

[Reprinted from *Planning and Environmental Law,* July 2005]

Glinda (Witch of the North):
Well, I'm a little muddled. The Munchkins called me because a new witch has just dropped a house on the Wicked Witch of the East. And there's the house, and here you are, and that's all. . . .[2]

Michael M. Berger (property rights lawyer):
When it issued its recent decision in *Lingle v. Chevron U.S.A. Inc.,* the U. S. Supreme Court untangled a quarter-century-old jurisprudential knot that it confessed probably was caused by its near absence from the field of takings law since 1922. . . . The most important thing about *Lingle* for the government was that—having taken the issue into the spotlight of a Supreme Court hearing—the government didn't lose. As little exposure as the theory had received in other parts of the country before now, a Chevron win would have encouraged more such litigation elsewhere. But that's a negative win, not a positive gain.[3]

Timothy J. Dowling (government lawyer):
Just three years ago, things looked bleak and uncertain for those who defend health, safety and environmental safeguards against regulatory taking challenges under the Fifth Amendment. . . . What a difference today! Last week, the Supreme Court took another huge step toward restoring logic to regulatory takings law in *Lingle v. Chevron.* . . . In a remarkable, unanimous ruling, the Court confessed error and thoroughly repudiated the notion that the Takings Clause authorizes the judiciary to evaluate the wisdom or efficacy of government action.[4]

• • •

The so-called *Agins* test for takings emerged fully formed, like Aphrodite, the goddess of love and beauty[5], in a 1980 decision by the U.S. Supreme Court involving a five-lot residential subdivision proposal in Tiburon, California.[6] The Court held that the property owner could not prove a facial taking. In the process of sending the plaintiffs packing, the Court made a general statement about takings principles cobbled together from words and phrases out of the dust bin of old decisions: "The application of a general zoning law to particular property effects a taking if the ordinance does not substantially advance legitimate state interests . . ., or denies an owner economically viable use of his land. . . ."[7]

This formulation created a two-part disjunctive test, or at least it seemed to do so, by which a regulation or government action could be held to cause a compensable taking under the Fifth Amendment if the law or its application did not substantially advance permissible governmental objectives or if the property owner was left with no "economically viable use" of the property.

This *Agins* either/or analysis appeared to be at odds with the multifactor test set forth in *Penn Central Transportation Co. v. City of New York* just two years earlier.[8] In that decision, the Court offered up a three-part framework that has come to be called the *Penn Central* test.[9] The three factors to be considered are: economic impact on the claimant; the extent to which the regulation or decision interferes with distinct investment-backed expectations; and the character of the government's action.[10]

The *Penn Central* test is plainly a more difficult one for someone claiming a taking than the first prong of *Agins*, which only requires that the regulation or its application not substantially advance a permissible governmental interest. Property-rights advocates liked the *Agins* test and government lawyers didn't.

It is against this background that *Lingle v. Chevron* arose.[11] We address the decision in four parts, starting with the history of the case, then the litigation, next the arguments before the Court, and concluding with an analysis of the decision itself. You know the end of the story already from the title and short quotes from people imaginary and real. The *Agins* test is dead, at least as it applies to takings.[12] It remains important, however, to understand the history, arguments, and decision to discern the probable impacts on land-use litigation in the future.

Background, Including Procedural History

At the center of this litigation is Act 257, a 1997 Hawaii statute limiting the maximum rent Chevron and other oil companies may charge dealers leasing company-owned service stations. In the conventional lessee-dealer arrangement, an oil company buys or leases property from a third party, constructs a gas station, and then leases the property and the facilities to an independent dealer. The oil company and the independent dealer also generally enter into a supply contract, where the independent dealer is obligated to purchase oil exclusively from the oil company at a set price.

Act 257 specifically limits the maximum rent that an oil company may charge an independent dealer to 15 percent of the dealer's gross profit from fuel sales plus 15 percent of the dealer's other gross sales. The stated purpose of the Act is to combat Hawaii's high retail gasoline prices, which Hawaii argued was a result of its highly concentrated markets for oil and oil products. Hawaii believed that the existence of a healthy number of independent lessee-dealerships is essential to maintaining competition and reasonable retail gasoline prices. This is a belief shared by the United States Congress. In 1978, Congress passed the Petroleum Marketing Practices Act (PMPA), which bars oil companies from directly converting leased stations to company-operated stations.[13] However, the PMPA does not preclude oil companies from raising rents in order to force out lessee-dealers and there is some evidence to suggest that oil companies have engaged in such anticompetitive behavior.[14] Hawaii argued that the rent caps in Act 257 would prevent such behavior and thus help preserve a multiplicity of independent lessee-dealerships.

Hawaii and Chevron debated the issue of whether the market for gasoline in Hawaii actually is highly concentrated. What is clear is that Chevron has a great deal of influence in the Hawaii oil markets and that Hawaii has been a very profitable place for Chevron to do business. Chevron is one of only two gasoline refiners and one of only six wholesalers in the state. In 1997, the year Act 257 was passed, Chevron controlled 60 percent of the market share for gasoline produced or refined in Hawaii. According to an article in the Honolulu *Star-Bulletin*, "Chevron's profits from gasoline sales through Hawaii dealers generated almost one-quarter of the company's nationwide profits from dealer sales between 1988 and 1995."[15]

On the other hand, there is also evidence to suggest that the Hawaii retail gasoline market in not quite the "oligopoly" described by the state. At the time of trial, gasoline was sold at about 300 different service stations in Hawaii. About half of these were lessee-dealer stations and approximately another 75 were open dealers. Chevron actually only operated six of its own stations in Hawaii, while selling to 64 lessee-dealer stations and six open dealers.

The Agins *test is dead, at least as it applies to takings. It remains important, however, to understand the history, arguments, and decision to discern the probable impacts on land-use litigation in the future.*

Following the enactment of Act 257, Chevron challenged its validity, arguing that the Act effected an unconstitutional regulatory taking. Chevron did not zero in on Act 257's adverse economic impact on it and other oil companies, but instead attacked the wisdom of such legislation. Chevron argued that the challenged legislation would not accomplish its intended effect—lowering gasoline prices for consumers. Chevron said that the rent cap would actually lead to an increase in retail gasoline prices. The district court agreed and Act 257 was struck down on the basis of the "substantially advances" inquiry announced in *Agins.*

Procedural history. Chevron was successful early on in this litigation in winning its motion for summary judgment and convincing the district court to grant injunctive relief against the enforcement of Act 257 on the basis of the "substantially advances" test.[16] We told you it was an easy test! The federal trial court found that because Act 257 would not have the effect of lowering retail gasoline prices, it failed to substantially advance a legitimate state interest and thus constituted a regulatory taking.[17]

Hawaii immediately appealed this decision, challenging the standard used to evaluate Chevron's regulatory takings claim. The Ninth Circuit upheld the "substantially advances" test used by the district court, relying primarily on the Supreme Court's opinion in *Yee v. City of Escondido,*[18] and its own opinion in *Richardson v. City and County of Honolulu.*[19] "These cases teach that the application of the 'substantially advances' test is appropriate where a rent control ordinance creates the possibility that an incumbent lessee will be able to capture the value of the decreased rent in the form of a premium."[20] Nevertheless, the Ninth Circuit held that the court erred in granting summary judgment because there remained issues of material fact central to the outcome of the case. The court reversed and remanded.[21]

Before returning to the district court, Hawaii filed a petition for rehearing, asserting that Chevron's challenge to Act 257 should be analyzed under the Due Process Clause and not the Takings Clause. The Ninth Circuit rejected Hawaii's petition for rehearing and the U.S. Supreme Court subsequently denied Hawaii's petition for certiorari.

Chevron II. Chevron won again at the trial level, as all factual issues were resolved in its favor. For the second time, the district court held that Act 257 effected an uncompensated regulatory taking in violation of the Just Compensation Clause.[22] The court found that the rents charged to lessee-dealers were not the cause of high retail gasoline prices in Hawaii; that dealers would not pass along any rent reductions to consumers in the form of lower gasoline prices; and that there was no evidence that oil companies were likely to try to eliminate lessee dealers by charging excessive rent.[23] Hawaii, as expected, appealed to the Ninth Circuit.

The Ninth Circuit held that Hawaii's argument—that the district court should have analyzed Chevron's claim under a more deferential standard—was barred by the law of the case doctrine.[24] The court "explicitly addressed and rejected this argument when it was raised for the first time in Hawaii's petition for rehearing, and implicitly did so in *Chevron I* when [it] endorsed the 'substantially advances' test over the more deferential test urged by Hawaii."[25] Hawaii's remaining arguments failed as well.

Issues before the U.S. Supreme Court. The Supreme Court granted certiorari on October 12, 2004. There were two questions before the Court. Ultimately, it was only necessary for the Court to answer the first one:

1) Whether the Just Compensation Clause authorizes a court to invalidate state economic legislation on its face and enjoin enforcement of the law on the basis that the legislation does not substantially advance

a legitimate state interest, without regard to whether the challenged law diminishes the economic value or usefulness of any property.

2) Whether a court, in determining under the Just Compensation Clause whether state economic legislation substantially advances a legitimate state interest, should apply a deferential standard of review equivalent to that traditionally applied to economic legislation under the Due Process and Equal Protection Clauses, or may instead substitute its judgment for that of the legislature by determining de novo, by a preponderance of the evidence at trial, whether the legislation will be effective in achieving its goals.

These questions forced the Supreme Court to decide once and for all if the "substantially advances" test originally articulated in *Agins* was a true "regulatory takings" precedent or was simply dicta loosely parroted over the years. While Hawaii argued that the "substantially advances" test was completely at odds with the basic principles of takings jurisprudence, Chevron maintained that this inquiry has been an ingrained component of the takings doctrine since at least *Penn Central*. In their battle over *Agins*, the parties took opposing views on four main points:

1) Is a regulation's economic impact on a claimant the central and predominant focus of regulatory takings analysis?

2) Is the "substantially advances" test simply a "mistaken transposition of substantive due process into takings law"?

3) Is such an inquiry inconsistent with the understanding that the Just Compensation Clause is not meant to place substantive barriers on government appropriation of private property, but to ensure that compensation is paid when such action is taken?

4) Should economic regulation that affects private property be evaluated under a traditional rational basis review or should it receive some form of heightened scrutiny?

The Arguments Before the Court

It is about economics, not effectiveness. The petitioner, Hawaii, asserted that the central focus of regulatory takings doctrine is the economic impact of a regulation on the claimant and that the "substantially advances" inquiry is invalid because it focuses solely on the effectiveness of the government action. Hawaii pointed to *Lucas v. South Carolina Coastal Council*,[26] and *Penn Central*, both landmark regulatory takings cases, to support this proposition. In *Lucas*, the court held that a regulation effects a taking if it denies an owner "all economically viable" use of his property.[27] If a regulation does not constitute a *Lucas*-type per se taking, that is, it causes a partial, not complete, diminution in value, courts generally use the *Penn Central* three-part balancing test.

Hawaii argued that the central focus of the *Penn Central* framework is economic impact. Under *Penn Central*, a court must look at the "economic impact of the regulation on the claimant and, particularly, the extent to which the regulation has interfered with distinct investment backed expectations." The Ninth Circuit held that Act 257 constituted a taking solely on the basis of the efficiency of the legislation, despite Chevron's stipulation that it would still receive "a return that satisfies any Constitutional standards on its investment in lessee dealer stations in Hawaii."[28] Hawaii argued such "means/ends scrutiny . . . is out of place in regulatory takings doctrine."[29]

While Hawaii argued that the "substantially advances" test was completely at odds with the basic principles of takings jurisprudence, Chevron maintained that this inquiry has been an ingrained component of the takings doctrine since at least Penn Central.

Chevron disputed Hawaii's assertion that the economic impact of a regulation is the predominant factor in takings analysis. It argued that without the "substantially advances" test, private property owners will not be protected from unreasonable government action unless such regulation completely destroys their property value.[30] Chevron believed that "the 'substantially advances' test focuses on whether the government has improperly singled out individual property owners whose property is not the source of the social condition the government is seeking to address."[31] In support of its position, Chevron cited both the *Penn Central* balancing test and the "substantially advances" test articulated in *Agins*. Chevron made express reference to the portion of the *Penn Central* balancing test directing courts to consider the "character of the government action" in deciding whether a regulation constitutes a taking. Chevron argued that the "substantially advances" test actually serves to isolate the situations in which the "character of the government action" requires compensation. However, in its reply brief, Hawaii countered that such an argument is completely unfounded: "The court has never suggested . . .that the alleged illegitimacy of a government action is a relevant aspect of the 'character' of the [government] action."[32]

During oral arguments, many of the Justices appeared to side with Hawaii: At least four times, Justice Breyer questioned why the effectiveness of the regulation should affect whether a regulation is a taking:

> Let me go back to my question because I haven't heard the answer. And I'm in a world, imaginative if you like, where Hawaii passes this statute, and what we're interested in is not whether they can do it, but whether they have to pay compensation. And my question is, what in heaven's name has the goodness or badness of their reason to do with that question?[33]

Justice Souter also seemed dismissive of this argument:

> I take it on your theory. . . if the rent control ordinance said, $5 an apartment, that's the top rent, fine with you because it's extraordinarily efficient. . . . That can't be the test.[34]

Chevron complained that the "state seeks a one-way ratchet, under which the nature of the government's interests works only in the government's favor."[35] Chevron offered *Nollan*[36] and *Dolan*[37] as cases where the courts have used a means/ends inquiry to find that a regulation constitutes a taking and argued that these precedents apply to all cases in which there is a regulation affecting private property. Surprise! Hawaii argued that the analysis and holdings in these cases are only limited to cases involving exactions.

Has the court really been confused for 25 years? In its brief, Chevron offered a parade of cases that have repeated and seem to endorse the "substantially advances" inquiry as an element of their takings analysis. Hawaii countered that the Court's repeated statements, that a government regulation may effect a taking if it does not "substantially advance legitimate state interests," is a "mistaken transposition of substantive due process doctrine into takings law." According to Hawaii, *Agins* relied on *Nectow v. Cambridge*,[38] and *Village of Euclid v. Ambler Realty Co.*,[39] both due process precedents, in formulating this inquiry. With the exception of exactions cases, said the state, neither the U.S. Supreme Court nor the U.S. courts of appeals have sustained a claim under this theory in the past 25 years, including the *Agins* court. It argued that the language in *Agins* was simply dicta because the effectiveness of the government's action was not at issue there. In Hawaii's view, the "substantially advances" test merely restates the traditional inquiry into the substantive validity of a regulation under the Due Process clause.

During oral argument, the Justices took issue with Hawaii's argument that the "substantially advances" test is not really a part of takings doctrine.

Justice Scalia: Well, we've said it a lot, though, haven't we? Why do we keep on saying it?[40]

Justice Breyer: What are we supposed to do with the fact that this appears—I counted about 12 cases, I mean, where it implicitly or explicitly appears, something like it. Are we supposed to just, oh, say all those cases were wrong and—what are we supposed to do about that?[41]

Chevron dismissed the fact that *Agins* was apparently based on due process precedents without addressing exactly why this was not an important factor and further asserted that the "substantially advances" test was not dicta. It also advanced several arguments why the "substantially advances" test is not a due process inquiry. Chevron argued that the "substantially advances" test is different from a substantive due process inquiry because it does not bar a government from acting. Also, such an inquiry focuses on the singling out of individual property owners, not the general wisdom of legislation.

Is the Just Compensation Clause only about compensation? Hawaii took the position that the "substantially advances" test is also inconsistent with takings jurisprudence because the Just Compensation Clause is not meant to place substantive barriers on government appropriation of private property, but to ensure that just compensation is paid when the government takes such action. It cited *First English Evangelical Lutheran Church of Glendale v. County of Los Angeles*,[42] a landmark Supreme Court case that held just that.

Chevron asserted, and Hawaii conceded, that there are exceptions to this general principle. The only recognized exceptions, according to Hawaii, are where it would be impossible for a government to remedy the alleged taking through payment of compensation and in situations where "government mandate[s] that one private party pay out funds to another private party, [such that] a suit may be brought under the Just Compensation Clause to prevent an enforcement of such obligation." The gas station rent control law was outside these narrow exceptions, according to the state.

By Chevron's reckoning, the remedies available under the "substantially advances" test are no different than the remedies available when any uncompensated taking is found. Finding that a regulation fails this inquiry does not preclude government action, said Chevron, but only requires that compensation be paid. In its reply brief, Hawaii pointed out that Chevron had not mentioned compensation until its brief to the Supreme Court and had sought only declaratory and injunctive relief in its complaint. The Ninth Circuit, said Hawaii, has "repeatedly affirmed that, unlike normal takings claims, claims under the substantially advances theory give rise to injunctive relief."[43] Chevron saw compensation as an alternative for a government facing an injunction. During oral arguments, at least two Justices were surprised that Chevron was arguing that this was an issue of compensation.

Mr. Stewart: We—we believe, Your Honor, that it is a compensation issue.

Justice Breyer: It's a compensation issue.

Justice Souter: So you want money? You want a money judgment? I thought you wanted them to stop it.[44]

Should economic regulation that affects private property receive more than traditional rational basis scrutiny? Striking down such legislation under heightened scrutiny, according to Hawaii, would be inconsistent with the great deference shown to legislatures in the economic sphere. Under the Supreme Court's current jurisprudence, economic regulations receive rational basis scrutiny. The application of the "substantially advances" test in such a manner is reminiscent of the *Lochner* era. Some readers may wish to go to this footnote for what *Lochner* is all about.[45]

Chevron refuted any connection between *Lochner* and the "substantially advances" inquiry. Chevron argued, for starters, that *Lochner* did not rely on an express constitutional provision; however, the "substantially advances" inquiry is an aspect of the Just Compensation Clause which is provided under the Bill of Rights. In addition, the oil company pressed the view that it is the character of the right, not the limitation, which determines what standard of scrutiny is appropriate. Economic regulation is not always evaluated under rational basis review when a specific constitutional right is involved. For instance, economic regulations that affect interstate commerce are evaluated under the Commerce Clause and economic regulations affecting the right to travel have been evaluated under the Privileges and Immunities Clause.

As opposed to the Due Process Clause, according to Chevron, the "substantially advances" test is limited to regulations affecting private property and does not extend to life or liberty. In its reply brief, Hawaii offered that *Lochner* fears are not unjustified, as any economic regulation potentially may be turned into a taking. Hawaii was not alone in this concern:

> **Justice Ginsburg**: "But there are so many things that you could dress up as being a taking. And—and so it seems to me that it's up to the artful pleader to say whether this is a due process excessive regulation or this is intrusive to the point where it amounts to a taking."[46]

The U.S. Supreme Court's Decision

Holding. On May 23, 2005, a unanimous Supreme Court (that means even Justice Scalia) reversed the Ninth Circuit. In a decision written by Justice O'Connor, the Court held that "the "substantially advances" formula announced in *Agins* is not a valid method of identifying regulatory takings for which the Fifth Amendment requires just compensation.[47] Although the "substantially advances" test was cited in several cases since *Agins*, the Court explained that the language selected in *Agins* was "regrettably imprecise."[48]

Development of takings doctrine. Before discussing *Agins* and the "substantially advances" test, the Court conducted a thorough examination of Fifth Amendment takings jurisprudence. The Court explains that the Takings Clause is not a prohibition against the taking of private property, but rather requires that the government provide compensation when it exercises such power. The primary rationale behind the Takings Clause, says the Court, is that the government should not force "some people alone to bear public burdens which, in all fairness and justice, should be borne by the public as a whole."[49] Until the Supreme Court's 1922 decision in *Pennsylvania Coal Co. v. Mahon*, [50] the takings doctrine was generally inapplicable to regulation of property. Rather, the Takings Clause was limited to direct government appropriations of property and the functional equivalent. However, in *Mahon*, "the Court recognizes that government regulation of private property may, in some instances, be so onerous that its effect is tantamount to a direct appropriation or ouster—and that such 'regulatory takings' may be compensable under the Fifth Amendment."[51] From the time since *Mahon*, the Court has noted that it has failed in establishing a precise formula to define the "instances" in which a regulation goes so far as to be recognized as a "regulatory taking." Courts generally look, however, to the factors set forth in *Penn Central*, in making such a determination.[52] The primary factors, as we described early on, include 1) the economic impact of the regulation on the claimant; 2) the extent to which the regulation has interfered with distinct investment-backed expectations; and 3) the character of the government action.

Outside the standard-based approach set forth in *Penn Central*, there are two areas where regulation may be considered a per se taking under the Fifth Amendment. One is when a government regulation causes a property owner to bear a "permanent physical invasion" of his or her property, such as in *Loretto v. Teleprompter Manhattan CATV Corp.*[53] *Loretto* held that a state law requiring landlords to permit cable companies to install cable facilities in their apartment buildings effected a taking even though the economic impact of the regulation was minimal and the regulation did not interfere with distinct "investment-backed expectations." The second area in which a regulation has been considered a per se taking is *Lucas*, where an owner is deprived of all "economically beneficial use" of his property.[54] *Lingle* doesn't change the law as to per se takings.

While the varying approaches to regulatory takings jurisprudence may be far from unified, Justice O'Connor convincingly articulates the "common touchstone" shared by the differing approaches, as reflected in *Penn Central*, *Loretto*, and *Lucas*.[55] "Each aims to identify regulatory actions that are functionally equivalent to the classic taking in which government directly appropriates private property or ousts the owner from his domain. Accordingly, each of these tests focuses directly upon the severity of the burden that government imposes upon private property rights."[56] The inquiries set out in both *Penn Central* and *Lucas* largely relate to the economic impact of a regulation on a private property owner. Similarly, the *Loretto* test focuses on the burden a regulation places upon an owner's property rights, specifically, the "owner's right to exclude others from entering and using her property—perhaps the most fundamental of all property interests."[57] Neither of these inquiries is grounded, at least in the first instance, on the reasonableness of the government's actions.

Agins. After its general discussion of regulatory takings doctrine, the Court addresses the *Agins* decision at length. In this discussion, Justice O'Connor acknowledges that the Court has recited the "substantially advances" inquiry several times and that it has often been read as a "stand-alone regulatory takings test that is wholly independent of Penn Central or any other test."[58] However, despite this history, Lingle holds that the "substantially advances" test "prescribes an inquiry in the nature of a due process, not a takings, test and that it has no proper place in [the Court's] takings jurisprudence."[59]

The *Lingle* decision parallels the petitioner's brief. In support of its position that the "substantially advances" test is invalid, the Court endorses almost every theory Hawaii put forward. First, it finds that the "substantially advances" inquiry was based on language from *Nectow* and *Euclid*, both due process precedents.[60] It explains that there was a "commingling of due process and taking inquiries" in the time of *Penn Central*.[61] *Lingle* appears to be the end of any such "commingling."

Next, the Court declares that a means/end test has no part in takings jurisprudence, but rather only holds logic under the Due Process Clause. It explains that the "substantially advances" inquiry reveals nothing about the magnitude or character of the burden a particular regulation imposes upon private property rights" and thus "does not help to identify those regulations whose effects are functionally comparable to a government appropriation or invasion of private property."[62] The Court also affirms that the "substantially advances" inquiry is inconsistent with Takings Doctrine because the focus of Takings Doctrine is providing compensation when private property is taken, not enjoining such action.[63] The Court rejects Chevron's claim that it brought suit in order

While the varying approaches to regulatory takings jurisprudence may be far from unified, Justice O'Connor convincingly articulates the "common touchstone" shared by the differing approaches, as reflected in Penn Central, Loretto, *and* Lucas.

to seek compensation, finding that Chevron was clearly seeking an injunction against the enforcement of a regulation. Finally, the Court finds that the level of scrutiny provided under the "substantially advances" inquiry is completely inconsistent with its prior precedents of deference to legislative judgments in the economic arena.

What Are the Implications?

Lingle does not disturb any prior Supreme Court holdings, other than *Agins*. *Nollan* and *Dolan* are special applications of the doctrine of unconstitutional conditions, which prohibits government from requiring a person to give up a constitutional right to receive a discretionary benefit where that benefit has no reasonable relationship to the property. This area of the law remains unchanged and, if anything, it is now even clearer that *Nollan* and *Dolan* are in a category unto themselves. It appears that *Nollan* and *Dolan* do not apply to impact fees or other exactions not involving physical invasions (remember that *Nollan* and *Dolan* were both cases where the government exacted an easement for public access). A physical invasion is still a per se taking and still compensable. But what about monetary exactions, such as impact fees—are these most likely to be treated as substantive due process cases?

The Court uses the term "adjudicative" when talking about the *Nollan/Dolan* exactions and we suspect this will reinforce the theory that legislative exactions that are broadly applicable and not specific to a particular parcel when enacted—such as those legislatively enacted at the local level—will be more easily defended.

We now have more clearly defined categories of what is a takings case and what is a substantive due process case. The *Penn Central* three-part test is the test for partial takings cases.[64] Permanent physical invasions and *Lucas*-type denial of all "economically viable use" regulations are still per se takings and the test is the same as always. The test for substantive due process cases is probably the widely used deferential rational or reasonable relationship test, which is a minimal threshold. The case of *Belle Terre* comes to mind.[65] There, the Court, deferring to local legislative judgment, upheld a narrow definition of family.

Higher levels of scrutiny may be applied under limited circumstances. One example is *Moore v. City of East Cleveland*, a counterpoint of sorts to *Belle Terre*, where the Court just three years later invalidated a definition of family as an "intrusive regulation of the family" when a grandmother couldn't live with her son and help raise her grandchildren.[66] Look at the seminal zoning enabling case, *Euclid v. Ambler*. The Court upheld zoning on a facial substantive due process challenge, applying a deferential rational relationship test.[67] Then, the Court said that it would use a higher standard for as-applied claims, and it did with the as-applied, single-lot case of *Nectow* two years later.[68]

Still, Justice O'Connor is clear about judicial deference to local legislative judgments and the decision seems to close the door to heightened scrutiny, but maybe—just maybe—with a site-specific, adjudicatory sort of as-applied claim . . . ?

> The *Agins* formula can be read to demand heightened means/ends review of virtually any regulation of private property. If so interpreted, it would require courts to scrutinize the efficacy of a vast array of state and federal regulations—a task for which courts are not well suited. Moreover, it would empower—and might often require—courts to substitute their predictive judgments for those of elected legislatures and expert agencies. Although the instant case is only the tip of the proverbial iceberg, it foreshadows the hazards of placing courts in this role. . . . We find the proceedings below

We now have more clearly defined categories of what is a takings case and what is a substantive due process case.

remarkable, to say the least, given that we have long eschewed such heightened scrutiny when addressing substantive due process challenges to government regulation. The reasons for deference to legislative judgments about the need for, and likely effectiveness of, regulatory actions are by now well established, and we think they are no less applicable here.[69]

We will know more about this later, especially in the Ninth Circuit, where substantive due process claims have been largely moribund since the *Agins* decision in 1980 and their forced transmogrification into takings. Plainly, we will now see more litigation of substantive due process claims. They will be married to, in most cases, a claim under the Civil Rights Act, Section 1983, for money damages and attorneys fees. We'll bet a richer, broader range of substantive due process tests will emerge.[70] Justice Kennedy penned a concurring opinion in which he says that a regulation might be so "arbitrary" and "irrational" as to violate due process.

Overall, can we now say that Justice O'Connor seems to have moved somewhat from a property rights position, to that of a swing vote, to perhaps a more government supportive position?[71] Perhaps not, after her vote in *Kelo v. New London*.[72]

One thing is certain—this is a well-reasoned and well-written decision that has an open tone and even a warm feeling to it, more like a friendly talk to an eager audience of land-use law aficionados. The basic message is—we on the Court were inartful at best; some have misinterpreted the language in *Agins*; it's not what we meant; and here is what the law is as to takings and substantive due process.

Were all appellate court decisions written like this. . . .

NOTES FOR "DING DONG, THE WITCH IS DEAD"

1. *See:* http://thewizardofoz.warnerbros.com/movie/cmp/r-lyrics.html; from the motion picture, *The Wizard of Oz*, Warner Brothers (1939).

2. *See:* http://www.un-official.com/The_Daily_Script/ms_wizoz.htm.

3. *Though No Blockbuster, 'Lingle' Disentangles Takings, Due Process*, Daily Journal. June 1, 2005. Why does this last sentence sound just a little like something Secretary of Defense Donald Rumsfeld might say? ("There are known knowns. These are things we know that we know. There are known unknowns. That is to say, there are things that we know we don't know. But there are also unknown unknowns. There are things we don't know we don't know." *Department of Defense news briefing (February. 12, 2002), see: http:// slate.msn.com/id/2081042/*

4. *High Court's Takings Decision Marks Restoration of Logic*, Daily Journal, June 1, 2005. Then again, Secretary Rumsfeld also said: "As you know, you go to war with the army you have. They're not the army you might want or wish to have at a later time."

5. Aphrodite is the daughter of Zeus and Dione (feminine form of Zeus in Greek) according to Homer (*Iliad*, Book V, 370). The poet Hesiod (Theogony, 188-198) says that the name Aphrodite is derived from aphros, or foam, from which the goddess was born. Titan Kronos castrated his father Ouranos, and then cast the severed genitals into the sea. From the foam that gathered around the member, Aphrodite emerged, fully formed. Some might argue that the *Agins* rule emerged from just as tortured circumstances. . . or that it was just as beautiful as Aphrodite. . . or as ugly as the Wicked Witch of the East. . . .

6. *Agins v. City of Tiburon*, 447 U.S. 255 (1980).

7. At 260.

8. 38 U.S. 104 (1978).

9. As the knowledgeable commentator, Homer Simpson, would say as to why it is called the Penn Central test: "D'oh." (pronounced "duh" but spelled "d'oh" in the cartoon; *see* usages including "Another common use is to suggest to someone that you are telling them something obvious, but you're telling them anyway. . . "
http://whatis.techtarget.com/definition/0,,sid9_gci212016,00.html.

10. At 124.

11. For a copy of the decision, go to http://www.supremecourtus.gov/opinions/04pdf/04-163.pdf.

12. Coroner:

> *As Coroner, I must aver*
> *I thoroughly examined her*
> *And she's not only merely dead,*
> *She's really, most sincerely dead.*

13. 15 USC Chapter 55.

14. S. Rep. No. 102-450, as 3-4, 6 (1992) (Senate Comm. on Judiciary).

15. *See* http://starbulletin.com/2003/05/08/news/story1.html.

16. Chevron U.S.A., Inc. v. Cayetano, 57 F. Supp. 2d 1003, 1014 (D. Haw., 1998).

17. *Id.*

18. *Chevron USA, Inc. v. Cayetano*, 224 F.3d 1030, 1037 (9th Cir., 2000) citing *Yee v. City of Escondido*, 503 U.S. 519, 118 L. Ed. 2d 153, 112 S. Ct. 1522 (1992).

19. *Chevron USA, Inc. v. Cayetano*, 224 F.3d 1030, 1037 (9th Cir., 2000) citing *Richardson v. City and County of Honolulu*, 124 F.3d 1150 (9th Cir. 1997), cert. denied, 525 U.S. 871, 142 L. Ed. 2d 137, 119 S. Ct. 168 (1998).

20. *Chevron USA, Inc. v. Lingle*, 363 F.3d 846, 849 (9th Cir., 2004).

21. *Chevron USA, Inc. v. Cayetano*, 224 F.3d 1030, 1042 (9th Cir., 2000).

22. *Chevron U.S.A., Inc. v. Cayetano*, 198 F. Supp. 2d 1182, 1193 (D. Haw., 2002).

23. *Id.* at 1192.

24. *Chevron USA, Inc. v. Lingle*, 363 F.3d 846, 850 (9th Cir., 2004).

25. *Id.*

26. 505 U.S. 1003, 1027 (U.S., 1992).

27. *Id.*

28. 2004 U.S. Briefs 163, 5.

29. *Id.* at 17.

30. 2004 U.S. Briefs 163, 9.

31. *Id.*

32. 2004 U.S. Briefs 163, 7.

33. Transcript of Oral Arguments at 26.

34. At 33.

35. 2004 U.S. Briefs 163, 7.

36. *Nollan v. Cal. Coastal Comm'n*, 483 U.S. 825, 834 (1987).

37. *Dolan v. City of Tigard*, 512 U.S. 374, 385 (1994).

38. 277 U.S. 183 (1928).

39. 272 U.S. 365 (1926).

40. Transcript of Oral Arguments at 6.

41. At 7.

42. 482 U.S. 304, 314 (1987).

43. 2004 U.S. Briefs 163, 11.

44. Transcript of Oral Arguments at 25.

45. For a mini-briefing on *Lochner*, *see* http://www.answers.com/topic/lochner-era. The *Lochner* era is a period in American legal history from roughly 1905 to 1937 where the United States Supreme Court made a series of judgments establishing a laissez-faire policy towards individual and group rights in favor of market self-regulation. During this period the court struck down a great deal of federal and state legislation designed to improve working conditions.

The eponymous 1905 case of *Lochner v. New York* was where the court struck down a law limiting the number of hours worked by bakers because it violated their "right to contract."

Other representative cases include *Hammer v. Dagenhart* (1918), where the court struck down legislation aimed at reducing child labor in factories where children under 14 worked; as well as *Adkins v. Children's Hospital* (1923), where the court struck down federal legislation that established a minimum wage level for women in D.C.

The era is considered to have ended with the overturning of *Adkins v. Children's Hospital* in the 1937 case of *West Coast Hotel Co. v. Parrish*.

Since that period the *Lochner* era is generally considered by both liberals and conservatives alike to be a regrettable period in U.S. jurisprudence, each for different reasons. Liberal-minded people considered it a shameful time for workers' rights and conservatives use it as an example of the inappropriate judicial activism.

"Lochnerizing" has developed into a verb used in the legal community to denote judicial activism.

46. Transcript of Oral Arguments at 41.

47. *Lingle v. Chevron U.S.A., Inc.*, 125 S. Ct. 2074 (U.S., 2005). For a copy of the opinion, *see* http://straylight.law.cornell.edu/supct/search/display.html?terms=lingle&url=/supct/html/04-163.ZO.html. Justice Scalia could see that *Agins* had to be discarded. During oral argument he asked: "I mean, so we have to eat crow no matter what we do, right?" At line 1, page 21.

48. At 25.

49. At 27; Citing *Armstrong v. United States*, 364 U.S. 40, 49, 4 L. Ed. 2d 1554, 80 S. Ct. 1563 (1960).

50. 260 U.S. 393, 67 L. Ed. 322, 43 S. Ct. 158 (2005).

51. *Id.*

52. At 8.

53. 458 U.S. 419, 73 L. Ed. 2d 868, 102 S. Ct. 3164.

54. *Lucas v. South Carolina Coastal Council*, 505 U.S. 1003, 1019, 120 L. Ed. 2d 798, 112 S. Ct. 2886.

55. At 9.

56. *Id.*

57. *Id.*

58. At 22.

59. *Id.*

60. At 4.

61. At 24.

62. At 26.

63. *At* 28.

64. Did *Lingle* alter the standards for the *Penn Central* test in any way, for example by suggesting some higher threshold for investment-backed expectations? Are invalid governmental actions now excluded from takings claims? Suppose a local legislative body enacts a hillside zoning ordinance prohibiting all development above a certain elevation, which a court later holds was not reasonably related to a permissible governmental objective under federal and state law, and little or no use remains when the law is applied to an individual's land. Is this a substantive due process case subject to invalidation or a takings case with just compensation potentially available?

65. *Village of Belle Terre v. Borass*, 416 U.S. 1 (1974).

66. *Moore v. City of East Cleveland*, 431 U.S. 494 (1977); *Also see City of Cleburne v. Cleburne Living Ctr.*, 473 U.S. 432 (U.S., 1985).

67. 272 U.S. 365 (1926).

68. 277 U.S. 183 (1928).

69. At 30-31.

70. *See* footnote 23 of Justice Brennan's dissenting opinion in *San Diego Gas & Elec. Co. v. San Diego*, 450 U.S. 621, 657 (U.S., 1981).

"A different case may arise where a police power regulation is not enacted in furtherance of the public health, safety, morals, or general welfare so that there may be no "public use." Although the government entity may not be forced to pay just compensation under the Fifth Amendment, the landowner may nevertheless have a damages cause of action under 42 U. S. C. Section 1983 for a Fourteenth Amendment due process violation."

71. Kennedy, J. Concurring Opinion, At 37.

72. *Kelo v. New London*, 545 U.S. ____ (June 23, 2005) (Dissenting Opinion, joined by Rehnquist, Scalia and Thomas). See Chapter 1 of this PAS Report for a detailed description of this case, including the text of the dissenting opinions.

LINGLE SUPREME COURT DECISION A STRONG WIN FOR PLANNERS AND LOCAL GOVERNMENTS (APA NEWS RELEASE, MAY 24, 2005)

The American Planning Association (APA) applauds the unanimous and clear opinion issued today in the U.S. Supreme Court case, Lingle v. Chevron. The court provided resounding support for the position advocated by APA and others concerned about this regulatory takings case.

In this decision, the court has rejected the "substantially advances" test, which has clouded regulatory takings cases for 25 years. Justice O'Connor, author of the decision, declared it is "not an appropriate test for determining whether a regulation effects a Fifth Amendment taking." She further stated in the opinion that, "Outside these two relatively narrow categories...[physical invasion and deprivation of all economically beneficial use...] regulatory takings challenges are governed by the standards set forth in Penn Central Transp. Co. v. New York City, 438 U.S. 104 (1978)."

The clarity of this decision is superb and it should provide the best guidance yet of what all the takings cases mean.

"This decision makes it very clear that while a regulation can be a taking, it is equally clear that the court's standard is high," said APA Executive Director, Paul Farmer, AICP.

In the case, Chevron had challenged Hawaii's legislation that "limits the rent oil companies may charge to dealers who lease service stations owned by the companies." Chevron claimed the legislation was an unconstitutional taking. Concerned about how the impacts of the decision would affect the planning profession, as well as state and local governments, APA filed an amicus brief in December 2004 urging the courts to jettison the "substantially advances test" in takings cases.

Law professor Tom Roberts, Wake Forest University Law School (Winston-Salem, North Carolina), collaborated with Edward Sullivan from Garvey Schubert Barer in Portland, Oregon, in drafting APA's amicus brief to the court.

In its amicus brief, APA argued that "[p]rinciple does not support moving the Fourteenth Amendment's substantially advances test into the Takings Clause of the Fifth Amendment. The question of the validity of governmental action is not a part of the takings inquiry, and it ought not become so based on the historical confusion between due process and takings. The adoption of legislation, particularly at the local government level, aided by the planning process, involves the participation of all segments of the community working to define the public interest. Allowing judges to second-guess legislation will undermine the public's role in the democratic process. Intermediate judicial scrutiny is neither needed nor justified to protect those who are well represented in legislative halls."

"The clarity of this decision is superb and it should provide the best guidance yet of what all the takings cases mean," said Farmer. "It's a virtual study guide to Lucas, Loretto, Dolan, Nollan, and Penn Central," Farmer stated, referring to related cases of the last 25 years. Regarding the 25-year-old Agins case, the case on which Chevron based its claim, the court said simply, "Today we correct course."

APA joined other organizations in support of the State of Hawaii, including the National Conference of State Legislatures, National Governors Association, Council of State Governments, National Association of Counties, National League of Cities, U.S. Conference of Mayors, International City/County Management Association, and International Municipal Lawyers Association.

CHAPTER 3

City of Rancho Palos Verdes v. Abrams

[125 S.Ct. 1453 (March 22, 2005)]

[*This overview is taken, in large part, from the August 2005 issue of* Zoning Practice, *which was written by Lora Lucero, editor of* Planning and Environmental Law.]

What remedies are available to a property owner if a municipality violates the Telecommunications Act of 1996 (TCA)? The Supreme Court answered this question in *Rancho Palos Verdes v. Abrams.*

Planners know that the TCA prohibits local governments from:

- unreasonably discriminating among providers of functionally equivalent services Section 332(c)(7)(B)(i)(I);

- taking actions that "prohibit or have the effect of prohibiting the provisions of personal wireless services," Section 332(c)(7)(B)(i)(II); or

- limiting the placement of wireless facilities "on the basis of the environmental effects of radio frequency emissions," Section 332(c)(7)(B)(iv).

Furthermore, local governments must:

- act on requests for authorization to locate wireless facilities "within a reasonable period of time," Section 332(c)(7)(B)(ii); and

- explain each decision denying such a request "in writing and supported by substantial evidence contained in a written record," Section 332(c)(7)(B)(iii), and "any person adversely affected by any final action or failure to act" may bring an action in court within 30 days after such action or failure to act. Section 332(c)(7)(B)(v).

Mark Abrams took the City of Rancho Palos Verdes, California, to court because the city denied him a conditional use permit for the second antenna tower he wanted to build on his residential hillside property. He successfully argued that the city had violated the TCA and the district court ordered the city to issue him a permit for the tower. When Abrams asked the court for money damages and attorneys fees pursuant to 42 U.S.C. Section 1983, the court refused because the TCA does not provide a remedy of money damages and attorneys fees.

Although Abrams won the right to build his second tower, he appealed the issue of money damages and attorneys fees to the Ninth Circuit Court of Appeals, which agreed with him, ruling that remedies from both the TCA and Section 1983 are available to successful plaintiffs. They sent the case back to the district court for a determination of money damages and attorneys fees. Then the city asked the U.S. Supreme Court to review the case.

What is 42 U.S.C. Section 1983? A person states a claim under 42 U.S.C. Section 1983 if he alleges that the defendant deprived him of a constitutional right while acting "under color" of state law. More importantly, Section 1983 provides money damages and Section 1988 provides attorneys fees to the successful litigant, which is different from the American Rule where litigants generally cover their own litigation costs.

Section 1983 was passed by Congress in 1871 but was rarely used until nearly 90 years later, when the U.S. Supreme Court gave private litigants a federal court remedy as a first resort rather than only in default of (or after) state action. [*Monroe v. Pape*, 365 U.S. 167 (1961)] Today, Section 1983 actions most commonly involve First Amendment issues like freedom of speech; Fourth Amendment issues like search and seizure or use of force; Eighth Amendment issues like cruel and unusual punishment; and Fourteenth Amendment claims of due process violations. But in this case, the Supreme Court was asked to decide whether Abrams was entitled to a Section 1983 remedy for a violation of the TCA.

AS ARGUED BY APA

APA joined many other organizations, including National League of Cities, National Association of Counties, International City/County Management Association, and others to show the Court the potentially serious impacts to local governments if property owners could claim money damages and attorneys fees for violations of the TCA:

> There are thousands of counties, municipalities, and townships in the United States, including many with few inhabitants, limited resources, and no full-time counsel. Faced with the threat of large claims for attorneys fees and damages by well-financed corporations represented by high-priced counsel, local governments may be deterred from vigorously protecting visual, aesthetic, and safety concerns. Such a result would defeat Congress's intention to allow local governments to retain "the flexibility to treat facilities that create different visual, aesthetic, or safety concerns differently to the extent permitted under generally applicable zoning requirements." H.R. Conf. Rep. No. 458, 104th Cong., 2d Sess. 208 1996.

In addition to the potential serious fiscal impacts, APA noted that the TCA provides a swift review of potential violations (30 days) while property owners would presumably have four years to bring a claim for damages under Section 1983. Congress patterned the TCA remedies after the state review mechanisms and took a deferential stance toward state and local zoning processes. APA discussed the State Zoning Enabling Act in detail to show the Court why Congress drafted the TCA the way it d*id.*

Resulting delays in obtaining final judgments—whether from a longer limitations period or slower judicial decision making—can harm local governments and the public. Such delays will slow the roll-out of personal wireless facilities and increase the adverse fiscal consequences that Section 1983 damages and Section 1988 attorneys fee liability poses to local governments.

THE COURT'S DECISION

In a unanimous decision written by Justice Antonin Scalia, the Supreme Court concluded that Congress did not intend for the judicial remedy provided by Section 332(c)(7) to coexist with an alternative remedy available in a Section 1983 action. This is a good decision for local governments and for planners because it means property owners who successfully challenge municipalities and counties on violations of the TCA can ask the court to remedy the violation and issue the permit but cannot obtain money damages and attorneys fees.

> *In addition to the potential serious fiscal impacts, APA noted that the TCA provides a swift review of potential violations (30 days) while property owners would presumably have four years to bring a claim for damages under Section 1983.*

CASE SYLLABUS

After petitioner City denied respondent Abrams permission to construct a radio tower on his property, he filed this action seeking, *inter alia*, injunctive relief under Section 332(c)(7)(B)(v) of the Communications Act of 1934, 47 U.S.C. Section 332(c)(7), as added by the Telecommunications Act of 1996 (TCA), and money damages under 42 U.S.C. Section 1983. Section 332(c)(7) imposes specific limitations on the traditional authority of state and local governments to regulate the location, construction, and modification of wireless communications facilities, and provides, in Section 332(c)(7)(B)(v), that anyone "adversely affected by any final action ... by [such] a ... government ... may ... commence an action in any court of competent jurisdiction." The District Court held that Section 332(c)(7)(B)(v) provided the exclusive remedy for the City's actions and, accordingly, ordered the City to grant respondent's application for a conditional-use permit, but refused respondent's request for damages under Section 1983. The Ninth Circuit reversed on the latter point.

Congress could not have meant the judicial remedy expressly authorized by Section 332(c)(7) to coexist with an alternative remedy available under Section 1983.

Held: **An individual may not enforce Section 332(c)(7)'s limitations on local zoning authority through a Section 1983 action. The TCA Section by providing a judicial remedy different from Section 1983 in Section 332(c)(7) itself Section precluded resort to Section 1983. Pp. 5–13.**

(a)   Even after a plaintiff demonstrates that a federal statute creates an individually enforceable right in the class of beneficiaries to which he belongs, see *Gonzaga Univ.* v. *Doe*, 536 U.S. 273, 285, the defendant may rebut the presumption that the right is enforceable under Section 1983 by, *inter alia*, showing a contrary congressional intent from the statute's creation of a "comprehensive remedial scheme that is inconsistent with individual enforcement under Section 1983," *Blessing* v. *Freestone*, 520 U.S. 329, 341. The Court's cases demonstrate that the provision of an express, private means of redress in the statute itself is ordinarily an indication that Congress did not intend to leave open a remedy under Section 1983. Pp. 5–8.

(b)   Congress could not have meant the judicial remedy expressly authorized by Section 332(c)(7) to coexist with an alternative remedy available under Section 1983, since enforcement of the former through the latter would distort the scheme of expedited judicial review and limited remedies created by Section 332(c)(7)(B)(v). The TCA adds no remedies to those available under Section 1983, and limits relief in ways that Section 1983 does not. In contrast to a Section 1983 action, TCA judicial review must be sought within 30 days after the governmental entity has taken "final action," and, once the action is filed, the court must "hear and decide" it "on an expedited basis." Section 332(c)(7)(B)(v). Moreover, unlike Section 1983 remedies, TCA remedies perhaps do not include compensatory damages, and certainly do not include attorney's fees and costs. The Court rejects Abrams's arguments for borrowing Section 332(c)(7)(B)(v)'s 30-day limitations period, rather than applying the longer statute of limitations authorized under 42 U.S.C. Section 1988 or 28 U.S.C. Section 1658 in Section 1983 actions asserting Section 332(c)(7)(B) violations. Pp. 8–12.

(c)   In concluding that Congress intended to permit plaintiffs to proceed under Section 1983, the Ninth Circuit misinterpreted the TCA's so-called "saving clause," which provides: "This Act... shall not be construed to ... impair... Federal... law." Construing Section 332(c)(7), as this Court does, to create rights that may be enforced only through the statute's express remedy, does not "impair" Section 1983 because it leaves Section 1983's pre-TCA operation entirely unaffected. Pp. 12-13.

354 F.3d 1094, reversed and remanded.

Justice Scalia delivered the opinion of the Court, in which Chief Justice Rehnquist and Justices O'Connor, Kennedy, Souter, Thomas, Ginsburg, and Breyer joined. Justice Breyer filed a concurring opinion in which Justice O'Connor, Souter, and Ginsburg joined. Justice Stevens filed an opinion concurring in the judgment.

OPINION OF THE SUPREME COURT OF THE UNITED STATES

Justice Scalia delivered the opinion of the Court.

We decide in this case whether an individual may enforce the limitations on local zoning authority set forth in Section 332(c)(7) of the Communications Act of 1934, 47 U.S.C. Section 332(c)(7), through an action under Rev. Stat. Section 1979, 42 U.S.C. Section 1983.

I

Congress enacted the Telecommunications Act of 1996 (TCA), 110 Stat. 56, to promote competition and higher quality in American telecommunications services and to "encourage the rapid deployment of new telecommunications technologies." *Ibid*. One of the means by which it sought to accomplish these goals was reduction of the impediments imposed by local governments upon the installation of facilities for wireless communications, such as antenna towers. To this end, the TCA amended the Communications Act of 1934, 48 Stat. 1064, to include Section 332(c)(7), which imposes specific limitations on the traditional authority of state and local governments to regulate the location, construction, and modification of such facilities, 110 Stat. 151, codified at 47 U.S.C. Section 332(c)(7). Under this provision, local governments may not "unreasonably discriminate among providers of functionally equivalent services," Section 332(c)(7)(B)(i)(I), take actions that "prohibit or have the effect of prohibiting the provision of personal wireless services," Section 332(c)(7)(B)(i)(II), or limit the placement of wireless facilities "on the basis of the environmental effects of radio frequency emissions," Section 332(c)(7)(B)(iv). They must act on requests for authorization to locate wireless facilities "within a reasonable period of time," Section 332(c)(7)(B)(ii), and each decision denying such a request must "be in writing and supported by substantial evidence contained in a written record," Section 332(c)(7)(B)(iii). Lastly, Section 332(c)(7)(B)(v), which is central to the present case, provides as follows:

> Any person adversely affected by any final action or failure to act by a State or local government or any instrumentality thereof that is inconsistent with this subparagraph may, within 30 days after such action or failure to act, commence an action in any court of competent jurisdiction.

Respondent Mark Abrams owns a home in a low-density, residential neighborhood in the City of Rancho Palos Verdes, California (City). His property is located at a high elevation, near the peak of the Rancho Palos Verdes Peninsula. *Rancho Palos Verdes* v. *Abrams*, 101 Cal. App. 4th 367, 371, 124 Cal. Rptr. 2d 80, 82 (2002). The record reflects that the location is both scenic and, because of its high elevation, ideal for radio transmissions. *Id.*, at 371–372, 124 Cal. Rptr. 2d, at 82–83.

In 1989, respondent obtained a permit from the City to construct a 52.5-foot antenna on his property for amateur use.[1] He installed the antenna shortly thereafter, and in the years that followed placed several smaller, tripod antennas on the property without prior permission from the City. He used the antennas both for noncommercial purposes (to provide an amateur radio service and to relay signals from other amateur radio operators) and for commercial purposes (to provide customers two-way radio communications from portable and mobile transceivers, and to repeat the signals of customers so as to enable greater range of transmission). *Ibid*.

In 1998, respondent sought permission to construct a second antenna tower. In the course of investigating that application, the City learned that respondent was using his antennas to provide a commercial service, in violation of a City ordinance requiring a "conditional-use permit" from the City Planning Commission (Commission) for commercial antenna use. See Commission Resolution No. 2000–12 ("A Resolution of the Planning Commission of the City of Rancho Palos Verdes Denying With Prejudice Conditional Use Permit No. 207 for the Proposed Commercial Use of Existing Antennae on an Existing Antenna Support Structure, Located at 44 Oceanaire Drive in the *Del Cerro* Neighborhood"), App. to Pet. for Cert. 54a. On suit by the City, Los Angeles County Superior Court enjoined re-

The court explained that the City could not rest its denial on aesthetic concerns, since the antennas in question were already in existence and would remain in place whatever the disposition of the permit application.

spondent from using the antennas for a commercial purpose. *Rancho Palos Verdes*, 101 Cal. App. 4th, at 373, 124 Cal. Rptr. 2d, at 84; App. to Pet. for Cert. 35a.

Two weeks later, in July of 1999, respondent applied to the Commission for the requisite conditional-use permit. The application drew strong opposition from several of respondent's neighbors. The Commission conducted two hearings and accepted written evidence, after which it denied the application. *Id.*, at 54a–63a. The Commission explained that granting respondent permission to operate commercially "would perpetuate . . . adverse visual impacts" from respondent's existing antennas and establish precedent for similar projects in residential areas in the future. *Id.*, at 57a. The Commission also concluded that denial of respondent's application was consistent with 47 U.S.C. Section 332(c)(7), making specific findings that its action complied with each of that provision's requirements. App. to Pet. for Cert. 61a–62a. The city council denied respondent's appeal. *Id.*, at 52a. See, generally, No. CV00–09071–SVW (RNBx) (CD Cal., Jan. 9, 2002), App. to Pet. for Cert. 22a–23a.

On August 24, 2000, respondent filed this action against the City in the District Court for the Central District of California, alleging, as relevant, that denial of the use permit violated the limitations placed on the City's zoning authority by Section 332(c)(7). In particular, respondent charged that the City's action discriminated against the mobile relay services he sought to provide, Section 332(c)(7)(B)(i)(I), effectively prohibited the provision of mobile relay services, Section 332(c)(7)(B)(i)(II), and was not supported by substantial evidence in the record, Section 332(c)(7)(B)(iii). Pet. App. 17a. Respondent sought injunctive relief under Section 332(c)(7)(B)(v), and money damages and attorney's fees under 42 U.S.C. Section 1983 and 1988. Plaintiff/Petitioner's Brief Re: Remedies and Damages, Case No. 00–09071–SVW (RNBx) (CD Cal., Feb. 25, 2002), App. to Reply Brief for Petitioners 2a-7a.

Notwithstanding Section 332(c)(7)(B)(v)'s direction that courts "hear and decide" actions "on an expedited basis," the District Court did not act on respondent's complaint until January 9, 2002, 16 months after filing; it concluded that the City's denial of a conditional-use permit was not supported by substantial evidence. App. to Pet. for Cert. 23a–26a. The court explained that the City could not rest its denial on aesthetic concerns, since the antennas in question were already in existence and would remain in place whatever the disposition of the permit application. *Id.*, at 23a–24a. Nor, the court said, could the City reasonably base its decision on the fear of setting precedent for the location of commercial antennas in residential areas, since adverse impacts from new structures would always be a basis for permit denial. *Id.*, at 25a. In light of the paucity of support for the City's action, the court concluded that denial of the permit was "an act of spite by the community." *Id.*, at 24a. In an order issued two months later, the District Court held that Section 332(c)(7)(B)(v) provided the exclusive remedy for the City's actions. Judgment of Injunction, No. CV00–09071–SVW (RNBx) (CD Cal., Mar. 18, 2002), App. to Pet. for Cert. 14a. Accordingly, it ordered the City to grant respondent's application for a conditional-use permit, but refused respondent's request for damages under Section 1983. Respondent appealed.

The Court of Appeals for the Ninth Circuit reversed on the latter point, and remanded for determination of money damages and attorney's fees. 354 F.3d 1094, 1101 (2004). We granted certiorari. 542 U.S. ___ (2004).

II

A

Title 42 U.S.C. Section 1983 provides:

> Every person who, under color of any statute, ordinance, regulation, custom, or usage, of any State or Territory . . . subjects, or causes to be subjected, any citizen of the United States or other person within the jurisdiction thereof to the deprivation of any rights, privileges, or immunities secured by the Constitution and laws, shall be liable to the party injured in an action at law, suit in equity, or other proper proceeding for redress.

In *Maine* v. *Thiboutot*, 448 U.S. 1 (1980), we held that this section "means what it says" and authorizes suits to enforce individual rights under federal statutes as well as the Constitution. *Id.*, at 4.

Our subsequent cases have made clear, however, that Section 1983 does not provide an avenue for relief every time a state actor violates a federal law. As a threshold matter, the text of Section 1983 permits the enforcement of "*rights,* not the broader or vaguer 'benefits' or 'interests.' " *Gonzaga Univ.* v. *Doe*, 536 U.S. 273, 283 (2002) (emphasis in original). Accordingly, to sustain a Section 1983 action, the plaintiff must demonstrate that the federal statute creates an individually enforceable right in the class of beneficiaries to which he belongs. See *id.*, at 285.

Even after this showing, "there is only a rebuttable presumption that the right is enforceable under Section 1983." *Blessing* v. *Freestone*, 520 U.S. 329, 341 (1997). The defendant may defeat this presumption by demonstrating that Congress did not intend that remedy for a newly created right. See *ibid.; Smith* v. *Robinson*, 468 U.S. 992, 1012 (1984). Our cases have explained that evidence of such congressional intent may be found directly in the statute creating the right, or inferred from the statute's creation of a "comprehensive enforcement scheme that is incompatible with individual enforcement under Section 1983." *Blessing, supra*, at 341.[2] See also *Middlesex County Sewerage Authority* v. *National Sea Clammers Assn.*, 453 U.S. 1, 19–20 (1981). "The crucial consideration is what Congress intended." *Smith, supra*, at 1012.

B

The City conceded below, and neither the City nor the Government as *amicus* disputes here, that Section 332(c)(7) creates individually enforceable rights; we assume, *arguendo*, that this is so. The critical question, then, is whether Congress meant the judicial remedy expressly authorized by Section 332(c)(7) to coexist with an alternative remedy available in a Section 1983 action. We conclude not.

The provision of an express, private means of redress in the statute itself is ordinarily an indication that Congress did not intend to leave open a more expansive remedy under Section 1983. As we have said in a different setting, "[t]he express provision of one method of enforcing a substantive rule suggests that Congress intended to preclude others." *Alexander* v. *Sandoval*, 532 U.S. 275, 290 (2001). Thus, the existence of a more restrictive private remedy for statutory violations has been the dividing line between those cases in which we have held that an action would lie under Section 1983 and those in which we have held that it would not.

We have found Section 1983 unavailable to remedy violations of federal statutory rights in two cases: *Sea Clammers* and *Smith*. Both of those decisions rested upon the existence of more restrictive remedies provided in the violated statute itself. See *Smith, supra*, at 1011–1012 (recognizing a Section

The provision of an express, private means of redress in the statute itself is ordinarily an indication that Congress did not intend to leave open a more expansive remedy under Section 1983.

1983 action "would . . . render superfluous most of the detailed procedural protections outlined in the statute"); *Sea Clammers, supra,* at 20 ("[W]hen a state official is alleged to have violated a federal statute which provides its own comprehensive enforcement scheme, the requirements of that enforcement procedure may not be bypassed by bringing suit directly under Section 1983" (internal quotation marks omitted)). Moreover, in *all* of the cases in which we have held that Section 1983 *is* available for violation of a federal statute, we have emphasized that the statute at issue, in contrast to those in *Sea Clammers* and *Smith, did not* provide a private judicial remedy (or, in most of the cases, even a private administrative remedy) for the rights violated. See *Blessing, supra,* at 348 ("Unlike the federal programs at issue in *[Sea Clammers and Smith],* Title IV–D contains no private remedySection either judicial or administrativeSection through which aggrieved persons can seek redress"); *Livadas* v. *Bradshaw,* 512 U.S. 107, 133–134 (1994) (there was a "complete absence of provision for relief from governmental interference" in the statute); *Golden State Transit Corp.* v. *Los Angeles,* 493 U.S. 103, 108–109 (1989) ("There is . . . no comprehensive enforcement scheme for preventing state interference with federally protected labor rights that would foreclose the Section 1983 remedy"); *Wilder* v. *Virginia Hospital Assn.,* 496 U.S. 498, 521 (1990) ("The Medicaid Act contains no . . . provision for private judicial or administrative enforcement" comparable to those in *Sea Clammers* and *Smith*); *Wright* v. *Roanoke Redevelopment and Housing Authority,* 479 U.S. 418, 427 (1987) ("In both *Sea Clammers* and *Smith* . . . , the statutes at issue themselves provided for private judicial remedies, thereby evidencing congressional intent to supplant the Section 1983 remedy. There is nothing of that kind found in the . . . Housing Act").

The Government as *amicus,* joined by the City, urges us to hold that the availability of a private judicial remedy is not merely indicative of, but conclusively establishes, a congressional intent to preclude Section 1983 relief. Brief for United States 17; Brief for Petitioners 35. We decline to do so. The ordinary inference that the remedy provided in the statute is exclusive can surely be overcome by textual indication, express or implicit, that the remedy is to complement, rather than supplant, Section 1983.

There is, however, no such indication in the TCA, which adds no remedies to those available under Section 1983, and limits relief in ways that Section 1983 does not. Judicial review of zoning decisions under Section 332(c)(7)(B)(v) must be sought within 30 days after the governmental entity has taken "final action," and, once the action is filed, the court must "hear and decide" it "on an expedited basis." Section 332(c)(7)(B)(v). The remedies available, moreover, perhaps do not include compensatory damages (the lower courts are seemingly in disagreement on this point[3]), and certainly do not include attorney's fees and costs.[4] A Section 1983 action, by contrast, can be brought much later than 30 days after the final action,[5] and need not be heard and decided on an expedited basis. And the successful plaintiff may recover not only damages but reasonable attorney's fees and costs under 42 U.S.C. Section 1988. *Thiboutot,* 448 U.S., at 9. Liability for attorney's fees would have a particularly severe impact in the Section 332(c)(7) context, making local governments liable for the (often substantial) legal expenses of large commercial interests for the misapplication of a complex and novel statutory scheme. See *Nextel Partners Inc.* v. *Kingston Township,* 286 F.3d 687, 695 (CA3 2002) (Alito, J.) ("TCA plaintiffs are often large corporations or affiliated entities, whereas TCA defendants are often small, rural municipalities"); *Primeco Personal Communications, Ltd. Partnership* v. *Mequon,* 352 F.3d 1147, 1152 (CA7 2003) (Posner, J.) (similar).

Respondent's only response to the attorney's-fees point is that it is a "policy argumen[t]," properly left to Congress. Brief for Respondent 35–36. That response assumes, however, that Congress's refusal to attach attorney's fees to the remedy that it created in the TCA does not *itself* represent a congressional choice. *Sea Clammers* and *Smith* adopt the opposite assumptionSection that limitations upon the remedy contained in the statute are deliberate and are not to be evaded through Section 1983. See *Smith*, 468 U.S., at 1011–1012, and n. 5; *Sea Clammers*, 453 U.S., at 14, 20.

Respondent disputes that a Section 1983 action to enforce Section 332(c)(7)(B) would enjoy a longer statute of limitations than an action under Section 332(c)(7)(B)(v). He argues that the rule adopted in *Wilson* v. *Garcia*, 471 U.S. 261 (1985), that Section 1983 claims are governed by the state-law statute of limitations for personal-injury torts, does not apply to Section 1983 actions to enforce statutes that themselves contain a statute of limitations; in such cases, he argues, the limitations period in the federal statute displaces the otherwise applicable state statute of limitations. This contention cannot be reconciled with our decision in *Wilson*, which expressly rejected the proposition that the limitations period for a Section 1983 claim depends on the nature of the underlying right being asserted. See *id.*, at 271–275. We concluded instead that 42 U.S.C. Section 1988 is "a directive to select, in each State, the one most appropriate statute of limitations for *all* Section 1983 claims." 471 U.S., at 275 (emphasis added); see also *Owens* v. *Okure*, 488 U.S. 235, 240–241 (1989) ("42 U.S.C. Section 1988 requires courts to borrow and apply to *all Section 1983 claims* the one most analogous state statute of limitations" (emphasis added)). We acknowledged that "a few Section 1983 claims are based on statutory rights," *Wilson, supra*, at 278, but carved out no exception for them.

Respondent also argues that, if 28 U.S.C. Section 1658 (2000 ed., Supp. II), rather than *Wilson*, applies to his Section 1983 action, see n. 4, *supra*, Section 1658's four-year statute of limitations is inapplicable. This is so, he claims, because Section 332(c)(7)(B)(v)'s requirement that actions be filed within 30 days falls within Section 1658's prefatory clause, "Except as otherwise provided by law."[6] We think not. The language of Section 332(c)(7)(B)(v) that imposes the limitations period ("within 30 days after such action or failure to act") is inextricably linked to—indeed, is embedded within—the language that creates the right of action ("may . . . commence an action in any court of competent jurisdiction"). It cannot possibly be regarded as a statute of limitations generally applicable to *any* action to enforce the rights created by Section 332(c)(7)(B). Cf. *Agency Holding Corp.* v. *Malley-Duff & Associates, Inc.*, 483 U.S. 143, 168 (1987) (Scalia, J., concurring in judgment) ("Federal statutes of limitations . . . are almost invariably tied to specific causes of action"). Respondent's argument thus reduces to a suggestion that we "borrow" Section 332(c)(7)(B)(v)'s statute of limitations and attach it to Section 1983 actions asserting violations of Section 332(c)(7)(B). Section 1658's "[e]xcept as otherwise provided by law"clause does not support this suggestion.

C

The Ninth Circuit based its conclusion that Congress intended to permit plaintiffs to proceed under Section 1983, in part, on the TCA's so-called "saving clause," TCA Section 601(c)(1), 110 Stat. 143, note following 47 U.S.C. Section 152. 354 F.3d, at 1099–1100. That provision reads as follows:

> (1) No implied effect—This Act and the amendments made by this Act shall not be construed to modify, impair, or supersede Federal, State, or local law unless expressly so provided in such Act or amendments.

The Court of Appeals took this to be an express statement of Congress's intent *not* to preclude an action under Section 1983, reasoning that to do so would be to " 'impair' " the operation of that section. 354 F.3d, at 1100.

We do not think this an apt assessment of what "impair[ment]" consists of. Construing Section 332(c)(7), as we do, to create rights that may be enforced only through the statute's express remedy, leaves the pre-TCA operation of Section 1983 entirely unaffected. Indeed, the crux of our holding is that Section 332(c)(7) has no effect on Section 1983 whatsoever: The rights Section 332(c)(7) created may not be enforced under Section 1983 and, conversely, the claims available under Section 1983 prior to the enactment of the TCA continue to be available after its enactment. The saving clause of the TCA does not require a court to go farther and permit enforcement under Section 1983 of the TCA's substantive standards. To apply to the present case what we said with regard to a different statute: "The right [Abrams] claims under [Section 332(c)(7)] did not even arguably exist before the passage of [the TCA]. The only question here, therefore, is whether the rights created by [the TCA] may be asserted within the *remedial* framework of [Section 1983]." *Great American Fed. Sav. & Loan Assn.* v. *Novotny*, 442 U.S. 366, 376–377 (1979).

This interpretation of the saving clause is consistent with *Sea Clammers*. Saving clauses attached to the statutes at issue in that case provided that the statutes should not be interpreted to " 'restrict any right which any person . . . may have under any statute or common law to seek enforcement of any . . . standard or limitation or to seek any other relief (including relief against the Administrator or a State agency).' 33 U.S.C. Section 1365(e)." 453 U.S., at 7, n. 10; see also *id.*, at 8, n. 11. We refused to read those clauses to "preserve" a Section 1983 action, holding that they did not "refer ... to a suit for redress of a violation of th[e] statutes [at issue]. . . ." *Id.*, at 20–21, n. 31.

• • •

Enforcement of Section 332(c)(7) through Section 1983 would distort the scheme of expedited judicial review and limited remedies created by Section 332(c)(7)(B)(v). We therefore hold that the TCASection by providing a judicial remedy different from Section 1983 in Section 332(c)(7) itselfSection precluded resort to Section 1983. The judgment of the Court of Appeals is reversed, and the case is remanded for further proceedings consistent with this opinion.

It is so ordered.

NOTES TO SUPREME COURT OPINION

1. The City's approval specified a maximum height of 40 feet, but, because of an administrative error, the permit itself authorized respondent to construct a tower 12.5 feet taller. 354 F.3d 1094, 1095 (CA9 2004).

2. This does not contravene the canon against implied repeal, see *Posadas* v. *National City Bank*, 296 U.S. 497, 503 (1936), because we have held that canon inapplicable to a statute that creates no rights but merely provides a civil cause of action to remedy "some otherwise defined federal right," *Great American Fed. Sav. & Loan Assn.* v. *Novotny*, 442 U.S. 366, 376 (1979) (dealing with a provision related to Section 1983, 42 U.S.C. Section 1985(3)). In such a case, "we are not faced ... with a question of implied repeal," but with whether the rights created by a later statute "may be asserted within the *remedial* framework" of the earlier one. *Great American Fed. Sav. & Loan Assn.*, 442 U.S., at 376–377.

3. Compare *Primeco Personal Communications, Ltd. Partnership* v. *Mequon*, 352 F.3d 1147, 1152–1153 (CA7 2003) (damages are presumptively available), with *Omnipoint Communications MB Operations, LLC* v. *Lincoln*, 107 F. Supp. 2d 108, 120–121 (D. Mass. 2000) ("[T]he majority of district courts ... have held that the appropriate remedy for a violation of the TCA is a mandatory injunction").

4. Absent express provision to the contrary, litigants must bear their own costs. *Alyeska Pipeline Service Co.* v. *Wilderness Society*, 421 U.S. 240, 249–250 (1975). The Communications Act of 1934 authorizes the award of attorney's fees in a number of provisions, but not in Section 332(c)(7)(B)(v). See, *e.g.*, 47 U.S.C. Section 206 325(e)(10), 551(f)(2)(C), 605(e)(3)(B)(iii).

5. The statute of limitations for a Section 1983 claim is generally the applicable state-law period for personal-injury torts. *Wilson* v. *Garcia*, 471 U.S. 261, 275, 276 (1985); see also *Owens* v. *Okure*, 488 U.S. 235, 240–241 (1989). On this basis, the applicable limitations period for respondent's Section 1983 action would presumably be one year. See *Silva* v. *Crain*, 169 F.3d 608, 610 (CA9 1999) (citing Cal. Civ. Proc. Code Ann. Section 340(3) (West 1999)). It may be, however, that this limitations period does not apply to respondent's Section 1983 claim. In 1990, Congress enacted 28 U.S.C. Section 1658(a) (2000 ed., Supp. II), which provides a 4-year, catchall limitations period applicable to "civil action[s] arising under an Act of Congress enacted after" December 1, 1990. In *Jones* v. *R. R. Donnelley & Sons Co.*, 541 U.S. 369 (2004), we held that this four-year limitations period applies to all claims "made possible by a post-1990 [congressional] enactment." *Id.*, at 382. Since the claim here rests upon violation of the post-1990 TCA, Section 1658 would seem to apply.

6. Title 28 U.S.C. Section 1658(a) provides as follows: "Except as otherwise provided by law, a civil action arising under an Act of Congress enacted after the date of the enactment of this section may not be commenced later than four years after the cause of action accrues."

JUSTICE BREYER'S CONCURRENCE

I agree with the Court. It wisely rejects the Government's proposed rule that the availability of a private judicial remedy *"conclusively establishes . . .* a congressional intent to preclude [Rev. Stat. Section 1979, 42 U.S.C.] Section 1983 relief." *Ante*, at 8 (emphasis added). The statute books are too many, federal laws too diverse, and their purposes too complex, for any legal formula to provide more than general guidance. Cf. *Gonzaga Univ.* v. *Doe*, 536 U.S. 273, 291 (2002) (Breyer, J., concurring in judgment). The Court today provides general guidance in the form of an "ordinary inference" that when Congress creates a specific judicial remedy, it does so to the exclusion of Section 1983. *Ante*, at 8. I would add that context, not just literal text, will often lead a court to Congress' intent in respect to a particular statute. Cf. *ibid.* (referring to "implicit" textual indications).

Context here, for example, makes clear that Congress saw a national problem, namely an "inconsistent and, at times, conflicting patchwork" of state and local siting requirements, which threatened "the deployment" of a national wireless communication system. H. R. Rep. No. 104–204, pt. 1, p. 94 (1995). Congress initially considered a single national solution, namely a Federal Communications Commission wireless tower siting policy that would pre-empt state and local authority. *Ibid.*; see also H. R. Conf. Rep. No. 104–458, p. 207 (1996). But Congress ultimately rejected the national approach and substituted a system based on cooperative federalism. *Id.*, at 207–208. State and local authorities would remain free to make siting decisions. They would do so, however, subject to minimum federal standards—both substantive and procedural—as well as federal judicial review.

The statute requires local zoning boards, for example, to address permit applications "within a reasonable period of time;" the boards must maintain a "written record" and give reasons for denials "in writing." 47 U.S.C. Section 332(c)(7)(B)(ii), (iii). Those "adversely affected" by "final action" of a state or local government (including their "failure to act") may obtain judicial review provided they file their review action within 30 days. Section 332(c)(7)(B)(v). The reviewing court must "hear and decide such action on an expedited basis." *Ibid.* And the court must determine, among other things, whether a zoning board's decision denying a permit is supported by "substantial evidence." Section 332(c)(7)(B)(iii).

This procedural and judicial review scheme resembles that governing many federal agency decisions. See H. R. Conf. Rep. No. 104–458, at 208 ("The phrase 'substantial evidence contained in a written record' is the traditional standard used for judicial review of agency actions"). Section 1983 suits, however, differ considerably from ordinary review of agency action. The former involve plenary judicial evaluation of asserted rights deprivations; the latter involves deferential consideration of matters within an agency's expertise. And, in my view, to permit Section 1983 actions here would undermine the compromise—between purely federal and purely local siting policies—that the statute reflects.

For these reasons, and for those set forth by the Court, I agree that Congress, in this statute, intended its judicial remedy as an exclusive remedy. In particular, Congress intended that remedy to foreclose—not to supplement—Section 1983 relief.

JUSTICE STEVENS'S CONCURRENCE

In this case the statute's text, structure, and history all provide convincing evidence that Congress intended the Telecommunications Act of 1996 (TCA) to operate as a comprehensive and exclusive remedial scheme.

When a federal statute creates a new right but fails to specify whether plaintiffs may or may not recover damages or attorney's fees, we must fill the gap in the statute's text by examining all relevant evidence that sheds light on the intent of the enacting Congress. The inquiry varies from statute to statute. Sometimes the question is whether, despite its silence, Congress intended us to recognize an implied cause of action. See, *e.g., Cannon* v. *University of Chicago*, 441 U.S. 677 (1979). Sometimes we ask whether, despite its silence, Congress intended us to enforce the pre-existing remedy provided in Rev. Stat. Section 1979, 42 U.S.C. Section 1983. See *Maine* v. *Thiboutot*, 448 U.S. 1, 4 (1980). And still other times, despite Congress' inclusion of specific clauses designed specifically to preserve pre-existing remedies, we have nevertheless concluded that Congress impliedly foreclosed the Section 1983 remedy. See *Middlesex County Sewerage Authority* v. *National Sea Clammers Assn.*, 453 U.S. 1, 13 (1981). Whenever we perform this gap-filling task, it is appropriate not only to study the text and structure of the statutory scheme, but also to examine its legislative history. See, *e.g., id.,* at 17–18; *Smith* v. *Robinson*, 468 U.S. 992, 1009 (1984); *Cannon*, 441 U.S., at 694.

In this case the statute's text, structure, and history all provide convincing evidence that Congress intended the Telecommunications Act of 1996 (TCA) to operate as a comprehensive and exclusive remedial scheme. The structure of the statute appears fundamentally incompatible with the private remedy offered by Section 1983.[1] Moreover, there is not a shred of evidence in the legislative history suggesting that, despite this structure, Congress intended plaintiffs to be able to recover damages and attorney's fees. Thus, petitioners have made "the *difficult showing* that allowing Section 1983 actions to go forward in these circumstances 'would be inconsistent with Congress' carefully tailored scheme.' " *Blessing* v. *Freestone*, 520 U.S. 329, 346 (1997) (emphasis added) (quoting *Golden State Transit Corp.* v. *Los Angeles*, 493 U.S. 103, 107 (1989)). I therefore join the judgment of the Court without reservation.

Two flaws in the Court's approach, however, persuade me to write separately. First, I do not believe that the Court has properly acknowledged the strength of our normal presumption that Congress intended to preserve, rather than preclude, the availability of Section 1983 as a remedy for the enforcement of federal statutory rights. Title 42 U.S.C. Section 1983 was "intended to provide a remedy, to be broadly construed, against all forms of official violation of federally protected rights." *Monell* v. *New York City Dept. of Social Servs.*, 436 U.S. 658, 700–701 (1978). "We do not lightly conclude that Congress intended to preclude reliance on Section 1983 as a remedy. . . . Since 1871, when it was passed by Congress, Section 1983 has stood as an independent safeguard against deprivations of federal constitutional and statutory rights." *Smith*, 468 U.S., at 1012. Although the Court is correct to point out that this presumption is rebuttable, it remains true that only an *exceptional* case—such as one involving an unusually comprehensive and exclusive statutory scheme—will lead us to conclude that a given statute impliedly forecloses a Section 1983 remedy. See *Wright* v. *Roanoke Redevelopment and Housing Authority,* 279 U.S. 418, 452 (1979) (statutory scheme must be "sufficiently comprehensive and effective to raise a clear inference that Congress intended to foreclose a Section 1983 cause of action"). While I find it easy to conclude that petitioners have met that heavy burden here, there will be many instances in which Section 1983 will be available even though Congress has not explicitly so provided in the text of the statute in question. See, *e.g., id.,* at 424–425; *Blessing,* 520 U.S., at 346–348.

Second, the Court incorrectly assumes that the legislative history of the statute is totally irrelevant. This is contrary to nearly every case we have decided in this area of law, all of which have surveyed, or at least acknowledged, the available legislative history or lack thereof. See, *e.g., Wright,* 479 U.S., at 424–426 (citing legislative history); *Smith,* 468 U.S., at 1009–1010 (same); *Sea Clammers,* 453 U.S., at 17–18 (noting that one of the relevant factors in the Court's inquiry "include[s] the legislative history"); *Cannon,* 441 U.S., at 694 (same).

Additionally, as a general matter of statutory interpretation, Congress' failure to discuss an issue during prolonged legislative deliberations may itself be probative. As The Chief Justice has cogently observed: "In a case where the construction of legislative language such as this makes so sweeping and so relatively unorthodox a change as that made here, I think judges as well as detectives may take into consideration the fact that a watchdog did not bark in the night." *Harrison* v. *PPG Industries, Inc.,* 446 U.S. 578, 602 (1980) (dissenting opinion). The Court has endorsed the view that Congress' silence on questions such as this one "can be likened to the dog that did not bark." *Chisom* v. *Roemer,* 501 U.S. 380, 396, n. 23 (1991) (citing A. Doyle, Silver Blaze, in The Complete Sherlock Holmes 335 (1927)). Congressional silence is surely probative in this case because, despite the fact that awards of damages and attorney's fees could have potentially disastrous consequences for the likely defendants in most private actions under the TCA, see *Primeco Personal Communications* v. *Mequon,* 352 F.3d 1147, 1152 (CA7 2003), nowhere in the course of Congress' lengthy deliberations is there any hint that Congress wanted damages or attorney's fees to be available. That silence reinforces every other clue that we can glean from the statute's text and structure.

For these reasons, I concur in the Court's judgment.

> *The Court incorrectly assumes that the legislative history of the statute is totally irrelevant. This is contrary to nearly every case we have decided in this area of law, all of which have surveyed, or at least acknowledged, the available legislative history or lack thereof.*

NOTE TO JUSTICE STEVENS'S CONCURRENCE

1. The evidence supporting this conclusion is substantial. It includes, *inter alia,* the fact that the private remedy specified in 47 U.S.C. Section 332(c)(7)(B)(v) requires all enforcement actions to be brought in any court of competent jurisdiction "within 30 days after such action or failure to act." Once a plaintiff brings such an action, the statute requires the court both to "hear and decide" the case "on an expedited basis." *Ibid.* As the Court properly notes, *ante,* at 9–10, the TCA's streamlined and expedited scheme for resolving telecommunication zoning disputes is fundamentally incompatible with the applicable limitations periods that generally govern Section 1983 litigation, see, *e.g., Wilson* v. *Garcia,* 471 U.S. 261 (1985), as well as the deliberate pace with which civil rights litigation generally proceeds. See, *e.g.,* H. R. Conf. Rep. No. 104–458, p. 208–209 (1996) (expressing the intent of the congressional Conference that zoning decisions should be "rendered in a reasonable period of time" and that Congress expected courts to "act expeditiously in deciding such cases" that may arise from disputed decisions). Like the Court, I am not persuaded that the statutory requirements can simply be mapped onto the existing structure of Section 1983, and there is nothing in the legislative history to suggest that Congress would have wanted us to do so. For these reasons, among others, I believe it is clear that Congress intended Section 332(c)(7) to operate as the exclusive remedy by which plaintiffs can obtain judicial relief for violations of the TCA.

Richard Ruda is Chief Counsel of the State and Local Legal Center in Washington, D.C., a position he has held since January 1991. The Legal Center files amicus briefs in support of states and local governments in the U.S. Supreme Court, conducts moot courts for attorneys arguing in the Supreme Court, and provides other assistance to states and local governments in connection with Supreme Court litigation. James I. Crowley is also an attorney with the State and Local Legal Center in Washington, D.C.

AMICUS CURIAE BRIEF

By Richard Ruda and James I. Crowley, State and Local Legal Center, Washington, D.C.

This brief was filed on behalf of The National League Of Cities, National Association Of Counties, International City/County Management Association, National Conference Of State Legislatures, Council Of State Governments, International Municipal Lawyers Association, and U.S. Conference of Mayors, joined by The National Association of Telecommunications Officers and Advisors and The American Planning Association, as Amici Curiae Supporting Petitioners

QUESTION PRESENTED
Whether the limits on state and local zoning and land-use authority established by 47 U.S.C. Section 332(c)(7)(B) can be enforced through an action for damages and attorney's fees under 42 U.S.C. Section 1983 and 1988.

INTEREST OF THE AMICI CURIAE
Amici National League of Cities, National Association of Counties, International City/County Management Association, National Conference of State Legislatures, Council of State Governments, International Municipal Lawyers Association, and U.S. Conference of Mayors are organizations whose members include state, county, and municipal governments and officials throughout the United States.[1]

Amicus National Association of Telecommunications Officers and Advisors (NATOA) has represented the telecommunications needs and interests of local governments for over 20 years. NATOA advises individuals and organizations responsible for telecommunications policies and services in local governments throughout the country.

Amicus American Planning Association (APA) is a nonprofit public interest and research organization founded in 1978 to advance the art and science of planning at the local, regional, state, and national levels. With more than 34,000 members nationwide, APA has a longstanding policy interest and involvement in the federal legislative debate concerning the Telecommunications Act to ensure that communities remain empowered to make appropriate, necessary, and citizen driven decisions about telecommunications infrastructure.

All of the amici have a compelling interest in the issue presented in this case: whether Congress intended that the remedy provided in 47 U.S.C. Section 332(c)(7)(B)(v) for challenging wireless facility zoning or permitting decisions that allegedly violate Section 332 be exclusive or whether such challenges can be brought under 42 U.S.C. Section 1983. While Congress imposed certain federal standards on wireless facility zoning and permitting decisions, it did so in a manner that is highly deferential to state and local government review processes. For example, while Congress created a right of judicial review, it imposed the same 30-day limitations period that exists in most States. Moreover, Congress adopted the same standard of judicial review that is used by state courts reviewing local land use decisions. Section 1983 suits are fundamentally incompatible with the remedial scheme Congress created in Section 332(c)(7)(B).

The court of appeals' holding that Section 1983 suits nonetheless are available to challenge local wireless facility zoning and permitting decisions undermines the scheme Congress created in Section 332(c)(7)(B) and will disrupt the state and local zoning review process. Amici accordingly submit this brief to assist the Court in its resolution of the case.

SUMMARY OF ARGUMENT

1. Section 332(c)(7), entitled "Preservation of local zoning authority," is designed to facilitate the rollout of wireless service in a way that is respectful of existing state and local zoning processes. Congress achieved this balance by adopting traditional state-law principles and limitations governing judicial review of zoning determinations. For example, Congress provided that a person seeking judicial review of any final action or failure to act by a state or local government must commence an action "within 30 days." 47 U.S.C. Section 332(c)(7)(B)(v). This 30-day limitation is derived from the Standard State Zoning Enabling Act of 1926, which was adopted by all 50 States and remains in effect in modified form in 47 States. Most States impose a relatively short time limit on persons seeking judicial review of zoning decisions, and 30 days is the most common state-imposed limit. Congress determined that the same 30-day requirement should apply when a challenge to a local zoning or permitting decision is based on the federal standards of Section 332(C)(7)(B).

The provision of Section 332(c)(7)(B)(v) that judicial review is available for "final" actions of state or local governments parallels similar "final agency action" requirements for judicial review of zoning decisions under state law. Likewise, the requirement that zoning decisions be "in writing and supported by substantial evidence contained in a written record," 47 U.S.C. Section 332(c)(7)(B)(iii), also follows typical state-law requirements governing judicial review of zoning decisions.

The Court has recognized that when a federal statute does not expressly authorize particular remedies, it is presumed that courts are authorized to award any *appropriate* relief. *Franklin v. Gwinnett County Pub. Schs.*, 503 U.S. 60, 73 (1992). Congress's decision to adopt the existing framework for state judicial review of zoning decisions strongly indicates that the appropriate remedies for violations of the standards of Section 332(c)(7)(B) are those generally available when a court reviews a zoning decision under state law. Consistent with traditional appellate review of agency action, those remedies may include injunctive or declaratory relief setting aside or modifying the administrative decision, but not damages or attorney's fees. Indeed, most States grant local governments and municipalities immunity from damages liability for zoning decisions. Those grants of immunity should be respected under the 1996 Act's saving clause, which provides that the Act "shall not be construed to modify, impair, or supersede Federal, State, or local law unless expressly so provided . . . ." 47 U.S.C. Section 152 (note).

The practical consequences of allowing Section 1983 actions could be significant. There are thousands of counties, municipalities, and townships in the United States, including many with few inhabitants, limited financial resources, and no full-time counsel.

2. Allowing suits under 42 U.S.C. Section 1983 would upset the careful balance struck by Congress in the 1996 Act. If Section 1983 actions are available to redress violations of the federal standards of Section 332(c)(7)(B), then the 30-day limitations period is ineffective, because plaintiffs would have up to four years to commence an action under Section 1983. See 28 U.S.C. Section 1658. In addition, if Section 1983 actions are available private parties may obtain damages and attorney's fees awards under 42 U.S.C. Section 1988, neither of which are available under Section 332(c)(7)(B)(v). There is persuasive evidence that Congress did not intend to saddle local and state governments with this liability.

The practical consequences of allowing Section 1983 actions could be significant. There are thousands of counties, municipalities, and townships in the United States, including many with few inhabitants, limited financial resources, and no full-time counsel. Faced with the threat of large claims for attorney's fees and damages by well-financed corporations represented by high-priced counsel, local governments may be deterred from vigorously protecting visual, aesthetic, and safety concerns. Such a result would defeat Congress' intention to allow local governments to retain "the flexibility to treat facilities that create different visual, aesthetic, or safety concerns differently to the extent permitted under generally applicable zoning requirements." H.R. Conf. Rep. No. 458, 104th Cong., 2d Sess. 208 (1996).

This Court's decisions point towards reversal of the court of appeals' decision in this case. Where this Court has held that Section 1983 actions are available, the federal statute that creates the federal rights at issue has not expressly provided individuals with a private right of action to vindicate those rights. In contrast, where Congress has expressly provided for a private right of action in the statute that creates the federal rights at issue, this Court has held that actions under Section 1983 are foreclosed. In enacting Section 332(c)(7), Congress created an express private right of action that parallels the judicial review of zoning and permitting decisions that is traditionally available under state law. In these circumstances, allowing resort to Section 1983 would contravene the intent of Congress.

ARGUMENT

In the Telecommunications Act of 1996, Congress imposed federal standards on local zoning authorities' "decisions regarding the placement, construction, and modification of personal wireless service facilities." 47 U.S.C. Section 332(c)(7)(A). Substantively, Congress prohibited local zoning authorities (1) from "unreasonably discriminat[ing] among providers of functionally equivalents services" (*id.* Section 332(c)(7)(B)(i)(I)); (2) from "prohibit[ing] . . . the provision of personal wireless services" (*id.* Section 332(c)(7)(B)(i)(II)); and (3) from regulating the placement, construction, and modification of personal wireless service facilities based on "the environmental effects of radio frequency emissions to the extent that such facilities comply with the [FCC's] regulations" (*id.* Section 332(c)(7)(B)(iv)). Procedurally, Congress required zoning authorities (1) to "act on any request for authorization to place, construct, or modify personal wireless service facilities within a reasonable period of time, . . . taking into account the nature and scope of the request" (*id.* Section 332(c)(7)(B)(ii)) and (2) to ensure that decisions "deny[ing] a request . . . be in writing and supported by substantial evidence contained in a written record" (*id.* Section 332(c)(7)(B)(iii)).

The 1996 Act expressly provides private parties with "a mechanism for judicial relief from zoning decisions that fail to comply with" these requirements. H.R. Conf. Rep. No. 458, 104th Cong., 2d Sess. 208 (1996). Specifically, 47 U.S.C. Section 332(c)(7)(B)(v) allows "[a]ny person adversely affected by any final action or failure to act by a State or local government . . . that is inconsistent with [the federal standards listed above], within 30 days after such action or failure to act, [to] commence an action in any court of competent jurisdiction." Congress viewed such actions as "appeal[s]" of "final" zoning and permitting decisions (H.R. Conf. Rep. No. 458, *supra*, at 209), and required courts to "hear and decide [them] on an expedited basis" (47 U.S.C. Section332(c)(7)(B)(v)).[2]

Despite Congress' decision to provide a specific avenue for private parties to seek judicial enforcement of these federal standards via Section 332(c)(7)(B)(v), the court of Appeals held that private parties can enforce the same federal standards under 42 U.S.C. Section 1983 as well. The court ruled that Section 1983 actions are cognizable (and Section 1983 remedies are available) because Section 332(c)(7)(B)(v)—the very "mechanism for judicial relief" (H.R. Conf. Rep. No. 458, *supra*, at 208) that Congress chose to include in the 1996 Act—"does not explicitly provide for any types of remedies such as damages, injunctions, attorney's fees, or costs[,]" and "grants no remedies beyond procedural rights." Pet. App. at 5a, 6a. The court further reasoned that Section 332(c)(7)(B)(v)'s 30-day limitations period "imposes a burden on an aggrieved plaintiff, not a benefit" and that "[t]he only benefit to an aggrieved plaintiff is expedited judicial review," which "does nothing to remedy a TCA violation in itself." *Id.* at 8a-9a.

In so holding, the court of appeals misconstrued the scope and effect of Section 332(c)(7)(B)(v), as well as Congress' intent in the 1996 Act to minimize disruption to state and local zoning decisions. As amici will show, the judgment below should be reversed for two reasons. *First*, examination of the text, structure, and legislative history of the Act confirms that Congress designed Section 332(c)(7)(B)(v) to provide for judicial review of wireless facility zoning and permitting decisions that parallels, in terms of timing, scope, and remedies, the review that is available in nearly every State for zoning and permitting decisions. Contrary to the views of the court of appeals, Section 232(c)(7)(B)(v) authorizes courts to order appropriate remedies, such as declaratory and injunctive relief, upon a determination that a local zoning authority's decision fell afoul of the 1996 Act's requirements. *Second*, allowing private parties to sue under Section 1983, and thereby circumvent the prescribed limits on Section 332(c)(7)(B)(v) actions, upsets Congress' carefully designed scheme; could have significant, negative consequences for local governments that Congress sought to avoid; and is contrary to this Court's precedents on the availability of Section 1983 remedies.

I. Section 332(C)(7)(B)(V) provides for judicial review of wireless facility zoning decisions that is analogous to the review traditionally available for state and local zoning decisions.

With Section 332(c)(7)(B), Congress sought to facilitate the rollout of wireless service in a manner that is respectful of existing state and local zoning processes. Section 332(c)(7) is entitled "Preservation of local zoning authority." See also H.R. Conf. Rep. No. 458, *supra*, at 208 (Congress did not intend "to give preferential treatment to the personal wireless service industry in the processing of requests, or to subject their requests to any but the generally applicable time frames for zoning decisions."). Other than the nondiscrimination and procedural requirements that are set forth in Section 332(c)(7)(B) and described above, Congress disavowed any intent to "limit or affect the authority of a State or local government or instrumentality thereof over decisions regarding the placement, construction, and modification of personal wireless service facilities." 47 U.S.C. Section 332(c)(7)(A); H.R. Conf. Rep. No. 458, *supra*, at 207-08 (1996 Act "preserves the authority of State and local governments over zoning and land use matters except in the limited circumstances set forth" in Section 332).[3]

A. Congress Patterned Section 332(7)(B)(v) after State Review Mechanisms. The judicial review provision of Section 332(c)(7)(B)(v) reflects Congress' deferential stance toward state and local zoning processes. Strikingly, both it and Section 332(c)(7)(B)(iii)'s requirement that zoning decisions be "in writing and supported by substantial evidence contained in a written record" parallel requirements contained in state enabling acts that create, and define the scope of, private parties' rights to obtain judicial review of zoning determinations in state court.

1. Section 332(c)(7)(B)(v) follows the lead of most states and the Standard State Zoning Enabling Act in restricting the time for seeking judicial review to 30 days. The court of appeals characterized Section 332(c)(7)(B)(v) as establishing a "short" statute of limitations for review of local zoning authority decisions. Pet. App. 5a. But Congress did not select the 30-day limitations period from thin air. Thirty-day limits have a venerable provenance in early zoning law and continue to be widely used in state zoning law review schemes.

"Statutes and ordinances prescribing the time limitations to initiate judicial review are often patterned after the Standard State Zoning Enabling Act," which was adopted in final form in 1926 and published by the U.S. Department of Commerce. 8 Patrick J. Rohan, *Zoning and Land Use Controls* Section 52.04[2] (2004) (footnote omitted).[4] Section 7 of the Zoning Enabling Act authorized the appointment of boards of adjustment to decide such matters as appeals from administrative orders and requests for special exceptions and variances. See U.S. Dep't of Commerce, A Standard State Zoning Enabling Act, *supra,* at 9-11. Section 7 provided that "[a]ny person . . . aggrieved by any decision of the board of adjustment . . . may present to a court of record a petition . . . setting forth that such decision is illegal . . . . Such petition *shall be presented to the court within 30 days after the filing of the decision in the office of the board." Id.* at 11 (emphasis added).

The Zoning Enabling Act was subsequently "adopted by all 50 states and is still in effect, in modified form, in 47 states." Stuart Meck, *Model Planning and Zoning Enabling Legislation: A Short History* 3, in 1 American Planning Association, *Modernizing State Planning Statutes* 3 (1996). When the American Law Institute published its Model Land Development Code, it suggested:

> four weeks as a reasonable time in which to commence legal proceedings to challenge the validity of orders issued by a Land Development Agency. Most states that currently provide for statutory judicial review of local administrative zoning decisions prescribe a 30-day time period for such actions to be initiated." Model Land Dev. Code Section 9-107, at 423 (Reporters Note) (1975). See also *id.* Section 9-107(1), at 422 ("The validity of an order of a Land Development Agency granting or denying development permission or an enforcement order shall not be questioned in any legal proceeding commenced more than [four weeks] after notice of the order was given. . . .").

Even today, while "[t]he time restrictions range from 10 to 60 days, most require[e] that proceedings be commenced within 30 days of the decision in issue." 4 Kenneth H. Young, Anderson's American Law of Zoning Section 27.24, at 572 (4th ed. 1997 & 2004 Supp.). See, e.g., Del. Code Ann. Tit. 22, Section 328(a) (30 days); Fla. Stat. Ann. Section 120.68(2)(a) (same); N.Y. Town Law Section 267-c (same); N.C. Gen. Stat. Section 160A-381 (same); Pa. Stat. Ann. Tit. 53, Section 11002-A (same).

2. Section 332(c)(7)(B)(v)'s requirement that State or local government action be "final" as a condition of review accords with typical state requirements for zoning decision review. Similarly, Congress' decision to restrict judicial review to "final" state or local government decisions emulates state judicial review provisions. Nearly every state review scheme is identical, in that virtually all allow parties "aggrieved" or "affected" by a "final" state administrative zoning or permitting decision to challenge the decision in court. See, e.g., Haw. Rev. Stat. Section 91-14(a); 55 Ill. Comp. Stat. Ann. Section 5/5-12012; Ky. Rev. Stat. Section 100.347(1); N.H. Rev. Stat. Ann. Section 677:4; N.M. Stat. Ann. Section 3-21-9; Tenn. Code Ann. Section 27-9-101. That Congress chose to follow the state-law model for challenges to wireless facilities zoning decisions demonstrates its intent to preserve the integrity of local zoning and permitting processes, while ensuring that private parties have an effective method of securing compliance with federal standards through judicial actions under Section 332(c)(7)(B)(v). The particular balance Congress struck in this regard was carefully considered. See H.R. Conf. Rep. No. 458, *supra,* at 208 (rejecting alternative that aggrieved parties must exhaust any "independent State *court* remed[ies]," in addition to obtaining "final administrative action at the State or local government level" before commencing an action under Section 332(c)(7)(B)(v)) (emphasis added).

3. Section 332(c)(7)(B)(iii)'s requirement that decisions denying requests be "in writing and supported by substantial evidence contained in a written record" replicate zoning review standards used throughout the states. Congress' decision to require that zoning decisions be "in writing and supported by substantial evidence contained in a written record" (47 U.S.C. Section332(c)(7)(B)(iii)) also follows typical state review mechanisms. Most States apply the same standard. See, e.g., Alaska Stat. Section 29.40.060(b); N.M. Stat. Ann. Section 39-3-1.1(D)(2); Utah Code Ann. Section 10-9-708(6); see also *Nevada Contractors v. Washoe Cty.*, 792 P.2d 31, 33 (Nev. 1990) (substantial evidence test).

The Conference Report for the 1996 Act confirms that Congress intended the "phrase 'substantial evidence contained in a written record'" to be construed as "the traditional standard used for judicial review of agency actions." H.R. Conf. Rep. No. 458, *supra*, at 208. *See also id.* at 209 (describing Section 332(c)(7)(B)(v) action as an "appeal" of state or local administrative decision). As contemplated by Congress, the scope of judicial review under Section 332(c)(7)(B)(v) parallels certiorari review of administrative zoning boards in state courts. See *Anderson's American Law Of Zoning, supra*, Section 27.07, at 507 (The "writ is traditionally confined to the review by a judicial tribunal of a decision of an inferior tribunal, on the record made by the latter."). As another authority explains, "[a] challenge to a quasi-judicial determination brought by way of certiorari or appeal is similar to the appeal of a judicial decision to a higher court. The appellate court will, of course, correct any errors of law by the lower tribunal." Rohan, *Zoning and Land Use Controls, supra*, Section 52.05[3].

Moreover, the appellate court will overturn a board's decision where it "has failed to follow procedures required by state statutes or its own prescribed procedures." *Id.* (footnote omitted). A reviewing court, however, "will not weigh the evidence but will examine the record to determine whether there is any legal or competent evidence in the record to support the decision." *Anderson's American Law Of Zoning, supra*, Section 27.30, at 614 (footnotes omitted). As a leading authority explains:

> In the instance that the board's decision is supported by 'substantial evidence' the board will be generally upheld.....[A]s a rule the courts limit their inquiry of the administrative record to ascertain that the zoning board decision was neither irrational nor clearly erroneous. It is in fact error for the trial court to amplify its review beyond such findings.

Rohan, *Zoning and Land Use Controls, supra*, Section 52.05[2] (footnotes omitted). See also *Anderson's American Law Of Zoning, supra*, Section 27.30, at 610-11 & n.45 ("While a court reviewing a decision of a board of adjustment may not substitute its judgment for that of the board, it will examine the record upon which the board's decision is based to determine whether the findings of the board are supported by substantial evidence.")(footnotes omitted); Model Land Development Code, Section 9-110(1) & (f), at 422 (A "court may declare the order ... invalid ... if it determines that ... the order is not based on findings of fact which are supported by substantial evidence.").

Likewise, the commentary to the Model Land Development Code explains, "[i]f findings of fact were made by a prior administrative agency, the courts are not free to disregard the weight given the evidence by the agency." *Id.* at 433. Accord *Pacifica Corp v. City of Camarillo*, 149 Cal. App.3d 168, 178 (Ct. App. 1983); *Education Dev. Center, Inc. v. West Palm Beach Zoning Bd. of Apps.*, 541 So.2d 106, 108 (Fla. 1989); *Turner v. Hammond*, 310 A.2d 543, 553 (Md. 1973); *Younger v. City of Portland*, 752 P.2d 262, 263 (Or. 1988).

B. Section 332(c)(7)(B)(v) allows private parties to obtain federal remedies that are consistent with congressional intent. As the foregoing discussion demonstrates, Congress provided for judicial review in Section 332(c)(7)(B)(v) that mirrors the review process for zoning decisions that is widely used throughout the States. The court of appeals acknowledged that Section 332(c)(7)(B)(v) "provides for a private right of action by allowing aggrieved plaintiffs the right to bring an action in any court of competent jurisdiction." Pet. App. 6a. But the court nonetheless concluded that Section 332(c)(7)(B)(v) "does not provide for any type of relief." *Id.* at 7a. In its view, "[t]he only benefit to an aggrieved plaintiff [in Section 332(c)(7)(B)(v)] is expedited judicial review," which "does nothing to remedy a TCA violation in itself." *Id.* at 8a-9a. The lower court's interpretation of Section 32(c)(7)(B)(v) is contrary to all indicia of congressional intent and common sense.

1. Declaratory and injunctive relief are available in actions brought under Section 332(c)(7)(B)(v). Contrary to the view of the court of appeals, it is of no consequence that Section 332(c)(7)(B)(v) does not itemize the remedies available to private parties for a violation of federal standards. As this Court has long recognized, "[t]hat a statute does not authorize the remedy at issue 'in so many words is no more significant than the fact that it does not in terms authorize execution to issue on a judgment.'" *Franklin v. Gwinett County Pub. Schs.*, 503 U.S. 60, 68 (1992) (quoting *Deckert v. Independence Shares Corp.*, 311 U.S. 282, 288 (1940)). Rather, there is a "traditional presumption in favor of any *appropriate relief* for violation of a federal right." *Franklin*, 503 U.S. at 73 (emphasis added). See also 3 W. Blackstone, Commentaries 23 (1783) (quoted in Franklin, 503 U.S. at 66) (It is "'a general and indisputable rule, that where there is a legal right, there is also a legal remedy, by suit or action at law, whenever that right is invaded.'")).

"[A]ppropriate relief," within the meaning of *Franklin*, includes "forms of relief traditionally available in [analogous] suits." *Barnes v. Gorman*, 536 U.S. 181, 187 (2002). Congressional intent remains the touchstone for determining what relief is "appropriate." See *Gebser v. Lago Vista Indep. School Dist.*, 524 U.S. 274, 285 (1998) (general rule that all "appropriate relief" is available "must be reconciled with congressional purpose" of the statute); *id.* at 284 (consideration of "the statutory structure and purpose" is "pertinent . . . to [determination of] the scope of the available remedies").

Errors in state zoning decisions are typically remedied by relief setting aside or modifying the order of the lower tribunal. The Model Land Development Code states:

> [T]he Court may, in a proceeding involving an order, affirm the decisions of the agency, set aside the order, remand the matter for further proceedings before the agency in accordance with directions contained in the opinion or order of the Court, or enter an order that might have been entered by the agency issuing the order and that the court could order the agency to issue. Model Land Dev. Code, *supra*, Section 9-111(2), at 434. See Standard State Zoning Enabling Act, *supra*, Section 7, at 12 ("The court may reverse or affirm, wholly or partly, or may modify the decision brought up for review."); Rohan, *Zoning and Land Use Controls, supra*, Section 52.05[3] ("A court will overturn a zoning determination which is beyond the ambit of the board's legislatively prescribed powers . . ., or where the lower tribunal has failed to follow procedures required by state statutes or its own prescribed procedures.") (footnotes omitted).

Nearly every state zoning review scheme provides for the same specific remedies.[5] Given Congress' decision to pattern Section 332(c)(7)(B)(v) after these state models, Section 332(c)(7)(B)(v) clearly embraces these traditional remedies.

Indeed, the district court had little problem fashioning a comprehensive remedy for the violation of federal right, which it found to have occurred in this case. Respondent obtained complete relief when the district court enjoined the city council "to set aside its earlier resolution denying [respondent's] application" and ordered it "to adopt a new resolution granting . . . a Conditional Use Permit" subject to "reasonable conditions." Pet. App. 14a. A federal court order that sets aside a local government's zoning determination on the ground that it violates federal law and further commands local officials to grant a conditional use permit subject to certain conditions is not merely "procedural." *Id.* at 9a (Ct. App. Op). Quite the opposite, the district court's order "remed[ies] a TCA violation in itself." *Id.* at 8a-9a.

2. Damages and attorney's fees are not "appropriate relief" under Section 332(c)(7)(B)(v) and would contravene Congress' unambiguous intent not to modify, impair, or supersede state and local immunity laws. Violations of Section 332(c)(7)(B) occur as a result of the exercise of a quasi-judicial function. See Rohan, *Zoning and Land Use Controls, supra*, at Section 52.01 (noting "the adjudicatory power to enforce [zoning] ordinances and to grant or deny, on an individual basis, permits, exceptions, nonconforming uses and variances under the ordinances"). As explained above, see *supra* pp. 11-12, "[a]ppeal and certiorari are the usual avenues of review open to a party aggrieved by the quasi-judicial decision of zoning boards." Rohan, *Zoning and Land Use Controls, supra*, Section 52.05[1]. See also *Anderson's American Law Of Zoning, supra*, Section 27.07, at 507 ("the writ of certiorari is probably the most common device for reviewing the decisions of administrative boards"); *id.* at 27.06, at 504 ("The courts are in apparent agreement that a decision of a legislative body is subject to review by certiorari or appeal where such decision is an administrative or quasi-judicial one."). Moreover, "[a] challenge to a quasi-judicial board determination brought by way of certiorari or appeal is similar to the appeal of a judicial decision to a higher court." Rohan, *Zoning and Land Use Controls, supra*, at Section 52.05[3].

Just as a trial court's ruling that violates a party's rights does not give rise to damages when it is overturned on appeal, damages are traditionally unavailable where a board of adjustment or city council has incorrectly denied a permit, special use exception, or request for a variance. See, e.g., *Torromeo v. Town of Fremont*, 813 A.2d 389, 392 (N.H. 2002). ("[Q]uasi-judicial . . . acts of a town ordinarily do not subject it to claims for damages. . . . [P]laintiffs are not entitled to damages, and . . . their only remedy is issuance of the erroneously-denied building permits.") (internal quotation and citation omitted). Consistent with the "American Rule," see *Alyeska Pipeline Service Co. v. Wilderness Society*, 421 U.S. 240, 247 (1975), attorney's fees generally are not recoverable either. Consequently, neither damages nor attorney's fees would constitute "appropriate relief" in actions brought under Section 332(c)(7)(B)(v). See *Barnes*, 536 U.S. at 187; *Gebser*, 524 U.S. at 285.

Interpreting Section 332(c)(7)(B)(v) not to allow damages and attorney's fee recoveries is also required by Section 601(c)(1) of the 1996 Act. See 47 U.S.C. Section 152 (reprinting Section 601(c)(1) in historical and statutory notes). In that provision, Congress admonished that the 1996 Act "shall not be construed to modify, impair, or supersede Federal, State, or local law unless expressly so provided. . . ." Most States by statute grant local governments immunity from damages liability for zoning decisions.[6] If damages and fee-shifting were deemed available under Section 332(c)(7)(B)(v), those "State [and] local law[s]" would, contrary to Section 601(c)(1), be "impair[ed] or supersed[ed]" by the 1996 Act in the absence of an "express[]" provision.[7]

Permitting challenges to zoning decisions to be filed up to four years after the fact and dispensing with expedited review would deprive local governments of the certainty afforded by Section 332(c)(7)(B)(v)'s speedier processes.

II. Interpreeting the 1996 Act to Allow Suits Under Section 1983 Would Upset Congress' Carefully Chosen Enforcement Scheme and Run Counter to *Sea Clammers* and Its Progeny

The Ninth Circuit reasoned that actions to enforce Section 332(c)(7)(B)'s requirements with respect to zoning decisions are cognizable under Section 1983 because Section 332(c)(7)(B)(v)'s enforcement provisions do not contain a sufficiently "comprehensive" remedial scheme to overcome the "presumption" that respondent is entitled to Section 1983 remedies. Pet. App. 4a-5a. In reaching this conclusion, the Ninth Circuit lost sight of the "crucial consideration" this Court has identified for determining whether Section 1983 actions are available—"what Congress intended." *Smith v. Robinson*, 468 U.S. 992, 1012 (1984). Allowing private parties to assert claims under Section 1983 to enforce federal standards for wireless zoning and permitting decisions is fundamentally incompatible with Congress' desire to preserve existing state and local zoning processes and place limits on enforcement actions brought under Section 332(c)(7)(B)(v). Cases such as *Middlesex County Sewerage Auth. v. National Sea Clammers Ass'n*, 453 U.S. 1 (1981), further support the conclusion that Section 1983 actions are unavailable under Section 332(c)(7).

A. Section 1983 actions are fundamentally inconsistent with the mechanism for judicial relief that Congress chose to include in 1996 act. As discussed *supra*, pp. 8-13, Congress patterned Section 332(c)(7)(B)(v)'s review provisions after those typically available under state law as part of its effort to facilitate provision of wireless services while minimizing disruption to existing zoning processes. If the door to Section 1983 actions is opened to private parties that challenge wireless zoning and permitting decisions, important limits on Section 332(c)(7)(B)(v) review would be circumvented, thereby frustrating congressional intent.

1. Plaintiffs proceeding under Section 1983 could circumvent the 30-day limitations period governing actions under Section 332(c)(7)(B)(v) and prevent expedited judicial review. A key feature of Section 332(c)(7)(B)(v) review is its 30-day limitations period. See *supra* pp. 8-10 (discussing the zoning law origins of the 30-day limit). This short limitations period reduces the amount of time local governments need worry about whether a particular zoning decision will be challenged and helps bring about swifter resolution of disputes. It is particularly beneficial to local governments as they deal with the proliferation of litigation concerning the scope of Section 332(c)(7)'s substantive requirements. Lower courts have recognized that the statute "fairly bristles with potential issues." *Cellular Tel. Co. v. Town of Oyster Bay*, 166 F.3d 490, 494 (2d Cir. 1999). As wireless networks continue to expand in terms of geographic reach and competitors, the number of disputes continue to rise. See Pet. 26-28 (describing explosion of Section 332(c)(7) litigation).

If Section 1983 actions are available, however, plaintiffs "would be freed of the short 30-day limitations period and would instead presumably have four years to commence the action." *Nextel Partners, Inc. v. Kingston Township*, 286 F.3d 687, 695 (3d Cir. 2002) (citing 28 U.S.C. Section 1658).[8] In this same vein, it should be noted that parties to a Section 1983 suit, unlike those in a Section 332(c)(7)(B)(v) appeal, would not be entitled to have courts "hear and decide [the] action on an expedited basis." 47 U.S.C. Section 332(c)(7)(B)(v). The consequences would be significant. Permitting challenges to zoning decisions to be filed up to four years after the fact and dispensing with expedited review would deprive local governments of the certainty afforded by Section 332(c)(7)(B)(v)'s speedier processes. Furthermore, it would delay local zoning authorities' receipt of timely, much-needed guidance from courts about how to comply with Section 332(c)(7). If private parties can invoke Section 1983's generous time-frame, local government decision makers may not learn that they have a good-faith but erroneous view of Section 332(c)(7) until many years, and many other similarly mistaken decisions, later. Resulting delays in obtaining final judgments—whether from a longer limitations period or slower judicial decision making—can harm local governments and the public. Such delays will slow the roll-out of personal wireless facilities and increase the adverse fiscal consequences that Section 1983 damages and Section 1988 attorney's fee liability poses to local governments.

2. Plaintiffs proceeding under Section 1983 could subject local governments to monetary judgments and attorney's fee awards. Allowing private parties to bring Section 1983 suits to enforce Section 332(c)(7) would also allow litigants to seek monetary damages and attorney's fee awards, neither of which are available under Section 332(c)(7)(B)(v). As discussed above, all available indicia of legislative intent strongly suggest that Congress affirmatively did not wish to saddle local governments with potential liability for damages and attorney's fees for zoning and permitting decisions. In addition to these indicia of congressional intent, it is worth considering the real-world consequences that are likely to follow from a judicial decision to expose local governments to liability for damages and attorney's fees under Section 1983 and 1988.

There are thousands of local governments that potentially would be affected by a decision holding them liable under Section 1983 for violations of zoning and permitting requirements under the 1996 Act. See *The Municipal Year Book* xi (2004) (reprinting 2002 U.S. census data regarding number of county and municipal governments). The vast majority of these jurisdictions have less than 50,000 inhabitants. *Id.* at xii-xiii. Many do not have full-time counsel or significant financial resources.

Damages and attorney's fees awarded under Section 1983 would reduce the amount these local governments otherwise would spend on services for their communities, such as police and fire protection, infrastructure, and general services. Governments would pay either directly, from their general revenue, or indirectly, through increased insurance premiums or contributions to insurance alternatives, such as municipal liability pools.

A recent survey of attorney's fee awards in California civil rights cases found that federal courts awarded attorney's fees at an average billable rate of $253.44 per hour. Michael Kao, *Calculating Lawyers Fees: Theory and Reality*, 51 U.C.L.A. L. Rev. 825, 841 (2004). Moreover, in four of the sixteen federal cases reviewed in the survey, the fee award exceeded $290,000. *Id.* at 840-41. Attorney's fees in civil rights cases can substantially exceed the monetary damages awarded to plaintiffs. See *City of Riverside v. Rivera*, 477 U.S. 561, 564-65 (1986) (upholding fee award of $245,456 where plaintiff recovered total damages of $33,350). Substantial attorney's fees are also awarded in cases involving declaratory and injunctive relief.[9]

If anything, these figures likely understate the potential amounts involved in Section 332(c)(7) disputes. Typical plaintiffs in these suits are large telecommunications companies who hire sophisticated counsel and have the resources to litigate aggressively. Even though Respondent does not fit this mold, the potential damage and fee amounts in this case are staggering. See Josh Cohen, *Supreme Court to Hear City's Antenna Case*, Palos Verdes Peninsula News, Oct. 1, 2004, (Respondent "told the News that 'based upon attorney's fees, court costs and the loss of my revenue,' the court could grant him upward of $15 million"), available at http://pvnews.nminews.com/articles/2004/10/01/local_news/news1.txt. See

Damages and attorney's fees awarded under Section 1983 would reduce the amount these local governments otherwise would spend on services for their communities, such as police and fire protection, infrastructure, and general services.

also Nick Green, *High Court to Rule on RVP Tower Issue*, The Daily Breeze, Sept. 29, 2004, at 1 (reporting that Respondent "said he is seeking more than $3 million").

Given their often razor-thin budgets, many local governments may conclude that visual, aesthetic, and safety concerns are not worth fighting for in view of the threat of a damages or fee award being entered against them. Such a result would undermine Congress' intent to leave authority for local zoning decisions in the hands of state and local governments and compromise local governments' ability to protect their citizens. Cf. H.R. Conf. Rep. No. 458, *supra*, at 208 (expressing intent that municipalities retain "the flexibility to treat facilities that create different visual, aesthetic, or safety concerns differently to the extent permitted under generally applicable zoning requirements").

Given their often razor-thin budgets, many local governments may conclude that visual, aesthetic, and safety concerns are not worth fighting for in view of the threat of a damages or fee award being entered against them.

B. This court's precedents further demonstrate that Section 1983 remedies should not be engrafted onto the 1996 Act. The court of appeals interpreted this Court's decisions in cases such as *Wright v. City of Roanoke Redev. and Hous. Auth.*, 479 U.S. 418 (1987), *Blessing v. Freestone*, 520 U.S. 329 (1997), and *Middlesex County Sewerage Auth. v. National Sea Clammers Ass'n*, 453 U.S. 1 (1981), to support its conclusion that Section 1983 remedies were available. See Pet. App. 3a-12a. In fact, this Court's decisions support the opposite result. In no case where Congress expressly created a private right of action against state officials has the Court held that a Section 1983 remedy is available.

Most of this Court's cases addressing whether private parties have a cause of action under Section 1983 did not involve statutory schemes closely analogous to the scheme at issue here. In several cases, the Court examined statutes that created enforceable federal rights, but did not, in contrast to Section 332(c)(7)(B)(v), expressly provide individuals with the means to vindicate those rights in court. In each of these cases, the Court concluded that "'the availability of administrative mechanisms to protect the plaintiff's interests' " did not defeat the plaintiff's ability to seek judicial review via Section 1983. *Blessing*, 520 U.S. at 347 (quoting *Golden State Transit Corp. v. City of Los Angeles*, 493 U.S. 103, 106 (1989)).

For example, *Wright* examined an amendment to the United States Housing Act that gave petitioners, tenants living in low-income housing, an enforceable right to pay rent commensurate with their income, but did not expressly provide petitioners with a cause of action to enforce the statutory limit. The court of appeals had inferred that Congress' failure to include a specific provision giving petitioners access to court while investing the Department of Housing and Urban Development with audit and budgeting authority indicated that petitioners had to rely on the Secretary to ensure compliance. See 479 U.S. at 428. This Court reversed, holding that provisions granting an administrator "generalized [auditing and oversight] powers [were] insufficient to indicate a congressional intention to foreclose Section 1983 remedies." *Id.* at 428.

Likewise, *Wilder v. Virginia Hosp. Ass'n*, 496 U.S. 498, 521 (1990), examined the Medicaid Act, which "contain[ed] no . . . provision for private judicial or administrative enforcement" of a hospital's statutory right to reasonable and adequate reimbursement rates. Again, the Court concluded that statutory provisions granting the Secretary of Health and Human Services general budget and oversight authority and requiring States to adopt certain administrative review schemes were not "sufficiently comprehensive to demonstrate a congressional intent to withdraw the private remedy of Section 1983." *Id.* at 522. *Blessing* similarly held that provisions of Title IV-D of the Social Security Act that granted the Secretary limited powers to audit and cut federal funding, but did not provide private parties with a private cause of action, did not create a remedial scheme "comprehensive enough to close the door on Section 1983 liability" for violations of rights that were secured by the statute. 520 U.S. at 348. *Accord Golden State*, 493 U.S. at 108-09 (Section 1983 action available where National Labor Relations Board "ha[d] no authority to address conduct protected by the NLRA against governmental interference" and no provision of the NLRA authorized private suits for that purpose); *Livadas v. Bradshaw*, 512 U.S. 107 (1994) (same).

In stark contrast to *Wright, Wilder,* and *Blessing* are cases such as *Sea Clammers and Smith v. Robinson*, 468 U.S. 992 (1984). Both examined whether Section 1983 remedies remained available to plaintiffs where the statutory scheme at issue, like Section 332(c)(7) of the 1996 Act, expressly provided for a right of action to enforce federally secured rights. In both cases, this Court found Section 1983 actions foreclosed. See also *Wright*, 479 U.S. at 427 ("congressional intent to supplant the Section 1983 remedy" is evidenced where "the statute[] at issue . . .provide[s] for private judicial remedies").

In *Sea Clammers*, plaintiff-respondent, an association of commercial fishermen, claimed that the Environmental Protection Agency and the Army Corps of Engineers allowed defendant-petitioners to dump pollutants in violation of Federal Water Pollution Control Act and Marine Protection, Research, and Sanctuaries Act of 1972 and caused its members to suffer $250 million in damages. See 453 U.S. at 5. Both "Acts contain[ed] unusually elaborate enforcement provisions" that allowed "private citizens" to "seek judicial review . . . of various particular actions by the Administrator, including establishment of effluent standards and issuance of permits for discharge of pollutants," and "citizen-suit provisions authoriz[ing] private persons to sue for injunctions," but not damages. *Id.* at 13-14 & n.24.

Looking at the statutory remedies as a whole, the Court "found it 'hard to believe that Congress intended to preserve the Section 1983 right of action when it created so many specific statutory remedies, including the two citizen-suit provisions.'" *Blessing*, 520 U.S. at 347 (quoting 453 U.S. at 200). It "therefore concluded that the existence of these express remedies demonstrate[ed] . . . that [Congress] intended to supplant any remedy that otherwise would be available under Section 1983" to enforce federal statutory claims. *Sea Clammers*, 453 U.S. at 21. As in this case, the absence of a provision expressly authorizing private parties to recover damages did not warrant a different result.

In *Smith* the Court confronted a similar issue: whether the existence of a statutory enforcement provision under the Education of the Handicapped Act (EHA) (20 U.S.C. Section 1400 et seq.) precluded petitioners from seeking relief under Section 1983 for a "constitutional deprivation[]" that was "virtually identical" to statutory claims redressable under the EHA. *Id.* at 1008-09. Although the EHA's judicial review provision did not state that it foreclosed Section 1983 actions, the *Smith* Court nonetheless had "little difficulty concluding that Congress intended the EHA to be the exclusive avenue" for enforcement of claims "to a publicly financed special education." *Id.* at 1009. The Court's holding was based on the recognition that allowing Section 1983 suits to proceed would bypass the carefully tailored statutory scheme Congress intended to ensure that children receive a free appropriate public education. See *id.* at 1011.

This case falls squarely within the *Sea Clammers-Smith* line of decisions. In enacting Section 332(c)(7), Congress did not simply leave it to federal administrative officials to enforce its provisions. Rather, Congress expressly created a private right of action to challenge zoning decisions that violate the federal standards set forth in Section 332(c)(7)(B). Congress' decision to provide in Section 332(c)(7)(B) a "mechanism for judicial relief," H.R. Conf. Rep. No. 458, *supra*, at 208, that parallels, in terms of timing, scope, and remedies, the review that is available in nearly every State for zoning and permitting decisions is conclusive evidence of its intent to foreclose resort to Section 1983.[10]

CONCLUSION

The judgment of the court of appeals should be reversed.

NOTES TO AMICUS BRIEF

1. The parties have consented to the filing of amicus curiae briefs in this case and have filed blanket consent letters with the Clerk of the Court. This brief was not authored in whole or in part by counsel for a party, and no person or entity other than amici or their members has made a monetary contribution to the preparation or submission of this brief.

2. The Act further allows persons who claim a local zoning authority's decision was impermissibly based on radio frequency emissions the option of petitioning the Federal Communications Commission or a court for relief. 47 U.S.C. Section 332(c)(7)(B)(v).

3. A House amendment to the bill would have required the FCC to issue specified siting regulations and to create a "negotiated rulemaking committee comprised of State and local governments, public safety agencies and the affected industries . . . to have attempted to develop a uniform policy to propose to the Commission for the siting of wireless tower sites." H.R. Conf. Rep. No. 458, *supra*, at 207. This amendment was rejected by the conferees in favor Section 332'smore deferential approach to existing land use processes. *Id.*

4. The Act was the product of a committee of leading lawyers, engineers, and housing and planning experts, which was appointed by then Secretary of Commerce Herbert Hoover. See U.S. Dep't of Commerce, A Standard State Zoning Enabling Act Under Which Municipalities May Adopt Zoning Regulations (1926). The Act's principal drafter was Edward M. Bassett, an attorney who was instrumental in the creation of New York City's "pioneering zoning code in 1916." Stuart Meck, *Model Planning and Zoning Enabling Legislation: A Short History* 1, in 1 American Planning Association, *Modernizing State Planning Statutes* 1 (1996).

5. See, e.g., Cal. Gov. Code Section 65009(c)(1)(E) (authorizing suit "[t]o attack, review, set aside, void, or annul any decision" on applications for conditional use permits and variances made by a zoning board of adjustment or zoning board of appeals, "or to determine the reasonableness, legality, or validity of any condition attached to a variance, conditional use permit, or any other permit"); Mich. Comp. Laws Section 125.293a(3) ("the court may affirm, reverse, or modify the decision of the board of appeals"); N.Y. Town Law Section267-c(4) ("The court may reverse or affirm, wholly or partly, or may modify the decision brought up for review determining all questions which may be presented for determination."); Or. Rev. Stat. Section197.850(9) ("The court may affirm, reverse or remand the order."); Pa. Stat. Ann. Tit. 53, Section11006-A(a) ("In a land use appeal, the court shall have power to declare any ordinance or map invalid and set aside or modify any action, decision or order of the governing body, agency or officer of the municipality brought up on appeal."); R.I. Gen. Laws Section45-24-69(d) ("The court may affirm the decision of the zoning board of review or remand the case for further proceedings, or may reverse or modify the decision. . . ."); Tex. Local Gov't Code Section 211.011(f) ("The court may reverse or affirm, in whole or in part, or modify the decision that is appealed.");Wash. Rev. Code Section 36.70C.140 ("The court may affirm or reverse the land use decision under review or remand it for modification or further proceedings.").

6. See, e.g., Ala. Code Section 11-47-190; Cal. Gov. Code Section 818.4; Del. Code Ann. Tit. 10, Section 4011(a)(2); Idaho Code Section 6-904B(3); Or. Rev. Stat. Section 30.265(3)(c); S.C. Code Ann. Section 15-78-60(1) & (2); Tenn. Code Ann. Section 29-20-201.

7. Any conclusion that damages and attorney's fees are appropriate relief under Section 332(c)(7)(B)(V) would rest on the implausible premise that Congress—while deferring to the traditional authority of state and local governments over zoning matters—nonetheless intended to subject their decision-making process to the extraordinary and unprecedented prospect of damages suits and fee shifting for merely misapplying federal law. Being subject to damages suits and fee shifting would create a strong incentive for local governments to abdicate their authority over the zoning and permitting of wireless facilities. Given the continued need of wireless service providers to expand their networks and build additional towers, the liability could be substantial in comparison to typical municipal budgets. See, infra, pp. 21-23 (discussing budgetary consequences for local governments of damages and fee awards).

8. Section 1658 provides that "[e]xcept as otherwise provided by law, a civil action arising under an Act of Congress enacted after [December 1, 1990] may not be commenced later than 4 years after the cause of action accrues." Last Term, this Court held that "a cause of action 'aris[es] under an Act of Congress enacted' after December 1, 1990—and therefore is governed by Section 1658's 4-year statute of limitations period—if the plaintiff's claim was made possible by a post-1990 enactment." *Jones v. R.R. Donnelly & Sons Co.*, 124 S. Ct. 1836, 1845 (2004). A Section 1983 action brought to enforce rights secured by Section 332(c)(7)(B) is "made possible by" Section 332(c)(7)(B), a post-1990 enactment.

9. To place such awards in context, police officers and sheriff's deputies had median annual base earnings of $42,270 in 2002, and firefighters approximately $36,000 during the same time period. See U.S. Dep't of Labor, *Bureau of Labor Statistics, Occupational Outlook Handbook* (2004), available at http://stats.bls.gov/oco/ocos160.htm and http://stats.bls.gov/oco/ocos158.htm.

10. For the numerous reasons explained above, Congress intended that Section 332(c)(7)(B)(v) provide the exclusive remedy for violations of Section 332(c)(7)(B) (i)-(iv). There is thus no merit to the court of appeals' contention that the savings clause of the 1996 Act (Pub. L. No. 104-104, Section 601, 110 Stat. 143, reprinted in 47 U.S.C. Section 152 (note)) evidences congressional intent to preserve Section 1983 remedies for violations of Section 332(c)(7)(B). See Pet. App. 10a-12a. Recognizing the exclusivity of the Section 332 remedy does not impair Section 1983, as the latter remains available to redress violations of federal rights whenever Congress did not intend to foreclose its use. And as explained above at p. 17, authorizing damages actions for violations of Section 332 would impair state laws denying damages liability and attorney's fees for erroneous zoning and permitting decisions.

COMMENTARY AND REACTION

HIGH COURT LIMITS CITIES' LIABILITY UNDER TELCOM ACT: UNANIMOUS DECISION SUPPORTS APA AMICUS BRIEF

Last week the United States Supreme Court issued a unanimous ruling in *City of Rancho Palos Verdes v. Abrams*. The ruling in a case closely watched by local officials limited liability of municipalities under the federal Telecommunications Act (TCA). The Court's decision that judicial remedy under Sec. 1983 is not available to an individual seeking judicial review of a zoning decision under the Telecommunications Act reverses a 9th Circuit Court of Appeals ruling.

In November 2004, APA joined a number of other groups to file an amicus brief in the U.S. Supreme Court asking the Court to limit the judicial remedies available when someone seeks review under the Telecommunications Act (TCA). When Congress passed the TCA, it specifically adopted a 30-day statute of limitations governing judicial review of zoning determinations. But the 9th Circuit Court of Appeals ruled earlier that money damages under a civil rights statute (Section 1983) were also available to a plaintiff who successfully challenged denial of a conditional use permit under the TCA. Since the statute of limitations is much longer for a Section 1983 claim, the two remedies are inconsistent.

This is a good decision for local governments and for planners because it harmonizes the provisions of the TCA with the requirements in most states that zoning decisions be appealed within 30 days, as well as precluding money damages for land use permitting errors made under the TCA.

This is a good decision for local governments and for planners because it harmonizes the provisions of the TCA with the requirements in most states that zoning decisions be appealed within 30 days, as well as precluding money damages for land use permitting errors made under the TCA. The alternative would have exposed communities and local officials to the threat of significant financial liability in TCA litigation.

APA joined the National League of Cities, the International Municipal Lawyers Association, the National Association of Counties, the National Conference of State Legislatures, the Council of State Governments, the U.S. Conference of Mayors, International City/County Management Association, and the National Association of Telecommunications Officers and Advisors on the brief.

CHAPTER 4

San Remo Hotel, L.P. v. City and County of San Francisco

[125 S. Ct. 2491 (June 20, 2005)]

[*This overview is taken, in large part, from the August 2005 issue of* Zoning Practice, *which was written by Lora Lucero, editor of* Planning and Environmental Law.]

Which court should decide what? And when? That was the conundrum presented to the U.S. Supreme Court in *San Remo*.

To set the stage, remember that our judicial system is made up of both the federal courts (which include both trial and appellate courts divided into 13 circuits) and the state courts (which also include trial and appellate courts and the state supreme courts). Above it all is the United States Supreme Court.

Generally, the federal courts handle cases involving federal laws and the U.S. Constitution, while the state courts handle cases involving state laws and the state constitutions. Decisions from a trial court might be appealed to an appellate court so there is an opportunity to review and correct mistakes. But imagine the chaos that would ensue if a litigant, dissatisfied with the decision from one court, could simply take his case to another court, not to review the first court's decision, but to make his arguments anew! What a boon for the lawyers, but a mess for everyone else who want some closure and finality to these disputes.

Our Founding Fathers anticipated such mischief when they included the "full faith and credit clause" in the U.S. Constitution. Article IV, Section 1 demands that

> Full Faith and Credit shall be given in each State to the public Acts, Records, and judicial Proceedings of every other State. And the Congress may by general Laws prescribe the Manner in which such Acts, Records and Proceedings shall be proved, and the Effect thereof.

Once a landowner has received a fair hearing, to grant a request for a second hearing in a different forum "would unfairly put two hammers to the heads of local officials."

Congress passed the full faith and credit statute in 1790 to implement Article IV, Section 1. The modern version of the statute, 28 U.S.C. Section 1738, provides that "judicial proceedings...shall have the same full faith and credit in every court within the United States and its Territories and Possessions as they have by law or usage in the courts of such State . . .".

In this case, the owner of the San Remo Hotel in San Francisco asked the Supreme Court to make an exception to the full faith and credit statute. He wanted to bring his federal takings claims into federal court after the state court had already entered a final judgment denying him just compensation. San Remo's argument went this way. Since takings claims based on the U.S. Constitution against a state or local government cannot be brought into federal court until the property owner has been denied just compensation in state court [see *Williamson County v. Hamilton Bank*, 473 U.S. 172 (1985)], a federal takings claim might never be heard in federal court unless the state court's decision is disregarded. San Remo argued that the federal courts should hear the takings claim anew. The U.S. Supreme Court, in a decision written by Justice Stevens in which all the Justices joined, rejected San Remo's argument.

AS ARGUED BY APA

The American Planning Association filed an amicus curiae brief to share with the Court why it would be unfair to communities if developers were given two bites at the litigation apple:

> Ninety percent of American municipalities have less than 10,000 people and cannot afford a full-time municipal lawyer. For these municipalities, defending against a single takings suit by a wealthy developer can result in debilitating costs. For example, Hudson, Ohio, a community of 22,000, had to spend more than $400,000 in an ultimately successful effort to defend against a challenge to the city's growth management ordinance spearheaded by the Home Builders Association of Greater Akron. . . . Litigation costs for small communities have soared in recent years."

APA acknowledged that "Landowners deserve a fair forum and a full hearing for their constitutional claims." But once a landowner has received a fair hearing, to grant a request for a second hearing in a different forum "would unfairly put two hammers to the heads of local officials."

THE COURT'S DECISION

The Court agreed with the position advanced by APA and others and refused to create an exception to the full faith and credit statute. Congress had not expressed an intent to create such an exception when it passed the full faith and credit act, the Court said, and the "weighty interests in finality and comity trump the interest in giving losing litigants access to an additional appellate tribunal."

Justice Stevens concluded his opinion by stating, "State courts are fully competent to adjudicate constitutional challenges to local land-use decisions. Indeed, state courts undoubtedly have more experience than federal courts do in resolving the complex factual, technical, and legal questions related to zoning and land-use regulations."

State courts are fully competent to adjudicate constitutional challenges to local land-use decisions. Indeed, state courts undoubtedly have more experience than federal courts do in resolving the complex factual, technical, and legal questions related to zoning and land-use regulations.

CASE SYLLABUS

Petitioners, hoteliers in respondent city, initiated this litigation over the application of an ordinance requiring them to pay a $567,000 fee for converting residential rooms to tourist rooms. They initially sought mandamus in California state court, but that action was stayed when they filed suit in Federal District Court asserting, *inter alia*, facial and as-applied challenges to the ordinance under the Fifth Amendment's Takings Clause. Although the District Court granted the city summary judgment, the Ninth Circuit abstained from ruling on the facial challenge under *Railroad Comm'n of Tex.* v. *Pullman Co.*, 312 U.S. 496, because the pending state mandamus action could moot the federal question. The court did, however, affirm the District Court's ruling that the as-applied claim was unripe. Back in state court, petitioners attempted to reserve the right to return to federal court for adjudication of their federal takings claims. Ultimately, the California courts rejected petitioners' various state-law takings claims, and they returned to the Federal District Court, advancing a series of federal takings claims that depended on issues identical to those previously resolved in the state courts. In order to avoid being barred from suit by the general rule of issue preclusion, petitioners asked the District Court to exempt their federal takings claims from the reach of the full faith and credit statute, 28 U.S.C. Section 1738. Relying on the *Williamson County Regional Planning Comm'n* v. *Hamilton Bank of Johnson City*, 473 U.S. 172, 195, holding that takings claims are not ripe until a State fails "to provide adequate compensation for the taking," petitioners argued that, unless courts disregard Section 1738 in takings cases, plaintiffs will be forced to litigate their claims in state court without any realistic possibility of ever obtaining federal review. Holding, *inter alia*, that petitioners' facial attack was barred by issue preclusion, the District Court reasoned that Section 1738 requires federal courts to give preclusive effect to any state-court judgment that would have such effect under the State's laws. The court added that because California courts had interpreted the relevant substantive state takings law coextensively with federal law, petitioners' federal claims constituted the same claims the state courts had already resolved. Affirming, the Ninth Circuit rejected petitioners' contention that general preclusion principles should be cast aside whenever plaintiffs must litigate in state court under *Pullman* and/or *Williamson County*.

Held: **This Court will not create an exception to the full faith and credit statute in order to provide a federal forum for litigants seeking to advance federal takings claims. Pp. 11–23.**

(a) The Court rejects petitioners' contention that whenever plaintiffs reserve their federal takings claims in state court under *England* v. *Louisiana Bd. of Medical Examiners*, 375 U.S. 411, federal courts should review the reserved federal claims *de novo*, regardless of what issues the state court may have decided or how it may have decided them. The *England* Court's discussion of the "typical case" in which reservations of federal issues are appropriate makes clear that the decision was aimed at cases fundamentally distinct from petitioners'. *England* cases generally involve federal constitutional challenges to a state statute that can be avoided if a state court construes the statute in a particular manner. *Id.,* at 420. In such cases, the purpose of abstention is not to afford state courts an opportunity to adjudicate an issue that is functionally identical to the federal question, but to avoid resolving the federal question by encouraging a state-law determination that may moot the federal controversy. See *id.,* at 416–417, and n. 7. Additionally, the Court made clear that the effective reservation of a federal claim was dependent on the condition that plaintiffs take no action to broaden the scope of the state court's review beyond deciding the antecedent state-law issue. *Id.,* at 419. Because the Ninth Circuit invoked *Pullman* abstention after determining that a ripe federal question existed as to the petitioners' facial takings challenge, they were entitled to insulate from preclusive effect that one federal issue while they returned to state court to resolve their mandamus petition. Petitioners, however, chose to advance broader issues than the limited ones in the mandamus petition, putting forth facial and as-applied takings challenges to the city ordinance in their state action. By doing so, they effectively asked the state court to resolve the same federal issue they had previously asked it to reserve. *England* does not support the exercise of any such right. Petitioners' as-applied takings claims fare no better. The Ninth Circuit found those claims unripe under *Williamson County,* and therefore affirmed their dismissal. They were never properly before the District Court, and there was no reason to expect that they could be relitigated in full if advanced in the state proceedings. Pp. 11–17.

(b) Federal courts are not free to disregard Section 1738 simply to guarantee that all takings plaintiffs can have their day in federal court. Petitioners misplace their reliance on the Second Circuit's *Santini* decision, which held that parties who are forced to litigate their state-law takings claims in state court pursuant to *Williamson County* cannot be precluded from having those very claims resolved by a federal court. The *Santini* court's reasoning is unpersuasive for several reasons. First, both petitioners and *Santini* ultimately depend on an assumption that plaintiffs have a right to vindicate their federal claims in a federal forum. This Court has repeatedly held to the contrary. See, *e.g., Allen* v. *McCurry,* 449 U.S. 90, 103–104. Second, petitioners' argument assumes that courts may simply create exceptions to Section 1738 wherever they deem them appropriate. However, this Court has held that no such exception will be recognized unless a later statute contains an express or implied partial repeal. *E.g., Kremer* v. *Chemical Constr. Corp.,* 456 U.S. 461, 468. Congress has not expressed any intent to exempt federal takings claims from Section 1738. Third, petitioners have overstated *Williamson County's* reach throughout this litigation. Because they were never required to ripen in state court their claim that the city ordinance was facially invalid for failure to substantially advance a legitimate state interest, see *Yee* v. *Escondido,* 503 U.S. 519, 534, they could have raised the heart of their facial takings challenges directly in federal court. With respect to those federal claims that did require ripening, petitioners are incorrect that *Williamson County* precludes state courts from hearing simultaneously a plaintiff's request for compensation under state law together with a claim that, in the alternative, the denial of compensation would violate the Fifth Amendment of the Federal Constitution. Pp. 17–23. 364 F.3d 1088, affirmed.

Justice Stevens delivered the opinion of the Court, in which Justices Scalia, Souter, Ginsburg, and Breyer. Chief Justice Rehnquist filed an opinion concurring in the judgment, in which Justices O'Connor, Kennedy, and Thomas joined.

OPINION OF THE SUPREME COURT

Justice Stevens delivered the opinion of the Court.

This case presents the question whether federal courts may craft an exception to the full faith and credit statute, 28 U.S.C. Section 1738 for claims brought under the Takings Clause of the Fifth Amendment.

Petitioners, who own and operate a hotel in San Francisco, California (hereinafter City), initiated this litigation in response to the application of a city ordinance that required them to pay a $567,000 "conversion fee" in 1996. After the California courts rejected petitioners' various state-law takings claims, they advanced in the Federal District Court a series of federal takings claims that depended on issues identical to those that had previously been resolved in the state-court action. In order to avoid the bar of issue preclusion, petitioners asked the District Court to exempt from Section 1738's reach claims brought under the Takings Clause of the Fifth Amendment.

Petitioners' argument is predicated on *Williamson County Regional Planning Comm'n* v. *Hamilton Bank of Johnson City*, 473 U.S. 172 (1985), which held that takings claims are not ripe until a State fails "to provide adequate compensation for the taking." *Id.*, at 195. Unless courts disregard Section 1738 in takings cases, petitioners argue, plaintiffs will be forced to litigate their claims in state court without any realistic possibility of ever obtaining review in a federal forum. The Ninth Circuit's rejection of this argument conflicted with the Second Circuit's decision in *Santini* v. *Connecticut Hazardous Waste Management Service*, 342 F.3d 118 (2003). We granted certiorari to resolve the conflict, 543 U.S. ___ (2004),[1] and now affirm the judgment of the Ninth Circuit.

I

The San Remo Hotel is a three-story, 62-unit hotel in the Fisherman's Wharf neighborhood in San Francisco. In December 1906, shortly after the great earthquake and fire destroyed most of the city, the hotel—then called the "New California Hotel"—opened its doors to house dislocated individuals, immigrants, artists, and laborers. The City officially licensed the facility to operate as a hotel and restaurant in 1916, and in 1922 the hotel was given its current name. When the hotel fell into financial difficulties and a "dilapidated condition" in the early 1970's, Robert and Thomas Field purchased the facility, restored it, and began to operate it as a bed and breakfast inn. See *San Remo Hotel, L. P.* v. *City and County of San Francisco*, 100 Cal. Rptr. 2d 1, 5 (Cal. App. 2000) (officially depublished).

In 1979, San Francisco's Board of Supervisors responded to "a severe shortage" of affordable rental housing for elderly, disabled, and low-income persons by instituting a moratorium on the conversion of residential hotel units into tourist units. San Francisco Residential Hotel Unit Conversion and Demolition Ordinance (hereinafter Hotel Conversion Ordinance or HCO) Sections 41.3(a)–(g), Pet. for Cert. 195a–197a. Two years later, the City enacted the first version of the Hotel Conversion Ordinance to regulate all future conversions. San Francisco Ordinance No. 330–81, codified in Section 41.1 *et seq.* Under the 1981 version of the HCO, a hotel owner could convert residential units into tourist units only by obtaining a conversion permit. And those permits could be obtained only by constructing new residential units, rehabilitating old ones, or paying an "in lieu" fee into the City's Residential Hotel Preservation Fund Account. See Sections 41.12–41.13, Pet. for Cert. 224a–231a. The City substantially strengthened the HCO in 1990 by eliminating several exceptions that had existed in the 1981 version and increasing the size of the "in lieu" fee hotel owners must pay when converting residential units. See 145 F.3d 1095, 1099 (CA9 1998).

The genesis of this protracted dispute lies in the 1981 HCO's requirement that each hotel "file an initial unit usage report containing" the "number of residential and tourist units in the hotel[s] as of September 23, 1979." Section 41.6(b)(1), Pet. for Cert. 206a. Jean Iribarren was operating the San Remo Hotel, pursuant to a lease from petitioners, when this requirement came into effect. Iribarren filed the initial usage report for the hotel, which erroneously reported that all of the rooms in the hotel were "residential" units.[2] The consequence of that initial classification was that the City zoned the San Remo Hotel as "residential hotel"—in other words, a hotel that consisted entirely of residential units. And that zoning determination ultimately meant that, despite the fact that the San Remo Hotel had operated in practice as a tourist hotel for many years, 145 F.3d, at 1100, petitioners were required to apply for a conditional use permit to do business officially as a "tourist hotel," 27 Cal. 4th 643, 654, 41 P.3d87, 94 (2002).

After the HCO was revised in 1990, petitioners applied to convert all of the rooms in the San Remo Hotel into tourist use rooms under the relevant HCO provisions and requested a conditional use permit under the applicable zoning laws. In 1993, the City Planning Commission granted petitioners' requested conversion and conditional use permit, but only after imposing several conditions, one of which included the requirement that petitioners pay a $567,000 "in lieu" fee.[3] Petitioners appealed, arguing that the HCO requirement was unconstitutional and otherwise improperly applied to their hotel. See *id.*, at 656, 41 P.3d, at 95. The City Board of Supervisors rejected petitioners' appeal on April 19, 1993.

In March 1993, Petitioners filed for a writ of administrative mandamus in California Superior Court. That action lay dormant for several years, and the parties ultimately agreed to stay that action after petitioners filed for relief in Federal District Court.

Petitioners filed in federal court for the first time on May 4, 1993. Petitioners' first amended complaint alleged four counts of due process (substantive and procedural) and takings (facial and as-applied)[4] violations under the Fifth and Fourteenth Amendments to the United States Constitution, one count seeking damages under Rev. Stat. Section 1979, 42 U.S.C. Section 1983 for those violations, and one pendent state-law claim. The District Court granted respondents summary judgment. As relevant to this action, the court found that petitioners' facial takings claim was untimely under the applicable statute of limitations, and that the as-applied takings claim was unripe under *Williamson County*, 473 U.S. 172.

On appeal to the Court of Appeals for the Ninth Circuit, petitioners took the unusual position that the court should not decide their federal claims, but instead should abstain under *Railroad Comm'n of Tex.* v. *Pullman Co.*, 312 U.S. 496 (1941), because a return to state court could conceivably moot the remaining federal questions. See App. 67–68; see also 145 F.3d, at 1101. The Court of Appeals obliged petitioners' request with respect to the facial challenge, a request that respondents apparently viewed as an "outrageous act of chutzpah." *Id.*, at 1105. That claim, the court reasoned, was "ripe the instant the 1990 HCO was enacted," *id.*, at 1102, and appropriate for *Pullman* abstention principally because petitioners' "entire case" hinged on the propriety of the planning commission's zoning designation—the precise subject of the pending state mandamus action, 145 F.3d, at 1105.[5] The court, however, affirmed the District Court's determination that petitioners' as-applied takings claim—the claim that the application of the HCO to the San Remo Hotel violated the Takings Clause—was unripe. Because petitioners had failed to pursue an inverse condemnation action in state court, they had not yet been denied just compensation as contemplated by *Williamson County.* 145 F.3d, at 1105.

At the conclusion of the Ninth Circuit's opinion, the court appended a footnote stating that petitioners would be free to raise their federal takings claims in the California courts. If, however, they wanted to "retain [their] right to return to federal court for adjudication of [their] federal claim, [they] must make an appropriate reservation in state court." *Id.,* at 1106, n. 7 (citations omitted).[6] That is precisely what petitioners attempted to do when they reactivated the dormant California case. Yet petitioners advanced more than just the claims on which the federal court had abstained, and phrased their state claims in language that sounded in the rules and standards established and refined by this Court's takings jurisprudence. Petitioners claimed, for instance, that "imposition of the fee 'fails to substantially advance a legitimate government interest' and that '[t]he amount of the fee imposed is not roughly proportional to the impact' of the proposed tourist use of the San Remo Hotel." 27 Cal. 4th, at 656, 41 P.3d, at 95 (quoting petitioners' second amended state complaint).[7] The state trial court dismissed petitioners' amended complaint, but the intermediate appellate court reversed. The court held that petitioners' claim that the payment of the "in lieu" fee effected a taking should have been evaluated under heightened scrutiny. Under more exacting scrutiny, the fee failed this Court's "essential nexus" and "rough proportionality" tests because, *inter alia*, it was based on the original flawed designation that the San Remo Hotel was an entirely "residential use" facility. See *id.,* at 657–658, 41 P.3d, at 96–97 (summarizing appellate court opinion).

The California Supreme Court reversed over the partial dissent of three justices.[8] The court initially noted that petitioners had reserved their federal causes of action and had sought no relief for any violation of the Federal Constitution. *Id.,* at 649, n. 1, 41 P.3d, at 91, n. 1.[9] In the portion of its opinion discussing the Takings Clause of the California Constitution, however, the court noted that "we appear to have construed the clauses congruently." *Id.,* at 664, 41 P.3d, at 100–101 (citing cases). Accordingly, despite the fact that petitioners sought relief only under California law, the state court decided to "analyze their takings claim under the relevant decisions of both this court and the United States Supreme Court." *Ibid.,* 41 P.3d, at 101.[10]

The principal constitutional issue debated by the parties was whether a heightened level of scrutiny applied to the claim that the housing replacement fee " 'does not substantially advance legitimate state interests.' " *Ibid.* (quoting *Lucas* v. *South Carolina Coastal Council,* 505 U.S. 1003, 1016 (1992)). In resolving that debate the court focused on our opinions in *Nollan* v. *California Coastal Comm'n,* 483 U.S. 825 (1987), and *Dolan* v. *City of Tigard,* 512 U.S. 374 (1994). Rejecting petitioners' argument that heightened scrutiny should apply, the court emphasized the distinction between discretionary exactions imposed by executive officials on an ad hoc basis and " 'generally applicable zoning regulations'" involving " 'legislative determinations.'" 27 Cal. 4th, at 666–668, 41 P.3d, at 102–104 (quoting, *e.g., Dolan,* 512 U.S., at 385, 391, n. 8). The court situated the HCO within the latter category, reasoning that the ordinance relied upon fixed fees computed under

Accordingly, despite the fact that petitioners sought relief only under California law, the state court decided to "analyze their takings claim under the relevant decisions of both this court and the United States Supreme Court."

a formula that is generally applicable to broad classes of property owners.[11] The court concluded that the less demanding "reasonable relationship" test should apply to the HCO's monetary assessments, 27 Cal. 4th, at 671, 41 P.3d, at 105.

Applying the "reasonable relationship" test, the court upheld the HCO on its face and as-applied to petitioners. As to the facial challenge, the court concluded that the HCO's mandated conversion fees "bear a reasonable relationship to the loss of housing . . . in the *generality* or *great majority* of cases. . . ." *Id.*, at 673, 41 P.3d, at 107. With respect to petitioners' as-applied challenge, the court concluded that the conversion fee was reasonably based on the number of units designated for conversion, which itself was based on petitioners' own estimate that had been provided to the City in 1981 and had remained unchallenged for years. *Id.*, at 678, and n. 17, 41 P.3d, at 110–111, and n. 17. The court therefore reversed the appellate court and reinstated the trial court's order dismissing petitioners' complaint.

Petitioners did not seek a writ of certiorari from the California Supreme Court's decision in this Court. Instead, they returned to Federal District Court by filing an amended complaint based on the complaint that they had filed prior to invoking *Pullman* abstention.[12] The District Court held that petitioners' facial attack on the HCO was not only barred by the statute of limitations, but also by the general rule of issue preclusion. See Pet. for Cert. 85a–86a.[13] The District Court reasoned that 28 U.S.C. Section 1738 requires federal courts to give preclusive effect to any state court judgment that would have preclusive effect under the laws of the State in which the judgment was rendered. Because California courts had interpreted the relevant substantive state takings law coextensively with federal law, petitioners' federal claims constituted the same claims that had already been resolved in state court.

The Court of Appeals affirmed. The court rejected petitioners' contention that general preclusion principles should be cast aside whenever plaintiffs "must litigate in state court pursuant to *Pullman* and/or *Williamson County.*" 364 F.3d 1088, 1096 (CA9 2004). Relying on unambiguous Circuit precedent and the absence of any clearly contradictory decisions from this Court, the Court of Appeals found itself bound to apply general issue preclusion doctrine. Given that general issue preclusion principles governed, the only remaining question was whether the District Court properly applied that doctrine; the court concluded that it did. The court expressly rejected petitioners' contention "that California takings law is not coextensive with federal takings law," *id.*, at 1096, and held that the state court's application of the "reasonable relationship" test was an " 'equivalent determination' of such claims under the federal takings clause," *id.*, at 1098.[14] We granted certiorari and now affirm.

II

Article IV, Section 1, of the United States Constitution demands that "Full Faith and Credit shall be given in each State to the public Acts, Records, and judicial Proceedings of every other State. And the Congress may by general Laws prescribe the Manner in which such Acts, Records and Proceedings shall be proved, and the Effect thereof." In 1790, Congress responded to the Constitution's invitation by enacting the first version of the full faith and credit statute. See Act of May 26, 1790, ch. 11, 1 Stat. 122.[15] The modern version of the statute, 28 U.S.C. Section 1738 provides that "judicial proceedings . . . shall have the same full faith and credit in every court within the United States and its Territories and Possessions as they have by law or usage in the courts of such State ... ." This statute has long been understood to encompass the doctrines of res judicata, or "claim preclusion," and collateral estoppel, or "issue preclusion." See *Allen* v. *McCurry*, 449 U.S. 90, 94–96 (1980).[16]

The general rule implemented by the full faith and credit statute—that parties should not be permitted to relitigate issues that have been resolved by courts of competent jurisdiction—predates the Republic.[17] It "has found its way into every system of jurisprudence, not only from its obvious fitness and propriety, but because without it, an end could never be put to litigation." *Hopkins* v. *Lee*, 6 Wheat. 109, 114 (1821). This Court has explained that the rule "is demanded by the very object for which civil courts have been established, which is to secure the peace and repose of society by the settlement of matters capable of judicial determination. Its enforcement is essential to the maintenance of social order; for, the aid of judicial tribunals would not be invoked for the vindication of rights of person and property, if, as between parties and their privies, conclusiveness did not attend the judgments of such tribunals in respect of all matters properly put in issue and actually determined by them." *Southern Pacific R. Co.* v. *United States*, 168 U.S. 1, 49 (1897).

As this case is presented to us, under our limited grant of certiorari, we have only one narrow question to decide: whether we should create an exception to the full faith and credit statute, and the ancient rule on which it is based, in order to provide a federal forum for litigants who seek to advance federal takings claims that are not ripe until the entry of a final state judgment denying just compensation. See *Williamson County,* 473 U.S. 172.[18]

The essence of petitioners' argument is as follows: because no claim that a state agency has violated the federal Takings Clause can be heard in federal court until the property owner has "been denied just compensation" through an available state compensation procedure, *id.,* at 195, "federal courts [should be] required to disregard the decision of the state court" in order to ensure that federal takings claims can be "considered on the merits in . . . federal court." See Brief for Petitioners 8, 14. Therefore, the argument goes, whenever plaintiffs reserve their claims under *England* v. *Louisiana Bd. of Medical Examiners*, 375 U.S. 411 (1964), federal courts should review the reserved federal claims *de novo*, regardless of what issues the state court may have decided or how it may have decided them.

We reject petitioners' contention. Although petitioners were certainly entitled to reserve some of their federal claims, as we shall explain, *England* does not support their erroneous expectation that their reservation would fully negate the preclusive effect of the state-court judgment with respect to any and all federal issues that might arise in the future federal litigation. Federal courts, moreover, are not free to disregard 28 U.S.C. Section 1738 simply to guarantee that all takings plaintiffs can have their day in federal court. We turn first to *England*.

III

England involved a group of plaintiffs who had graduated from chiropractic school, but sought to practice in Louisiana without complying with the educational requirements of the State's Medical Practice Act. 375 U.S., at 412. They filed suit in federal court challenging the constitutionality of the Act. The District Court invoked *Pullman* abstention and stayed the proceedings to enable the Louisiana courts to decide a preliminary and essential question of state law—namely, whether the state statute applied at all

> *The general rule implemented by the full faith and credit statute—that parties should not be permitted to relitigate issues that have been resolved by courts of competent jurisdiction—predates the Republic.*

to chiropractors. 375 U.S., at 413.[19] The state court, however, reached beyond the state-law question and held not only that the statute applied to the plaintiffs but also that its application was consistent with the Fourteenth Amendment to the Federal Constitution. The Federal District Court then dismissed the federal action without addressing the merits of the federal claim.

On appeal, we held that when a federal court abstains from deciding a federal constitutional issue to enable the state courts to address an antecedent state-law issue, the plaintiff may reserve his right to return to federal court for the disposition of his federal claims. *Id.*, at 419. In that case, the antecedent state issue requiring abstention was *distinct* from the reserved federal issue. See *id.*, at 418–419. Our discussion of the "typical case" in which reservations of federal issues are appropriate makes clear that our holding was limited to cases that are fundamentally distinct from petitioners'. "Typical" *England* cases generally involve federal constitutional challenges to a state statute that can be avoided if a state court construes the statute in a particular manner.[20] In such cases, the purpose of abstention is not to afford state courts an opportunity to adjudicate an issue that is functionally identical to the federal question. To the contrary, the purpose of *Pullman* abstention in such cases is to avoid resolving the federal question by encouraging a state-law determination that may moot the federal controversy. See 375 U.S., at 416–417, and n. 7.[21] Additionally, our opinion made it perfectly clear that the effective reservation of a federal claim was dependent on the condition that plaintiffs take no action to broaden the scope of the state court's review beyond decision of the antecedent state-law issue.[22]

Our holding in *England* does not support petitioners' attempt to relitigate issues resolved by the California courts. With respect to petitioners' facial takings claims, the Court of Appeals invoked *Pullman* abstention after determining that a ripe federal question existed—namely, "the facial takings challenge to the 1990 HCO." 145 F.3d, at 1105.[23] It did so because " 'land use planning is a sensitive area of social policy' " and because petitioners' pending state mandamus action had the potential of mooting their facial challenge to the HCO by overturning the City's original classification of the San Remo Hotel as a "residential" property. *Ibid.* Thus, petitioners were entitled to insulate from preclusive effect one federal issue—their facial constitutional challenge to the HCO—while they returned to state court to resolve their petition for writ of mandate.

Petitioners, however, chose to advance broader issues than the limited issues contained within their state petition for writ of administrative mandamus on which the Ninth Circuit relied when it invoked *Pullman* abstention. In their state action, petitioners advanced not only their request for a writ of administrative mandate, 27 Cal. 4th, at 653, 41 P.3d, at 93, but also their various claims that the HCO was unconstitutional on its face and as applied for (1) its failure to substantially advance a legitimate interest, (2) its lack of a nexus between the required fees and the ultimate objectives sought to be achieved via the ordinance, and (3) its imposition of an undue economic burden on individual property owners. *Id.*, at 672–676, 41 P.3d, at 106–109. By broadening their state action beyond the mandamus petition to include their "substantially advances" claims, petitioners effectively asked the state court to resolve the same federal issues they asked it to reserve. *England* does not support the exercise of any such right.

Petitioners' as-applied takings claims fare no better. As an initial matter, the Court of Appeals did not abstain with respect to those claims. Instead, the court found that they were unripe under *Williamson County*. The court therefore affirmed the district court's dismissal of those claims. 145 F.3d, at 1106. Unlike their "substantially advances" claims, petitioners' as-applied claims were never properly before the District Court, and there was no reason to expect that they could be relitigated in full if advanced in the state proceedings. See *Allen*, 449 U.S., at 101, n. 17. In short, our opinion in *England* does not support petitioners' attempt to circumvent Section 1738.

IV

Petitioners' ultimate submission, however, does not rely on *England* alone. Rather, they argue that federal courts simply should not apply ordinary preclusion rules to state-court judgments when a case is forced into state court by the ripeness rule of *Williamson County*. For support, petitioners rely on the Court of Appeals for the Second Circuit's decision in *Santini*, 342 F.3d, at 130.

In *Santini*, the Second Circuit held that parties "who litigate state-law takings claims in state court involuntarily" pursuant to *Williamson County* cannot be precluded from having those very claims resolved "by a federal court." 342 F.3d, at 130. The court did not rest its decision on any provision of the federal full faith and credit statute or our cases construing that law. Instead, the court reasoned that "[i]t would be both ironic and unfair if the very procedure that the Supreme Court required [plaintiffs] to follow before bringing a Fifth Amendment takings claim . . . also precluded [them] from ever bringing a Fifth Amendment takings claim." *Ibid.* We find this reasoning unpersuasive for several reasons.

First, both petitioners and *Santini* ultimately depend on an assumption that plaintiffs have a right to vindicate their federal claims in a federal forum. We have repeatedly held, to the contrary, that issues actually decided in valid state-court judgments may well deprive plaintiffs of the "right" to have their federal claims relitigated in federal court. See, *e.g., Migra* v. *Warren City School Dist. Bd. of Ed.*, 465 U.S. 75, 84 (1984); *Allen*, 449 U.S., at 103–104. This is so even when the plaintiff would have preferred not to litigate in state court, but was required to do so by statute or prudential rules. See *id.*, at 104. The relevant question in such cases is not whether the plaintiff has been afforded access to a federal forum; rather, the question is whether the state court actually decided an issue of fact or law that was necessary to its judgment.

In *Allen*, the plaintiff, Willie McCurry, invoked the Fourth and Fourteenth Amendments in an unsuccessful attempt to suppress evidence in a state criminal trial. After he was convicted, he sought to remedy his alleged constitutional violation by bringing a suit for damages under 42 U.S.C. Section 1983 against the officers who had entered his home. Relying on "'the special role of federal courts in protecting civil rights'" and the fact that Section 1983 provided the "only route to a federal forum," the court of appeals held that McCurry was entitled to a federal trial unencumbered by collateral estoppel. 449 U.S., at 93. We rejected that argument emphatically.

> The actual basis of the Court of Appeals' holding appears to be a generally framed principle that every person asserting a federal right is entitled to one unencumbered opportunity to litigate that right in a federal district court, regardless of the legal posture in which the federal claim arises. But the authority for this principle is difficult to discern. It cannot lie in the Constitution, which makes no such guarantee, but leaves the scope of the jurisdiction of the federal district courts to the wisdom of Congress. And no such authority is to be found in Section 1983 itself . . . . There is, in short, no reason to believe that Congress intended to provide a person claiming a federal right an unrestricted opportunity to relitigate an issue already decided in state court simply because the issue arose in a state proceeding in which he would rather not have been engaged at all. *Id.*, at 103–104.[24]

As in *Allen*, we are presently concerned only with issues *actually decided* by the state court that are dispositive of federal claims raised under Section 1983. And, also as in *Allen*, it is clear that petitioners would have preferred not to have been forced to have their federal claims resolved by issues decided in state court. Unfortunately for petitioners, it is entirely *unclear* why their preference for a federal forum should matter for constitutional or statutory purposes.

The only distinction between this case and *Allen* that is possibly relevant is the fact that petitioners here originally invoked the jurisdiction of a Federal District Court, which abstained on *Pullman* grounds while petitioners returned to state court. But petitioners' as-applied takings claims were never properly before the District Court because they were unripe. And, as we have already explained, the Court of Appeals invoked *Pullman* abstention only with respect to petitioners' "substantially advances" takings challenge, which petitioners then gratuitously presented to the state court. At a bare minimum, with respect to the facial takings claim, petitioners were "in an offensive posture in [their] state court proceeding, and could have proceeded first in federal court had [they] wanted to litigate [their "substantially advances"] federal claim in a federal forum." *Migra*, 465 U.S., at 85, n. 7. Thus, the only distinction between this case and *Allen* is a distinction of no relevant significance.

The second reason we find petitioners' argument unpersuasive is that it assumes that courts may simply create exceptions to 28 U.S.C. Section 1738 wherever courts deem them appropriate. Even conceding, *arguendo*, the laudable policy goal of making federal forums available to deserving litigants, we have expressly rejected petitioners' view. "Such a fundamental departure from traditional rules of preclusion, enacted into federal law, can be justified only if plainly stated by Congress." *Kremer* v. *Chemical Constr. Corp.*, 456 U.S. 461, 485 (1982). Our cases have therefore made plain that "an exception to Section 1738 will not be recognized unless a later statute contains an express or implied partial repeal." *Id.*, at 468 (citing *Allen*, 449 U.S., at 99). Even when the plaintiff's resort to state court is involuntary and the federal interest in denying finality is robust, we have held that Congress "must 'clearly manifest' its intent to depart from Section 1738." 456 U.S., at 477.

The same concerns animate our decision here. Congress has not expressed any intent to exempt from the full faith and credit statute federal takings claims. Consequently, we apply our normal assumption that the weighty interests in finality and comity trump the interest in giving losing litigants access to an additional appellate tribunal. As we explained in *Federated Department Stores, Inc.* v. *Moitie*, 452 U.S. 394, 401 (1981), "we do not see the grave injustice which would be done by the application of accepted principles of res judicata. 'Simple justice' is achieved when a complex body of law developed over a period of years is evenhandedly applied. The doctrine of res judicata serves vital public interests beyond any individual judge's ad hoc determination of the equities in a particular case. There is simply 'no principle of law or equity which sanctions the rejection by a federal court of the salutary principle of *res judicata*' " (quoting *Heiser* v. *Woodruff*, 327 U.S. 726, 733 (1946)).

Third, petitioners have overstated the reach of *Williamson County* throughout this litigation. Petitioners were never required to ripen the heart of their complaint—the claim that the HCO was facially invalid because it failed to substantially advance a legitimate state interest—in state court. See *Yee* v. *Escondido*, 503 U.S. 519, 534 (1992). Petitioners therefore could have raised most of their facial takings challenges, which by their nature requested relief distinct from the provision of "just compensation," directly

Congress has not expressed any intent to exempt from the full faith and credit statute federal takings claims.

in federal court.[25] Alternatively, petitioners had the option of reserving their facial claims while pursuing their as-applied claims along with their petition for writ of administrative mandamus. Petitioners did not have the right, however, to seek state review of the same substantive issues they sought to reserve. The purpose of the *England* reservation is not to grant plaintiffs a second bite at the apple in their forum of choice.

With respect to those federal claims that did require ripening, we reject petitioners' contention that *Williamson County* forbids plaintiffs from advancing their federal claims in state courts. The requirement that aggrieved property owners must seek "compensation through the procedures the State has provided for doing so," 473 U.S., at 194, does not preclude state courts from hearing simultaneously a plaintiff's request for compensation under state law and the claim that, in the alternative, the denial of compensation would violate the Fifth Amendment of the Federal Constitution. Reading *Williamson County* to preclude plaintiffs from raising such claims in the alternative would erroneously interpret our cases as requiring property owners to "resort to piecemeal litigation or otherwise unfair procedures." *MacDonald, Sommer & Frates* v. *Yolo County*, 477 U.S. 340, 350, n. 7 (1986).

It is hardly a radical notion to recognize that, as a practical matter, a significant number of plaintiffs will necessarily litigate their federal takings claims in state courts. It was settled well before *Williamson County* that "a claim that the application of government regulations effects a taking of a property interest is not ripe until the government entity charged with implementing the regulations has reached a final decision regarding the application of the regulations to the property at issue." 473 U.S., at 186. As a consequence, there is scant precedent for the litigation in federal district court of claims that a state agency has taken property in violation of the Fifth Amendment's takings clause. To the contrary, most of the cases in our takings jurisprudence, including nearly all of the cases on which petitioners rely, came to us on writs of certiorari from state courts of last resort.[26]

Moreover, this is not the only area of law in which we have recognized limits to plaintiffs' ability to press their federal claims in federal courts. See, *e.g.*, *Fair Assessment in Real Estate Assn., Inc.* v. *McNary*, 454 U.S. 100, 116 (1981) (holding that taxpayers are "barred by the principle of comity from asserting Section 1983 actions against the validity of state tax systems in federal courts"). State courts are fully competent to adjudicate constitutional challenges to local land-use decisions. Indeed, state courts undoubtedly have more experience than federal courts do in resolving the complex factual, technical, and legal questions related to zoning and land-use regulations.

At base, petitioners' claim amounts to little more than the concern that it is unfair to give preclusive effect to state-court proceedings that are not chosen, but are instead *required* in order to ripen federal takings claims. Whatever the merits of that concern may be, we are not free to disregard the full faith and credit statute solely to preserve the availability of a federal forum. The Court of Appeals was correct to decline petitioners' invitation to ignore the requirements of 28 U.S.C. Section 1738 . The judgment of the Court of Appeals is therefore affirmed.

It is so ordered

Most of the cases in our takings jurisprudence, including nearly all of the cases on which petitioners rely, came to us on writs of certiorari from state courts of last resort.

NOTES TO THE SUPREME COURT OPINION

1. Although petitioners asked this Court to review two separate questions, our grant of certiorari was limited exclusively to the question whether "a Fifth Amendment Takings claim [is] barred by issue preclusion based on a judgment denying compensation solely under state law, which was rendered in a state court proceeding that was required to ripen the federal Takings claim?" Pet. for Cert. i. Thus, we have no occasion to reach

petitioners' claim that, under California law, the substantive state takings law decision of the California Supreme Court was not entitled to preclusive effect in federal court. See Brief for Petitioners 19–21.

2. It seems that despite this initial classification, the San Remo Hotel has operated as a mixed hotel for tourists and long-term residents since long before the HCO was enacted. According to the California Supreme Court, in "a 1992 declaration by [petitioners], Iribarren filed the 'incorrect' initial unit usage report without their knowledge. They first discovered the report in 1983 when they resumed operation of the hotel. They protested the residential use classification in 1987, but were told it could not be changed because the appeal period had passed." 27 Cal. 4th 643, 654, 41 P.3d 87, 94 (2002).

3. The application specifically required petitioners (1) to pay for 40 percent of the cost of replacement housing for the 62 lost residential units; (2) to offer lifetime leases to any then-current residential users; and (3) to "obtain variances from floor-area ratio and parking requirements." *Id.*, at 656, 41 P.3d, at 95.

4. Specifically, count 3 alleged that the HCO was facially unconstitutional under the Takings Clause because it "fails to substantially advance legitimate government interests, deprives plaintiffs of the opportunity to earn a fair return on its investment, denies plaintiffs economically viable use of their property, and forces plaintiffs to bear the public burden of housing the poor, all without just compensation." First Amended and Supplemental Complaint, No. C–93–1644–DLJ (D. Cal., Jan. 24, 1994), p. 20, ¶49. Count 4, which advanced petitioners' as-applied Takings Clause violation, was predicated on the same rationale. *Id.*, at 21.

5. The Court of Appeals did not answer the question whether this claim was barred by the statute of limitations, as the District Court had held.

6. The reservation discussed in the Ninth Circuit's opinion was the common reservation of federal claims made in state litigation under *England v. Louisiana Bd. of Medical Examiners*, 375 U.S. 411, 420–421 (1964).

7. With respect to claims that a regulation fails to advance a legitimate state interest, see generally *Lingle v. Chevron U.S.A. Inc.*, 544 U. S. ___, (2005) (slip op., at 6–15). With respect to "rough proportionality" claims, see generally *Nollan v. California Coastal Comm'n*, 483 U.S. 825 (1987); *Dolan v. City of Tigard*, 512 U.S. 374 (1994).

8. Justice Baxter and Justice Chin opined that because some hotel rooms had been previously rented to tourists, the "in lieu" payment was excessive. 27 Cal. 4th, at 691, 41 P.3d, at 119–120. Justice Brown opined that a 1985 statute had effectively superseded the HCO and disagreed with the majority's analysis of the constitutional issues. *Id.*, at 699, 700–704, 41 P.3d, at 125–128.

9. "Plaintiffs sought no relief in state court for violation of the Fifth Amendment to the United States Constitution. They explicitly reserved their federal causes of action. As their petition for writ of mandate, as well, rests solely on state law, no federal question has been presented or decided in this case." Ibid.

10. See also *id.*, at 665, 41 P.3d, at 101 ("[I]t is the last mentioned prong of the *high court's takings analysis* that is at issue here" (emphasis added)).

11. See *id.*, at 669, 41 P.3d, at 104 (noting that the "HCO is generally applicable legislation in that it applies, without discretion or discrimination, to every residential hotel in the city" and that "no meaningful government discretion enters into either the imposition or the calculation of the in lieu fee"). The court noted that the general class of property owners included more than 500 properties containing over 18,000 rooms, *id.*, at 669, n. 12, 41 P.3d, at 104, n. 12, and concluded that the HCO "applies to all property in the class logically subject to its strictures, that is, to all residential hotel units; no more can rationally be demanded of local land use legislation in order to qualify for deferential review," *id.*, at 669, 41 P.3d, at 104.

12. The third amended complaint, which was filed on November 14, 2002, alleged two separate counts. See App. 88–93. Count 1 alleged that the HCO was facially unconstitutional and unconstitutional as-applied to petitioners because (a) it failed "to substantially advance legitimate government interests"; (b) it forced petitioners "to bear the public burden of housing the poor"; and (c) it imposed unreasonable conditions on petitioners' request for a conditional use permit (the in lieu fee and the required lifetime leases to residential tenants). *Id.*, at 88–89. Count 2 sought relief under 42 U.S.C. Section 1983 based on (a) extortion through the imposition of the $567,000 fee; (b) an actual taking of property under *Penn Central Transp. Co. v. New York City*, 438 U.S. 104 (1978); (c) the failure of the HCO as applied to petitioners to advance legitimate state interests; (d) the City's requirement that petitioners bear the full cost of providing a general public benefit (public housing) without just compensation.

13. The District Court found that most of petitioners' as-applied claims amounted to nothing more than improperly labeled facial challenges. See Pet. for Cert. 82a–85a. The remainder of petitioners' as-applied claims, the court held, was barred by the statute of limitations. *Id.*, at 84a–85a.

14. California courts apply issue preclusion to a final judgment in earlier litigation between the same parties if "(1) the issue decided in the prior case is identical with the one now presented; (2) there was a final judgment on the merits in the prior case, and (3) the party to be estopped was a party to the prior adjudication." 364 F.3d 1088, 1096 (CA9 2004). The court reasoned that the California Supreme Court's decision satisfied those criteria because petitioners' takings challenges "raised in state court are identical to the federal claims . . . and are based on the same factual allegations." *Ibid.* Our limited review in this case does not include the question whether the Court of Appeals' reading of California preclusion law was in error.

15. "This statute has existed in essentially unchanged form since its enactment just after the ratification of the Constitution. . . ." *Allen* v. *McCurry*, 449 U.S. 90, 96, n. 8 (1980).

16. "Under res judicata, a final judgment on the merits of an action precludes the parties or their privies from relitigating issues that were or could have been raised in that action. Under collateral estoppel, once a court has decided an issue of fact or law necessary to its judgment, that decision may preclude relitigation of the issue in a suit on a different cause of action involving a party to the first case." *Id.*, at 94 (citations omitted).

17. "The authority of the *res judicata*, with the limitations under which it is admitted, is derived by us from the Roman law and the Canonists." *Washington, Alexandria, & Georgetown Steam-Packet Co.* v. *Sickles*, 24 How. 333, 341 (1861); see also *id.*, at 343 (noting that the rule also has its pedigree "[i]n the courts upon the continent of Europe, and in the courts of chancery and admiralty in the United States and Great Britain, where the function of adjudication is performed entire by a tribunal composed of one or more judges . . .").

18. We did not grant certiorari on many of the issues discussed by the parties and *amici*. We therefore assume for purposes of our decision that all other issues in this protracted controversy have been correctly decided. We assume, for instance, that the Ninth Circuit properly interpreted California preclusion law; that the California Supreme Court was correct in its determination that California takings law is coextensive with federal law; that, as a matter of California law, the HCO was lawfully applied to petitioners' hotel; and that under California law, the "in lieu" fee was imposed evenhandedly and substantially advanced legitimate state interests.

19. We stressed in *England* that abstention was essential to prevent the district court from deciding " 'questions of constitutionality on the basis of preliminary guesses regarding local law.' " 375 U.S., at 416, n. 7 (quoting *Spector Motor Service, Inc.* v. *McLaughlin*, 323 U.S. 101, 105 (1944)).

20. 375 U.S., at 420 (describing the "typical case" as one in which "the state courts are asked to construe a state statute against the backdrop of a federal constitutional challenge").

21. As we explained in *Allen*, 449 U.S., at 101–102, n. 17, "[t]he holding in *England* depended entirely on this Court's view of the purpose of abstention in such a case: Where a plaintiff *properly invokes* federal-court jurisdiction in the first instance on a federal claim, the federal court has a duty to accept that jurisdiction. Abstention may serve only to postpone, rather than to abdicate, jurisdiction, since its purpose is to determine whether resolution of the federal question is even necessary, or to obviate the risk of a federal court's erroneous construction of state law." (Emphasis added and citations omitted.)

22. 375 U.S., at 419 ("[I]f a party freely and without reservation submits his federal claims for decision by the state courts, litigates them there, and has them decided there, then . . . he has elected to forgo his right to return to the District Court").

23. Petitioners' facial challenges to the HCO were ripe, of course, under *Yee* v. *Escondido*, 503 U.S. 519, 534 (1992), in which we held that facial challenges based on the "substantially advances" test need not be ripened in state court—the claims do "not depend on the extent to which petitioners are deprived of the economic use of their particular pieces of property or the extent to which these particular petitioners are compensated." *Ibid.*

24. We expressed similar views in *Migra* v. *Warren City School Dist. Bd. of Ed.*, 465 U.S. 75, 84 (1984): "Although such a division may seem attractive from a plaintiff's perspective, it is not the system established by Section 1738. That statute embodies the view that it is more important to give full faith and credit to state-court judgments than to ensure separate forums for federal and state claims. This reflects a variety of concerns, including notions of comity, the need to prevent vexatious litigation, and a desire to conserve

judicial resources." In all events, petitioners may no longer advance such claims given our recent holding that the " 'substantially advances' formula is not a valid takings test, and indeed . . . has no proper place in our takings jurisprudence." *Lingle*, 544 U.S., at ___ (slip op., at 18).

25. See, *e.g., Dolan*, 512 U.S., at 383; *Yee*, 503 U.S., at 526; *Nollan*, 483 U.S., at 830; *First English Evangelical Lutheran Church of Glendale* v. *County of Los Angeles*, 482 U.S. 304, 310–311 (1987); *Penn Central*, 438 U.S., at 120–122. Indeed, Justice Holmes' famous "too far" formulation, which spawned our regulatory takings jurisprudence, was announced in a case that came to this Court via a writ of certiorari to Pennsylvania's highest court. *Pennsylvania Coal Co.* v. *Mahon*, 260 U.S. 393, 415 (1922).

CHIEF JUSTICE REHNQUIST'S CONCURRENCE

I agree that the judgment of the Court of Appeals should be affirmed. Whatever the reasons for petitioners' chosen course of litigation in the state courts, it is quite clear that they are now precluded by the full faith and credit statute, 28 U.S.C. Section 1738, from relitigating in their 42 U.S.C. Section 1983 action those issues which were adjudicated by the California courts. See *Migra* v. *Warren City School Dist. Bd. of Ed.*, 465 U.S. 75, 84 (1984); *Allen* v. *McCurry*, 449 U.S. 90, 103–105 (1980). There is no basis for us to except from Section 1738's reach all claims brought under the Takings Clause. See, *e.g., Kremer* v. *Chemical Constr. Corp.*, 456 U.S. 461, 485 (1982). I write separately to explain why I think part of our decision in *Williamson County Regional Planning Comm'n* v. *Hamilton Bank of Johnson City*, 473 U.S. 172 (1985), may have been mistaken.

In *Williamson County*, the respondent land developer filed a Section 1983 suit in federal court alleging a regulatory takings claim after a regional planning commission disapproved respondent's plat proposals, but before respondent appealed that decision to the zoning board of appeals. *Id.*, at 181–182. Rather than reaching the merits, we found the claim was brought prematurely. *Id.*, at 200. We first held that the claim was "not ripe until the government entity charged with implementing the regulations [had] reached a final decision regarding the application of the regulations to the property at issue." *Id.*, at 186. Because respondent failed to seek variances from the planning commission or the zoning board of appeals, we decided that respondent had failed to meet the final-decision requirement. *Id.*, at 187–191. We then noted a "second reason the taking claim [was] not yet ripe": "respondent did not seek compensation through the procedures the State [had] provided for doing so." *Id.*, at 194. Until the claimant had received a final denial of compensation through all available state procedures, such as by an inverse condemnation action, we said he could not "claim a violation of the Just Compensation Clause." *Id.*, at 195–196.

It is not clear to me that *Williamson County* was correct in demanding that, once a government entity has reached a final decision with respect to a claimant's property, the claimant must seek compensation in state court before bringing a federal takings claim in federal court. The Court in *Williamson County* purported to interpret the Fifth Amendment in divining this state-litigation requirement. See, *e.g., id.*, at 194, n. 13 ("The nature of the constitutional right . . . requires that a property owner utilize procedures for obtaining compensation before bringing a Section 1983 action"). More recently, we have referred to it as merely a prudential requirement. *Suitum* v. *Tahoe Regional Planning Agency*, 520 U.S. 725, 733–734 (1997). It is not obvious that either constitutional or prudential principles require claimants to utilize all state compensation procedures before they can bring a federal takings claim. Cf. *Patsy* v. *Board of Regents of Fla.*, 457 U.S. 496, 516 (1982) (holding that plaintiffs suing under Section 1983 are not required to have exhausted state administrative remedies).[1]

The Court today attempts to shore up the state-litigation requirement by referring to *Fair Assessment in Real Estate Assn., Inc. v. McNary*, 454 U.S. 100 (1981). *Ante*, at 22–23. There, we held that the principle of comity (reflected in the Tax Injunction Act, 28 U.S.C. Section 1341) bars taxpayers from asserting Section 1983 claims against the validity of state tax systems in federal courts. 454 U.S., at 116. Our decision that such suits must be brought in state court was driven by the unique and sensitive interests at stake when federal courts confront claims that States acted impermissibly in administering their own tax systems. *Id.*, at 102–103, 107–113. Those historically grounded, federalism-based concerns had led to a longstanding, "fundamental principle of comity between federal courts and state governments . . . , particularly in the area of state taxation," a principle which predated the enactment of Section 1983 itself. *Id.*, at 103, 107–114. We decided that those interests favored requiring that taxpayers bring challenges to the validity of state tax systems in state court, despite the strong interests favoring federal-court review of alleged constitutional violations by state officials. *Id.*, at 115–116.

The Court today makes no claim that any such longstanding principle of comity toward state courts in handling federal takings claims existed at the time *Williamson County* was decided, nor that one has since developed. The Court does remark, however, that state courts are more familiar with the issues involved in local land-use and zoning regulations, and it suggests that this makes it proper to relegate federal takings claims to state court. *Ante*, at 23. But it is not apparent that any such expertise matches the type of historically grounded, federalism-based interests we found necessary to our decision in *Fair Assessment*. In any event, the Court has not explained why we should hand authority over federal takings claims to state courts, based simply on their relative familiarity with local land-use decisions and proceedings, while allowing plaintiffs to proceed directly to federal court in cases involving, for example, challenges to municipal land-use regulations based on the First Amendment, see, *e.g.*, *Renton v. Playtime Theatres, Inc.*, 475 U.S. 41 (1986); *Young v. American Mini Theatres, Inc.*, 427 U.S. 50 (1976), or the Equal Protection Clause, see, *e.g.*, *Cleburne v. Cleburne Living Center, Inc.*, 473 U.S. 432 (1985); *Village of Belle Terre v. Boraas*, 416 U.S. 1 (1974). In short, the affirmative case for the state-litigation requirement has yet to be made.

Finally, *Williamson County*'s state-litigation rule has created some real anomalies, justifying our revisiting the issue. For example, our holding today ensures that litigants who go to state court to seek compensation will likely be unable later to assert their federal takings claims in federal court. *Ante*, at 22. And, even if preclusion law would not block a litigant's claim, the *Rooker-Feldman* doctrine might, insofar as *Williamson County* can be read to characterize the state courts' denial of compensation as a required element of the Fifth Amendment takings claim. See *Exxon Mobil Corp. v. Saudi Basic Industries Corp.*, 544 U.S. ___ (2005). As the Court recognizes, *ante*, at 22, *Williamson County* all but guarantees that claimants will be unable to utilize the federal courts to enforce the Fifth Amendment's just compensation guarantee. The basic principle that state courts are competent to enforce federal rights and to adjudicate federal takings claims is sound, see *ante*, at 23, and would apply to any number of federal claims. Cf. 28 U.S.C. Section 2254 (providing for limited federal habeas review of state-court adjudications of alleged violations of the Constitution). But that principle does not explain why federal takings claims in particular should be singled out to be confined to state court, in the absence of any asserted justification or congressional directive.[2]

> *The basic principle that state courts are competent to enforce federal rights and to adjudicate federal takings claims is sound . . . and would apply to any number of federal claims.*

• • •

I joined the opinion of the Court in *Williamson County*. But further reflection and experience lead me to think that the justifications for its state-litigation requirement are suspect, while its impact on takings plaintiffs is dramatic. Here, no court below has addressed the correctness of *Williamson County*, neither party has asked us to reconsider it, and resolving the issue could not benefit petitioners. In an appropriate case, I believe the Court should reconsider whether plaintiffs asserting a Fifth Amendment takings claim based on the final decision of a state or local government entity must first seek compensation in state courts.

NOTES TO CHIEF JUSTICE REHNQUIST'S CONCURRENCE

1. In creating the state-litigation rule, the Court, in addition to relying on the Fifth Amendment's text, analogized to *Ruckelshaus* v. *Monsanto Co.*, 467 U.S. 986 (1984), and *Parratt* v. *Taylor*, 451 U.S. 527 (1981). As several of petitioners' *amici* in this case have urged, those cases provided limited support for the state-litigation requirement. See Brief for Defenders of Property Rights et al. as *Amici Curiae* 9–12; Brief for Elizabeth J. Neumont et al. as *Amici Curiae* 10–14.

2. Indeed, in some States the courts themselves apply the state-litigation requirement from *Williamson County Regional Planning Comm'n* v. *Hamilton Bank of Johnson City*, 473 U.S. 172 (1985), refusing to entertain any federal takings claim until the claimant receives a final denial of compensation through all the available state procedures. See, *e.g.*, *Breneric Assoc.* v. *City of Del Mar*, 69 Cal. App. 4th 166, 188–189, 81 Cal. Rptr. 2d 324, 338–339 (1998); *Melillo* v. *City of New Haven*, 249 Conn. 138, 154, n. 28, 732 A. 2d 133, 138, n. 28 (1999). This precludes litigants from asserting their federal takings claim even in *state* court. The Court tries to avoid this anomaly by asserting that, for plaintiffs attempting to raise a federal takings claim in state court as an alternative to their state claims, *Williamson County* does not command that the state courts themselves impose the state-litigation requirement. *Ante*, at 21–22. But that is so only if *Williamson County*'s state-litigation requirement is merely a prudential rule, and not a constitutional mandate, a question that the Court today conspicuously leaves open.

AMICUS CURIAE BRIEF

This brief was filed by Timothy J. Dowling and Douglas T. Kendall of the Community Rights Counsel, Washington, D.C., on behalf of The Community Rights Counsel, The California State Association of Counties, The League of California Cities, and the American Planning Association.

INTEREST OF THE AMICI CURIAE[1]

Community Rights Counsel is a nonprofit, public interest organization that assists government officials in defending against constitutional challenges to federal, state, and local protections. It has filed *amicus* briefs with this Court and federal and state courts across the country in many regulatory takings cases, including *Brown v. Legal Found. of Wash.*, 538 U.S. 216 (2003), *Tahoe-Sierra Pres. Council, Inc. v. Tahoe Reg'l Planning Agency*, 535 U.S. 302 (2002), and *Palazzolo v. Rhode Island*, 533 U.S. 606 (2001).

The California State Association of Counties (CSAC) is a nonprofit corporation, with membership consisting of all 58 counties in the State of California. CSAC sponsors a Litigation Coordination Program administered by the County Counsels' Association of California and overseen by the Association's Litigation Overview Committee, com-posed of county counsel throughout the State. The Litigation Overview Committee monitors litigation of concern to counties statewide and has determined that this case is a matter affecting all counties in California.

The League of California Cities is an association of 476 cities united in promoting the general welfare of cities and their citizens. The League is ad-

Timothy J. Dowling is the Chief Counsel of the Community Rights Counsel in Washington, D.C. He has represented local government clients in state and federal appellate courts around the country. He served as counsel of record for the APA and International Municpal Lawers Association in *Palazzolo v. Rhode Island* case. Douglas T. Kendall is the founder and executive director of the Community Rights Counsel. He is the coauthor of CRC's *Takings Litigation Handbook: Defending Takings Challenges to Land Use Regulations* (American Legal Publishing 2000).

vised by its Legal Advocacy Committee, which is composed of 24 city attorneys representing all 16 divisions of the League from all parts of the State. The committee monitors appellate litigation affecting municipalities and identifies those cases that are of statewide significance.

The American Planning Association (APA) is a nonprofit public interest and research organization founded in 1978 to advance the art and science of planning at the local, regional, state, and national levels. It represents more than 37,000 practicing planners, officials, and citizens involved, on a day-to-day basis, in formulating and implementing planning policies and land use regulations. The organization has 46 regional chapters, as well as 19 divisions devoted to specialized planning interests. The APA's members work for development interests as well as state and local governments.

The question presented involves the intersection of the federal Full Faith and Credit Act, 28 U.S.C. ◊ 1738, with *Williamson County Reg'l Planning Comm'n v. Hamilton Bank*, 473 U.S. 172 (1985). As organizations that represent government officials and planners, *amici* have a strong interest in ensuring that state and local governments retain their ability to regulate property to promote public health, safety, and welfare. Their ability to do so would be significantly constrained if takings claimants were allowed, in contravention of the Full Faith and Credit Act, to relitigate issues of law and fact already fully litigated in state courts.

SUMMARY OF ARGUMENT

1. To clarify the issues presented in this case, this Court first should reaffirm that when a landowner seeks compensation in state court as required by Williamson County, it may do so only under state law because no federal takings claim exists when the landowner files in state court. In the words of *Williamson County Reg'l Planning Comm'n v. Hamilton Bank*, 473 U.S. 172 (1985), "if a State provides an adequate procedure for seeking just compensation, the property owner cannot claim a violation of the Just Compensation Clause until it has used the procedure and been denied just compensation." *Id.* at 195.

The *Williamson County* Court rested this analysis on the language of the Just Compensation Clause and the very nature of the constitutional right. It also drew from parallel doctrines regarding the need to pursue statutory remedies prior to filing a federal takings claim against the United States under the Tucker Act, as well as requirements to pursue post-deprivation remedies under the Due Process Clause. Although certain takings cases have reached this Court on appeal from state court rulings on federal takings claims, the parties in those cases did not question whether the federal claim was properly filed in state court, and thus this Court had no occasion to address the issue.

The first principles articulated in *Williamson County* have direct consequences for the application of the Full Faith and Credit Act. Because no federal takings claim against a state or local official exists until the state court denies compensation under state law, claim preclusion generally would not apply once the *Williamson County* state-compensation requirement is fulfilled. As a result, there is no need for so-called "*England* reservations" to protect federal takings claims from claim preclusion.

The Full Faith and Credit Act requires the application of state issue preclusion law to matters resolved in state court. But a landowner may return to federal court to argue that the federal Constitution is more protective than state law. This process ensures that federal courts, including this Court, remain the ultimate arbiter of the scope of federal takings law.

In many communities, the playing field for land-use disputes already is tilted in favor of developers and other potential takings claimants. . . . Granting developers and other takings claimants two bites at the apple, in contravention of the Full Faith and Credit Act, would unfairly shift the playing field further to their advantage.

2. San Remo argues that the Full Faith and Credit Act unfairly leaves it without an unfettered opportunity to litigate its federal takings claims in federal court. But it fails to reconcile this argument with a series of cases where this Court, following the mandate of the Full Faith and Credit Act, has applied preclusion even where the result is to deprive a federal claimant of a federal forum. In *Allen v. McCurry*, 449 U.S. 90 (1980), the Court explicitly rejected San Remo's argument "that every person asserting a federal right is entitled to one unencumbered opportunity to litigate that right in a federal district court." *Id.* at 103.

Cases governing the application of the Full Faith and Credit Act to federal claims regarding workplace discrimination reaffirm that preclusion principles promote essential principles of repose, federalism, judicial economy, and comity between state and federal courts. San Remo has failed altogether to offer any plausible explanation as to why state judges would treat property owners unfairly.

In many communities, the playing field for land-use disputes already is tilted in favor of developers and other potential takings claimants. Pro-development professionals serve in disproportionate numbers on planning and zoning boards. Developers commonly use litigation, or the mere threat of litigation, as a tool for advancing their interests in land-use negotiations. Granting developers and other takings claimants two bites at the apple, in contravention of the Full Faith and Credit Act, would unfairly shift the playing field further to their advantage.

3. Issues concerning the continued viability of Williamson County's longstanding, repeatedly reaffirmed state-compensation requirement are not raised in San Remo's petition or merits brief. Addressing them without adequate notice and briefing would be fundamentally unfair to municipalities and the public at large.

ARGUMENT

I. A federal takings claim against a state or local government does not exist until the state courts deny just compensation

As a threshold matter, the Court should clarify the nature of the claim to be filed in state court under *Williamson County*. This issue pertains directly to the question presented, and reaffirmation of applicable first principles would greatly assist in elucidating precisely how the Full Faith and Credit Act applies to takings claimants that file in federal court after seeking just compensation in state court.

Simply put, when a takings claimant files in state court as required by *Williamson County*, the claimant may seek compensation *only* under state law. The claimant may not simultaneously file a federal takings claim in state court. As discussed below, this reading of the federal Just Compensation Clause and this Court's takings precedents differs markedly from that adopted by several federal appellate courts. We respectfully submit, however, that the analysis below is the only one consistent with this Court's longstanding pronouncements.

Williamson County itself could not be clearer on this point: "[I]f a State provides an adequate procedure for seeking just compensation, the property owner cannot claim a violation of the Just Compensation Clause until it has used the procedure and been denied just compensation." 473 U.S. at 195. This principle flows directly from the text of the Constitution: "The Fifth Amendment does not proscribe the taking of property; it proscribes taking without just compensation." *Id.* at 194. In other words, the state-compensation requirement is compelled by the very nature of the protected right: "The nature of the constitutional right therefore requires that a property owner utilize [state] procedures for obtaining compensation *before* bringing a Section 1983 action." *Id.* at 194 n.13 (emphasis added). The "special nature" of this right makes it different from other constitutional rights in a way that requires special treatment. *Id.* at 196 n.14.

This analysis makes plain that *Williamson County* does not send federal takings claimants to state court. Rather, it sends property owners who do *not* have a federal takings claim to state court, precisely because they do not have a federal claim. And their federal takings claim does not arise upon their mere appearance in state court. It arises, in the words of *Williamson County*, only after the landowner has "been denied just compensation" in state court under state law. *Id.* at 195.

In explaining this conclusion, *Williamson County* relied on cases requiring exhaustion of federal statutory compensation schemes prior to filing a federal takings claim under the Tucker Act, 28 U.S.C. Section 1491. In *Ruckelshaus v. Monsanto Co.*, 467 U.S. 986 (1984), for example, the Court held that takings claimants challenging actions under the federal pesticide laws must first pursue compensation remedies under those laws as a "precondition" to a federal takings claim under the Tucker Act. *Id.* at 1018. Because the Just Compensation Clause does not require payment in advance of, or even contemporaneously with, the taking, there is no cognizable federal constitutional claim against the United States unless the claimant is denied compensation under available statutory compensation procedures. *Id.* at 1016-19. Likewise, where a reasonably adequate compensation process exists in state court, "the property owner 'has no [federal] claim against the Government' for a taking" until that process is tested. *Williamson County*, 473 U.S. at 194-95 (quoting *Monsanto*, 467 U.S. at 1018 n.21).

Williamson County also drew an analogy to due process claims, observing that for those claims "the State's action is not 'complete' in the sense of causing a constitutional injury 'unless or until the state fails to provide an adequate postdeprivation remedy for the property loss.' " *Williamson County*, 473 U.S. at 195 (quoting *Hudson v. Palmer*, 468 U.S. 517, 532 n.12 (1984)). In the same way, because the Just Compensation Clause is satisfied by an adequate process for obtaining compensation, "the State's action here is not 'complete' [in the sense of causing constitutional injury] until the State fails to provide adequate compensation for the taking." *Williamson County*, 473 U.S. at 195.

This Court repeatedly has reaffirmed these bedrock principles in a way that shows that no federal constitutional violation occurs until the property owner seeks and is denied compensation through available procedures. In *United States v. Riverside Bayview Homes, Inc.*, 474 U.S. 121 (1985), the Court stressed that "so long as compensation is available for those whose property is in fact taken, the governmental action is not unconstitutional." *Id.* at 128 (citing *Williamson County*). In *Preseault v. ICC*, 494 U.S. 1 (1990), the Court reiterated that if the government provides a process for obtaining just compensation, "then the property owner 'has no [federal] claim against the Government for a taking.' " *Id.* at 11 (quoting *Williamson County*). And in *Suitum v. Tahoe Reg'l Planning Agency*, 520 U.S. 725 (1997), the Court quoted with approval *Williamson County*'s central premise that " 'if a State provides an adequate procedure for seeking just compensation, the property owner cannot claim a violation of the Just Compensation Clause until it has used the procedure and been denied just compensation.' " *Id.* at 734 (quoting *Williamson County*).

The Court's most recent reaffirmation of these principles came in *City of Monterey v. Del Monte Dunes at Monterey, Ltd.*, 526 U.S. 687 (1999), where the majority insisted that a landowner "suffer[s] no constitutional injury from the taking alone" so long as a state court is available to provide just compensation. *Id.* at 710 (citing *Williamson County*); *accord, id.* at 714 (plurality) ("If the condemnation proceedings do not, in fact, deny the landowner just compensation, the government's actions are neither unconstitutional nor unlawful."). For this reason, a federal court "cannot entertain a takings claim under Section 1983 unless or until the complaining landowner has been denied an adequate postdeprivation remedy." *Id.* at 721. This analysis was an integral part of the *Del Monte Dunes* ruling that because the statutory takings suit there "sounded in tort and sought legal relief, it was an action at law." *Id.* at 710-11.

These basic principles apply with equal force to direct condemnations. Many states have enacted "quick-take" statutes that provide for ouster of condemnees well before the award of compensation by state commissioners or state court. *See* 6 Julius L. Sackman, Nichols on Eminent Domain Section 24.10 (3d ed. 2002). If the Just Compensation Clause were deemed violated immediately upon the taking of property, these statutes would give rise to immediate federal court actions that could be used to circumvent established state remedies. As recognized in *Williamson County*, however, a violation of the Just Compensation Clause is not "complete" until the claimant is denied just compensation through available state court procedures.

The obligation to pursue available state-compensation procedures prior to filing a federal claim in federal court is not limited to relief available in state courts, but extends to administrative processes as well. The Court made this explicit in *MacDonald, Sommer & Frates v. County of Yolo*, 477 U.S. 340 (1986), stating that a federal court "cannot determine whether a municipality has failed to provide 'just compensation' until it knows what, if any, compensation the responsible administrative body intends to provide." *Id.* at 350. The Congress, too, may authorize an administrative agency to determine just compensation in the first instance, subject to judicial review. The Federal Communications Commission, for instance, routinely determines compensation for physical takings of utility pole space authorized by the federal Pole Attachment Act, 47 U.S.C. Section 224, a process that comports with the federal Constitution so long as adequate judicial review is available. *See Gulf Power Co. v. United States*, 187 F.3d 1324, 1331-37 (11th Cir. 1999) (citing *Williamson County*).[2]

Cases involving administrative determinations do not raise the same preclusion issues as the instant case, but they reaffirm that property owners may not simply bypass established administrative processes and seek compensation directly in federal district court instead. Other statutes that authorize administratively determined compensation, subject to judicial review, would be gutted if property owners could simply sidestep the agency and sue for compensation in federal district court. These procedures are especially common during times of war.[3] Their pervasiveness is difficult to estimate, but to cite just one example, with respect to compelled utility interconnections many physical takings claims might be filed immediately in federal district court, without the benefit of an administrative record, if claimants could circumvent FCC and other federal administrative processes for the determination of just compensation.[4]

We acknowledge that several takings cases have reached this Court on appeal from state court rulings that addressed federal takings claims. *E.g., Palazzolo v. Rhode Island*, 533 U.S. 606 (2001); *Lucas v. South Carolina Coastal Council*, 505 U.S. 1003 (1992). On the reading of the Fifth Amendment presented in *Williamson County*, these cases might be viewed as anomalous because no federal claim should have been asserted in state court. Perhaps this Court's role in those cases could be explained by the heavy reliance on federal precedents by the state court rulings being reviewed.[5] But more to the point, the parties in these cases did not question whether the federal claim was appropriately filed in state court, and thus this Court had no occasion to address the issue. Cases that do not speak to the issue cannot justify abandoning the repeated holdings of *Williamson County* and other cases that directly address it. On the reading of the Fifth Amendment set forth in *Williamson County* and its progeny, review by this Court might occur after the state court ruling (*see* note 5), and would certainly be available after the claimant returns to federal court (*see* pp. 13-15, *infra*).

Because *Williamson County* and similar rulings make clear that no federal constitutional violation exists until a state court denies just compensation, the state court claim required to be filed by *Williamson County* is a claim for compensation under state law, and only under state law. *See Bakken v. City of Council Bluffs*, 470 N.W.2d 34, 37 (Iowa 1991) ("Bakken's claim for a taking under section 1983 is not ripe for adjudication in this action until the remedy of inverse condemnation, or an equivalent state remedy, is first pursued.") (citing *Williamson County*); *Impink v. City of Indianapolis*, 612 N.E.2d 1125, 1127 (Ind. Ct. App. 1993) (where landowners filed both federal and state takings claims in state court, federal claim was premature under *Williamson County*); *Drake v. Town of Sanford*, 643 A.2d 367, 369 (Me. 1994) (same).

This straightforward reading of *Williamson County* has direct consequences for the application of preclusion principles under the Full Faith and Credit Act. Because no federal takings claim against a state or local official exists until the state court denies compensation under state law, claim preclusion generally would not apply once the *Williamson County* state-compensation requirement is fulfilled. Claim preclusion generally would not apply in these circumstances because state preclusion law typically is inapplicable to claims that had not accrued at the time of the prior litigation.[6] And because there is no claim preclusion, there is no need for so-called "*England* reservations" to protect federal takings claims from claim preclusion.

Unfortunately, several federal appellate courts have ignored this Court's teachings and assumed takings claimants may file federal takings claims in state court while they are fulfilling the *Williamson County* state-compensation requirement. This approach has resulted in an unnecessarily complicated system of *England*-like reservations in certain circuits.[7] A clear reaffirmation of *Williamson County*'s theoretical underpinnings in the instant case would remove this needlessly complex underbrush.

Notwithstanding the overheated rhetoric by San Remo and its *amici*, *Williamson County* does not create a "trap" (Pet. Br. 14) that forever "slams" the federal courthouse door on takings claimants (Home Builders Br. 17). To be sure, as explained in Section II below, the Full Faith and Credit Act requires the application of state issue preclusion law to matters litigated and resolved in state court. This issue preclusion would apply to factual findings, as well as legal conclusions to the extent the federal court determines that state and federal takings law are coextensive. But a landowner may return to federal court to argue that the federal Constitution is more protective than state law, a process that often involves a legal analysis of federal takings law as comprehensive as a merits determination.

That is precisely what San Remo did here. Notwithstanding the California Supreme Court's rejection of heightened judicial scrutiny, San Remo returned to federal court to argue that federal takings law is more protective than California law. Specifically, regarding its claim that the law at issue does not substantially advance a legitimate state interest, San Remo argued that federal takings law subjects legislatively imposed fees to rough-proportionality review under *Dolan v. City of Tigard*, 512 U.S. 374 (1994).

San Remo contended that because state and federal law are not equivalent regarding the application of *Dolan*, issue preclusion does not apply to its *Dolan* theory. The federal district and appeals courts gave this scope-of-*Dolan* argument as much consideration as they would have given if the *Dolan* issue had been presented to them in the first instance. After full deliberation, they ruled against San Remo, applying an analysis virtually indistinguishable from a merits determination, concluding that *Dolan* does not apply to legislatively imposed fees under federal takings law. Pet. App. 17a-21a, 44a-48a, 91a-94a. San Remo then petitioned this Court for *certiorari* on the *Dolan* issue, which was denied when the Court limited review to the procedural question presented. J.A. 129. To say that *Williamson County* slammed the federal courthouse door on San Remo is to ignore reality.

Other takings claimants have been treated in similar fashion. For example, in *Dodd v. Hood River County*, 136 F.3d 1219 (9th Cir. 1998), the Ninth Circuit applied issue preclusion as required by the Full Faith and Credit Act to a takings claimant that sought compensation in Oregon state court and then returned to federal court to litigate its federal takings claim. In determining the appropriate scope of the issue preclusion, the Ninth Circuit considered whether federal takings law is more protective than Oregon takings law. Because Oregon takings law does not recognize a claim under the multi-factor test articulated in *Penn Central Transp. Co. v. City of New York*, 438 U.S. 104 (1978), the Ninth Circuit ruled that federal takings law is more protective and that the claimant was entitled to a full hearing on the merits of its *Penn Central* theory of liability in federal court. *Dodd*, 136 F.3d at 1228-30. The *Dodd* court addressed the *Penn Central* claim on the merits and ultimately rejected it. *Id.*

Moreover, where a state court invokes federal precedent to resolve the state law takings claims, this Court retains the ability to review that determination directly. *See* note 5, *supra.* And under *Williamson County*, takings claimants are not required to file in state court at all where state-compensation procedures are inadequate. 473 U.S. at 194-95.[8]

• • •

In short, where a landowner alleges a taking by state or local officials, *Williamson County* requires the claimant to seek compensation in state court under state law, and no parallel federal takings claim may be filed in that proceeding. A federal takings claim does not arise until the claimant is denied just compensation in state court under state law. Reaffirmation of these first principles would clarify the law by eliminating concerns about claim preclusion and dispensing with the need for *England*-type reservations.

We show in the next section that, if the claimant files in state court, loses, and then files a federal takings claim in federal court, the federal Full Faith and Credit Act requires the application of state law on issue preclusion. If the Full Faith and Credit Act means anything, it means this lengthy litigation has finally run its course.

If the Full Faith and Credit Act means anything, it means this lengthy litigation has finally run its course.

II. San Remo's Effort to Secure Two Forums for Its Takings Claim Is Barred by the Full Faith and Credit Act, This Court's Case Law, and Fundamental Principles of Comity, Federalism, and Judicial Economy

Amicus Neumont warns this Court to anticipate a "chorus from respondents and their amici about how the state procedures requirement is a pillar of Western Civilization and how overruling it will usher in a new Dark Ages." Neumont Br. 23. But it is San Remo and its *amici* who are guilty of overplaying their rhetorical hand. San Remo cites unidentified "commentators" who describe *Williamson County* as "pernicious," "riddled with obfuscation and inconsistency," and "a Kafkaesque maze." Pet. Br. 16. *Amicus* Neumont accuses this Court of "fabricating the state procedures requirement" in *Williamson County* and calls the case "a jurisprudential embarrassment." Neumont Br. 2, 4. *Amicus* Kottschade ridicules the application of *Williamson County* by the lower courts, calling it "a tragic-comic parody of law." Kottschade Br. 28.

It is nothing of the sort. *Williamson County*, as applied by the court below, is both straightforward and fair. Takings claimants must file their claims first in state court under state law. Where the state court provides a full and fair opportunity to litigate particular takings issues, claimants are not permitted to relitigate these issues in federal court.

San Remo's argument reduces to a single proposition: this framework unfairly leaves it without an unfettered opportunity to litigate its federal takings claims in federal court. As discussed above, San Remo *was* allowed to return to federal court to argue that federal takings law subjects legislatively imposed fees to the *Dolan* test. But more fundamentally, San Remo overstates its case in two basic respects. First, it fails to confront a series of cases where this Court, following the mandate of the Full Faith and Credit Act, has applied preclusion even where the result is to deprive a federal claimant of a federal forum. Second, San Remo ignores the unfairness of the outcome it proposes, which would give two bites at the apple to developers. We address each point in turn.

A. San Remo is not entitled to two bites at the litigation apple. San Remo and its *amici* assert that *Williamson County*, as applied by the lower court, has made takings claimants a "poor relation" to other federal claimants because they alone are denied an unfettered opportunity to litigate their federal claim in a federal forum. Pet. Br. 15. But this Court has faithfully applied preclusion law even when the claimant was in a state forum involuntarily and where the result was to deprive a claimant of a federal forum altogether.

The leading example is *Allen v. McCurry*, 449 U.S. 90 (1980). Police allegedly violated McCurry's Fourth Amendment rights in the course of searching his apartment prior to his arrest. McCurry raised this violation in defending against a state criminal trial and his claim was upheld in part and rejected in part. He thereafter at-tempted to bring a Section 1983 claim in federal court to obtain damages. McCurry argued against application of preclusion doctrines by asserting that, because he was forced into state court involuntarily, he was entitled to a federal forum for his federal constitutional claim.

This Court rejected McCurry's argument, finding it irreconcilable with the Full Faith and Credit Act. *Id.* at 99. The Court also rejected what lies at the heart of San Remo's argument here: the "generally framed principle that every person asserting a federal right is entitled to one unencumbered opportunity to litigate that right in a federal district court." *Id.* at 103. The Court held that the basis for this argument "cannot lie in the Constitution, which makes no such guarantee," *id.* at 103, and also cannot be rooted in "a general distrust of the capacity of the state courts to render correct decisions on constitutional issues." *Id.* at 105. Rather, the Court expressed its "emphatic reaffirmation . . . of the constitutional obligation of the state courts to uphold federal law, and its . . . confidence in their ability to do so." *Id.* (citing *Stone v. Powell*, 428 U.S. 465, 493-494 n.35 (1976)).

Those alleging discrimination in the workplace are subject to similar preclusion rules, as shown by *Kremer v. Chemical Constr. Corp.*, 456 U.S. 461 (1982), and *University of Tennessee v. Elliott*, 478 U.S. 788 (1986). *Kremer* and *Elliot* apply preclusion in the context of Title VII of the Civil Rights Act of

1964, 42 U.S.C. Section 2000e, *et seq.*, notwithstanding Congress's express concern with preserving a federal forum for victims of workplace discrimination. As the Court recognized in *Kremer*, Title VII "implemented the national policy against employment discrimination by creating an array of substantive protections and remedies which generally allows federal courts to determine the merits of a discrimination claim." 456 U.S. at 463. Nonetheless, in *Kremer*, Justice White, perhaps the Court's foremost nationalist during his time on the Court,[9] wrote for the Court that "traditional rules of preclusion, enacted into federal law" required preclusion even though the result was to deprive Kremer of a federal forum for his federal claims. *Id.* at 485.

Kremer, like San Remo, possessed a federal claim that he hoped to litigate in federal court. But like the Just Compensation Clause, Title VII routed Kremer first to a state forum. Specifically, Title VII requires that the Equal Employment Opportunity Commission refer charges of employment discrimination first to state administrative agencies with authority to provide relief. *Id.* at 469. A federal proceeding can begin only after affording the state agency the opportunity to resolve the complaint. *Id.*

After a New York administrative tribunal rejected Kremer's state law claims, he appealed the tribunal's ruling in the New York courts. After losing this appeal, he attempted to litigate his Title VII claim in federal court. The district court dismissed Kremer's case under the Full Faith and Credit Act, and this Court affirmed. *Id.* at 485.

The result in *Kremer* is strikingly similar to the result complained about by San Remo here. Kremer was forced into a state forum. After receiving a full hearing in state court, he was not permitted to get a second bite at the litigation apple in federal court. This result, the Court held, was compelled by the Full Faith and Credit Act, which, as stressed by Justice White throughout his opinion, is one of Congress's most enduring and important laws because it promotes "the comity between state and federal courts that has been recognized as a bulwark of the federal system." *Id.* at 467 n.6 (quoting *Allen*, 449 U.S. at 96).

Elliott takes *Kremer* one step further. Like Kremer, Elliott pursued his employment discrimination claim first in a Tennessee administrative tribunal. Unlike Kremer, Elliott elected against a state court appeal and sued immediately in federal court, where he asserted federal claims under Title VII and other statutory and constitutional provisions. The question presented in *Elliott* was what, if any, preclusive effect should be given to the findings of the state administrative tribunal. The *Elliott* Court recognized that the Full Faith and Credit Act does not mandate preclusion with respect to "unreviewed findings of state administrative agencies," 478 U.S. at 793, but nevertheless concluded that Elliott's non-Title VII claims were precluded by the Tennessee administrative adjudication. The Court held the "parties' interest in avoiding the cost and vexation of repetitive litigation and the public's interest in conserving judicial resources" mandated preclusion. *Id.* at 798.

Allen, *Kremer*, and *Elliott* expose a critical flaw at the center of San Remo's case. As these three cases illustrate, the desire of a federal claimant for a federal forum is frequently trumped by concerns of repose, comity, federalism, and judicial economy, and by the need to adhere to the Full Faith and Credit Act. *See also Migra v. Warren City School Dist. Bd. of Educ.*, 465 U.S. 75, 84 (1984) ("[I]t more important to give full faith and credit to state-court judgments than to ensure separate forums for federal and state claims."). In *Williamson County*, this Court ruled as a matter of constitutional law that takings claimants must first seek compensation in state court. Where a state court provides a takings claimant with a full and fair hearing, the federal Full Faith and Credit Act requires that this Court give those state rulings their full preclusive effect.

As *Elliott* demonstrates, even absent the mandates of the federal Full Faith and Credit Act, San Remo would bear a heavy burden in proposing that this Court waive application of issue preclusion in the context of a case litigated first in state court pursuant to *Williamson County*. As Justice Marshall wrote for the Court in *Montana v. United States*, 440 U.S. 147 (1979), preclusion "is central to the purpose for which civil courts have been established, the conclusive resolution of disputes within their jurisdictions." *Id.* at 153. San Remo has offered this Court no compelling reason for waiving the application of this central and eminently sensible doctrine.

San Remo complains about being "consigned to the state courts." Pet. Br. 14. *Amicus* Kottschade goes further, strangely suggesting that the application of the Full Faith and Credit Act here would "lead to a *sub rosa* resuscitation of the discredited 'interposition doctrine' that reared its head briefly in the wake of *Brown v. Board of Education*." Kottschade Br. 8 n.5. But San Remo has not provided this Court with *any* evidence that property owners are systematically mistreated in state court.[10]

Indeed, San Remo has failed even to offer an explanation as to why state judges would be biased against claims by property owners or more hostile to property claims than their federal counterparts.[11] As Judge Easterbrook has recognized, this proposition defies common sense:

> Federal courts are not boards of zoning appeals. This message, oft-repeated, has not penetrated the consciousness of property owners who believe that federal judges are more hospitable to their claims than are state judges. Why they should believe this we haven't a clue; none has ever prevailed in this circuit, but state courts often afford relief on facts that do not support a federal claim. *River Park, Inc. v. City of Highland Park*, 23 F.3d 164, 165 (7th Cir. 1994).

Even were there evidence that a particular state court had mistreated takings claimants, a federal court could address this inequity while remaining in full compliance with the Full Faith and Credit Act. As this Court explained in *Allen*, preclusion applies only where a litigant has "full and fair opportunity" to litigate in state court. 449 U.S. at 101. Thus, the *Allen* Court instructed lower courts not to apply preclusion where "state law did not provide fair procedures for the litigation of constitutional claims, or where a state court failed to even acknowledge the existence of the constitutional principle on which a litigant based his claim." *Id.*

But San Remo does not claim that the hearing it received in the California courts was unfair, nor could it. Instead, San Remo asserts that every claimant should get a full and fair hearing in state court and then, if it loses, another full hearing in federal court. As explained above, this result is prohibited by the Full Faith and Credit Act and the fundamental principles of comity, federalism, and judicial economy that underlie the Act.

B. Giving takings claimants two bites at the apple would give developers an unfair advantage in dealing with local officials. While San Remo and its *amici* imply that state agencies and state courts systemically mistreat developers and other property owners, the reality is exactly the opposite.

Pro-development professionals serve in disproportionate numbers on planning and zoning boards. *See* Jerry L. Anderson & Erin Sass, *Is the Wheel Unbalanced? A Study of Bias on Zoning Boards*, 36 Urb. Law. 447, 466 (2004). And developers have become adept at using litigation, and often just the threat of litigation, as a tool for advancing their interests.

Ninety percent of American municipalities have less than 10,000 people and cannot afford a full-time municipal lawyer. *See* S. Rep. No. 105-242, at

Indeed, San Remo has failed even to offer an explanation as to why state judges would be biased against claims by property owners or more hostile to property claims than their federal counterparts.

44-45 (1998) (minority views). For these municipalities, defending against a single takings suit by a wealthy developer can result in debilitating costs. For example, Hudson, Ohio, a community of 22,000, had to spend more than $400,000 in an ultimately successful effort to defend against a challenge to the city's growth management ordinance spearheaded by the Home Builders Association of Greater Akron. *See* Eliza Newlin Carney, *Power Grab*, Nat'l J., Apr. 11, 1998, at 798, 800.

Litigation costs for small communities have soared in recent years. The "'explosion in the non-traditional use of civil rights statutes—most important, Section 1983 of the Civil Rights Act of [1871]—to include cases involving such areas as zoning and land development'" is a "driving factor" in these increased costs. Susan A. MacManus, *The Impact of Litigation on Municipalities: Total Cost, Driving Factors, and Cost Containment Mechanisms*, 44 Syracuse L. Rev. 833, 836-840 (1993) (citation omitted).

Litigation costs for small communities have soared in recent years.

Not surprisingly, the fear of big litigation bills alters the behavior of local officials. For example, a California Research Bureau study found that cities that have been sued for takings are twice as likely to report having changed their regulatory behavior as those who have not been sued. *See* Daniel Pollak, *Have the U.S. Supreme Court's 5th Amendment Takings Decisions Changed Land Use Planning in California?*, 27 (California Research Bureau, 2000). The report concluded that "takings objections, litigation threats, and even lawsuits have become a common aspect of land use planning discussions." *Id.*

For small municipalities, a lawsuit in an often distant, unfamiliar, federal court represents an even greater threat to community interests and resources. To litigious developers, this means that the threat of a federal suit is a bigger club. This is at least part of the reason *amici* National Association of Home Builders (NAHB) asserted that federal bills intended to overrule *Williamson County* were its "main legislative initiatives" during the 105th and 106th Congresses. John J. Delaney and Duane J. Desiderio, *Who Will Clean Up the "Ripeness Mess"? A Call for Reform So Takings Plaintiffs Can Enter the Federal Courthouse*, 31 Urb. Law. 195, 195 (1999). The current Chief Executive Officer of the NAHB candidly called one such bill a much-needed "hammer to the head" of state and local officials. *See* Brody Mullins, *Property Takings Bill Set For House Fight*, National Journal's Congress-Daily AM (March 14, 2000).

Landowners deserve a fair forum and a full hearing for their constitutional claims. San Remo received its fair hearing already.

Landowners deserve a fair forum and a full hearing for their constitutional claims. San Remo received its fair hearing already. To grant San Remo's request in this case would unfairly put two hammers to the heads of local officials.

III. Williamson County Should Not Be Overruled

Evidently recognizing that the Full Faith and Credit Act requires application of issue preclusion here, certain *amici* supporting San Remo urge this Court to overrule *Williamson County*. Significantly, however, San Remo neither raised this issue in its Petition nor addressed it in its merits brief. As the Court observed in *Yee*, "it is the petitioner himself who controls the scope of the question presented. The petitioner can generally frame the question as broadly or as narrowly as he sees fit." 503 U.S. at 535. As in *Yee*, San Remo's failure to raise the issue should dispose of the matter.

Moreover, in the past this Court has not viewed issues regarding the soundness and viability of existing precedents to be fairly included within questions presented regarding the application of those precedents. *See Del Monte Dunes*, 526 U.S. at 704 ("declin[ing] the suggestions of *amici* to revisit [applicable] precedents" where the city did not challenge them); *Thornton v. United States*, 124 S. Ct. 2127, 2132 & n.4 (2004) (refusing to overrule established constitutional precedent governing automobile searches because the petitioner had not argued that prior precedent be limited).

We will resist the urge to rebut in comprehensive fashion the eristic arguments proffered by San Remo's *amici*, but we mention a few responses in summary fashion because they provide additional reasons not to address the issue at all. Briefly put, *Williamson County*'s state-compensation requirement is longstanding rule of law that has been repeatedly reaffirmed. It is based on controlling authorities extending back more than 100 years. 473 U.S. at 194. It is expressly predicated on the text of the Just Compensation Clause. *Id.* Its analysis is drawn from, and inextricably intertwined with, parallel lines of authorities that govern cases brought under the Tucker Act (*id.* at 194-95) and the Due Process Clause (*id.*), and should not be revisited without full consideration of how changes would influence those lines of cases. Much of the academic literature agrees with the Court's reading of the Fifth Amendment articulated in *Williamson County*.[12] Finally, addressing the status of *Williamson County* at the eleventh hour in this case, without adequate notice, would be tremendously unfair to state and local officials and the public at large.

CONCLUSION
The judgment of the court of appeals should be affirmed.

COMMENTARY AND REACTION

SAN REMO SUPREME COURT DECISION A WIN FOR PLANNERS AND LOCAL GOVERNMENTS

The American Planning Association (APA) applauds the opinion issued today in the U.S. Supreme Court case, *San Remo Hotel v. City and County of San Francisco*, California (No. 04-340). The unanimous court agreed with the position advocated by APA and others that takings claims resolved by state courts should not be relitigated in federal court.

Under this decision, the courts cannot create an exception to the "full faith and credit" statute. Congress enacted the full faith and credit statute (28 U.S.C. § 1738) in order to give equal weight and recognition to opinions between different state and federal courts. If a state court issues an opinion in the case, then the federal courts must acknowledge and abide by the decision.

Justice Stevens, author of the opinion wrote: ". . . we find petitioner's argument unpersuasive [in] that it assumes the courts may simply create exceptions to [the full faith and credit statute] wherever the courts deem appropriate ... we have held that Congress must 'clearly manifest' its intent to depart from [the full faith and credit statute]." He further stated in the opinion that "[p]etitioners did not have the right, however, to seek state review of the same substantive issues they sought to reserve. The purpose of the *England* reservation is not to grant plaintiffs a second bite at the apple in their forum of choice."

"This decision supports the principle of basic fairness," said Paul Farmer, AICP, APA's Executive Director and CEO. "Takings claims, like all other legal disputes, deserve a day in court, but taxpayers deserve resolution once that claim is heard, not the prospect of endless litigation. This ruling protects local taxpayers from repeated lawsuits over development and planning decisions."

"The justices realized that it simply isn't right to allow one side to keep playing until they win—or force communities to back down in the face of costly legal expenses."

In this case, San Remo Hotel challenged San Francisco's ordinance requiring a "conversion fee" to change hotel rooms from the designation of resident use to tourist use. The California Supreme Court decided there

Takings claims, like all other legal disputes, deserve a day in court, but taxpayers deserve resolution once that claim is heard, not the prospect of endless litigation. This ruling protects local taxpayers from repeated lawsuits over development and planning decisions.

was no takings based on both the California and U.S. Constitutions. The hotel then asked the federal court to consider the issue. The U.S. Court of Appeals, 9th Circuit, ruled that it could not because of the "full faith and credit" statute. However, the 2nd Circuit (in a different case with similar issues) ruled that the full faith and credit statute didn't apply.

The U.S. Supreme Court agreed to hear the case because of the conflicting opinions. APA filed an amicus brief in February 2005 urging the courts not to permit relitigation, given the concern that the claimant would be allowed a second suit in federal court that could further hinder local government's planning ability and give developers an unfair advantage in dealing with local officials.

Timothy Dowling of Community Rights Counsel drafted APA's amicus brief to the court.

In its amicus brief, APA argued that "landowners deserve a fair forum and a full hearing for their constitutional claims. San Remo received its fair hearing already. To grant San Remo's request in this case would unfairly put two hammers to the heads of local officials."

Justice Stevens stated in the opinion that "state courts are fully competent to adjudicate constitutional challenges to local land-use decisions. Indeed, state courts undoubtedly have more experience than federal courts do in resolving complex factual, technical, and legal questions related to zoning and land-use regulations."

APA joined other organizations in support of the City of San Francisco, including the California State Association of Counties and the League of California Cities.

Afterword

The recently concluded term of the U.S. Supreme Court was historic for planning. Not in recent memory has the court weighed in on important planning issues with four significant decisions in a single term, each of which supported good planning principles. In the wake of these landmark rulings, the question that arises is where the planning movement goes from here.

*The four decisions—*Kelo, Lingle, San Remo, *and* Rancho Palos Verdes*—share some important characteristics. In each case, the court rejected attempts to take away established tools and techniques used by communities in planning and development, and endorsed the concept that, if well used, these tools actually add value for citizens.*

The four decisions—*Kelo, Lingle, San Remo,* and *Rancho Palos Verdes*— share some important characteristics. In each case, the court rejected attempts to take away established tools and techniques used by communities in planning and development, and endorsed the concept that, if well used, these tools actually add value for citizens. The four rulings also acknowledge that development decisions are best made locally by officials accountable directly to citizens. Each of these decisions can be read as an endorsement of good planning that protects citizens and strengthens neighborhoods.

These cases have real impacts on local planning. The court has brought needed clarity to the arena of regulatory takings by eliminating the *Agins* "substantially advances" test and rejecting the notion that federal judges and endless litigation are the best means of guiding local decisions. Efforts to tie the hands of local communities through re-litigating settled cases in federal court or under different laws were rightly rejected. The new clarity resulting from *Lingle* and the "one bite at the apple" standard in *San Remo* reaffirm fairness and due process in resolving takings disputes and should strengthen local planning.

The decisions represent a victory for planning and communities, but we must be mindful that our challenge is greater than individual victories in court. Our work continues. The court has stopped those who sought to hobble the efforts of planners and local officials to build communities of lasting value. The court preserved tools and a fair process, but the effort to use planning to improve communities continues.

Our challenge now is to continue our longstanding effort to improve planning practice and laws. Good planning produces a fair system that preserves the rights of citizens, increases choices, and promotes the vitality and livability of communities. States and localities need to establish the framework and guidelines that meet this vision.

The public outcry in the aftermath of the *Kelo* decision has been substantial but is mostly overblown rhetoric and outright inaccuracies masquerading as genuine debate. In spite of this fact, the heightened public consciousness and scrutiny offers planners an opportunity to advance an agenda for reform.

In his opinion for the court's majority, Justice Stevens expressly invited a "public debate" on "the necessity and wisdom of using eminent domain for economic development." States are clearly rising to his challenge and eager to take up redevelopment issues. In the weeks since the *Kelo* decision, at least half of all state legislatures have seen some bill or resolution introduced addressing eminent domain. Unfortunately, too many of these proposals give in to the temptation to simply eliminate the tool without thought to the consequences (intended or otherwise), the broader context of redevelopment, or the unique local situation. All too often, the focus is limited to eminent domain without a willingness to examine the complexity of a comprehensive redevelopment process.

The legislative fallout from *Kelo* will likely not be limited to addressing eminent domain. For years, proponents of takings bills have turned to state legislators, hoping to use the guise of property rights to gut the ability of municipalities to plan and enforce regulations that protect people, their property, and the environment. Those efforts may well gain momentum in many states.

In the past, these initiatives have usually been rejected because legislators of both parties come to understand the dramatic threat they pose. To avoid the scrutiny of the legislative process, the special interests behind takings bills may well attempt turn the debate over redevelopment reform into support for ballot initiatives that undermine good planning. The line connecting Susette Kelo and Dorothy English, the public relations face of Oregon's Measure 37, is clear.

The debate will now unfold in state legislatures, and perhaps ballot boxes, across the nation. It is a debate we should welcome, and one we must inform and influence with principles for good planning. We should promote legislation that embraces a comprehensive approach to redevelopment, improves planning practice, and increases quality of life.

Debate at the state level over eminent domain provides an opportunity to improve the redevelopment process in a way that bolsters the future of our communities while allaying the fears of property owners. As in so many areas of state law related to planning, redevelopment statutes in many states are out-dated, ill conceived, or nonexistent. A cornerstone of positive reform should be a focus on creating a planning process that is democratic, inclusive, accountable, comprehensive, and empowering. Our vision of redevelopment must lead to communities of lasting value. Creation of such communities is the best guarantor of everyone's property rights and values.

What does "redevelopment done right" look like? Redevelopment, including any use of eminent domain, should be directly linked to a plan. Redevelopment plans should be consistent with adopted comprehensive plans. Both plans should be subject to rigorous public involvement. Legislation governing redevelopment authorities should include a clearly defined process for designating redevelopment areas. Whenever possible, a designated and well-defined redevelopment authority should be a prerequisite to eminent domain use. Public-private partnerships for redevelopment should be constructed to ensure they are fair, open, equitable, transparent, and accountable for acting in the public interest. Public notice and participation processes should be required and expanded. Outreach should include citizens, property owners, businesses, and civic institutions.

Compensation reform for eminent domain should also be on our agenda. As we argued in our brief to the Supreme Court in *Kelo*, eminent domain compensation should in certain circumstances exceed the fair market value standard. If we really care about the social equity implications of eminent domain, we should adopt policies that provide support for displaced renters.

In addition to these changes, we must work with states to address the lingering problems with blight definitions and designations. Virtually none of the legislative remedies proposed thus far address the use of eminent domain for blight. This is in spite of the fact that blight is the most common rationale for eminent domain and, low-income citizens are vastly more likely to be affected by blight designations than economic development.

Eminent domain is a difficult and often vexing issue. APA acknowledged in our amicus brief that it is a "harsh power" and one to be used only as a last resort. We share concerns about impacts on low-income communities and inadequate public involvement. That is why we must work to improve the whole system of planning and redevelopment statutes.

Throwing out the tool will not solve our larger problems. I am reminded of former President Clinton's words on affirmative action, "mend it; don't end it." The same can safely be said of eminent domain. Without this tool, many projects consistent with local plans and providing positive local impacts will be lost due to absentee landlords, vacant properties with uncertain ownership, and individual holdouts. Neighborhoods in cities from coast-to-coast have benefited from projects where eminent domain was essential.

As states debate the best approach for their state, it is important to keep in mind that redevelopment, including eminent domain, is critical for job

The debate will now unfold in state legislatures, and perhaps ballot boxes, across the nation. It is a debate we should welcome, and one we must inform and influence with principles for good planning.

Court victories are important and these cases have clarified and improved legal standards in a way that will enhance local planning. Now, we turn to the court of public opinion. To be successful, we must be leaders in advocacy for the reform and modernization of planning practices nationwide.

creation, economic revitalization, and improved quality of life. Eminent domain is a powerful tool and its prudent use, when exercised in the sunshine of public scrutiny, can help achieve a greater public good that benefits the entire community.

Looking ahead, planners face a so-called property rights movement and a public that demands results. The Supreme Court's decisions have raised the stakes for planning. The most successful approach to countering bad bills and ballot measures is, in part, seizing the opportunity to play a vital role in promoting both local vitality and protecting citizens.

Planners need to move beyond simply defending individual tools or regulations to promoting our ideas and policies for improving communities. People want a process that helps them understand and manage change in way that advances their vision and values. Planning can help citizens choose the future they want. If we meet this objective, planners will find natural support for the process and rules that underlie the plan.

We are more than regulators, more than stewards of zoning maps. The regulations necessary to good planning are important, but they will only be maintained through planning that is engaged and visionary. We must strive for planning that increases choices and guarantees fairness.

In the mid 1990s, federal takings legislation emerged as a serious threat to planning. Congress repeatedly came near to passing bills that would have undermined local planning authority. Yet, in some ways, out of those battles emerged passionate advocates for better planning and great communities. Is it a coincidence that the smart growth movement really gained prominence later in the decade? Perhaps the coming state debates will spur new energy and innovation in the planning movement.

As we face the political battles ahead, APA will be a leader in the campaign for property fairness and community value. We will develop and provide the communications and advocacy tools necessary to influence the debate. To be successful, individual planners, local officials, and engaged citizens have to get involved. Websites, toolkits, and information are vital, but successful campaigns are driven by grassroots involvement and action.

Where do we go from here? Our work is only beginning. Court victories are important and these cases have clarified and improved legal standards in a way that will enhance local planning. Now, we turn to the court of public opinion. To be successful, we must be leaders in advocacy for the reform and modernization of planning practices nationwide.

Paul Farmer, AICP
Executive Director and CEO, APA

MAKING GREAT COMMUNITIES HAPPEN

The American Planning Association provides leadership in the development of vital communities by advocating excellence in community planning, promoting education and citizen empowerment, and providing the tools and support necessary to effect positive change.

480/481. Modernizing State Planning Statutes: The Growing Smart^{SM} Working Papers. Volume 2. September 1998. 269pp.

482. Planning and Zoning for Concentrated Animal Feeding Operations. Jim Schwab. December 1998. 44pp.

483/484. Planning for Post-Disaster Recovery and Reconstruction. Jim Schwab, et al. December 1998. 346pp.

485. Traffic Sheds, Rural Highway Capacity, and Growth Management. Lane Kendig with Stephen Tocknell. March 1999. 24pp.

486. Youth Participation in Community Planning. Ramona Mullahey, Yve Susskind, and Barry Checkoway. June 1999. 70pp.

489/490. Aesthetics, Community Character, and the Law. Christopher J. Duerksen and R. Matthew Goebel. December 1999. 154pp.

493. Transportation Impact Fees and Excise Taxes: A Survey of 16 Jurisdictions. Connie Cooper. July 2000. 62pp.

494. Incentive Zoning: Meeting Urban Design and Affordable Housing Objectives. Marya Morris. September 2000. 64pp.

495/496. Everything You Always Wanted To Know About Regulating Sex Businesses. Eric Damian Kelly and Connie Cooper. December 2000. 168pp.

497/498. Parks, Recreation, and Open Spaces: An Agenda for the 21st Century. Alexander Garvin. December 2000. 72pp.

499. Regulating Home-Based Businesses in the Twenty-First Century. Charles Wunder. December 2000. 37pp.

500/501. Lights, Camera, Community Video. Cabot Orton, Keith Spiegel, and Eddie Gale. April 2001. 76pp.

502. Parks and Economic Development. John L. Crompton. November 2001. 74pp.

503/504. Saving Face: How Corporate Franchise Design Can Respect Community Identity (revised edition). Ronald Lee Fleming. February 2002. 118pp.

505. Telecom Hotels: A Planners Guide. Jennifer Evans-Crowley. March 2002. 31pp.

506/507. Old Cities/Green Cities: Communities Transform Unmanaged Land. J. Blaine Bonham, Jr., Gerri Spilka, and Darl Rastorfer. March 2002. 123pp.

508. Performance Guarantees for Government Permit Granting Authorities. Wayne Feiden and Raymond Burby. July 2002. 80pp.

509. Street Vending: A Survey of Ideas and Lessons for Planners. Jennifer Ball. August 2002. 44pp.

510/511. Parking Standards. Edited by Michael Davidson and Fay Dolnick. November 2002. 181pp.

512. Smart Growth Audits. Jerry Weitz and Leora Susan Waldner. November 2002. 56pp.

513/514. Regional Approaches to Affordable Housing. Stuart Meck, Rebecca Retzlaff, and James Schwab. February 2003. 271pp.

515. Planning for Street Connectivity: Getting from Here to There. Susan Handy, Robert G. Paterson, and Kent Butler. May 2003. 95pp.

516. Jobs-Housing Balance. Jerry Weitz. November 2003. 41pp.

517. Community Indicators. Rhonda Phillips. December 2003. 46pp.

518/519. Ecological Riverfront Design. Betsy Otto, Kathleen McCormick, and Michael Leccese. March 2004. 177pp.

520. Urban Containment in the United States. Arthur C. Nelson and Casey J. Dawkins. March 2004. 130pp.

521/522. A Planners Dictionary. Edited by Michael Davidson and Fay Dolnick. April 2004. 460pp.

523/524. Crossroads, Hamlet, Village, Town (revised edition). Randall Arendt. April 2004. 142pp.

525. E-Government. Jennifer Evans–Cowley and Maria Manta Conroy. May 2004. 41pp.

526. Codifying New Urbanism. Congress for the New Urbanism. May 2004. 97pp.

527. Street Graphics and the Law. Daniel Mandelker with Andrew Bertucci and William Ewald. August 2004. 133pp.

528. Too Big, Boring, or Ugly: Planning and Design Tools to Combat Monotony, the Too-big House, and Teardowns. Lane Kendig. December 2004. 103pp.

529/530. Planning for Wildfires. James Schwab and Stuart Meck. February 2005. 126pp.

531. Planning for the Unexpected: Land-Use development and Risk. Laurie Johnson, Laura Dwelley samant, and Suzanne Frew. February 2005. 59pp.

532. Parking Cash Out. Donald C. Shoup. March 2005. 119pp.

533/534. Landslide Hazards and Planning. James C. Schwab, Paula L. Gori, and Sanjay Jeer, Project Editors. September 2005. 209pp.

535. The Four Supreme Court Land-Use Decisions of 2005: Separating Fact from Fiction. August 2005. 193pp.

# of special interest

E-Government

PAS 525. Jennifer Evans–Crowley and Maria Manta Conroy. 2004. 41 pp.

A useful guide to creating websites that provide efficient and cost-effective public service. The report examines the range of electronic citizen-participation tools and products used by cities and, in particular, planning departments to streamline tasks; provide in-depth information on plans, projects, and visioning exercises; and make sites accessible to persons with disabilities.

Street Graphics and the Law

PAS 527. Daniel Mandelker with Andrew Bertucci and William Ewald. 2004. 133 pp.

The updated edition of this seminal report outlines a street-graphics system that ensures on-premise signs are expressive, appropriate, legible, and compatible with the character of the community. The system is a legally enforceable regulatory framework that makes good design possible. The CD-ROM includes a model ordinance, links to community sign ordinances, samples of signs, and more.

Parking Cash Out

PAS 532. Donald C. Shoup. 2005. 119 pp.

Free parking is the most common fringe benefit offered to workers in the U.S. Is it any wonder, then, that 91 percent of them drive to work—or that most of them drive solo? The cost of this parking subsidy is about 1 percent of the gross national product and four times the amount of funding for public transit. This report, a complement to Shoup's *The High Cost of Free Parking*, shows how employers who offer their employees the option to cash out their parking subsidies can discourage solo driving and its attendant social, environmental, and infrastructure costs. It also suggests ways planners can bring this option to their communities.